Grammatology and Literary Modernity in Turkey

Grammatology and Literary Modernity in Turkey

Nergis Ertürk

OXFORD
UNIVERSITY PRESS

OXFORD
UNIVERSITY PRESS

Oxford University Press is a department of the University of Oxford.
It furthers the University's objective of excellence in research,
scholarship, and education by publishing worldwide.

Oxford   New York
Auckland   Cape Town   Dar es Salaam   Hong Kong   Karachi
Kuala Lumpur   Madrid   Melbourne   Mexico City   Nairobi
New Delhi   Shanghai   Taipei   Toronto

With offices in
Argentina   Austria   Brazil   Chile   Czech Republic   France   Greece
Guatemala   Hungary   Italy   Japan   Poland   Portugal   Singapore
South Korea   Switzerland   Thailand   Turkey   Ukraine   Vietnam

Oxford is a registered trade mark of Oxford University Press in the UK
and certain other countries.

Published in the United States of America by
Oxford University Press
198 Madison Avenue, New York, NY 10016

© Oxford University Press 2011

First issued as an Oxford University Press paperback, 2013.

Library of Congress Cataloging-in-Publication Data
Ertürk, Nergis.
Grammatology and literary modernity in Turkey / Nergis Ertürk.
    p.   cm.
Includes bibliographical references.
ISBN 978-0-19-974668-2 (hardcover); 978-0-19-934977-7 (paperback)
1. Turkish literature—20th century—History and criticism.
2. Turkish literature—19th century—History and criticism.
3. Modernism (Literature)—Turkey. 4. Language and culture—Turkey—History. I. Title.
PL216.E77   2011
894.3'509112—dc22   2010040318

1 3 5 7 9 8 6 4 2

Printed in the United States of America
on acid-free paper

Brian'a . . .

CONTENTS

PREFACE: NATIONALISM, COMPARATISM, AND THE COLONIZATION OF THE OUTSIDE

"The Orient and the Occident, for centuries . . . have been looking for the universal religion" (24), wrote Auguste Comte, the founding philosopher of positivism, in an enthusiastic letter dated 4 February 1853 and delivered to the reformist Ottoman Grand Vizier Mustafa Reşid Pasha. An invitation to the Ottomans to join his positivist "religion of humanity," Comte's letter praised Islam for its simplicity and pragmatism, arguing that Muslims could evolve from the theology of Islam toward the "cult of humanity" without risking the social chaos erupting in the West. Comte imagined the modernization projects of the Ottoman state as the promise of a historical synthesis of the two worlds of the Muslim Orient and the Christian Occident.

A more broadly generalized (yet no less positivist) understanding of Turkey as a bridge between the East and the West, or the cultures of Eastern Islam and Western Christianity, is still alive and well more than 150 years later, at a historical conjuncture placing the Republic of Turkey at the center of national and transnational elite-liberal geopolitical fantasies. Within the frame of this understanding, the global reception of literature in Turkish, today, is substantively circumscribed by the critical field of "new symbols for the clash and interlacing of cultures"[1]—a circumscription itself both reflecting, and reproducing, such fantasies. In the first phase of the 2003 military occupation of Turkey's geographic and cultural neighbor Iraq, the metonymic appropriation of Turkish literature, as an agent of reconciliation of essentialized cultural difference, made possible the warding off of fundamental questions concerning the economic, political, and human realities of the war. It served, as well, in the political climate of the years that followed, to resituate the Turkish model of "moderate Islamic democracy" as an acceptable compromise for a world unified by just the *right* measure of difference.

One of my goals in *Grammatology and Literary Modernity in Turkey* is to interrupt this globalized fantasy of reconciliation, condensed as it is, now, onto a single charismatic Turkish Nobel laureate forced into the role of representative *and* critic of his nation, and the trail of mostly poorly comprehended, mostly irremediable local *and* transnational controversies he trails in his wake. Reminding my readers

---

[1] These, of course, are the words of the Nobel committee, announcing the 2006 award in literature to Orhan Pamuk. Pamuk's novel *Snow* can be read as something of a metanovel devoted to problematizing this excessively interested appropriation of Turkish literary production by the world literary market. On this point, see my "Those Outside the Scene: *Snow* in the World Republic of Letters."

(of all persuasions) of the force of Pamuk's own claim that literary modernism conceived on the European model "did not take place" in Turkey,[2] I propose that we rethink the history of modern Turkish literature, from the late nineteenth century through the mid-twentieth, against the critical conceit through which modern Turkish literature is tutored by European genres, such as the novel, and European literary currents or movements, such as realism and Romanticism. In place of such received wisdom, this book offers a particular shift of focus, to the transformation of Turkish writing by the rise of new print and translational technologies and the historical shifts in the practice of writing they accompanied.

Among such agents of transformation, I emphasize the lexical and grammatical simplification of Ottoman Turkish, during the nineteenth century, and the extensive language reforms of the twentieth, which saw the new Turkish Republic undertaking to thoroughly rationalize modern Turkish, overcoming the gap separating its spoken from its written registers. Situating the 1928 replacement of Perso-Arabic script with the Latin phonetic alphabet and the subsequent expurgation of Arabic and Persian loanwords in a longer history of modern phonocentrism, or the programmatic privileging of spoken language over its written forms, I suggest that the unreconciled contradictions of Turkish literary modernity, as we know it today, are best explored in the context of these historically determined changes in the practice of writing.

In scholarship on Turkish literature no less than of any other, genre and movement- or current-based literary historiography too often takes for granted the simple fact of the linguistic *mediation* of the conventions of any given literary genre or pattern of transmission. Moving against unreflective assumptions of self-evidence, where the objectivity of literary production is concerned, *Grammatology and Literary Modernity in Turkey* suggests that the historical emergence of the Turkish novel as a form of fiction, conjoining an inner narrative voice with an external objective world, only becomes possible, in the first place, with the ascendance of modern Turkish linguistic phonocentrism. What is more, both thematic and structural reflection on the mediation of literary production, by the historical transformation of writing, can be seen to compose a critical element of many works of modern Turkish literature, themselves. The literary works of which I present readings, in *Grammatology and Literary Modernity in Turkey,* offer us both illustrations and enactments of the process through which the modern literary archive in the Turkish case, profoundly self-conscious of rapid and violent change in the historical determination of its own conditions of possibility, reflects continuously on the writing practices that bring it into being. In that, I suggest, such works present their own, potentially competing historical accounts of the nationalization of the Turkish language. Where the prevailing tendency in Eurocentrist critical discourse is to minimize the extra-European difference of Turkish linguistic and literary history, on the one hand, and to idealize it as the culmination of a successful will to rational

---

[2] Pamuk, "Ahmet Hamdi Tanpınar ve Türk Modernizmi" 43.

modernity, on the other, the literary texts I read here suggest another critical narrative altogether. That is a narrative of profound self-alienation, even what we might call "self-surgery," at the very limit or limits of modernity. Belonging purely neither to the imperial, nor to the anti-colonial histories of nationalist language reform in the world-historical twentieth century, modern Turkish grammatology, I am suggesting, emerges as a limit narrative about the self-consummating violence of the modern: a violence that can no longer be either obscured, or disinherited.

There is yet another reason to revisit the history of Turkish literary modernity, in just this way, at the current conjuncture. One very important component in the recent redevelopment of contemporary global or world literary and cultural studies, in the United States, has been the recovery of Turkey (in particular, the interwar academic milieu of the city of Istanbul) as the generously imagined true birthplace of postwar comparative literature. It is through modern Turkey, as a historical transition and limit site, that comparative literary studies locates itself, today, in the legacy of the philological criticism of Jewish intellectuals exiled from Germany during the Nazi period, who held teaching posts at Istanbul University before emigrating to the United States. Long ago, now, it was Edward W. Said who made the fact and conditions of Erich Auerbach's Turkish exile foundational to his vision of comparative literature, as it is practiced in the U.S. today.[3] More recently, Emily Apter has explored what she calls "the volatile crossing of Turkish language politics with European philological humanism" (50) in the Turkish exile of Auerbach's colleague Leo Spitzer. In so far as Spitzer, unlike Auerbach, apparently learned during his sojourn in Turkey to read and write in the Turkish language, for Apter, it is Spitzer's "linguistic cosmopolitanism," set against the backdrop of a historically radical transformation of language itself in Republican Turkey, that testifies to the translational-transnational globality of comparative literature at its most recent inception.[4]

As determinedly as it engages the scholarship of Turkish literature in the more restricted sense, *Grammatology and Literary Modernity in Turkey* engages

---

[3] See the Said of *The World, the Text, and the Critic*, observing that Auerbach's *Mimesis* "owed its existence to the very fact of Oriental, non-Occidental exile and homelessness. . . . *Mimesis* itself is not, as it has so frequently been taken to be, only a massive reaffirmation of the Western cultural tradition, but also a work built upon a critically important alienation from it" (8). For Said, Auerbach in exile is the paradigmatic "secular" intellectual, making his cultural alienation the ground of a new worldly criticism.

[4] Apter suggests that the Turkish translation of Spitzer's essay entitled "En apprenant le turc," published in the journal *Varlık* in three segments in 1934 and 1935, marks Spitzer as "the forerunner of postcolonial humanism" (53) and "'worlded' minoritarian comparatism" (45). While the recovery of Spitzer's essay certainly helps to articulate a productively complex legacy for twentieth-century comparative literature, it would be unwise to overlook the Orientalism at play in the essay (to which Apter herself gives little attention). As an encounter of Romance philological hermeneutics with Orientalist linguistics, "En apprenant le turc" records the philologist's "love" for a language that he understands, without strenuous qualification, as baldly more emotional, less abstract and less logical, than Indo-European languages in general. Unsurprisingly, Spitzer's primary sources in this essay include such key texts of European Turcology as Deny, *Grammaire de la langue turque* (1921) and Sandfeld, *Linguistique balkanique* (1930).

this generally more diffuse body of work figuring Turkey as a site of translational-transnational disciplinarity at scale. In some ways, it is in seeking their very most substantive point of contact, here, that this book aims to open a new space for negotiation, with and among the work it invites to dialogue. At this level, my goal here is to appraise the simultaneously substantial and spectralized non-place, or "absent presence," of Turkish literature in Said's and Apter's comparative-critical histories, which by choice or by necessity converge on the activities of European exiles in Istanbul. It should go without saying that such appraisal must come to stand for something more substantial, in both critical and comparative terms, than the restitutional integration of Turkish literature into the disciplinary space of an exilic-Europeanized literary-critical Turkey. Any account of the nationalization of the Turkish language and its literatures in their late imperial and Republican transformation, I contend, is also and necessarily a history of its transnational "outside." This claim, in turn, carries with it consequences for both our conceptual understanding *and* our practical disciplinary application of the methodological gesture of comparatism.

The term and concept "comparatism," in *Grammatology and Literary Modernity in Turkey*, marks the irreducible power of language to receive and to transmit messages, from unknown sources, in a universal omni-directionality. We might say that the very condition of possibility of the discipline of comparative literature, as we know it today, is itself nothing but this force of language as a medium, in its traffic or intercourse in space and time. To the extent that mid-nineteenth century Ottoman print culture is my key historical point of departure, here, that is because its emergence, in a massive amplification of print and translational practices in Ottoman imperial institutional and everyday life, marks an unprecedented intensification of both the activity of communication and the conditions of possibility of *communicability, as a linguistic and literary problem*. Benedict Anderson has memorably marked the conjunction of historically new writing practices with accelerated vernacularization, under such conditions, with the image of "newspapers everywhere tak[ing] 'this world of mankind' as their domain no matter how partially they read it" (*The Spectre of Comparisons* 33).

My readings of early works of Ottoman Turkish literature suggest that the reception, through translative writing practices, of messages from "outside" awakens powerful new modes of desire, able to remediate and consume immediate hierarchies of legal and literary authority. As I employ it, the term and concept "literary modernity" marks the discovery of the "native" vernacular, itself, as an uncanny communications medium, within the historical intensification of translation and dissemination. Such discovery of course can and does produce intense *fear,* of a sort that too often welcomes, even demands the panicky restoration of (new) hierarchies of authority. Shadowing the national evolution of vernacularization, such fear enables the nationalistic reception of phonocentric technologies devised (or manipulated) for the demarcation of a fixed "inner" national domain of life and reference. At the transnational or global scale, meanwhile, it abets what we might call the colonization of the linguistic outside by Orientalist philology, the disciplined nineteenth-century European production of knowledge of languages of the East. I understand modern Orientalism, as diagnosed and reimagined in Edward W. Said's body of work, as entailing this colonization of the linguistic outside, above all else. We might say that by far the most detrimental consequence of what Said called Orientalism is the foreclosure it enacts, on the futurity of the plural and heterogeneous "chatter" of the world of the nineteenth century: a foreclosure achieved through the demarcation of a world stage, or totalized representative space, detaching the "Western" body of civilization from its "Eastern" other. To the extent that the earlier, Eurocentric institutionalization of comparative literature itself, in its late nineteenth century moment, is an effect of just such a colonization of the linguistic outside, it, too, carries in itself this structural foreclosure on all literary powers of imagination of the future.[5]

It is certainly the case that all national literatures do address and position themselves in relation to such a "world stage,"[6] in one way or another. The history of the modern Turkish language and its literatures is unquestionably profoundly shaped by Orientalism, and in unique ways. One might point first of all to the development of Turkist cultural nationalism from within European Turcology, itself, during the last quarter of the nineteenth century, as one unmistakable manifestation of such influence. Another is rendered in the sociologist Meltem Ahıska's analysis of governmentality in Turkey as profoundly structured by the projection of the social imaginary of the "West."[7] It is through this imaginary, in its workings at the subjective level, that the symbolist poet Ahmet Haşim came to celebrate (albeit ambivalently) the alphabet reform imposing the Latin alphabet on Turkish, for abolishing the Perso-Arabic script convention of writing from right to left. (Haşim relates how, standing before a monkey cage during a visit to a Paris zoo in 1928,[8] openly taking notes in the old script, he realized all at once that the spectacular fascination of the Parisians surrounding him had turned from the zoo animals, to himself.)

Motivated, actuated, and shaped by Orientalism, modern nationalism in the Turkish case abets the colonization of the linguistic outside, by policing internally the very conditions of (internal) communication. The late nineteenth- and early twentieth-century reform measures devised for "linguistic modernization" set and violently defended limits to the possibilities opened up by the omni-directional

---

[5] This formulation of Orientalism as the colonization of the linguistic outside draws on Aamir R. Mufti's "Orientalism and the Institution of World Literatures," which I first heard as a talk delivered at Istanbul Bilgi University on 20 December 2008.

[6] On this point, see Rutherford, "Why Papua Wants Freedom" 345–359. Pascale Casanova's recent *La république mondiale des lettres/The World Republic of Letters* can be read as a kind of theory *and* critical enactment of a world literary "stage." For an elaboration of this point, see my "Those Outside the Scene."

[7] See Ahıska, "Occidentalism."

[8] See Ahmet Haşim, "Sağdan Yazı" 316.

travels of Turkish writing from within the nation. Haunted doubly by the external difference of an encroaching "Europe" and by the internal difference of atrophied and mortified Ottoman imperial multilingualism, Turkish modernity is distinguished by the extremity of measures taken for the control of writing, in the establishment of an impossibly self-same or self-identical identity. It is in this light, I will suggest, that we can read the struggle for the nationalization of modern Turkish writing and literature, in a determinedly *double* reading, as one history of a wider struggle to contain the "comparative" futurity inherent in the communications revolution of the world-historical mid-nineteenth century. At a time when the theory of critical comparison is too often eclipsed by its impulsive practice, in a rush to practical judgment reconfusing Orientalist philology with more demanding imaginations of a multilingual humanism, my hope is that this rereading of modern Turkish literature, for a readership imagined as neither completely oblivious to it, nor determined to adapt or appropriate it to something else, might serve to remind us of the spectrality of comparison, itself.

ACKNOWLEDGMENTS

In many ways, this book is the product of a unique interdisciplinary conversation ongoing at Columbia University during my graduate work in the Center (now Institute) for Comparative Literature and Society from 1999 to 2006—a conversation involving faculty, graduate students, research affiliates, and invited guests of Columbia's Department of English and Comparative Literature, Department of Middle East and Asian Languages and Cultures, and Department of Anthropology. From the very start, David Damrosch, Ursula Heise, and Nader Sohrabi have steadfastly supported my work on this project. Martin Puchner and Sibel Erol offered valuable comments at an early stage of the book's inception. Gayatri Chakravorty Spivak has been an important influence, and I am especially grateful for the postdoctoral fellowship I held at the Center for Comparative Literature and Society in spring 2007. Work on the book was further advanced during a residency at the Cogut Center for the Humanities at Brown University during the fall semester 2008. I am grateful to Michael Steinberg, the staff of the Cogut Center, and the members of the 2008 Fellows' Seminar for their parts in ensuring an unforgettable semester at Brown.

I would not have been able to make this book all I wished it to be without the support of my colleagues in the Department of Comparative Literature at Binghamton University, SUNY and the Department of Comparative Literature at Pennsylvania State University, as well as in Penn State's Department of English. Luiza Moreira, Gisela Brinker-Gabler, and Elif Şendur were tremendously kind and generous during my time at Binghamton. I completed the book during my first two years at Penn State, where Carey Eckhardt generously and attentively secured me the valuable research and writing time I required. In more ways than I could ever properly thank them for, Juana Celia Djelal and Djelal Kadir have provided me with a home away from home in central Pennsylvania. The support of Eric Hayot and Jonathan Eburne, who always left their office doors open to me, has been essential. The members of my graduate seminar "Specters of Comparison," taught at Binghamton, Brown, and Penn State, helped me to reread and rethink the strands of theoretical text and discourse that inform this book. In their approaches to modern Turkish literature, Beyza Atmaca and Veli Yashin have been a special inspiration.

Sanja Bahun, Nader Sohrabi, Shaden Tageldin, Harriet Stone, Jeffrey Sacks, Pericles Lewis, David Damrosch, Elias Khoury, and Özen Nergis Dolcerocca provided me with opportunities to present my work to audiences at the Modernist Studies Association 2006 annual meeting, the Columbia University Seminar in Ottoman and Turkish Studies, the Berlin-Brandenburg Academy of Sciences and Humanities program

"Europa im Nahen Osten—Der Nahe Osten in Europa," Washington University in St. Louis, the American Comparative Literature Association annual meetings of 2008 and 2009, Istanbul Bilgi University, and the Kevorkian Center for Near Eastern Studies at New York University/Eugene Lang College, The New School. I thank Aamir Mufti and Paul Bové, for inviting me to contribute to the journal *boundary 2*, as well as the members of the *boundary 2* editorial collective, for stimulating and inspiring conversation during a visit to the University of Pittsburgh.

At Oxford University Press, I thank Shannon McLachlan, for her enthusiastic support of this project, and Brendan O'Neill, for the patience with which he answered all of my questions. I also would like to thank Rick Stinson for overseeing the production process. I am grateful to two of the anonymous reviewers for Oxford University Press, for the meticulous professionalism with which they responded to an earlier draft of this book. I have made extensive use of their comments and suggestions in preparing its final draft. I also thank Tufan Buzpınar, for putting me in touch with Tuna Baltacıoğlu, and Tuna Baltacıoğlu and Tansı Baltacıoğlu Yıldırımer for their permission to reproduce the charts created by Ismayil Hakkı Baltacıoğlu on the cover and in the body of this book.

In fundamental ways, this book is marked by my decade-long friendship with Özge Serin, whose rare analytical *and* creative theoretical acumen has opened new worlds of thought to me. I am indebted to her for the ethic of friendship that marks our ongoing conversation, conducted by telephone, e-mail, and during transoceanic flights. Suzan Yalman, with whom I have traveled so many stages on life's way, is a tremendously generous personal and intellectual friend, who never hesitates to dig through her library in response to my many queries. I am grateful to each and every one of countless other friends in Turkey, the United States, and elsewhere, for having patiently given me ear while I was writing this book: to name only a few, Zeynep Akon, Elif Akçalı, Ben Conisbee Baer, Angela Bayer, Constantine Caramanis, Güliz Dinç, Maureen Hickey, Esma İçen, Zeynep İnanoğlu, Olgu İçöz, Paul Lekas, Göze Saner, Siona Wilson, and Chad Wolfe.

Cantagallos, Lennons, and Angels have welcomed me into their families as one of them; words cannot express my thanks for the generosity and kindness of Linda Cantagallo and Karen and Michael Lennon. Ertürks, Çamlıcas, and Duras—most especially my parents, Feza and Nejat Ertürk, and my grandmothers, Enise Çamlıca and Suzan Ertürk—supported me unconditionally during this unending "literature quest," even when it failed to make sense. To be able to give, with no strings attached to the gift, in the face of an utterly unknown foreign horizon, is the ultimate test of love. This book is a conversation I've been having with each and every one of them in another language, all these many years.

This book is dedicated to Brian Lennon, whom I met on a street of books, in another city, in another time at the end of the twentieth century. Ever since then, we have given each other language.

The views expressed herein are exclusively my own, as is the responsibility for any errors.

A NOTE ON TRANSLATION, TRANSLITERATION, AND USAGE

Unless otherwise noted, throughout this book, translations from Ottoman Turkish and modern Turkish into English are my own. For English equivalents for Turkish words, the dictionary I have most frequently consulted is the *Redhouse Türkçe/Osmanlıca-İngilizce Sözlük* (*Redhouse Turkish/Ottoman-English Dictionary*). I have followed the modern Turkish orthography used by *Redhouse* in transliterating titles and other words in Ottoman Turkish. In those cases where titles and quotations have been drawn from existing transliterations, the orthographic conventions of those transliterations, as cited, have been retained. In rendering Ottoman Turkish names, I have followed the most common transliterations used by scholars in Turkish studies. For my Anglophone readers who are unfamiliar with Turkish, the following is a pronunciation guide for the extended Latin character set used for writing and typesetting modern Turkish:

c, C = pronounced *j,* as in "Jane"
ç, Ç = pronounced *ch,* as in "child"
ğ = a "soft" *g* (in Turkish, "yumuşak *g*"), which lengthens the vowel preceding it, rather than being pronounced separately. This "soft" *g* never appears at the beginning of a word.
ı, I = pronounced like the second *e* in "legend," in U.S. English pronunciation
i, İ = pronounced sometimes like the *i* in "bit," sometimes like the *ee* in "meet"
ö, Ö = pronounced *ö,* as in the German "können"
ü, Ü = pronounced *ü,* as in the German "über"
ş, Ş = pronounced *sh,* as in "she"

A circumflex mark (^) is added over a vowel in words of Arabic and Persian origin to mark the palatalization of a preceding *g, k,* or *l.* It may also be used to indicate long vowels in Arabic and Persian loanwords.

In 1934, the Surname Law (Soyadı Kanunu) was passed, requiring all Turkish citizens to adopt Western-style family names. It was at this time that Nâzım Hikmet became Nâzım Hikmet Ran, Ahmet Hamdi became Ahmet Hamdi Tanpınar, and so on. Throughout, these adopted surnames are enclosed in square brackets, following scholarly convention in Turkish studies. This book otherwise follows the Modern Language Association (MLA) documentation style used in language and literature studies in the United States. Where I'm citing work by an author who has adopted a surname, all publications by that author are listed in the Works Cited under one entry for that surname. As for Ottoman writers who lacked Western-style family names (Ahmed Midhat Efendi, Ömer Seyfeddin), bibliographic information for an author is listed under an entry for the author's first name in the list of Works Cited.

Where publications were originally dated using the Islamic or Rumi calendars, I have included those publication dates in the Works Cited.

Portions of the Introduction and Chapter 2 appeared in modified form as "Phonocentrism and Literary Modernity in Turkey," *boundary 2* 37.2 (Summer 2010), 155–185, published by Duke University Press.

Grammatology and Literary Modernity in Turkey

Introduction: اول, Be or Die: The Stakes of Phonocentrism

Utopias afford consolation: although they have no real locality there is nevertheless a fantastic, untroubled region in which they are able to unfold; they open up cities with vast avenues, superbly planted gardens, countries where life is easy, even though the road to them is chimerical. *Heterotopias* are disturbing, probably because they secretly undermine language, because they make it impossible to name this *and* that, because they shatter or tangle common names, because they destroy 'syntax' in advance, and not only the syntax with which we construct sentences but also that less apparent syntax which causes words and things (next to and also opposite one another) to 'hold together.'

—Michel Foucault, *The Order of Things*

It is as if we are witnessing the reconstruction of old ruined streets with broken pavements, their opening up into boulevards. On these new streets, old words in nightcaps and bathrobes will not be able to walk without looking laughable. We await the pleasure of watching new ideas stroll back and forth on these modern avenues.

—Ahmet Haşim, "Lisan İmari"

In *The Turkish Language Reform: A Catastrophic Success*, Geoffrey Lewis refers to what he calls a "shrewd" observation made by the British diplomat Sir Charles Eliot (1862–1931), author (under the pseudonym Odysseus) of the political history *Turkey in Europe,* regarding the difficulties posed for Ottoman Turkish speakers by the Perso-Arabic script in which the language was written. Eliot observed that because the script's vowels were insufficient for rendering Turkish pronunciation, the Turkish word اولدی, as written in what Eliot called the Arabic alphabet, could be read in two blatantly and mutually contradictory ways: as either *oldu* (he became), or *öldü* (he died) (103–104).[1] In Eliot's view, Arabic script, naturally "adapted to the Arabic

---

[1] *O, u, ö,* and *ü* were indicated in combination of the letters *elif* and *vav,* at the head of a Turkish word, and by *vav,* at its middle and end.

language, which has a multiplicity of strange consonants and a peculiar grammatical system which renders it unnecessary to write the vowels fully," was the "least fitted" of all possibilities for writing Turkish, with its "few consonants and many vowels" (103).

In its devotion to the exemplary, I will suggest in this book, such commentary is staked on a broader discourse shaping the fundamentals of Turkish linguistic modernization through its various stages. What entices the contemporary Orientalist, approaching his subject as (in this case) something of a source of entertainment for the reader less than familiar with the history of the Turkish language, is the seemingly quintessential and definitive dimension of the given example. Still, we might observe that there is something in the particular example chosen by Eliot (and reanimated by Lewis, here), that places intense pressure on the concept and the comparative logic of exemplariness, itself. The literally invisible contrast, in written Ottoman Turkish, between the developmental or progressive assertion "he became" and the decadent assertion "he died" suggests not a positive linguistic-historical fact, readily appropriable for critical-historiographic illustration, but rather something of a twilight world, the world of life and writing in a language *itself* dead and alive, at the same time. In returning our attention to the annihilating power of death, in a modernity that strenuously seeks to fix writing's ability to record and guarantee the stable "life" of knowledge or truth, Eliot's example invokes an uneasiness that is not easy to shake off.

Indeed, the astonished laughter intended to be evoked, by Lewis's highly scripted management of this exoticized anecdote, might be compared with that described by Foucault in *The Order of Things,* where it is occasioned by a passage from Jorge Luis Borges's "The Analytical Language of John Wilkins" regarding a "certain Chinese encyclopedia" constructed with arbitrary categories of classification. Such laughter has its uncomfortable source, Foucault writes, in

> the suspicion that there is a worse kind of disorder than that of the *incongruous*, the linking together of things that are inappropriate; I mean the disorder . . . of the *heteroclite* . . .: in such a state, things are 'laid,' 'placed,' 'arranged' in sites so very different from one another that it is impossible to find a place of residence for them, to define a *common locus* beneath them all.[2]

For Foucault, such "shattering," "disturbing," and "threatening" uneasiness is profoundly related to the "distress of those whose language has been destroyed," in their "loss of what is 'common' to place and name. Atopia. Aphasia."[3]

Read against the grain, Lewis's juxtaposition (through Eliot) of life with death, in the non-place of a "heteroclitic" modern writing, suggests that the real energies

---

[2] Foucault, *Order* xvii–xviii; *Mots* 9.
[3] Foucault, *Order* xviii–xix; *Mots* 10.

of Turkish linguistic modernization were never directed solely at writing in the narrowest technical sense of the term. Above and beyond such positive objects and goals, the Turkish language reforms disclosed a kind of mad fantasy, which is in no way unique to the Turkish context—though the foundation of the Turkish Republic does give us a specific form or model of its intensity. That fantasy is modern man's fantasy of immobilizing the threat of that constitutive (and fatal) indeterminacy that is always immanent in writing, and of creating, through writing's reform, an ontology freed of death. Without a doubt, in the same way that this irreducible alterity is externalized, for Borges and for Foucault, in the figure of "a certain Chinese encyclopedia," and for Eliot and Lewis in the exotic life/death confusion of Arabic writing, Turkish linguistic modernization, I will suggest, necessarily touches the discomfiting question of ethnocentrism. For we might say that the fear of illegible writing, in the world of discourse, is always a symptom of the fear of the "illegible" social other(s) within the social body itself. That is also a question that bears on the special particularities of what we call literature, and its study in what are always and unavoidably universalizing critical modes. Despite and against the attempt to disavow literature, in the challenge it poses to those modes, in a very much active and ongoing contemporary strife of the faculties, I will suggest that the "strange institution called literature" comprises a unique archive of the violent effects of this mad modern fantasy.[4]

Overview: Phonocentrism in Turkey

This book begins by tracing the emergence in Turkey of "phonocentrism," or the privileging of speech and oral language, as well as the problematics of representation that accompanied it, in the mid-nineteenth century, when the Ottoman Empire was integrated into the geopolitical network of global capitalist modernity. The period between 1851 and 1950, in Turkey, saw the publication of a wide range of works on the general science of writing that Jacques Derrida, writing of its counterpart in Hellenist European culture, has called "grammatology."[5] Animating this corpus of Turkish grammatology is the question of the discursive commensurability of modern Turkish language and literature with Western European representational practices.

The peripheral integration of the Ottoman Empire into the capitalist world system did not, of course, involve direct European colonial rule; the struggle

---

[4] On this point, see Derrida, "'This Strange Institution Called Literature,'" especially 42–43.

[5] I take as my starting point here 1851, when the Ottoman statesman and historian Ahmed Cevdet Pasha (1822–1895) made the first proposal to reform Ottoman Turkish writing, in his grammar *Medhal-i Kavâ'id*. 1950 marks a corresponding ending point, with the end of the single-party regime of the Republican period in 1946 and the change in the official language policies of the state with the election of the populist Democratic Party in 1950.

between a residually resilient Ottoman imperial bureaucracy and a newly emerging bourgeois class, at a time of intensified rivalry among the European powers for control of Ottoman territories, shaped what Çağlar Keyder terms the "integration of the Ottoman economy into capitalist networks, namely those of trade, debt, and direct investment" (Keyder 47).[6] It is important to understand that Ottoman modernization programs, beginning at the end of the eighteenth century with the adoption of European military techniques, were extended into other sectors of Ottoman society for the protection and reinforcement of the Ottoman state against foreign (European and Russian) powers and local ruling formations.[7] It is equally important to stress the gradual character of these transitions: at every point in the process, which continued through the reign of Sultan Abdülhamid II (1876–1909), the combination of the "traditional" and the "new" can be seen to have produced many different hybrid cultural forms and practices.[8] Nowhere was this more the case, we might say, than in the development of reform projects focused on the Ottoman Turkish language, which Ahmet Hamdi Tanpınar (1901–1962), by consensus the most important writer of the Republican period, emphasized retrospectively as a fundamental register of the ambiguities and tensions of the transformation of the Ottoman cultural and political spheres at large. "The change of civilizations [from East to West]," Tanpınar wrote, "manifests itself undoubtedly as a real crisis [*kriz*] in language" ("Türk" 103).

An admixture of Turkish with Persian and Arabic vocabulary, written in a script combining Arabic and Persian letter forms,[9] Ottoman Turkish had developed as a written language from the fourteenth century on, with its cultivated use formed by intense training.[10] The politics attending its use were already complex by the end of the fifteenth century, with the dramatic expansion of a linguistic gap separating the speech and writing of the learned class (*havas*) from that of the commoners (*avam*). While vernacular Turkish also borrowed from Persian and Arabic—a quality obscured by the nationalist myth of a pure vernacular—the formal and colloquial registers of Ottoman Turkish diverged

---

[6] For an authoritative macrosociological analysis of Ottoman peripheralization, see Keyder 25–40. Keyder's analysis explores the emergence of a new bourgeois class mediating between the local economy and the European system, with focus on "the overdetermination of the class conflict . . . with religious and ethnic difference" (33). The rise of a non-Muslim bourgeoisie, and the social unrest resulting from increasing income disparity between Muslims and non-Muslims, became crucial in the formation of strong separatist nationalist movements, leading eventually to the collapse of the empire.

[7] For a historical overview of such measures, see the first part of Zürcher, *Turkey.*

[8] Reexamining Ottoman educational policy during the reign of Abdülhamid II (1876–1909), Benjamin Fortna, in *Imperial Classroom,* has argued that the "combination of elements of 'modernity' with those of 'tradition' necessarily altered both as they were fused into a system that functioned across the breadth of the far-flung empire on a daily basis" (5).

[9] In addition to Arabic letters, Ottoman Turkish used the Persian letters *pe* (پ), *çim* (چ), *je* (ژ), and *gef* (گ). A variant of the Arabic *kef* (ك), *sağır kef* (ڭ)—was also used occasionally, to represent the Turkish sound *ñ*.

[10] Turkic populations had been living in Anatolia since the eleventh century. The Anatolian Seljuks, who preceded the Ottoman Turks, used Persian as the language of the state. According to Develi, the adoption of Turkish as the language of the state, by the Ottoman Turks, is one cultural consequence of the thirteenth-century Mongol invasions, which provoked the westward migration of large Turkish-speaking populations into Anatolia (46–47).

significantly as its written forms developed under the literary and linguistic influence of Arabic and Persian traditions, producing what some historians have described as a culture of diglossia.[11] Frequently charged (anachronistically) with great artificiality and obscurity, the development of "high" Ottoman Turkish is perhaps best explained, as İhsan Fazlıoğlu has recently explained it, in terms of the translation practices of the classical period and their constitution by an Islamic philosophy of language.[12]

Fazlıoğlu shows how Ottoman scholars of the classical period regarded Arabic as both the medium of divine revelation, as materialized in the Quran, and the medium of divine will, as materialized in Being; Arabic was understood as the "house of Divine Logos [*kelâm-ı ilâhî*]," and was formalized and studied as a "half-symbolic language" (153–154).[13] Fazlıoğlu draws at length on the writings of the well-known Ottoman philosopher and madrasa teacher Taşköprülüzâde Ahmed (1495–1561), who viewed language study as a fundamental instrument (*âlet*) of the knowledge of Being and God. For Taşköprülüzâde, Being manifested itself in four different forms: the physical actuality of an entity; the conceptual image of that entity; the oral or verbal name of the conceptual image; and the written image of the name.[14] These four different ontological spheres formed a unity, for Taşköprülüzâde, in the chain linking the written indication of the verbal, the verbal indication of the conceptual, and the conceptual indication of the physical. For Taşköprülüzâde, while verbal and written images will necessarily vary across cultures and in history, conceptual images, and the physical entities they

---

[11] On Ottoman Turkish diglossia, see Strauss, "Diglossie." Charles Ferguson defines diglossia as

> a relatively stable language situation in which, in addition to the primary dialects of the language (which may include a standard or regional standards), there is a very divergent, highly codified (often grammatically more complex) superposed variety, the vehicle of a large and respected body of written literature, either of an earlier period or in another speech community, which is learned largely by formal education and is used for most written and formal spoken purposes but is not used by any sector of the community for ordinary conversation. (336; also paraphrased in French in Strauss 230)

Strauss's use of the term "diglossia," which I have followed here, is meant to recognize and to mark a real linguistic tension in broad terms, not to absolutize a divide between the two linguistic registers. The learned elite in the empire was also raised on the tales and epics of vernacular culture, and the literary production of these two domains overlapped significantly when it came to matters of content. Fahir İz (and following İz, Şerif Mardin) resists the notion of diglossia, preferring a tripartite division of "ornamental" and "middle" from "simple" prose styles (İz, *Eski* v; Mardin, "Playing" 119). Rather than imagining three such discrete linguistic "consciousnesses," we might regard the "middle" style as a marker of the loose hybridity of the culture of diglossia in itself.

[12] See Fazlıoğlu, "Osmanlı Döneminde 'Bilim' Alanındaki Türkçe Telif ve Tercüme Eserlerin Türkçe Oluş Nedenleri ve Bu Eserlerin Dil Bilincinin Oluşmasındaki Yeri ve Önemi" ("On the Significance of Original and Translational Works Written in Turkish in the Field of 'Science' during the Ottoman Period and On the Role of these Works in the Formation of Language Consciousness").

[13] Fazlıoğlu remarks that Arabic was studied as the "formal-categorical" language of Being during the classical period, much as we might say the symbolic language of mathematics is studied today. Arabic was only "half-symbolic," in this sense, since it was not regarded as a human-created, but rather as a divine language. On the significance of the Arabic language in classical Ottoman scholarship, see also Şükran Fazlıoğlu, "*Manzûme*" 108.

[14] See Taşköprülüzâde's encyclopedic *Miftâh el-sa'âde ve misbâh el-siyâde*, written in Arabic. The Ottoman Turkish translation of this work is entitled *Mevzuat'ül Ulûm.*

indicate, remain universal and unchanging. Fazlıoğlu argues that it was this immutability of concepts, in Taşköprülüzâde's schema, which legitimized *certain* kinds of translation projects from Arabic into other languages, including Turkish, for the transfer, through instruction, of that universal truth to students without knowledge of Arabic (155).

Although the translation practice this legitimated, in targeting specific pupils, formed a relatively limited field of influence, it did contribute to the development of a composite written register in Turkish, called *Türkî-i fasîh* or "eloquent Turkish," as distinct from spoken *kaba* or "vulgar" Turkish. Because Ottoman intellectuals (who organized their compositions, or *inşa,* according to the rules of Arabic and Persian rhetoric) remained doubtful of the translatability of "lawless," "hard," and "sterile" plain Turkish, they purposefully left certain Arabic and Persian words untranslated when translating Arabic and Persian original sources into Turkish (159). Fazlıoğlu also notes examples of works written initially in "archaic Turkish" (*üslûb-ı kadim*) later to be recopied in Istanbul into a "corrected" Turkish meeting the standard of *Türkî-i fasîh* (162). For many such Ottoman intellectuals, the profusion of Arabic and Persian loanwords in Ottoman Turkish served not to obscure meaning, but on the contrary as refining, "clarifying" and "sweetening" it, refining it toward the symbolic function of Arabic.

The translation practices of the classical period were not restricted to scientific texts. Saliha Paker has demonstrated that the "poet-translators" who moved within and between Persian and Turkish, performing a wide range of translational (*terceme*) activities—including both the "literal/substitutive" translation of texts and creative forms such as "parallel and competitive poetry" or *nazire*—also contributed to the emergence of a hybrid "Ottoman interculture" with a mixed language ("Translation" 140).[15] The domain of *Türkî-i fasîh* covered a wide range of generic categories, from highly codified forms of prose and poetry to less elaborate prose texts including mystical narratives, biographies, geographies, and travel writings, among others.[16] Although significant literary production was recorded in *basît* or plain Turkish, the adoption of *Türkî-i fasîh* by the state bureaucracy solidified the political power of this formation of written language against *Türkî-i basît.*[17] What is retrospectively called Ottoman Turkish, today, to distinguish it from modern Turkish, was simply called *lisan-ı Rûm* or *lisan-ı Türkî-i Rûm* until at

---

[15] For a general overview of translation practices prior to the mid-nineteenth century, see Paker, "Turkish Tradition." For Paker's analysis of the "intercultural" translation practices of Ottoman poet-translators, see her "Translation as *Terceme* and *Nazire.*" I return to the notion of *nazire* (*imitatio* or rewriting) in Chapter 4. For now, let me emphasize the importance of Paker's scholarship for new directions in Ottoman Turkish studies. Often viewed, through the lens of Republican ideology, as imitative, artificial, and impure, the hybrid Ottoman Turkish language and its literatures are cast in an entirely new light by Paker's reconceptualization of *terceme.*

[16] On the diversity of prose texts in the classical period, see İz, *Eski.*

[17] On the language of state documents, see Kütükoğlu, *Osmanlı Belgelerinin Dili.* On poetry in *Türkî-i basît,* see Mehmed Fuad [Köprülü], *Millî Edebiyat Cereyânının İlk Mübeşşirleri ve Divân-ı Türkî-i Basit.*

least the mid-nineteenth century (Develi 68).[18] Although the plurilingual populations of the empire were permitted freedom of religious practice and vernacular
language rights under the Ottoman social administrative system,[19] many of those
who sought to rise in social rank learned this Turkish.

Arguably, the nineteenth century is unique in the intensity of pressure created by
the state's modernization programs, which posed problems of translation in the dissemination of reform to the subjects of the empire. Chapter 1 of this book explores
the unprecedented intensification of translational and print practices, in the mid-
nineteenth century, and the consequent emergence of Ottoman Turkish itself as a
kind of telecommunications technology, a carrier of news and a connector across
greater and greater distances.[20] Newspapers played a fundamental role in the simplification of vocabulary and grammar, spurring the attempt to eliminate what was now
understood to be a problematic gap between spoken and written language. Referred
to, by mid-nineteenth century intellectuals, as *Osmanlıca* (Ottoman), this new vernacularized public written language differed both qualitatively and quantitatively
from the old *Türkî-i fasîh*. No longer a half-symbolic instrument (*âlet*) for the mediation of the truth of a universal higher ontological reality, writing was now an arbitrary representational and translational medium for the transmission of a variety of
different, and sometimes conflicting, messages from unfamiliar sources.

Unsurprisingly, it is during this period that debates about the insufficiency of
"Arabic" writing to represent "Turkish" sounds first decisively emerge, and that a
new phonocentric conception of writing begins to take hold. While the orthography of Arabic and Persian loanwords mostly followed the conventions of the source
languages, orthography in Ottoman Turkish was complicated by the representation
of the eight distinct vowel sounds of Turkish by the four letters of Arabic. *Elif* was

---

[18] The term *Rûm* is a geographical term used to refer to western Anatolia and the Balkans, the territory of
the former Byzantine Empire. Develi and Fazlıoğlu agree that neither register of the language was called "Ottoman" (*Osmanlıca*) prior to the rise of Ottoman nationalism, in the mid-nineteenth century. During the classical
period, the term *Osmanlı* was used strictly to describe the ruling group or the state itself. While the eloquent
register could be distinguished as *Türkî* or *Rûm* in its difference from Arabic and Persian, the term *lisan-ı Türkî*
(Turkish language), when used alone, often referred to the spoken *kaba Türkçe* or "vulgar Turkish" of common
Anatolian people (Develi 69). The Istanbul elite often used the term "Turk" in the pejorative, to distinguish
themselves from the "uncultivated" peasants of Anatolia. On the complexity of Turkish linguistic identity during
the classical period, see also Mardin, "Playing."

[19] Until the nineteenth century, Ottoman administration of its multiethnic populations was based in the
millet system. First established by Mehmed II in 1453, the *millet* system segmented the subjects of the empire
into coexisting, semi-autonomous, corporate religious communities. Although the subjects were ruled by the
Sultan and taxed by the Ottoman state, they belonged to religious communities (communities without national
definition) administered by their own ecclesiastical hierarchies, with rabbis, bishops and kadis presiding over
courts, managing civil affairs, and assuming responsibility for collecting taxes. The legal basis of this system
was the Islamic *dhimmi* concept, which recognized Christians and Jews as the "peoples of the Book" and extended protection to them as second-class subjects, in exchange for a special tax payment. For a more detailed
analysis of this system as "the outcome of the Ottoman effort to reconcile the ethnic and linguistic realities of
their realm with the commandments of Islam" (149), see Karpat's "*Millets* and Nationality." It would be inac-
curate, in any case, to understand the *millet* system as one of strict segregation. For a range of essays on the
relations between different *millets*, see Braude and Lewis's *Christians and Jews in the Ottoman Empire.*

[20] I take up theoretical aspects of this conceptualization of Ottoman Turkish later in my discussion, here.
On writing as telecommunications technology, see Derrida, "Signature Event" 311–321.

used to indicate the initial, medial, and final *a* and initial *e, o, u, ö, ü,*[21] while the letter *he,* representing the consonant *h,* was used to mark the final *e* and *a. Vav,* representing the consonant *v,* was used to represent the medial and final *o, u, ö,* and *ü,* while *ye,* representing the consonant *y,* was employed for the medial and final *ı* and *i.* As in Arabic and Persian writing, it was uncommon to represent every vowel, and while the diacritical vocalization markers known as *hareke* could be used to index missing vowels, such usage was generally rare after the sixteenth century.[22] In a well-known 1862 speech to the Cemiyet-i İlmiye-yi Osmâniyye (Ottoman Scientific Society), the translator and statesman Mehmed Münif Pasha (1828–1910) offered two solutions to the problem of ambiguous or multiplied legibility. What ought to be done, Münif Pasha suggested, was either to introduce new vocalization diacritics designating each distinct vowel sound, or to space the letters of each word individually, instead of writing cursively, and insert the necessary diacritics on the line as in "the languages of the foreigners" (224). Although many such proposals were not realized, in the aggregate they register clearly the unprecedented emergence of a new, phonetically biased discourse both in and about Ottoman Turkish, in which for the first time, words are imagined to possess thing-like objectivity, and the one-to-one correspondence between the written word and its signified referent is made the focus of regulation.

It is important to acknowledge that what one might, following Derrida, call "logocentrism," or a metaphysical privileging of speech over writing (which one would have to distinguish from modern phonocentrism), did characterize Ottoman Turkish writing in the period prior to the nineteenth century.[23] In *The Calligraphic State* (1993), Brinkley Messick argues that "in Muslim societies, a culturally specific logocentrism, as Derrida terms this privileging of the spoken word, has had widespread institutional implications, many of which are connected to the recitational cast of the basic texts" (25). The ground of this "recitational logocentrism" (25), as Messick terms it, which also informed pedagogical practice, is the Quran, received

---

[21] A common way to distinguish the initial *a* was to write it with the diacritical sign *med,* a tilde-like mark placed above *elif.* The initial *o, u, ö,* and *ü* were distinguished by the addition of *vav* after the initial *elif.* A later practice of differentiating initial *ı* and *i* was to add *ye* after the initial *elif.* For more information on orthography in Ottoman Turkish, see Levend 51–59 and Develi 52–58.

[22] Diacritical markers in Ottoman Turkish included the *üstün,* a small diagonal line placed over a letter and representing *a, e;* the *ötre,* a hook placed over a letter and representing *o, u, ö, ü;* and the *esre,* a diagonal line placed under a letter and representing *ı* and *i.*

[23] "Phonocentrism," here, refers specifically to the impulse behind projects to overcome the gap between speech and writing, during the nineteenth and twentieth centuries. The word "logocentrism," as I use it throughout, in a culturally specific sense, describes the metaphysics of the spoken word in the Ottoman context prior to the nineteenth century. Derrida himself does not make such historical distinctions, defining logocentrism rather more generally as the (Western) "metaphysics of phonetic writing (for example, of the alphabet)" (3). In his early readings of works by Plato, Rousseau, Lévi-Strauss, and Saussure, among others, Derrida detected a persistent prioritization of speech as the primary, immediate, and natural conveyor of a metaphysical "truth" against a demoted writing. *Of Grammatology* deconstructed this hierarchy by exposing the ways in which speech is structured—spaced and temporalized—as writing; it demonstrates how signs, rather than bearing any direct relation to an originary "truth," assume meaning as an effect of the unmotivated, differential relation with other signs.

and transmitted orally by the Prophet as the spoken word of God. Because recitation (*qira'a*) from memory is the primary mode served by the Quran as a ritual text, the written form of sacred language is understood as secondary to its original, recitational form.

The function of "strings of unvoweled consonants" is best understood in the context of this "recitational logocentrism" (26). Messick explains that "the act of voweling, whether by marking in the vowel signs over and under the consonantal string or by voicing them in recitation, is an interpretive act . . ." (26). In this context, the Arabic word *ḥaraka*, used to designate such "voweling," literally means the movement of the mouth and the vocal cord, "moving" the written letters in a particular way so as to render meaning.[24] The anecdote Lewis takes over from Eliot regarding the scriptorial convergence of *oldu* with *öldü* demonstrates that because the written word permits widely (in this case) diverging possible vocalizations, it is especially important to know the original sense of a written text as intended by the author. To the extent that the final and true signification of the written word resides in the voice of an authorial (or any other authoritative) presence, this practice of writing, Messick argues, may be accurately characterized as logocentric. One may note a similar elevation of the spoken over the written word in Taşköprülüzâde's classification of Being, where the ability of writing to sustain and preserve communication across space and time is subordinated to the oral-linguistic as more proximate to, and immediate of, conceptual meaning (*Mevzuat'ül* 98).

The Calligraphic State demonstrates how this "recitational complex," accompanied by a distrust of authorial absence in "that dangerous supplement," writing, shaped educational practice at the level of both primary instruction and advanced learning in the Muslim world. As Messick puts it, the basic instructional mode, common to Quranic schools and to the authoritative transmission of knowledge in the core disciplines of law, hadith, and grammar, "proceeded ideally from an initial oral recitation (or dictation) by the teacher to the listening student," who "repeated the text segment on his own" until he was ready to reproduce the original recitation for the teacher (21–22). Writing, here, played a secondary, if otherwise decisive role.[25] In the Ottoman case, it was the recitational complex that substantively shaped the educational system. If the goal of elementary Quranic schools (*mekteb*)—often endowed by wealthy subjects or government officials as part of neighborhood mosque complexes—was to teach the recitation of the Quran to young children, the aim of the Ottoman madrasa (*medrese*) was to train the students of higher learning in the knowledge of God through a program of the instrumental and spiritual sciences. In each of these institutions, the instructor—in the Quranic school, the *hoca,*

---

[24] On *ḥaraka*, see Arnaldez.
[25] Messick acknowledges that the private practice of silent reading and writing, as distinct from recitation, prevailed in fields of study such as history, theology, and medicine (28). See also his "Genealogies of Reading and the Scholarly Cultures of Islam."

in the madrasa, the *müderris*—transmitted the correct interpretations of written texts to his students through oral recitation.[26] (The dominance of recitation was hardly limited to the educational domain where Arabic was predominant: the Ottoman scribes and poets who worked in *Türkî-i fasîh* reproduced the hegemonic power of recitation in their devotion to the metrics and rhyme of *seci'*, in prose, and of *arûz,* in poetry.[27])

What is the relation of such earlier classical forms of logocentrism to the mid-nineteenth phonocentrism of the late Ottoman Empire? The answer requires reflection on not only given concepts and models of historical relation within defined fields, areas, and periods of inquiry, but also on those suitable for comparative work across such codified zones, bound by their own limits. We might regard modern phonocentrism as at least partly the radicalization of a *fear* of writing already existent in classical writing, which enters the configuration of radically new historical circumstances with the "communications revolution" of the nineteenth century.[28] The mid-nineteenth-century is characterized by the emergence of the Ottoman Turkish language as an unpredictable and autonomous telecommunicative medium serving as a carrier of "foreign" messages from around the world. The ambiguity of Arabic writing, in its inability to accurately represent Turkish speech, emerges as a problem precisely at the time that written language, newly (dis)embodied in the mass-distributed print medium of the newspaper, begins to "free" itself ever more energetically from the recitative authority of the author's vocal presence. As I will argue at some length, in Chapter 1, the discourse on phonocentric writing was ambiguous and inchoate at first, in its mid-nineteenth century inception (propelled as it was by the desire to expand and accelerate the translative and communicative powers of writing). Yet it took on more self-consciously repressive political dimensions toward the last quarter of the nineteenth century, as the fear generated by the seductive enchantments and "illegibilities" of this revolutionary liberation of writing spurred the subjection of writing to a new and different kind of voice: a nonlocalized figure of vocal subjectivity produced and shaped by new disciplinary mechanisms of power.

---

[26] On the educational background of Ottoman scribes on the eve of the nineteenth-century bureaucratic reforms, see Findley, *Ottoman Civil Officialdom* 51–56. For a comprehensive history of Ottoman Turkish educational history from the fifteenth century through the Republican period, see Ergin, *İstanbul Mektepleri ve İlim, Terbiye ve San'at Müesseseleri Dolayısıyla Türkiye Maarif Tarihi.* (See volume 1 regarding Ottoman educational institutions prior to the nineteenth-century reforms.) On the Ottoman madrasas, see Uzunçarşılı, *Osmanlı Devletinin İlmiye Teşkilatı.* On the role of the madrasa instructor, see also Şükran Fazlıoğlu, "Language as a Road to the Being" 7–12.

[27] The Ottoman Turkish *seci'* and *arûz* derive from the Arabic *sadj'* and *'arūḍ,* respectively. See Fahd et al., "Sadj'" and Weil and Meredith-Owens, "'Arūḍ," in English. See Olgun, *Edebiyat Lügatı* 20, on *arûz,* and 131–132, on *seci',* in Turkish.

[28] This is not just a "peculiarity" of Perso-Arabic writing; there is no writing, perhaps, that can completely free itself of this fear. In "Freud and the Scene of Writing," Derrida observes that "Logo-phonocentrism is not a philosophical or historical error which the history of philosophy, of the West, that is, of the world, would have rushed into pathologically, but is rather a necessary, and necessarily finite, movement and structure: the history of the possibility of symbolism *in general . . .*" (197).

Decisive as they were, however, the upheavals of the mid-nineteenth century must not be regarded as a historical ground zero. I want to suggest that in a way, the historically chronological posteriority of phonocentric writing, in the Ottoman Empire of the nineteenth century, can be understood as an "anterior posteriority," a complex temporal relation that marks something more than simple derivation in time, and whose effects are *epistemic,* in the sense of that term developed by Foucault.[29] Neither progressive nor derivative evolution, in the strict and simple sense, nor a radical rupture with the past, such epistemic change is rather a violent, contingent intersection of large-scale historical formations. I am suggesting that in this instance, the mid-nineteenth century liberation and recapture of writing is grounded in the discursive convergence of Ottoman Turkish writing practices with those of Western Europe. It is equally important to note that despite the logocentrism that marked its dominance by recitation, the classical Ottoman Turkish practice of writing *did* preserve a certain awareness of writing's *inherent* multivalence and irreducible indeterminacy.[30] Where the phonocentric fantasy of representational writing, consolidated by the late nineteenth century, attempted to create and regulate the direct correspondence of signifying words to their signified referents, the written word, in classical Ottoman Turkish writing, was regarded as a nondeterminative starting point for interpretations that might vary, even if not all interpretations would ultimately carry authority. This interpretive indeterminacy built into classical Ottoman Turkish writing practice was a crucial condition of possibility for the development of Ottoman Turkish as an imperial composite and cosmopolitan language.

Chapter 1, entitled "Words Set Free," explores the historical developments of the second half of nineteenth century through a close reading of two Ottoman Turkish novels thematizing the communications revolution from alternate sides of Ottoman Turkish diglossia. My argument here is that conventional critical models of literary influence, which turn on the dissemination of European genres such as the novel or European literary currents such as realism, Romanticism, and modernism, are incapable of explaining the emergence of new Ottoman Turkish literary forms, which are *foremost* contingent on the transformation of writing practices accompanying their development. Focusing on a well-known early novel, *Müşahedat* ("Observations," 1891), written in the voice of a *meddah* storyteller by Ahmed Midhat Efendi (1844–1912), a popularizer of the novel form, I suggest that for a brief period, authorship meant not the original invention of a story, but the transcription of the news of a "freed" language. Here, the role played by the novel was that of a general mode of giving ear to the world. Midhat's vernacular writing, both enchanted by *and* fearful of open communicability and translatability in Ottoman Turkish, finally instrumentalizes literature for the containment of the revolutionary

---

[29] For this particular interpretation of the Foucauldian epistemic shift, see Morris, *In the Place of Origins* 46–47.
[30] For an analysis of the logic of signification in Arabic writing, see Mitchell 142–154.

possibilities inherent in the linguistic upheavals of the mid-nineteenth century. With Midhat, I argue, modern literature becomes a means to the end of a closed, proto-national public in a domesticated phonocentric vernacular.

In the second part of Chapter 1, I turn to Recâizâde Mahmud Ekrem's *Araba Sevdası* ("The Carriage Affair," 1896), which I argue marks the ascendance of a new writing practice in the demise of classical Ottoman Turkish poetic writing. The melancholic realist narrator of *Araba Sevdası* instrumentalizes words as abstract one-to-one labels for an external reality, while the failed poetic trials of his dandy double (in mistranslations of French Romantic and Ottoman poetry) work to overcome phonocentric representation. We can say that in contrast with Midhat, Ekrem reconciles himself, in the end, to the freedom inherent in language. In Ekrem, modern literature emerges as an extraordinary domain through which writing momentarily escapes the determinations of *both* classical logocentrism and modern phonocentrism, folding back on itself in a movement of repetition marked by irreducible otherness.[31]

If this book traces the emergence of modern phonocentrism and its new representational writing to the second half of the nineteenth century, this is not to suggest that the language reforms of the Turkish Republic were somehow historically inevitable, but rather to counter a general tendency to overemphasize the reforms' uniqueness as watersheds of twentieth century Turkish modernity. *Grammatology and Literary Modernity in Turkey* argues that the language reforms found their conditions of possibility in the semiotic reorganization of the second half of the nineteenth century, and that the question of phonocentrism subsequently takes only new forms, not originary substance.

Chapter 2, "The Grammatology of Nationalism," will show that the communications revolution of the mid-nineteenth century, which freed "Ottoman" from the cultural authority of Arabic and Persian, paved the way for its demise at the same time. The identitarian logic of modern phonocentrism, which aims to control communicability by fixing writing, is intolerant above all of what we might call mingled supranational affiliation. The late nineteenth- and early twentieth-century rise of Turkish nationalism saw the recoding, through the Orientalist discipline of Turcology, of a "vulgar" Turkic linguistic element (in counterposition with "cultivated" Arabic and Persian) as the foundation of Turkish-speaking Muslim identity. My reading of the literary and journalistic writings of Ömer Seyfeddin (1884–1920), in the first part of Chapter 2, suggests that a key goal of Turkish national grammatology during the first two decades of the twentieth century was to code the communicative and translative exchange of the Turkish language with other languages as death, so as to foreclose on non-national

---

[31] On the sense of the "fold" I am invoking here, see Deleuze, *Foucault* 94–123.

alternative possibilities of being and to unify a religiously identified, heterogeneous, multilingual population as a nation. If this production of Turkish national
identity, immediately preceding and following through the outbreak of the First
World War, demanded the policing of communications with the extra-Turkish
linguistic "outside," the Republican period that succeeded it was marked by the
attempt to liquidate the internal oral and written difference of the new nation.
The real historical specificity of the Republican language reforms, as the historian
Erik Zürcher has observed, is their epistemic extremity within a program for secularization and nationalization devoted to the production of the impossibly pure
and "self-same."

Under the presidency of Mustafa Kemal [Atatürk] (1881–1938), the Republican government set up after the 1919–1922 *Kurtuluş Savaşı* (War of Independence)
initiated a series of reforms including abolishing the caliphate (1924), banning
Ottoman traditional attire and encouraging the wearing of European-style clothing
(1925), and closing religious orders (1925), along with the switch to the Latin alphabet (1928).[32] I argue in Chapter 2 that the reformers never overcame their own fear
of a freed language, going so far as to make Turkish-speaking Muslim populations
(along with remaining ethno-religious minorities) the very target of Republican
phonocentrism in its constitution of a new national self. Against the ideologues of
nationalism, Chapter 2 will argue that vernacularization and phoneticization are
never merely acts of transcription of authentic national speech. Rather, they enact
the generalization of one specific variant of one vernacular, as a standard, through
new alphabetic technologies, for the nationalization of an otherwise heterogeneous,
multilingual population.

Lewis recounts that in June 1928, when Mustafa Kemal was presented with
five- and fifteen-year timetables for the alphabet reform, he replied, "Either this
will happen in three months or it won't happen at all" (34). Introduced to the
public on 9 August 1928, at a gala hosted by the ruling Republican People's Party
(CHP), the Latin alphabet for modern Turkish was adopted by the Grand National Assembly on 1 November 1928.[33] Ten days later, on November 11, a law was
passed requiring all male and female citizens between the ages of 16 and 40 to take
a literacy course at the national public schools, or Millet Mektepleri, then being
created across the Republic. By 1932, the Türk Dili Tetkik Cemiyeti (Society for
the Study of Turkish Language) had been founded to manage a program of linguistic modernization including the elimination (*tasfiye*) of Arabic and Persian

---

[32] For a history of the nationalist resistance, see Stanford Shaw's six-volume *From Empire to Republic.*
For a critical historical survey of the establishment of the Republic and the Kemalist reforms, see Zürcher
166–195. A scholarly biography of Atatürk is Mango, *Atatürk.* In the language debates of the Republican
period, the new alphabet was described as the "Latin alphabet." To avoid confusion, I use this historical term
throughout this book, rather than "Roman alphabet" as is more usual in contemporary scholarship
in linguistics.
[33] For the details of this law, see "Türk Harflerinin Kabul ve Tatbiki Hakkındaki Kanun."

borrowings and their substitution with new Turkish neologisms whenever existing Turkish equivalents could not be found.[34] Especially noteworthy is the nationwide *söz derleme seferberliği* or word-collection mobilization of 1932, undertaken to compile words currently in use—a spectacular project of archiving, in which an immensely heterogeneous active cultural idiom was uprooted from its particularity, converted to dictionary form, and lexicalized in abstract equivalence for the Arabic or Persian language element (itself part of that active cultural idiom).[35] By 1936, the society was officially promulgating the famous Güneş-Dil Teorisi, or Sun-Language Theory, which identified Turkish as the original source of all other human languages.[36]

I will argue in Chapter 2 that the epistemic violence of these reforms is not merely a local historical expression of the nationalist and secularist project of the Kemalist revolutionary elite in Turkey, but must be understood as an hyperbole of modernity's key dynamic itself: what Foucault in *The Order of Things* called "the enormous thrust of a freedom, a desire, or a will" in transgression.[37] From the mid-nineteenth century on, each project for the reformation of Ottoman Turkish is succeeded by one still more ambitious, each taking as a kind of unattainable object the radical indeterminancy of freed writing. We might say, with Foucault, that the Turkish language reforms' "great narrative" is a narrative of "desire, violence, savagery, and death," in "the glittering table of representation"[38]—a project whose form is a kind of self-referential modern madness "just as lacking in reason as that of Don Quixote, when he believed himself to be progressing . . . but was in fact getting more and more entangled in the labyrinth of his own representations."[39] Part I of this book, comprising the first two chapters, tells a tale of the violent subordination of the real to the represented (and its primacy), in the production of an impossible linguistic and ontological purity.

In Part II of this book, I turn to works of literature produced in a linguistic field profoundly overdetermined by the national grammatology of the first half of the twentieth century. Profoundly self-conscious regarding both local *and* global forces aiming to bind language, the literary texts I read in Part II of this book offer their own accounts of the violent control of writing. What they narrate is not, in the least, a

---

[34] The society was named the Türk Dili Araştırma Kurumu (Society for Research in Turkish Language) in 1934 and changed to the Türk Dil Kurumu (Turkish Language Society) in 1936.

[35] I am borrowing Gayatri Chakravorty Spivak's special use of the term "lexicalization" here. "To *lexicalize*," she writes, "is to separate a linguistic item from its appropriate grammatical system into the conventions of another grammar" ("Harlem" 118). Spivak's example is from W. E. B. DuBois, *The Souls of Black Folk:* "At the head of each chapter, DuBois takes a line of African spiritual and writes it in European musical notation. There we have the desire to convert the performative into performance—an active cultural idiom lexicalized into the encyclopedia or the museum—that is at the core of it" (125).

[36] The Sun-Language Theory will be discussed in detail in Chapter 2.

[37] See Foucault, *Order* 209; *Mots* 222.

[38] See Foucault, *Order* 210; *Mots* 223.

[39] See Foucault, *Order* 210–211; *Mots* 223.

pleasant story. Still, I think we would be mistaken to approach the thematization of writing in these very *literary* texts as merely mimetic historical allegories, of one form or another. More than a mere second-order ideological representation, literature is also a linguistic *act* that distinguishes itself from other linguistic acts in its "free" mediation of writing independent of a fixed referent. Against phonocentric forces aiming to control language, I argue, such fictive—and therefore figurative, nontransparent, and multifarious—acts of writing reopen the closed channels of linguistic travel. Despite and against the extremity of measures for nationalization, in this case, such self-reflexive literary *stagings* demonstrate that no control of linguistic communication is ever complete.

Tanpınar's 1954 novel *Saatleri Ayarlama Enstitüsü* (*The Time Regulation Institute*) for example, which I take up in Chapter 3, provides us with an indispensable critique of the presumptuous thought that we "dictate" our own language at will. Constructed as the autobiography of a writer-citizen surviving the transition from empire to republic, the novel registers writing in a "cut" Turkish, deprived of its Arabic and Persian elements, as a profoundly uncanny experience, offering a literary embodiment (more than a mere representation) of the self-estranging subjective and social effects of the reforms. Unable to recognize himself as the source of his own words, the novel's protagonist wanders from one temporal-historically absurd and senseless situation to the next, ending up as the assistant director of a fictive Clock-Setting Institute established to synchronize all the private and public clocks in Republican Turkey. The significance of this novel, I suggest, lies in the way it both examines and resists the cultural effects of the reforms, without simultaneously generating a new logocentrism domesticating the uncanniness it comes to understand as immanent in language.

In Chapter 4, meanwhile, I examine another exemplary novel, *Matmazel Noraliya'nın Koltuğu* ("Mademoiselle Noralia's Armchair," 1949), by the journalist, novelist, and critic Peyami [Safa] (1899–1961). In a narrative and discursive idiom animated by regional colloquialisms, French medical and psychoanalytic terminology, archaic Ottoman Turkish, Arabic prayer words, and Kurdish borrowings, Safa's novel provides yet another account of the failure of the nationalist phonocentric project to meet its ideal goal. Unlike *The Time Regulation Institute,* however, *Matmazel Noraliya'nın Koltuğu* (which is organized by scenes of the translation and rewriting of such texts as Rimbaud's "L'Éternité" and Aldous Huxley's *The Perennial Philosophy*), can be said to aspire to the transcendence of linguistic difference and the reconstitution of a new order of national signification. My reading of Safa's novel emphasizes the *collapse* of this assimilating authorial agenda, but affirms it, at the same time, as a mark of the ineradicable internal heterogeneity of the Turkish language.

The book concludes with an analysis of language politics in the work of Nâzım Hikmet [Ran] (1901–1963). Affiliated with the post-revolutionary Soviet Futurists, Nâzım distinguished himself from both Safa and Tanpınar in his embrace of vernacularization. We should not, however, take Nâzım's embrace of vernacular-ization for an embrace of official state nationalism. Where nationalist phonocen-trism sought to control writing for the production of a pure national essence, Nâzım's vernacular writing aimed to expand and augment the revolutionary power of communication without any compensation in or by cultural essentialism. In an analysis of scenes of reading, writing, and translation in Nâzım's extended prose poems from the 1930s and 1940s, "Şeyh Bedreddin Destanı" ("The Epic of Sheik Bedreddin," 1936), "Taranta-Babu'ya Mektuplar" ("Letters to Taranta-Babu," 1935), and *Memleketimden İnsan Manzaraları* (*Human Landscapes from My Country*), I show that vernacularization, for Nâzım, is the opening up of language to the difference of other languages and linguistic registers, for the formation of an impure and boundless collectivity.

The works I have selected here do not by themselves give anything like a com-plete picture of Turkish literary modernity. Other critics have demonstrated at length how the work of such other prominent Republican writers as Halide Edib [Adıvar] (1884–1964), Yakup Kadri [Karaosmanoğlu] (1889–1974), and Reşat Nuri [Güntekin] (1889–1956), served the ends of reformist nationalism.[40] In Chapter 2 of this book, I examine the instrumentalization of literature toward the end of Turkish linguistic nationalism in the work of Ömer Seyfeddin. A work of literature is a powerful technology of nationalism in so far as it stakes a claim on using language fictively, outside the determination of rules binding statements.[41] In writing a fiction, an author willfully abstracts her or his own authorship, as-suming the voice of a narrator (or characters) who, "existing" only in language, can never be the *presences* of a nonfictional speaking situation. Here, as James T. Siegel has put it, "the origin of speech . . . shift[s] to a place whose locus is uncer-tain" (Siegel, *Naming* 80). Nationalism mobilizes on the level of culture by appro-priating such indeterminate and arguably *quasi*-religious literary communicability for its own ends.

While it is essential to recognize this nationalist appropriation of literature for what it is, it is equally important to observe that not *all* acts of literature willingly surrender themselves to such absorption. The works of fiction I examine in Part II of this book are of special importance, in this respect, in so far as they both thema-tize *and* free language from the binding control of phonocentrism. For me, these works affirm the ineradicable indiscipline of Turkish in and for itself, pointing to the possibility of an alternative, non-possessive relation to the "mother tongue" marked by an irreducible otherness.

---

[40] See Seyhan 41–79.

[41] Of course, the institution of literature maintains its own laws (generic, and otherwise). My point here is simply that literature is *more* than its laws. On this point, Derrida wrote of "literature as historical institution with its conventions, rules, etc., but also this institution of fiction which gives *in principle* the power to say everything, to break free of the rules, to displace them, and thereby to institute, to invent and even to suspect the traditional difference between nature and institution, nature and conventional law, nature and history" ("This Strange" 37).

With and Beyond Genres and Movements

At this point, the extent to which Orhan Pamuk's receipt of the 2006 Nobel Prize in Literature has greatly intensified interest in modern Turkish literature, in the transnational literary market, is beyond doubt. At the Frankfurt Book Fair of 2008, Turkey was celebrated as the fair's official "Guest of Honor," a distinction that extended the lionization of several of Turkey's most visibly embattled writers, and which has already clearly spurred a growth in English translations of twentieth-century and contemporary Turkish literature.[42] This growing interest, and the urgent curiosity to which it testifies, now confronts a real paucity of scholarship in Turkish literary studies available in English. Influential scholarship available to North American Anglophone readers has long been limited to two well-regarded studies of Ottoman poetry (Walter G. Andrews's 1985 *Poetry's Voice, Society's Song: Ottoman Lyric Poetry* and Victoria Rowe Holbrook's 1994 *The Unreadable Shores of Love: Turkish Modernity and Mystic Romance*) and three important studies of the Ottoman Turkish novel (Robert P. Finn's 1978 *The Early Turkish Novel*, Ahmet Ö. Evin's 1983 *Origins and Development of the Turkish Novel*, and those portions of Jale Parla's seminal 1990 *Babalar ve Oğullar* that appear in her journal articles "The Object of Comparison" and "Car Narratives: A Subgenre in Turkish Novel Writing"). Azade Seyhan's *Tales of Crossed Destinies: The Modern Turkish Novel in a Comparative Context,* which appeared in 2008 as part of the Modern Language Association of America's publication series "World Literatures Reimagined," is the first substantive overview of the twentieth-century Turkish novel available to Anglophone readers.

One of my goals in *Grammatology and Literary Modernity in Turkey* is to supplement this important body of work, by considering the relevance of modern Turkish literature to contemporary critical debates around questions of disciplinarity and methodology in comparative literature and world literature studies. While the early influence-based genre and movement historiographies of Finn and Evin have provided invaluable close readings of many early Ottoman Turkish novels, I will suggest that their readings are at times too solidly grounded in unquestioning reference to the paradigms of European literary realism. Realism, Romanticism, and modernism, I will suggest—and as a matter of fact, the very form of the novel itself—are in and of themselves empty categories when essentialized and (largely involuntarily) transposed onto Ottoman Turkish literary history in this way. It is

---

[42] Perhaps the most noteworthy recent example is Ahmet Hamdi Tanpınar's 1949 novel *A Mind at Peace*; in *Istanbul: Memories and the City,* the memoir that earned Pamuk the Nobel, Pamuk acknowledged Tanpınar as one of his most important influences. In United States-based literary studies, this interest is also confirmed by the recent publication of a cluster of articles devoted to Turkey and Turkish literature in the January 2008 of *PMLA,* the peer-reviewed journal of the Modern Language Association of America, whose historical focus has always been on Anglo-American literature. One might also note the Spring/Summer 2003 issue of the journal *South Atlantic Quarterly* entitled *Relocating the Fault Lines: Turkey Beyond the East-West Divide,* edited by Sibel Irzık and Güven Güzeldere.

not a matrix or pattern of positive comparability which links the European and Ottoman Turkish literary domains and their objects, but the discursive context of phonocentrism itself.

One might consider, in this context, Franco Moretti's mapping of the world novel as a project in genre studies that arguably relinquishes the Eurocentrist evolutionary teleology of the scholarship preceding it. Grouping the Ottoman Turkish novelist Namık Kemal with Ignacy Krasicki, José Rizal, and René Maran, Moretti has suggested these writers as typical of a "compromise" between Western plot, "local *characters,*" and "local *narrative voice*" (65) that marks in fact the *conventional,* not the exceptional factor in the rise of the novel generally. The "uneasiness" of a local narrative voice, in this schema, is the formal register of uneven economic development itself, in all its dynamism and violence, rather than some Orientalized evolutionary plateau of "backwardness." Although Moretti's worldly sociological formalism generates a methodological alternative to the more conventional mode of Eurocentrist literary genre studies, it reaches its limits, in my view, when it comes to the real and unavoidable complexities of linguistic mediation, which serves as the very condition of possibility for any such literary registration. Where it cannot be supplemented by a *literary* materialism taking the transformation of the medium of literary registration, itself, as a locus of (fundamentally complex) desire, the new genre studies disproportionately inspired by Moretti's work might be said to redenominate extra-European writing, in a reverse ethnocentrist mode masking a persistent ethnocentrism.

Those of my readers familiar with Parla's *Babalar ve Oğullar* ("Fathers and Sons"), which fundamentally transformed the study of its subject, will recognize her inspiration in my arrangement of materials here. Reconstructing Ottoman Turkish literary history as a genealogical narrative linking fathers to sons, Parla argued that the first-generation Ottoman Turkish novelists, writing in the two decades from the 1870s to the 1890s, took on paternalistic roles as the guardians of a new society, largely reproducing the absolutist-idealist ideology of their classical precursors. While I have followed Parla's work, here, in its move away from reductively narrow models of literary influence, my own discursive history of phonocentrism might be said to take Parla's counterposition of an essentially "empirical realistic" European epistemology to its "aprioristic and idealistic" Ottoman counterpart ("Car Narratives" 538) in another direction.[43] In my own reading, writers like Midhat assumed "paternal" or paternalistic roles in and for Turkish literary history not in their imperviousness to the foreign "messages" they received, but in precisely their *response* to the transgressions of their own seduction by translative language.[44] If, along with Parla, I regard Ekrem's *Araba Sevdası* as a seminal moment in modern Turkish prose literature, that, in my own reading, is not because the novel portrays what Parla calls

---

[43] For Parla's first detailed discussion of Ekrem, see *Babalar* 105–124.
[44] For a condensed version of Parla's argument on this point, see "The Object of Comparison."

"the fruitlessness of *Tanzimat* writers' labors to represent and communicate" (538), but also, or perhaps rather, because it demonstrates the Ottoman intellectual's masterful *command* of phonocentric representational writing. Where Parla narrates the epistemic shift of the late-nineteenth century in the "death" of absolutist literary fathers (such as Midhat) and the consequent breakdown of orphaned literary sons (such as Ekrem), I have found that that the uncanny ascendance of phonocentrism suggests precisely the *inversion* of genealogical sequencing.

Readers familiar with Turkish literary history will note that the literary-historical periodization structuring my work, in this book, fails to reproduce rigidly the conventional form of such periodization, grounded in denominated literary-historical movements in the Ottoman Empire and Republican Turkey.[45] There is nothing especially pernicious about such routine forms of criticism; but there ought not to be any prohibition on imagined alternatives, either. Fundamentally, for my work in this book, the historical determination of Turkish literary modernity is a function of shifts in the history of writing itself—not groupings of individual authors understood (or misunderstood) as historical actors. It is to this end that I emphasize the emergence of the discourse of phonocentrism itself, in Chapter 1, among intellectuals in the second half of the nineteenth century; the nationalization of the vernacular, in Chapter 2, in the early twentieth century; and the adoption of phonocentrism as state policy, in the second part of Chapter 2, with the establishment of the Republic of Turkey.

With that said, the arrangement of some material here (such as that structuring Chapters 3, 4, and 5) is thematic, and not (or not solely) historically chronological. Where my arrangement of themes breaks ranks with the regiment of historical publication dates, that is because the temporality of literature does not always coincide perfectly with the temporality of political history. If strictly speaking, the publication dates of Tanpınar's and Safa's novels fall under the period of "multi-party politics" following the end of the single-party rule, in 1946, implicit in my method, here, is the notion that these novels offer something of a long view of the transformation of Turkish society, from the late-nineteenth through the mid-twentieth century, and that they must be read with the historical *imagination* they themselves invoke.

---

[45] I recognize here the consensual historical distinctions between the literature of the post-1839 *Tanzimat* (Reorganization) period, the national literature of the Young Turk period (1908–1918), and the post-1923 literature of the Republican period. Each of these periods is conventionally divided into additional subcategories, which I also recognize—but which I do not take as a basis for organization of my materials, here. The conventional subdivisions include (but are not limited to) *Edebiyat-ı Cedide* ("New Literature," 1896–1901), an "art for art's sake" movement distinguished by its use of Arabisms and Persianisms, rather than the vernacular, and *Fecr-i Âti* ("Dawn of the New Age," 1909–1912), a Symbolist movement which emerged in reaction to *Edebiyat-ı Cedide* but did not depart from its principles in any significant way. *Millî Edebiyat Akımı* ("The National Literature Movement," 1911–1923) comprised various groupings of nationalist writers and poets advocating vernacularization. The period sometimes called simply "Literature of the Republican Period" is subdivided by the romantic nationalist literature of the 1920s and 1930s and the social realist literature of the 1940s and 1950s, with a wide array of traditionalist and avant-garde literary formations.

Such critical flexibility is recommended in dealing with the major sociological categories of literary, literary-critical and literary-historical subordination, as well. As first-generation Republican intellectuals representing widely divergent political blocs (those of conservatism, nationalism, and communism, respectively), Tanpınar, Safa and Nâzım have left their marks on Turkish political and cultural historiography, itself, in more ways than one. It is common (and not necessarily pernicious) to segment and segregate these three writers and their study by political affiliation, in a literary-historical reproduction of the political schisms of the Turkish national scene.[46] But this fundamentally typological approach is too limited for my critical project here, which begins with an understanding of literary modernity as a contestation of political projects and their schisms.[47] As I demonstrate in Chapter 2, despite official nationalism's success in producing an expansive new national written culture (along with the bureaucratic intelligentsia charged to administer and reproduce it), its control of linguistic communicability was always far from complete. In many ways, the real legacy of the language reforms was an intensified struggle, in itself, for the social reclamation and control of social communication. Where the *literary* works of iconic Turkish writers show us, despite and *with* their differences, the general ferocity of this struggle, they point also (and from within) to the limits of the logic of identity (including the identitarianism of political blocs), in their various ways of relinquishing their *own* desire to "fix" writing.

As a warning to those of my readers committed to misunderstanding me on this point, I want to be clear that to privilege the literary *act,* in this sense, is not necessarily also to make claims for its ethical purity. Some of the writers I discuss in Part II of this book attempt quite strenuously to reclaim the communicative powers of language for a conservative political counter-agenda every bit as violent as the agenda of official state nationalism that it opposes. Safa's *Matmazel Noraliya'nın Koltuğu* can be read (as I read it) as affirming the irreducible difference of writing only *despite* and *against* Safa's own purposes, in so far as these can be known and understood, both literary-critically and literary-historically. It is the power of literature's fictive performance *itself* to teach us how to relinquish the binding of language: a lesson that individual historical actor-authors are free to learn or not learn, as they see fit, but which might be both learned *and* taught by their work, irrespectively.

---

[46] See, for example, Belge et al., eds., *Modern Türkiye'de Siyasî Düşünce* ("Political Thought in Modern Turkey"), in nine volumes covering the thought of the late Ottoman period, Westernism, Kemalism, nationalism, conservatism, Islamism, liberalism, and leftism. Included are chapters devoted to the literary representation(s) of each major category of political history.

[47] Unavoidably, each political project will makes its own (counter) claim for the modern. I have found Arif Dirlik's essay "Modernity as History" particularly helpful in thinking through these issues. Commenting on contemporary discourses on Chinese modernity, Dirlik writes:

> Modernity in China, as it is globally, is a contested terrain where different experiences of the modern produce not a homogeneous modernity, but a cultural politics in which the conquest of the modern is the ultimate prize. . . . Modernity, to paraphrase Wittrock, is universal not because of shared goals, or how to reach them, but because it provides an idea to reach for, that becomes ever more elusive as it is decentered culturally, but still motivates a search for the modern. (33)

Between Literary Theory and Area Studies, From the Shore of Literature

Those who know well the early Derrida of *Of Grammatology* will have no trouble detecting his influence on my reading of literature and the history of writing here. It goes without saying that Derrida's work serves as an unpaved road, at best, to the disciplinary territory of national area studies, dominated as it is (now, as ever) by the unrepentant positivism of social science.[48] Declarations of a shared interdisciplinary interest in the study of language and literature notwithstanding, scholars in literary studies and area studies continue to this day to ignore each another—or worse (the concept of deconstruction associated with Derrida's work serves as a kind of disciplinary totem and scapegoat, in this respect). If I can say that *Grammatology and Literary Modernity in Turkey* aims to work through this contest between literary theory and area studies, that is because my rereading of modern Turkish literature, here, through the history of Turkish writing, suggests some potentially crucial methodological implications not only for work in literary studies, but for the interdisciplinary study of the culture of nationalism itself.

Many such opportunities have been missed. Benedict Anderson's observation, in *Imagined Communities* (1983; revised ed., 1991), that "the seeds of Turkish nationalism are easily detectable in the appearance of a lively vernacular press in Istanbul in the 1870s" (75), was an early reading of the dynamic of reformed languages as what I am calling a "telecommunications technology," in the "unself-conscious standardization of vocabulary" (*Spectre* 31) in newspaper culture. Anderson noted that under such pressure, languages are encouraged to become, so to speak, "transparent to each other," creating a "horizontal" reading public of "visible and invisible human beings" (31). For Anderson, this horizontality of representational writing—what he calls its "serialization"—disseminated by the novel and the newspaper is the ground of an unbound, emancipating nationalist imagination operating in a common abstract temporal and spatial continuum. The nation, for Anderson, is to be understood as a kind of sublation of the universalizing and excluding tendencies of phonocentrism, and as such, an entity carrying historical finality.

Anderson's critics have noted the extent to which serial translatability works almost too well, in this account of things, failing to generate anything that remains illegible either without or within the national frame.[49] Against Anderson's objectification of national language and literature as uniform material technologies, Partha Chatterjee (in *The Nation and Its Fragments*) has foregrounded the *spiritualization* of the linguistic medium under conditions of colonial rule, drawing our attention to the messy complexity of interiorizations of language by non-European subjects.

---

[48] For a critique of the predominance of positivist macromethodologies in Turkish studies, see Mardin, "Projects."

[49] As H. D. Harootunian and Partha Chatterjee, among others, have observed, the homogenizing and universalizing tendencies of global capitalist modernity are nowhere as successfully realized as Anderson makes them out to be. See Chatterjee's "Anderson's Utopia" and Harootunian's "Ghostly Comparisons."

Chatterjee observes that "anti-colonial nationalism creates its own domain of sovereignty within colonial society," demarcating a self-governing inner "spiritual" cultural domain against the accepted material and technological superiority of the West "outside" (6). Where a colonially educated bilingual intelligentsia, in Chatterjee's reading, supports nationalist political struggle against imperial powers threatening it from "outside," it launches a creative project in the inner, cultural domain: the determined fashioning of "a 'modern' national culture that is nevertheless not Western" (6). In Chatterjee's account, language and literature are ascribed to this inner cultural domain, where they are transformed and reconstructed by (Orientalist) practices of the national elite as modern *and* indigenous.[50]

Despite their differences, Anderson and Chatterjee's combined modernist-constructivist approach has had a profound critical impact, leaving the way open for a new mode of critical historiography of the making of the modern Turkish language. (Where such early work on the topic as Agâh Sırrı Levend's *Türk Dilinde Gelişme ve Sadeleşme Evreleri* [1949; 2nd ed. 1960; 3rd ed. 1972] could be said to have risked reproducing official state ideology, in excessively naturalizing the Turkish Republican language reforms, more recent studies by Şerif Mardin, Hüseyin Sadoğlu and İlker Aytürk have offered critical accounts of Turkish linguistic nationalism.) Nevertheless, where the study of nationalism more broadly is concerned, there has been very little meaningful contact with the deconstructive history of the mediation of study itself, including writing, that emanates from Derrida's work and the work of those who have built on it. Oblivious, it would seem, to the impact of forty years of post-structuralist critique of the formation and foundation of disciplines in the Euro-Atlantic university, scholars in national area studies too often persist, today, in taking language as a passive instrument, and literature as a second-order reflection of a first-order "outer" reality.[51] For their part, many scholars in literary studies (even those most committed to a theoretical and/or philosophical approach) still continue to argue for the privileged role of literary language, from a position of willed exteriority—to the point where they blind themselves to precisely those specific aspects of historical context most indispensable for their own work.

---

[50] Although Turkish nationalism fails in significant ways to converge with a range of Asian and African anti-colonial nationalisms, a similar demarcation between the "spiritual" "inside" and the "material" "outside" may be found, for example, in the seminal text of Turkish nationalism, *Türkçülüğün Esasları* (1923; *The Principles of Turkism*, trans. 1968) by Ziya Gökalp (1876-1924), its most prominent ideologue. There, Gökalp locates the Turkish language, and its literature, at the heart of the "inner" cultural domain, understood as simultaneously spiritual *and* national, and presumably unmarked by the transnationality of a technological civilization shared with other nations.

[51] As Rey Chow suggests, it is the so-called "self-referentiality" of literary theory (47)—what Paul de Man called its questioning of "the modalities of production and of reception of meaning and of value prior to their establishment" ("Resistance" 7)—that foregrounds the linguistic and discursive conditions of the very possibility of signification, which is what I am centrally concerned with in this book. To be sure, the task of chasing down actually and already existing empirical fact is both an essential task, not to be dismissed out of hand, and a genuinely diverting one. To suppose this task to be anything but difficult (even under the best possible conditions), however, is for a researcher to remain blind to her own historical and intellectual overdetermination by the unavoidably modern practice of research itself.

One especially noteworthy exception to this general rule of inertia is the pioneering work of Kojin Karatani (especially in *Nihon Kindai bungaku no kigen* [1980; *Origins of Modern Japanese Literature,* 1993] and "Nationalism and Écriture" [1995]), the influence of which coincided in many ways with that of Anderson in *Imagined Communities* and *The Spectre of Comparisons.* Deconstructing nationalist idealizations of the vernacular as "authentic" oral speech, Karatani placed on view some of the fundamental ethico-political implications of early Derridean "textualism," in a demonstration of the integral role of state regulation of the technologies of writing in the national standardization of one vernacular against (many) competing others.[52] Karatani could be said to have anticipated and shared Anderson's constructivist approach to the formation of the nation in and through vernacularization. Still, the project of bringing Karatani's and Anderson's respective projects into dialogue seems not to have held much appeal, during a period (the 1990s) marked by the energetic repudiation of deconstruction (as of "high" literary theory generally) and the opportune rise of a new globalist transnationalism as critical object *and* mode. One unfortunate consequence of this turn of events is the redigestion, as it were, of extra-European literatures by yet another (new, global) literary canon, coming as it always does at the expense of both literary *and* historico-institutional specificity. Let me suggest, as yet one more mode of approach to *Grammatology and Literary Modernity in Turkey,* that it is only by returning to some of this rigorously comparative work left incomplete, several decades ago (and to some extent, now eclipsed), that we can deal responsibly with the *best* of the somewhat more facile transnationalism that superseded it.

It is in this context that we might revisit, now, the concepts of writing and communication manipulated by both the ideologues and the critics of nationalism. The common understanding binding both such formations—of language as a *uniform* continuum transferring meaning, and of writing as a *continuous* registration of spoken language—marks nothing less than the persistence of the foundational Western philosophical discourse on writing treated by Derrida in *Of Grammatology* (and such other early essays as "Signature Event Context"). Neither the ideologue nor the critic of nationalism can do without the continuity of his object; *both* are driven to stabilize it, ignoring or erasing gaps or distance interrupting continuous communication. It is Derrida who reminds us of the plain and simple *impossibility* of any such uninterrupted travel, even where it is a question of one's own self-communication, in the autonomous repetition of a linguistic sign:

---

[52] Though Karatani's work has provided me with an important methodological model for my work here, I ought also to clarify some differences between our respective projects. First, I am tracing the emergence of modern phonocentrism, in the Turkish case, to the communications revolution and the global translation of the mid-nineteenth century. Second, modern literature, in my account, is not only a register of the discursive ascendance of phonocentrism, in itself, but additionally of that ascendance's limits and failures. One might say that the "interior exteriority" of *literary* writing is obscured, in Karatani's accounts—which are focused, perhaps too totalizingly, on the absorption of modern literature by the discursive complex of the modern nation-state.

> Let us consider any element of spoken language, a large or small unity. First
> condition for it to function: . . . a certain self-identity of this element (mark,
> sign, etc.) must permit its recognition and repetition. Across empirical vari-
> ations of tone, of voice, etc., eventually of a certain accent, for example, one
> must be able to recognize the identity, shall we say, of a signifying form.
> Why is this identity paradoxically the division or dissociation from itself. . .?
> It is because this unity of the signifying form is constituted only by its iter-
> ability, by the possibility of being repeated in the absence not only of its
> referent, which goes without saying, but of a determined signified or current
> intention of signification, as of every present intention of communication.[53]

Oral or written, any linguistic sign is available to, and exposed to, interminable
repetition. On the one hand, it necessarily offers a certain "sameness," as a minimal
condition of the recognizability required for it to be repeatable, in the first place. In
that repetition, on the other hand, any linguistic sign *also* separates from itself and
its self-sameness: any repetition of the same sign is a repetition in a new, different
context, necessarily distinct from its precedent.[54] For Derrida, the very "communicability" of a word, even as a mere and single repetition of the same word, is never
guaranteed; rather, it is always threatened by, indeed subject to disunity. Such
disunity is furthermore not anomalous, but rather routine: an effect of the very
structure of internal self-differentiation that makes meaning possible at all. It is in
this sense that for Derrida, the "force of breaking [with context] is not an accidental
predicate, but the very structure"[55] of language itself. And if such internal divisibility
is the very condition of possibility for the meaning of a word (for its meaning the
same, in different contexts), it is at the very same time the condition of possibility for
a word's deformation and resignification, as well as translation from and into other
languages.

No more so than in fields of national area studies focused on and/or operating
outside the Euro-Atlantic sphere of influence, ethnocentrist dismissals of Derrida's
work (for example, as an "alien" Judeo-Christian Euro-Atlantic export product)
have constrained the profound implications of this "foreigner's" writing for the
historiography of nationalism, which would find its grounding assumption—of
any given national language as nationally self-same—*productively* placed under
erasure there, if ever it dared to look. My own goal, in *Grammatology and Literary
Modernity in Turkey,* is to reconceive nationalism, through the insights provided to
me by Derrida's work, as a discovery and containment of the vernacular, itself, as

---

[53] Derrida, "Signature Event" 318; "Signature événement" 378.
[54] In *Of Grammatology*, Derrida names this minimal condition of repetition in difference "the trace":

Without a retention in the minimal unit of temporal experience, without a trace retaining the other
as other in the same, no difference would do its work and no meaning would appear. It is not the
question of a constituted difference here, but rather, before all determination of the content, of the
pure movement which produces difference. *The (pure) trace is différance.* (62; *De la grammatologie*
92)

[55] Derrida, "Signature Event" 317; "Signature événement" 377.

a deterritorialized other—especially in historical periods marked by the intensification of writing and translation. Popular nationalists and official elites alike require the "reform" of writing, for the national project, not because language appears to them, self-evidently, as an indubitable possession and practical instrument. The truth is the opposite: writing reform is driven by the experience of language as a threatening, uprooting *force,* generative of unforeseen consequences without end. Where I have used the epithet "translative" to qualify this *force,* I mean to emphasize the extent to which the transmission of "foreign" messages, in a "native" language, is radically generative in just this sense. An understanding of translation in this broadest sense, which would necessarily escape its own recuperation as an object (for example, of disciplinary translation studies), will point to a deeper understanding of both political *and* literary nationalization—as well as their real limits.

While I will place great emphasis, here, on the telecommunicative function of writing in the Turkish case, I will not presuppose any language's universal translatability in that function (as Anderson might be said to have done, in a portion of his work). Nor do I regard *any* possible formation of nationalism as achieving a clean temporal break in history, revolutionary or otherwise. At the same time, I have resisted the attempt to confine language and literature to the inner spiritual domain—itself a key tactic of both ideologues and critics of nationalism, when forced to confront language and literature. We might say that for my purposes in this book, at least, Chatterjee's valuable critique of Anderson dismissed somewhat too hastily the essential *strangeness* of a deterritorializing, translative language, in its continuous renegotiation of borders between "inside" and "outside."

One might argue, in fact, that at the level of language, at least, nationalism is best understood not as the realization of revolutionary change (however conceived), but on the contrary, as a struggle for *containment* of the revolutionary transvaluation of values through writing technologies (an idea I have found profitably pursued in the work of James T. Siegel and Vicente Rafael). Language as a telecommunications technology is effectively nationalized by new phonocentrist projects—that is, interiorized within a national frame, and so to speak "domesticated"—when the illegibility of the graphic sign, and the surplus of meaning it harbors in intensified communicative and translative activity, provokes an otherwise unmanageable fear of disorder.[56] The national spiritualization of language, in this way of thinking the problem, is an effect, rather than a cause or an origin, and the linguistically constituted nation is "haunted," in a way, from the very outset by the foreign outside it can never entirely dispel. As Messick, Mitchell, and Karatani have shown in their

---

[56] James T. Siegel's *Fetish, Recognition, Revolution* (1997) traces the emergence of Melayu in Indonesia, and Rafael's *The Promise of the Foreign* (2005) the role of Castilian in the Philippines, as lingua francas endowed with uncanny powers. Unlike Melayu or Castilian in these particular contexts, however, Turkish was the first language of a significant subject body of the Ottoman Empire (including the ruling elite). If the unsurpassable

work on nineteenth-century Yemen, Egypt, and Japan respectively, the national imagination of community is overdetermined by state management of the "impossible science" of grammatology, in the management of writing. This book argues that despite and against such ruthless phonocentrism, the "strange institution" called literature—"outside," as it were, in the archive of phonocentrism—harbors the possibility of another order of things.[57]

"foreignness" of Melayu, in the Indonesian case as Siegel describes it, was marked by its widespread use as a lingua franca (rather than as a first language)—and that of Castilian, in the Philippine case as Rafael examines it, by its identification with colonial power—the Turkish case involved a discovery of the *first language itself* as "foreign," under the historical conditions of its emergence as a translative medium.

[57] On literature as the displacement of the logic of immediacy and as a name for the sublimation of political violence, see Siegel's epilogue to *Fetish* 231–254.

PART ONE

Failed Revolution

1

Words Set Free

What the eye is to the lover—that particular, ordinary eye he or she is
born with—language—whatever language history has made his or her
mother-tongue—is to the patriot. Through that language, encountered at
mother's knee and parted with only at the grave, pasts are restored,
fellowships are imagined, and futures dreamed.

—Benedict Anderson, *Imagined Communities*

But what makes me remember the day especially was [Auntie Teïzé]
bringing out picture-books to show us during our visit to her apartments.
It was a strange sensation to me, those signs and the pictures out of
which a new world suddenly spoke. The book was a collection of African
travels, perhaps translated; I do not know. But she actually sat on the
floor and read to us the descriptions and explained the pictures. She had
not been a teacher in the palace for nothing, for, as granny said, she
could make a stone understand things. From that moment I gradually
began to find the palace lady very attractive. An uncontrollable desire to
learn to read began with the African travels that day.

—Halide Edib, *Memoirs of Halidé Edib*

Set in Istanbul around 1870, Recâizâde Mahmud Ekrem's *Araba Sevdası* ("The Carriage Affair," 1896) follows the overlapping topographic and textual adventures of a
"super-westernized" dandy, or *züppe,* through and along a chain of (mis)translations—
from an Ottoman Turkish sonnet by the late eighteenth-century poet Vâsıf-ı Enderunî,
to Jean-Jacques Rousseau's *Julie, ou la nouvelle Héloïse,* to the popular manual *Le
secrétaire des amants,* to Alphonso de Lamartine's *Graziella*—composing a love letter
to a fundamentally and continually misrecognized beloved.[1] Such intense linguistic

---

[1] On Bihruz as super-westernized dandy, see Mardin, "Super Westernization in Urban Life in the Ottoman Empire in the Last Quarter of the Nineteenth Century," and Moran, *Türk Romanına Eleştirel Bir Bakış*
73–86. In my use of the term "Ottoman Turkish," I am following the scholarly convention of referring to the
Turkish language of the Ottoman era as "Ottoman Turkish." This convention usefully marks the historical
specificity of this variation of the Turkish language, without essentializing it. "Ottoman" by itself refers to the
historical milieu of the Ottoman Empire; it may also refer to the discourse of Ottoman identity that emerged

performativity marks *Araba Sevdası* as an important record of the mid-nineteenth-century communications revolution, in its displacement of Ottoman lyric poetry.[2] We might say that Ekrem's novel registers the emergence of a new simplified phonocentric writing, freed of the linguistic, formal, and moral laws of classical writing, as the condition of possibility of its own novelization—while pointing to its tensions, contradictions, and deflections as such.

Araba Sevdası has often been singled out as a unique literary performance of modern linguistic self-consciousness in Turkey.[3] Arguably, however, it is neither unique nor unprecedented in its reflective staging of the communications revolution and its effects. The writings of Ekrem's prolific contemporary Ahmed Midhat Efendi (1844–1912), a popularizer of the novel form in the Ottoman Empire, provide us with material for an important internal comparison. Where Ekrem might be said to imagine the modern institutionalization of modern literature atop the ruins of the "high" divan poetry of a bygone age, Midhat, who composed, adapted, and translated more than 150 works in the vernacular voice of popular *meddah* storytelling, produced an archive of such institutionalization from the other side of diglossia. In an 1880 article in the periodical *Şark*, Midhat tapped the linguistic self-consciousness of an earlier scene of the Ottoman Turkish novel:

> If you're free one day, go to the Bridge and survey the faces passing by. You'll see a chic [*şık*] person dressed up from head to toe, jingling and walking like lightning despite the pain of his corns. If he runs into a friend, he does not stop to greet him; instead he signals ahead with his hand, face, in short with his complete physique and outfit, as if [*gûya*] he must hurry to attend something ahead. Of course, there is something very important ahead: There is the novel [*roman*] in that direction; he's running toward that novel. How can we dare to stop him? (Ahmed Midhat, "Romancı ve Hayat" 66)[4]

Foregrounded, here, is what we might call the comic publicity of the novelist traversing the Istanbul cityscape, crossing the bridge, linking the Europeanized and the more traditional Muslim neighborhoods on opposing banks of the Golden

---

in the context of nineteenth-century reforms. The first portion of the present chapter provides further reflection on nineteenth-century Ottoman identitarianism.

[2] "Ottoman lyric poetry" refers to a highly formalized poetic tradition administered by the educated elite in the Ottoman Empire. It developed along with *Türkî-i fasîh*, in the context of translational exchanges between Arabic, Persian, and Turkish. This poetic tradition is also commonly called "divan poetry" (a collection of poetry by an individual poet being referred to as a divan). For examples of this work in English translation, see Andrews et al., eds. and trans., *Ottoman Lyric Poetry*.

[3] For the first realist analysis of *Araba Sevdası*, see Dino, "Recaî-zade Ekrem'in *Araba Sevdası* Romanında Gerçekçilik." For a consideration of *Araba Sevdası* as a "significant stage from romanticism to realism" (144), see Evin, *Origins* 129–172. For the most influential modernist reading of the novel on record, see Parla, *Babalar* 105–124. Gürbilek's "Dandies and Originals" is an outstanding comparative reading of *Araba Sevdası* alongside *Madame Bovary*.

[4] The original version of the article published in the periodical *Şark* is untitled. The transliterated version was published with the title "Romancı ve Hayat."

Horn. We might say that the word *roman,* or novel, does not stand for the book of fiction authored by an individual writer, here, so much as it is a metonym for language as an autonomous force traversing the city in accelerated communication, escaping the control of its speakers and writers. Elsewhere in this article, Midhat discusses newspaper crime and suicide reporting as constituting "possible novels." For the inquisitive mind, he writes, there is a novel in the circumstances leading to the commitment of these crimes and their aftereffects. What novel writing really consists in, for Midhat, is this kind of public overhearing of the gossip, rumor and news of a language disseminated in oral and written media.

Midhat's epistemically variant use of the generic term "novel" is not the only thing striking in this passage. His comical narrative also counters a conventional instrumentalist understanding of language, staging traveling words themselves as unpredictable media. To the rumor-news of murder and suicide, as "possible novels," Midhat adds the story of a wealthy woman secretly giving birth with the help of a midwife (who if not exactly kidnapped, has been coerced into service), suggesting illicit copulation, with its consequences, as a figure for a compromised and "impregnated" language itself. Like the body of the woman in this rumored affair, language itself circulates in media, inseminated by news from the outside world and by translation from other languages, with socially unpredictable and indeterminable results. Enchanted by translative language, unable to manage the basic conventions of social greetings, Midhat's "chic" novelist is already on the verge of losing his self-control; in his intensified awareness of the gap separating appearance from reality, his public social appearance is very nearly compromised (he deflects the social encounter with his friend by making his body and clothing a kind of preemptive semaphore).

I begin with this scene of novel writing in order to underscore the entirely modern linguistic self-consciousness of early Ottoman Turkish novelists. Their various different points of departure notwithstanding (for Midhat, anonymous oral storytelling; for Ekrem, the ruins of divan poetry), these writers programmatically linked their work to the communications revolution and its freeing of language from the conventions of classical logocentrism and oral conversation. To grasp the dynamic of the semiotic reorganization transforming Ottoman Turkish literature (*edebiyat*) from a learned practice of ethical conduct into individualized aesthetic fiction, it is necessary to attend to the changes in writing practices thematized by Ekrem's *Araba Sevdası* and Midhat's 1891 novel *Müşahedat* ("Observations").

It is not merely an adjustment in literary-critical methodology that is required here, however. Midhat's and Ekrem's thematizations of the communications revolution are in fact supplements to a historiography of the nationalization of the Turkish language, in itself. Where historians of Turkish nationalism have tended to view the initial phase of phonocentrist vernacularization as a relatively unambiguous organic development, Midhat and Ekrem register nothing less than its self-estranging seductions and terrors. Foreignized by its interception of news, a disseminating language eventually comes into violent conflict with an extant social locality and its values, and how an estranged speaking or writing subject, caught up in the space of this conflict, ultimately "wears" his language will have decisive literary *and* political consequences. Like Midhat's chic novelist in his ill-fitting yet socially acceptable modern clothes, his response may be to seek to domesticate this uncanny medium in the production of a modern Ottoman identity. Or, he may vouch for a kind of "permanent revolution," leaving open the very conditions of communicability and translatability. In each case, the institutionalization of modern literature in and through modern identitarianism is inextricable from the emergence of Ottoman Turkish as an uncanny tele-communications medium.

1. "Communications Revolution" Revisited

What, following Şerif Mardin and Carter Findley, I am calling the "communications revolution" describes the generalization of writing in the Ottoman Empire with the intensification of print and translational activity.[5] Rooted in the eighteenth-century efforts of Ottoman scribes to facilitate communication within the chancelleries of the state, this communications revolution accelerated during the first half of the nineteenth century with the *Tanzimat* reforms[6] and culminated during its second half, with the expansion and reorganization of public education and the multiplication of independent readers and writers. The sequence of historical developments at issue here is in fact a complex and layered web of changes; I will mention only a few landmark events, by way of an overview.

In the eighteenth century, new lexicographic and grammatical reforms aimed to open up blocked communication channels within the state apparatus.[7] Crucial for bureaucratic reform was the replacement during the 1840s of the easily legible *nesih* script with the more "elastic" *rik'a* script written rapidly without lifting the pen (Akyıldız 107), increasing the speed and efficiency with which documents could

---

[5] See Findley, *Ottoman Civil Officialdom* 174–179; Mardin, "Some Notes on an Early Phase in the Modernization of Communications in Turkey"; and Mardin, "The Modernization of Social Communication."

[6] The Ottoman state initiated a range of modernization projects and programs for its own protection and reinforcement during the nineteenth century, as the empire was gradually and peripherally integrated into the economic and political sphere of global capitalist modernity. These included the foundation of military engineering (1773) and medical schools (1827) modeled on European institutions, the abolition of the Janissaries and their replacement with a modernized army (1826), and the transformation of scribes into modern bureaucrats. The Gülhane Hatt-ı Şerifi (Noble Edict of the Rose Chamber) reform of 1839, meanwhile, which granted guarantees of life, honor, and property to all Ottoman subjects of the sultan, replaced the traditional Ottoman social administration of its multiethnic population through the *millet* system. The Gülhane Hatt-ı Şerifi marks the beginning of what modern Turkish historiography calls the *Tanzimat* era. On the bureaucratic reforms, see Findley, *Bureaucratic Reform in the Ottoman Empire*. On the educational reforms, see Ergin, *İstanbul Mektepleri*. On the political and administrative reforms of the *Tanzimat*, see Davison, *Reform in the Ottoman Empire 1856–1876*.

[7] Mardin, "Some Notes" 254.

be processed. The printing press, which had first been introduced in 1726,[8] assumed new significance toward the turn of the nineteenth century, with the publication of translations of Arabic and French technical manuals for newly founded specialized army and navy schools.[9] But it is with newspaper publication that the printing press first assumed its truly "telecommunicative" aspect.

Devoted to documenting the affairs of the state, *Takvim-i Vekayi,* the first official newspaper, appeared in 1831 with editions printed in Ottoman Turkish as well as Arabic, Persian, Greek, Armenian, and French.[10] *Takvim-i Vekayi* was followed in 1840 by the launch (with government financial support) of the weekly *Ceride-i Havadis,* by an English expatriate, William Churchill. An important source of news during the Crimean War, *Ceride-i Havadis* introduced what later came to be known as the "journalistic language" (*gazeteci lisanı*): a simplified written register distinct from the lofty prose compositions (*inşa*) of court literature. The first privately owned Ottoman Turkish newspaper, İbrahim Şinasi's *Tercüman-ı Ahvâl,* would appear in 1860, also using this simplified language. In a *mukaddeme* or editorial statement in *Tercüman-ı Ahvâl's* first issue, Şinasi describes the newspaper as an essential way for the public to exercise its "earned" right to declare its opinions in the public interest. Defining speech (*kelâm*) as an "endowed might for the statement of one's objective" and writing (*kitâbet*), "the depiction of the word [*tasvir-i kelâm*] by pen," as "the most beautiful invention of the human mind," Şinasi announced that the writing in *Tercüman-ı Ahvâl* would "be understood easily by the members of the general public [*umûm halk*]" (1).[11] As a subtle but crucial turning point in Ottoman cultural history, Şinasi's inaugural editorial statement declared nothing less than the generalization of writing as a public medium. Henceforth, public writing concerning matters of political life and the state was no longer the exclusive province of the official (*resmi*) establishment.

In printing *Tercüman-ı Ahvâl,* Şinasi used an Ottoman Turkish type set reduced from approximately 500 to 112 forms (Tansel 248). This was no obstacle to the newspaper's coming to play a fundamental role in the formation of a *literary* reading public. Initially largely confined to military and technical documents translated by and for state institutions, translation activity in the nineteenth-century

---

[8] İnalcık notes that prior to the state establishment of the printing press in 1726, "in about 1590 a decree of Murâd III permitted the sale of non-religious books, printed in Italy in the Arabic alphabet. . . . By 1494 immigrant Jews had already established a non-Muslim press in Istanbul printing their own publications" (174). In *Türk Matbuatı,* Selim Nüzhet Gerçek notes that an Armenian press was established in 1567 in Istanbul.

[9] The Translation Office (Bâb-ı Âli Tercüme Odası) of the Sublime Porte, founded in 1821 and fully operational by 1833, trained French-speaking Muslim Ottoman government translators, many of who became the first novelists. On the establishment of the Translation Office, see Findley, *Bureaucratic Reform* 132–140. Findley notes that the Translation Office was founded to teach Muslim Ottomans the French language in order "to relieve the state once and for all of the need to rely on Greeks as translators" (133).

[10] On the multilingualism of Ottoman print culture, see Strauss, "Who Read What in the Ottoman Empire (19th–20th Centuries)?"

[11] On Şinasi's role in the formation of a new public sphere, see Mardin's influential *The Genesis of Young Ottoman Thought* 252–275.

Ottoman Empire expanded into the cultural domain with Şinasi's publication of translations from the French of Lamartine, Racine, La Fontaine, and Fénélon in 1859; Kirkor Çilingiryan's translation of Chateaubriand's *Atala* in 1860; and Yusuf Kâmil Pasha's translation of Abbé Fénélon's *Télémaque* in 1862. The 1860s and 1870s would see many serialized translations from French, including Hugo's *Les misérables* (1862), Bernardin de Saint-Pierre's *Paul et Virginie* (1870), Alexandre Dumas père's *Monte Cristo* (1871), Paul de Kock's *Monsieur Choublanc à la recherche de sa femme* (1873), and Eugène Sue's *Les mystères de Paris* (1875), among others.[12] As book production was costly, it was through the newspaper serial (*tefrika*) that readers first encountered much of this work. Without a doubt, the expansion of translation and publishing activity itself began to rediversify journalistic language, introducing new variations in lexical and formal style,[13] and the 1880s saw the appearance of a substantive popular literature in the vernacular on offer to the middle and lower classes.[14]

The generalization of the communications revolution during the second half of the nineteenth century did not go unchallenged or unchecked. During the absolutist reign of Sultan Abdülhamid II (1876–1909), strict censorship blocked the publication of writing determined to have slandered the state, the sultan, or the governing elite. Such censorship could not, on the other hand, ever possibly completely succeed in suppressing the "freeing" powers of translative language.[15] Not only did the last quarter of the nineteenth century see an increase in the sheer number of book and newspaper publications, but Abdülhamid II's own centralizing educational reforms arguably accommodated and accelerated the communications revolution, precisely by disseminating literacy. Regardless of the various levels of constraint under which the generalization of writing took place, the newly founded primary (*ibtidaî mektep*) and secondary (*i'dadîye mektebi*) public

---

[12] For a more complete list in English, see Evin, *Origins* 45. For a comparative discussion of these first translations in relation to their originals, see Özön, *Türkçede Roman Hakkında Bir Deneme* 144–185. For a survey of the critical literature on Ottoman translation, see Koç, "Osmanlı'da Tercüme Kavramı ve Tanzimat Dönemindeki Edebî Tercümelere Dair Çalışmalar." Literary translations made between 1860 and 1880 were primarily translations of Western classical and Romantic literature. In "Ludwig Büchner versus Nat Pinkerton: Turkish Translations from Western Languages, 1880–1914," Jitka Malečková notes that it is impossible to determine any single goal or initiative for the heterogeneous literary translation projects of the late nineteenth century. By 1880, translations accounted for 23 percent of all literary publication in the empire; 11 percent were from the Western classics, with popular genres such as French adventure and mystery novels holding a significant share. For Malečková, this is the historical turning point.

[13] On this point (and for examples), see Levend, *Türk Dilinde Gelişme ve Sadeleşme Evreleri* 85–95.

[14] With translations of works of drama, the second half of the nineteenth century also witnessed a vibrantly hybrid culture of theater. Literary historians tend to agree that the popularization of theater, during the third quarter of the nineteenth century, contributed significantly to the formation of a new vernacular literature. Strict governmental regulation of theater during the final quarter of the century, meanwhile, indirectly shaped literary history by forcing writers to shift from drama to the novel (Özön 139). On the history of the Ottoman theater, see And, *Türk Tiyatro Tarihi.*

[15] In 1888, Sultan Abdülhamid II issued the Matbaalar Nizamnamesi (Printing Houses Regulation), an extension and clarification of existing laws and statutes. Abdülhamid's excessive control of the press is a mark of his awareness of the subversive powers of print. On censorship laws, see Kabacalı, *Başlangıçtan Günümüze Türkiye'de Basın Sansürü* 54–82. For statistics tracking the increase in publications during the reign of Abdülhamid II, see Koloğlu, *Osmanlı'dan 21. Yüzyıla Basın Tarihi* 61–86.

schools certainly contributed significantly to the toppling of existent hierarchies of linguistic power.[16]

More than a merely quantitative change, then, the communications revolution must be understood in its epistemic dimension, as the intensified use of language as a *translative medium* displaced the discourse network of logocentrist classical rhetoric. As Ottoman Turkish was adopted as the medium of instruction in newly established schools, there appeared new grammar and rhetoric books in "Ottoman," including the lithographs of *Kavâ'id-i Osmâniyye* ("The Rules of Ottoman") and its simplified version, *Medhal-i Kavâ'id* ("Introduction to Grammar"), published in 1851 and prepared by a member of the newly founded Encümen-i Daniş (Academy of Sciences), Ahmed Cevdet Pasha (1822–1895).[17] These first projects of the Encümen-i Daniş for the preparation of literary, historical, and linguistic textbooks in Ottoman Turkish were modeled on the work of the Académie française and subsidized by the government. Although the activities of the Encümen-i Daniş had diminished in importance by 1863, other important grammar books followed, including the more simplified version of *Medhal-i Kavâ'id* entitled *Kavâ'id-i Türkiyye* (1871) and a revised version of *Kavâ'id-i Osmâniyye* entitled *Tertîb-i Cedîd Kavâ'id-i Osmâniyye* ("Revised Version of the Rules of Ottoman," 1885). Arguing for the necessity of the study of rhetoric along with grammar, Cevdet Pasha published his book of rhetoric, *Belâgat-ı Osmâniyye* ("Ottoman Rhetoric"), in 1880.[18]

The language referred to as *lisan-ı Osmanî* or "Ottoman," in these grammar books of the third quarter of the nineteenth century, is distinct in its "telecommunicative" instrumentalization from the language of the classical period, a time when the study of grammar (*sarf* and *nahv*) and rhetoric (*belâgat*) was focused on Arabic, rather than Turkish. While it is certainly true that these Ottoman grammar and rhetoric books of the mid-nineteenth century for the most part modeled the pedagogic structure of the older Arabic textbooks they displaced,[19] one might say that the study of grammar and rhetoric assumed a different function in the nineteenth century, as the distinction between the communicative and rhetorical functions of

---

[16] Findley notes that the literacy rate in the empire increased "perhaps from 1 percent in 1800 to 5–10 percent . . . in 1900," while noting that these numbers are only approximations (*Ottoman* 139). Donald Quataert notes a slightly higher rate of Muslim literacy: "2–3 percent in the early nineteenth century and perhaps 15 percent at its end" (169). It is important to understand that this reflects not only the establishment of specialized professional schools for a modernizing elite, but also the gradual centralization and secularization of the public educational system, from the 1870s on. On the nineteenth-century transformation of Ottoman public education, see Somel, *The Modernization of Public Education*.

[17] For a comprehensive historical account of Turkish-language grammar textbooks, including those published in Europe, see Dilâçar, "Gramer." For a short biography of Cevdet Pasha, see Bowen. *Kavâ'id-i Osmâniyye* was co-authored by Cevdet Pasha and Keçecizâde Fuad Pasha (1815–1869).

[18] On other books of rhetoric published during the second half of the nineteenth century, see Yetiş, *Belâgattan Retoriğe* 372–406. For a partial list of treatises on rhetoric in Ottoman Turkish prior to the mid-nineteenth century, see Yetiş, *Belâgattan Retoriğe* 367–371. The most well-known is İsmail Hakkı Ankaravî (d. 1631), *Miftâhu'l-Belâga ve Mısbâhu'l-Fesâha*.

[19] In *Medhal-i Kavâ'id*, for example, verb and pronoun conjugations begin with the third-person forms, instead of the first-person forms, as they would in an Arabic grammar textbook. Verbs are grouped into biliteral, triliteral, and quadriliteral consonantal roots (as in Arabic), and terminology is for the most part borrowed from Arabic practice. For a glossary of grammar terms, see Karabacak.

language assumed greater importance. According to the classical schema for scholarship, the study of *ilm-i sarf,* or morphology, and of *ilm-i nahv,* or the science of syntax, was succeeded by the science of rhetoric, which involved the study of such Arabic works as the *Miftāḥ al-'ulūm* of al-Sakkākī (d. 1226 or 1229), derived from the foundational work of the Arab rhetorician al-Djurdjānī; the *Talkhīṣ al-miftāḥ* of al-Ḳazwīnī (d. 1338), a summary of al-Sakkākī's *Miftāḥ*; and the long and short commentaries on the *Talkhīṣ,* the *Sharḥ muṭawwal* and *Sharḥ mukhtaṣar* of al-Taftāzānī (d. 1389). These three sciences were considered instrumental sciences, or *ulûm-ı âliyye,* deemed necessary but necessarily subservient to the higher spiritual sciences, or *ulûm-ı â'liyye.*[20]

The root of the Ottoman Turkish word for "rhetoric," *belâgat,* deriving from the Arabic *balagha,* means "to reach a goal."[21] Understood as the science of eloquent (*fasih*) speech that is fitting to the situation,[22] the communicative science of rhetoric subjugated the written to the spoken in its privileging of eloquence (*fesahat*) as a definitive criterion of *belâgat.* Divided into three branches, *belâgat* included, at the most basic level, *ilm-i meani,* or the science of ideas, in the study of the logical and situational appropriateness of speech utterances. *İlm-i beyan,* or "the science of expression," at the next level of complexity and prestige, sought to increase "the number of forms of expression and thereby . . . the accuracy and appropriateness of utterances," making use of the devices of simile (*teşbih*), metaphor (*istiare*), and allusion (*kinaye*) (Andrews 75). Finally, *ilm-i bedi,* "the science of poetic adornment," encompassed such figures of speech as contrast (*tezad*), hyperbole (*i'zam*), and anaphor (*tekrir*), used for poetic beautification (85–86). Although *ilm-i bedi* was considered less essential than *ilm-i meani* and *ilm-i beyan,*[23] the figurative and the communicative functions of language can be understood to have *supplemented* one another, in this system of relationships, rather than opposing each other in the larger field of rhetoric.

The mid-nineteenth century liberation or freeing of Ottoman Turkish as an everyday language was achieved through the opposition of these two functions. To echo a trope common in the reflective literature of the period, it is as if language had had to disrobe, to discard its "excessive adornments," in order to be able to traverse new historical contexts. That this polarization developed gradually, rather than interposing itself abruptly, is reflected in a diverse range of works in rhetoric published during the period, from Süleyman Pasha's French-influenced *Mebâni'l İnşâ* ("Foundations of Composition," 1871–1872) through Ali Cemâleddin's *Arûz-ı*

---

[20] On the significance of Arabic-language study, as well as of the grammar and rhetoric textbooks studied in Ottoman madrasas, see Şükran Fazlıoğlu, "Manzûme" 103–104 and 108. See also İzgi 163–183. For an historical overview of Arabic rhetoric, see Grunebaum. For an historical overview of the field of Arabic grammar, see Versteegh and Troupeau.

[21] In *An Introduction to Ottoman Poetry* (1976), Walter G. Andrews defined "*ilm-i belâgat*" as "the analysis of ways in which language is effective as a transmitter of ideas" (74).

[22] See Bilgegil 20.

[23] See Bilgegil 182.

Türkî ("Turkish Poetics," 1873) to Cevdet Pasha's Arabocentric *Belâgat-ı Osmâni-yye.* The debates generated by the latter work, in particular, reveal disagreement on a range of issues, including Cevdet's own descriptive vocabulary for his subject, which many argued should be called "Turkish," instead of "Ottoman."[24] It is note-worthy that even a work like Cevdet Pasha's, which adhered strictly to the rules of Arabic rhetoric, ultimately diverged in its valuation of that very adherence: where classical rhetoric aimed to "maximize the importance of any existing relationship to the extent of obliterating, or lessening, the distinction between the use and men-tion aspects of words" (Andrews 113), *Belâgat-ı Osmâniyye* argued for the subordi-nation of the signifier, or *lafız,* to the signified, or *mana.* Cevdet's hierarchization anticipates the rise of a new "phantasm," so to speak, of writing freed of the rheto-ricity always already immanent in it. (The 1882 publication of Ekrem's *Tâlim-i Edebiyat,* or "The Teaching of Literature," might be said to mark the displacement of rhetoric from "a *Kunstlehre,* an *ars dicendi*" into "an aesthetics in Plato's . . . sense, i.e., a *Schönheitslehre*" [Grunebaum].)

It is during this period of intensified communicability and translatability that a new discourse of phonocentrism emerged and matured, in the programmatic identification of the diglossia of Ottoman Turkish and its writing system as a prob-lem of inadequacy. If the process of vernacularization (as discussed above) formed one of this discourse's principal conditions of possibility, proposals for the phoneti-cization of Ottoman Turkish writing served as another. The earliest such proposal appears in Ahmed Cevdet Pasha's introductory textbook, *Medhal-i Kavâ'id,* which includes a special section ("Mu'allimîne Lâzım Olan Ma'lûmat," or "Instructions for Teachers") addressed to writing instructors, concerning the difficulties of reading and writing "Turkish" ("Türkî") in "Arabic" ("Arabî") letters and de-scribing supplementary diacritical marks used to distinguish Turkish vowels. Fol-lowing the practice of distinguishing the initial *a* from *e,* for example, by using the *med,~*, placed on the *elif* letterform, l, Cevdet marks the *o* vowel with ˘ placed below *vav,* ﺝ, and the *ö* vowel with ˘ placed above it; the vowel *u* with ˆ placed below *vav,* and the vowel *ü* with ˆ placed above it; *ı* with | placed below *ye,* ﺱ, and *i* with *ye* standing by itself (23–24).

A more systematic reform was advocated by the translator and statesman Mehmed Münif Pasha (1828–1910) in a 1862 speech he gave to the Cemiyet-i

---

[24] See Hacımüftüoğlu 203–209. Mid-nineteenth century phonocentrism achieved the freeing of "Otto-man" from its place in a cultural hierarchy dominated by Arabic and Persian, while establishing the conditions for its demise at the same time. Ali Cemâleddin's *Arûz-ı Türkî* ("Poetics of Turkish," 1873), Süleyman Pasha's *İlm-i Sarf-ı Türkî* ("Grammar of Turkish," 1875), and Şemseddin Sami's *Kâmus-ı Türkî* ("Dictionary of Turk-ish," 1899), are representative works of grammar and rhetoric refiguring a new language as "Turkish," rather than "Ottoman." One might say that the last quarter of the nineteenth century saw the first official efforts to appropriate this released Turkic element, for the purpose of reinstating Turkish Muslim hegemony. The decla-ration of Turkish (*lisan-ı Türkî*) as the official language (*lisan-ı resmî*) of a polyglot, multiethnic empire, in the 1876 constitution (*Kanun-i Esasi*), is an important moment of linguistic Turkification—though to be sure, it is not until the Young Turk period that the containment of the possibilities inherent in the communications rev-olution of the 1850s becomes plain.

İlmiye-yi Osmâniyye, or Ottoman Scientific Society.[25] Giving as examples "اون,
[which is] composed of merely three letters and can be pronounced in Turkish
[*Türkçe*] in three meaningful ways, and كورك six different forms," Münif Pasha
identifies as an "obstacle" ("mahzûr") the fact that "words can be read in five, ten
different ways" (224).[26] Where the first example demonstrates a widespread confusion concerning the reading of Turkish vowel sounds in general, the second registers the specific problem presented by the letter *kef*, ك, which can be read as any of
/k/, /g/, /y/, or /ny/. Because such problems do not, he says, occur "in the writing of
Europeans," Münif Pasha suggests that "six, seven-year old children, men, women,
servants, workers, and mothers" in Europe can all acquire literacy (224). Since, as
he puts it, "the available vowel signs [*harekât*] of Arabic language [*lisân-ı Arab*] are
insufficient" to eliminate such ambiguity, Münif Pasha suggests two solutions: (1)
the invention and codification of additional diacritical marks, capable of representing each vocalization in placement above or under the written word; (2) the
spacing of discrete letters in each word ("hurûf-ı makta'a ile tahrir"), rather than
joining them cursively, and the insertion of the necessary vowel signs in their place
on the line as is done in "the languages of the foreigners" (224). Despite the resistance he anticipates it provoking, Münif Pasha recommends the second proposal
as the better one, reasoning that the first would create insurmountable complica-
tions for print publishing. He advocates a trial period, with publication of booklets
and textbooks using the new system to be limited until the larger public accepts its
benefits (225).[27]

Münif Pasha is joined a year later in 1863 by Mirzâ Feth'ali Ahûndzâde
(Ahundov) (1812–1878), one of the architects of Azerbaijani modernization, who
submitted a proposal to Grand Vizier Fuad Pasha for the reformation of letters
used in "the Islamic world" ("memâlik-i İslâmiye").[28] The proposal, as transmitted
to the Cemiyet-i İlmiye-yi Osmâniyye for assessment, recommends the elimination
of the discrete graphic point (*nokta*) placed above and below certain consonants,
their replacement with new connective diacritical marks, and the adoption of new
signs to mark vowel sounds (emphasizing also that such reforms would not conflict
in any way with Islamic principles) ("Islâh-ı Resmi Hatta Dâir" 224). The report,
prepared by the society and published along with Münif Pasha's 1862 speech in the
society's journal *Mecmua-yı Fünun* ("The Journal of Sciences"), supports Ahûndzâde's proposal in principle, but objects to its adoption, stating that the suggested
changes would be insufficient to overcome difficulties encountered in printing (224).

---

[25] Cemiyet-i İlmiye-yi Osmâniyye was founded by Münif Pasha in 1862 to advance the study of natural
sciences in the Ottoman Empire. For a brief biography of Münif Pasha in English, see Mango.

[26] The first word can be read as *ün* (fame), *on* (ten), and *un* (flour), and the second as *kürek* (shovel), *gevrek*
(tender), *kürk* (fur), *körük* (bellows), *görk* (splendor), and *görün* (the imperative "Be seen").

[27] Grammar books by Ahmed Cevdet Pasha utilized the first method suggested by Münif Pasha.

[28] This phrase is taken from the published report of the Cemiyet-i İlmiye-yi Osmâniyye on Ahûndzâde's
proposal. For this report, see "Islâh-ı Resmi Hatta Dâir" 223.

Displeased by the failure of this initial attempt, Ahûndzâde subsequently (in the late 1860s) approached Grand Vizier Âli Pasha with a proposal for the abolishment of the "Islamic alphabet" ("İslam elifbası") and its replacement with Latin letters. This effort did not succeed either.[29]

Debates over orthography would continue in other *Tanzimat* journals through the 1860s and 1870s. A memorable exchange took place in 1869 between to Iran's ambassador to the Ottoman Empire, Malkum Khan (1833–1908), and the reformer, critic, poet, and translator Namık Kemal (1840–1888), an early literary experimenter with the novel form.[30] Reacting to Khan's 1869 open letter in Persian, in the Ottoman newspaper *Hürriyet* ("Freedom"), blaming "Arabic" letterforms for the problems of Islamic nations, Namık Kemal responded by conceding the necessity of writing reforms, while refusing to devolve the questions of arrested social, political, and economic development onto them.[31] In addition to recommending the addition of points above and below the letter *kef,* so as to distinguish between its various ways of being read, Kemal proposed marking words of Arabic origin with a line above the word and those of Persian origin with a line below, as cues for appropriate vocalization ("Kıraat" 35–36). Refusing the prospect of any overly abrupt change in script, Kemal instead directs his attention, in this response, to the existing gap between orthographic representation and actual pronunciation in the languages of the developed nations (England and the United States), and calls attention to the need for education reforms (32). In the same year, another public exchange takes place between the journalist Hayreddin Bey and the reformer Ebüzziya Tevfik (1849–1913) in the newspaper, *Terakkî* ("Progress"), with Hayreddin Bey arguing for the adoption of simplified lettering for use in the discursive domains of "science, administration, and trade," while allowing for the use of older letterforms in Quran study (31).

A Latin-based script designed by the Ottoman Albanian linguist, novelist, and reformer Şemseddin Sami Bey (1850–1904), who was actively involved in Turkicizing the Ottoman Turkish language during the late nineteenth century, was adopted in 1879 by the former members of the Cemiyet-i İlmiye-yi Arnavudiye (Albanian Society of Science) for publication and education in vernacular Albanian.[32] Although Latin orthography had already begun to establish itself in some domains

---

[29] On this point, see Aydın's introduction to "Mehmet Münif Paşa, Mirzâ Feth'ali Ahûndzâde." For a short biography of Ahûndzâde, see Brands.

[30] For a short biography of Malkum Khan, see Algar; on Namık Kemal, see Mardin, *Genesis* 283-336.

[31] For more on this exchange, see Tansel, "Arap Harflerinin Islahı." On improvement in writing instruction, see also Kemal's 1866 article "Usûl-i Tahsîlin Islâhına Dair" ("On Education Reform").

[32] On this alphabet as a "precursor to Turkish script reform," see Trix, "The Stamboul Alphabet of Shemseddin Sami Bey." A prominent advocate of renaming the language *lisan-ı Türkî*, rather than *lisan-ı Osmanî*, Şemseddin Sami published important Turkish dictionaries of the late nineteenth century, with such titles as *Kâmus-ı Türkî* (1899–1900) and *Kâmus-ı Fransevî* (an illustrated French-Turkish dictionary, 1901). Sami's binationalism is a mark of the complex ethnic politics of the Ottoman Empire.

of trade, transportation, and telecommunications,[33] no equivalent measure was taken in the Ottoman Turkish context, save for the publication of textbooks using the supplemental diacritics. We can nevertheless say that the debates of the 1860s, along with the adoption of new methods (*usûl-i cedid*) in the teaching of reading and writing,[34] mark the displacement of classical logocentrism and the emergence of a new phonocentric writing.

Despite their many differences, the respective projects of intellectuals of the period consistently identified an undesirable gap separating the spoken from the written, which they understood as blocking the direct communicative "travel" of words freed of authorial presence. The surplus value of writing—its inherent multiplicity and ambiguity, intensified, in this historical context, as an effect of the omnidirectional translatability of Ottoman Turkish—is refigured as something to be suppressed and controlled. One can no longer count on the determination of correct meaning by the use value of the word, in its local relation to what precedes and follows it (*siyak ü sibak*); the deterritorialized signifier now appears as something to be fixed to a single and universal meaning, in the abstract purity of exchange value. This means that just as the written word becomes a secondary, transparent *representation* of the spoken—itself an immediate representation of a conceptual meaning originating "outside" (from the speaker's mind or the world)—it is demanded that each letter (*harf*) and vowel sign (*hareke*) of the alphabet will be assigned one unequivocal phonemic value.[35] With the breakdown of the "necessary association between *ḥarf* and *ḥaraka*" in Perso-Arabic writing (Arnaldez), newly individualized letters, vowel signs, and words assume a

[33] See Şimşir 32–38. Latin letters were used on imported and exported packages. Mustafa Efendi used French Latin lettering as the basis for his design of Ottoman Turkish Morse code, in 1855. With the participation of the Ottoman Empire in the Universal Postal Union, in 1874, Ottoman postal stamps were lettered in Ottoman Turkish and in French in the Latin alphabet. The names of train stations were also frequently inscribed in both languages.

[34] Maarif-i Umumiye Nizamnamesi, the 1869 legislation regulating public education, can be understood as a turning point in the displacement of the "recitational complex" of classical learning—memorization, recitational "reading aloud," and authoritative listening, among other rituals presupposing an ambiguity inherent in writing—by new practices designed to prepare the student to read in "freedom" of context and authorial presence. One crucial change introduced by the important *Tanzimat* educator Selim Sâbit Efendi (1829–1910), in his instructional handbook entitled *Rehnüma-yı Muallimin* ("Guidebook for Instructors," 1870), concerns the teaching of syllable formation on the basis of sounds, rather than names of letters and their movements. The new pedagogy demanded that the student learn the syllable *cü*, for example, by sounding it in the combinatorial sequence "ce, ü, cü," rather than by reciting letter names ("cim, vav, ötre=cü"), in a departure from the methodology of the *Elifba Cüzü* ("Primer") used in elementary Quranic schools (*mekteb*) to teach Arabic lettering (Baymur 48). Other changes included the adoption of a reading comprehension method building on vocabulary already learned by the student (the names of days, seasons, animals, and vegetables, among other categories), rather than on the memorization of hitherto unfamiliar words (48). Instruction in reading, in Selim Sâbit's approach, is accompanied by instruction in writing, in a departure from the primary classical curricular emphasis centered on reading (49). Although such changes are often read anachronistically, as the abandonment of "rote" "Eastern" teaching methods for "Western" progressive ones, we might more accurately assess them in the context of discursive changes in historical writing practices. In so many ways, here as elsewhere, the deterritorializing democratization of writing in the modern episteme is accompanied by its reterritorializing subjection to new controlling mechanisms.

[35] Note that this was also an important criterion for the Latin-based alphabet designed by Şemseddin Sami (Trix 260).

thing-like objectivity.[36] Debate about "Islamic writing" as an abstract question of cultural value first becomes possible in the context of this discursive displacement of classical logocentrism.

This mid-nineteenth-century "freeing" of phonocentric writing has been understood as a first, crucial phase in the nationalization of the Ottoman Turkish language.[37] While the relationship between language and political identity, in this phase, can certainly not be described as fixed, scholars of Turkish modernity generally concur that it presents the institutional imaginary, as it were, of a state society bound by a common language.[38] If late nineteenth- and early twentieth-century Turkish nationalists were, in Mardin's words, able "to promote an argument about a 'Turkish' collectivity," that was because the vernacular literature of the second half of the nineteenth century had "provided them with a tacitly shared confirmation of the existence of an Ottoman society as a reality." With protagonists marked by the Islamic sensibilities of the lower and middle classes at their center, Midhat's novels could be said to have offered the first literary imaginations of a patriotic community in anonymity ("Some Consideration" 133–34).

If as Mardin suggests elsewhere, the role of language in Turkish nationalism "is not lost on anyone who has graduated from a Turkish lycée" ("Playing" 116), we might also say that historians and theorists of nationalism, even when they account carefully for the constructed nature of national identity, have tended to overlook the *extra*ordinariness of the structure that lies less than entirely examined in it. Both Anderson's constructivism and Mardin's "middle ground" between "philological classicism and Anderson's modernism" (116) require the imagination of a kind of minimal raw vernacular defining the mass of anonymous others in community.[39] My reading of Midhat's *Müşahedat* will suggest that vernacularization might best be thought not as the discovery of an unquestioned nativity, but rather as an encounter with a seductive and terrifying *Unheimlichkeit*. With the intensified use of language as a communicative and translative medium, the nativizing impulse of phonocentrist vernacularization paradoxically (re)exposed speakers and writers to a foreignness inherent in the "native" language itself.[40]

It must be emphasized that the source of linguistic alienation, here, is not merely the recognizable cultural and political threat of "the West." While *Müşahedat* and *Araba Sevdası* both foreground the dangers of the cultural and

---

[36] On this point, see also Mitchell, *Colonizing Egypt* 148.

[37] For examples, see Levend and Sadoğlu.

[38] I will return to this point in the following chapter. Suffice it to say, for the moment, that this imagined public was not necessarily set against the state establishment; while the semi-autonomous journalists of the empire were certainly critical of Abdülhamid's repressive policies, as Mardin has argued in *The Genesis of Young Ottoman Thought*, the reformist intelligentsia prioritized "sav[ing] the state" (398) above all.

[39] For another example, see Georgeon, *Osmanlı* 2–4.

[40] It is important to understand this putative "discovery" as an episode of repetition. The "otherness" in language is a universal structure of alterity constitutive of the human subject and its concept of meaning. Each historical period and culture organizes and names this structure differently. One way to define modernity is as the *generalization* of a consciousness of this structure's fundamental *indeterminacy*.

political hegemony of French, as the source language of most translation activity during this period, it would be an error to frame the alienation produced by such activity merely in terms of a split between the "Ottoman" self and the "Western" other. The subject of phonocentric writing assumes an estranged voice in these literary texts, I would like to suggest, because he recognizes the inherent arbitrariness, rather than essentiality, of all identity and its formation. If logocentrist classical rhetoric was able to answer questions of the origin of language as the grid of knowledge of Being and beings (and following them, questions about the relationship of Ottoman Turkish with Arabic), the breakdown of Islamic discursive networks produced the experience of language as a kind of intimate other, as the subject now claimed selfhood in a language whose origins were conspicuously unknown. The modern subject, enchanted by and yet fearful of this "disorder of identity," represses it in the embrace of the politics of identitarian essentialism.[41] The crucial point here is that no matter which compensatory identity (Ottomanism, Islamism, Turkism)[42] is embraced, the modern subject cannot escape a self-consciousness of the inherent otherness of the "I" assumed in an indeterminate language. The failure to reckon with this originary homelessness drives the extreme violence of language and social politics within a plurilingual and multireligious context.

If I emphasize this "foreignizing" aspect of what I am calling phonocentrism, that is by way of suggesting that we need to rethink the role of vernacularization and phoneticization in the shaping of nationalism, in the Turkish case as elsewhere. We might say that among other things, nationalism consists in the belated invention of a self-representation to domesticate a foreignness discovered after the fact, in the shared world of a common language and its translative idiom. While the discourse on phonocentrism assumes a solidly national character only after the turn of the twentieth century, its nationalization cannot be understood apart from an account of the mid-nineteenth-century "release" and subsequent containment of a freed language. The "contribution" of an emerging modern literature to these historical processes, during a historical period of semiotic reorganization, cannot be neglected. It might help to recall that the Ottoman Turkish word for literature, *edebiyat* (still in use in modern

---

[41] This phrase is taken from Derrida, *Monolingualism* 14; *Monolinguisme* 32. Naturally, the formation of *any* subject involves a degree of repression. By "identitarianism," I mean here a nativist politics that denies the irreducible otherness of the self.

[42] Ottomanism here denotes the nineteenth-century *Tanzimat* reform movement positing the equality of all subjects of the empire, independent of ethnic and religious affiliation. As a break with the *millet* system of the past, Ottomanism sought to reinforce the allegiance of non-Muslim communities to the Ottoman state, by establishing forms of supranational representation. Islamism here denotes different strains of anti-colonialist Islamic thought emerging in the late-nineteenth-century and aiming to reform the practice of Islam and foster unity among its followers around the world. Pan-Islamism became Ottoman state policy during the reign of Abdülhamid II, as the sultan sought to protect and strengthen the empire by promoting a common Muslim identity. Here and throughout, Turkism unites the different strains of Turkish nationalism emerging in the late nineteenth century and aiming to unify Turkish people on the basis of shared linguistic, historical, and/or racial identity. These discourses certainly overlap: Midhat, for example, embraced an imperial Ottoman identity in promoting the hegemony of Turkish-Islamic values.

Turkish), derives from the Arabic *adab,* denoting "the sum of knowledge which makes a man courteous and 'urbane'" (Gabrieli). By the sixteenth century, *edeb,* as the practice of an official of the state, marked a knowledge of classical rhetoric as well as familiarity with a canon of poetic and prose writings in Arabic, Persian, and Turkish traditions. Related to, and yet distinct from the *ilm* of higher learning in general, *edeb* meant the art of self-conduct, at once an ethic and an aesthetic.[43]

It has been argued that the breakdown of the Ottoman-Islamic discursive network reconstituted and reconfigured "literature," in this sense, in a new secularized field of influence. Generated neither strictly as the self-representation(s) of the Islamic palace, nor spontaneously as the expressive tale and epic of oral tradition, literature now comes to designate, in bare form, the practice of *mecaz,* or fiction writing.[44] Literature emerges as the only domain in the episteme of phonocentrism in which language travels independently of only fixed truth. It is true that individual authors working in this expanded literary field continued to produce hybrid discourses, shaped both by Ottoman *and* European epistemologies, on the aesthetic and political ends of literature as fiction—for example, as in the 1880s debate on *hakikiyun,* or realism, and *hayaliyun,* or Romanticism. Contiguously, Midhat's *Müşahedat,* as a meta-novel, makes the case for a literature subservient to essentialist identity politics, anticipating an all too commonly assumed trajectory of modern Turkish literature in the period that followed. But there is another modality of fiction writing, embodied in Ekrem's *Araba Sevdası,* which foregoes the impulse to control the freedom of that fiction. This other modality had specific effects of its own, as well.

2. Chasing Ottoman

Critics of modern Turkish literature have pointed out that the first Ottoman Turkish novelists of the 1870s, in their deliberate efforts to write novels (*roman,* or *hikâye,* used interchangeably) according to the European (primarily French) model, assumed the voice of the traditional *meddah* storyteller.[45] It is indeed necessary to explore this connection, in order to comprehend the emergence of the modern author in the Ottoman context as an author who, for monetary compensation,

---

[43] While the culture of *edeb* was a culture of state officials, it would be a mistake to understand it as completely disconnected from the cultural networks of ordinary subjects. Members of the ruling elite had after all been raised on the epics and tales of an oral culture, and the two cultures of diglossia had shared both themes and discursive spaces. See Özön, *Türkçede Roman* 133–137. For a detailed study of the poetics of *edeb,* see Andrews, *Poetry's Voice, Society's Song.*

[44] Traditionally, *mecaz,* meaning trope or metaphor, is studied as a component of *ilm-i beyan* (the science of expression). Distinguished from *hakikat* (truth) and *kinaye* (allusion), *mecaz* means the figurative use of a word, as distinct from its ordinary usage. I render it here as "fiction," because such figurative deviation is the very condition of possibility for fiction. For a detailed discussion of *mecaz,* see Bilgegil 130–134.

[45] An early articulation of this argument can be found in Boratav, "İlk Romanlarımız." On the relationship between Namık Kemal's *İntibâh* and the *meddah* story *Hançerli Hanım,* see Dino, *Türk Romanının Doğuşu* 35–40.

makes available the speech of an enlarged community to his audience. In the Otto-man literary tradition, at least since the seventeenth century, *meddah*s were profes-sional urban storytellers, who performed in coffeehouses, private households, or the palace, performing narratives of "types" or events in the everyday life of ordinary people in Istanbul and performing them in a conversational vernacular.[46] Critics have suggested that the first novelists adopted the *meddah* role primarily because they found its realism akin to that of the European novel, in their efforts to move away from the prose tradition of idealized love stories.[47] This is a persuasive ac-count of things, especially in light of Namık Kemal's definition of the novel, in "Mukaddime-i Celâl" ("Introduction to the play *Celâlettin Harzemşah,*" 1884–1885): "By a novel is understood . . . the description [*tasvir*] of an event, whose oc-currence is possible even if it has not yet taken place. . . . However, our stories thematize . . . subjects that lie altogether outside the realm of nature and reality [*hakîkat*], such as discovering treasure with the use of magic" (347). At the same time, one might suggest that the adoption of the role of *meddah*, as irreducible to a merely aesthetic "choice" of idealism or realism, is perhaps overdetermined by an-other historically specific element of the period: namely, the mid-nineteenth centu-ry's unprecedented explosion of technical communication. In a way, under such conditions, one could not help *but* be a *meddah* writer, with so many stories, as it were, tickling one's ear. In a world being brought by language, being *in* the world meant hearing and responding to it.

Let me open this up from a slightly different direction. In the adoption of the *meddah* role by the first novelists, what we observe is not the description of an event from a detached point of view by an original author, as in the European tradition of the novel (or as in Ekrem's interpretations). We have an author, rather, who medi-ates the stories of a community at large—now *including* Europe—in translations, adaptations, journal articles, and novels taken as real or potentially real narratives. The "origin of the story," here, is not the author so much as it is language itself, crossing distances and borders, including hierarchical borders, at the speed of the medium of print.[48] One appropriate word for this kind of autonomous, traversing

---

[46] The early *meddah*s functioned as actor-entertainers who would fabricate stories animating everyday life, in a tradition that went back to the Sassanid court and was adopted by the Anatolian Seljuks. They "were known as *kıssahan* (Persian *qissah'-khwan*, from the Arabic *qassas*, 'raconteur')" (Evin 29). In the fifteenth century, when the distinction between Ottoman divan literature (primarily in verse) and oral folk literature became more solidified, the *kıssahan*s were demoted. By the sixteenth century, we see the use of the word *med-dah* (praiser) in place of *kıssahan*. "By the seventeenth century, *meddah*s had become a professional group whose services were sought by the palace and the public alike. They were organized as a guild, had adopted a patron saint, and gained respectability as artisans" (30). *Meddah* stories had their source in real life, though many also borrowed themes or plot structures from folktales of love, revolved around illicit passions, and the-matized urban vices such as drinking and gambling. Performances were extemporaneous, and *meddah*s showed off their ability to mimic by imitating the different accents of the characters in their stories. For an informative short history in English, see Evin 29–40. For more detailed accounts and examples, see Nutku's *Meddahlık ve Meddah Hikâyeleri* and "On *Aşık*s (Tale Singers) and *Meddah*s (Story Tellers)."

[47] See Boratav 310.

[48] I have benefited from Siegel's account, in *Fetish, Recognition, Revolution,* of Melayu as a lingua franca in Indonesia. The case of the Turkish vernacular, as the first language of a dominant ethnic segment, differs

speech would of course be gossip; Midhat, whose writings are often retellings of local and foreign news or adaptations and summaries of European novels, explicitly theorizes the novel as originating from rumors and the "incidents of the public" ("vukuat-i umûmiye").[49]

Despite the oppressive political climate of the last quarter of the nineteenth century, the literary works of this period register the communications revolution as a powerful linguistic liberation. "Liberation," here, might best be understood not in terms of the historical dissemination of French Enlightenment political concepts of freedom and equality, but rather as an uprooting of the linguistic sign into omni-directional exchangeability. Language makes accessible distant speech (the speech of non-Muslim populations, as well as of the outside world more generally), bringing in the unseen and unheard world of the foreign and awakening a new kind of desire. My contention here is that the emergence of the novel in the Ottoman literary context cannot be understood apart from an early enchantment with (as well as fear of) this "freed" power of language. For a brief period, at a time of intensified communicability, authorship in the empire meant not the original invention of a story but the transcription of the news (*haber*; *rivayet*) of a freed language. Writing implied not the secondary representation of an "outer" reality, but a medium through which one indistinguishably found oneself in the world and in the text. The *meddah*-author was, in fact, so frequently taken over by the language he transcribed that he would insert himself into his stories, conversing with his readers, interpolating judgments, offering lengthy digressions on various subjects, and even weeping for his characters. In this context, "modern literature" must be understood as referring not to an *extra*ordinary aesthetic domain, but to a general mode of giving ear to the world, with the novel (*roman* or *hikâye*) assuming its significance as a hybrid form of satisfaction and regulation of newly awakened desires. If the question of the *actuality* of a story was secondary for an early writer like Midhat—such as in his classification of an adventure novel like Jules Verne's *Le tour du monde en quatre-vingts jours* (1873; trans. 1876) as realist (*realizm*)—this was not because he was incapable of distinguishing the imaginary (*hayali*) from the real (*hakiki*). Rather, what mattered to him was precisely that there was talk about such journeys in "geographies, maps, plans, travel guides, and travel literature" and that the author passed on *his* version of this talk.[50]

---

significantly from that of Melayu, a second language for the Dutch colonizers as well as for the colonized inhabitants of the Indies. Yet Siegel's insightful analysis of the emergence of the authorial function in Melayu has helped me to describe here an *analogous* situation in the early Ottoman Turkish novel, in which writers inserted themselves into their texts and spoke from within it. In the Ottoman case, these first "authors" were not copyists, but rather translators, or imperial bureaucrats who employed the *meddah* voice in their attempt to produce realist novels. See Siegel 13–26.

[49] See his 1880 article entitled "Romancı ve Hayat" 65.

[50] See his 1890 article entitled "Roman ve Romancılık Hakkında Mütaalamız" ("Our Analysis on the Novel and Novelism") 60.

This liberation of language pervades Midhat's *Müşahedat*, whose author was known as a "forty horsepower writing machine" (Findley, *Ottoman* 175).[51] Having begun his career as a journalist, Midhat was briefly exiled in 1873, and after his return to Istanbul he avoided controversial political discussions.[52] Also a novelist, translator, playwright, critic, and entrepreneur who owned his own printing house, he significantly shaped the formation of a wide reading public.[53] Far from tapping some primitive orality freed of convention (as twentieth-century nationalist ideologues have often construed vernacular writing), Midhat's conversational *meddah*-writing accentuates internal vernacular heterogeneity, juxtaposing the "eloquent" (*fasih*) Istanbul vernacular speech of the educated class with the "vulgar" (*kaba*) Turkish of the lower classes, with the Islamic ethics of sincerity (*samimiyet*) and respect (*hürmet*) serving as the social grammar of communicability.[54]

Serialized in 1891 in the newspaper *Tercüman-ı Hakikat* ("Interpreter of Truth"), *Müşahedat* textualizes the *meddah*-author function, inserting "Midhat" into the text in a staging of Midhat's own writing of *Müşahedat*. In a short address to the reader ("kariinle hasbıhal," or "conversation with the reader") at its very beginning, Midhat identifies this device of inserting himself into the text as his own invention (6). Critical of Emile Zola and other French naturalists for representing

---

[51] Findley cites Sabri Esat Siyavuşgil, "Ahmet Midhat Efendi," in *İslam Ansiklopedisi,* but notes "no source cited for the quotation about 'forty horsepower'" (Findley, *Ottoman* 175n7). Midhat tried his hand at virtually all subgenres of the novel, from the historical novel (*Yeniçeriler,* 1871) to novels of adventure (*Hasan Mellah,* 1874), to crime fiction (*Esrar-ı Cinâyat,* 1884). For recent bibliographies of Midhat's writings, see Koz, "Ahmet Mithat Efendi'nin Eserleri" and Esen, "Ahmet Mithat Bibliografyası." There are some inconsistencies between these two bibliographies, partly due to the difficulty of locating all of Midhat's work. For an analysis of the heterogeneity of those of Midhat's writings classified as translation, in these bibliographies, see Demircioğlu, "From Discourse to Practice" 213–286. According to Demircioğlu, for Midhat *terceme,* or translation, encompassed a wide range of activities, including summarizing (*telhis*), commentating (*şerh*), borrowing (*iktibas*), and conveying (*nakl*). Demircioğlu also notes that Midhat used interchangeably a diverse set of terms, such as translator (*mütercim*), author (*muharrir*), and summarizer (*mülahhis*), to refer to himself. We may further unravel the binary opposition between translation and original by recognizing that Midhat's writings, which do *not* fall under the category of *terceme* in these bibliographies, also had their sources in stories circulating in his community. In fact, *Müşahedat* itself is a strong example of such a category. Demircioğlu's reconceptualization of translation as discourse might be supplemented by an analogous historicization of *telif,* or original as a heterogeneous discursive practice.

[52] Midhat was exiled after publishing newspaper articles in *Dağarcık* seeking to reconcile Lamarckism (and other positivisms) with Islam (Tanpınar 438). At a time when Namık Kemal's vocal expressions of the Enlightenment ideals of freedom (*hürriyet*) and homeland (*vatan*) posed a threat to the reign of Sultan Abdülaziz, Midhat was sent to Rhodes along with Kemal and others. Midhat was not, however, a political revolutionary like Kemal. After his return to Istanbul in 1876, he made sure to maintain good relations with Sultan Abdülhamid. For a more detailed biography and a survey of Midhat's works, see Tanpınar, *Ondokuzuncu* 433–466. For a detailed study of Midhat's life and his approach to Westernization, see Okay, *Batı Medeniyeti Karşısında Ahmed Midhat Efendi.*

[53] Midhat was not alone in experimenting with the genre. Vartan Pasha's *Akabi Hikayesi* ("The Story of Akabi," 1851) in Armeno-Turkish (Ottoman Turkish written in Armenian script) and Evangelinos Misailidis's *Temaşa-i Dünya ve Cefakâr u Cefakeş* ("The Spectacle of the World and the Suffering of the Sufferer," 1872) in Karamanlı (Ottoman Turkish written in Greek letters) are the very first examples of the Ottoman novel. Emin Nihad's *Müsameretname* ("Night Entertainment,"1872–1875), Şemseddin Sami's *Taaşuk-ı Talât ve Fitnat* ("The Love of Talât and Fitnat,"1872), and Namık Kemal's *İntibah* ("Awakening," 1876) are other important examples of the early Ottoman novel.

[54] On the culture of oral conversation, including its *meddah* entertainments, see Strauss, "Konuşma." For an analysis of the social language of familiarity and intimacy used in oral conversations, see Meeker, "Oral" and "Once."

only the dark, decadent mores of Parisian life (3), Midhat claims here to have developed a more complete "naturalist" ("tabiî") picture of reality—not only in terms of the novel's content (5), but also through use of a device "unprecedented in Europe" (113), inserting himself into the text as its author (6). As a realization of *meddah*-like storytelling in the medium of the Ottoman Turkish novel, this device is neither necessarily innovative in the sense that demands novelty and surprise, as Midhat and his critics suggest, nor "postmodern," along the same lines.[55] Nor should we be persuaded by the rather anachronistic argument that *Müşahedat* anticipates Luigi Pirandello's *Sei personaggi in cerca d'autore* (1921) and André Gide's *Les faux-monnayeurs* (1925) in its technique of involving its characters as writers (Moran 71). *Müşahedat* is rather best read as an apotheosis of the early *Tanzimat* novel, with the author dislocating his technique from an earlier genealogy and reregistering it as an unprecedented authorial innovation comparable to that of his European contemporaries. Such abstraction and realization of the *meddah* technique, I am saying, occurs only after the fact, anticipating the disappearance of the *meddah*-author in later novels of the period. At the same time, it leaves the readers of *Müşahedat* what we might call a theoretical image of the early Ottoman Turkish novel.

The narrative begins with the figure of Midhat the journalist-writer conversing with his readers while traveling on a ferryboat across the Bosphorus in Istanbul for work: "As you know, this humble author is from Beykoz. He travels summer and winter, morning and evening between Beykoz and Istanbul" (7). Speaking from within the text about the public experience of travel on the new ferryboats, Midhat situates himself in the same linguistic milieu as his readers. The story to be narrated emerges spontaneously from this milieu, as Midhat, in the novel's next section, overhears an excited conversation in "almost perfect French" between two young Armenian women, concerning the abandonment of one of them by a ruthless man (25). While the women assume Midhat "a clumsy man"—probably a "Turkish ferryboat guide" ("Türk pilotu") who would not speak French (26)—Midhat has already "given ear [*kulak vermek*] to their conversation" (25), translating it into the vernacular so as to share it with his readers. At the end of this exchange, the figure of Midhat announces to his readers:

> Huuuuu! Not only is this a great novel [*roman*], but even . . . a naturalist novel! Indeed a perfect one! . . .

[55] For an analysis of the novelties of the technique used in *Müşadehat,* see Moran 59–72. See also Parla, *Babalar ve Oğullar* 43–64, reading the author-centeredness of the novel as an effect of the aprioristic, absolutist, idealist Ottoman epistemology in which Midhat himself was formed (63). For a narratological analysis of how Midhat "personalizes the narrative point of view" (141), see Esen, "The Narrator and the Narratee in Ahmet Mithat." "Ahmet Mithat was using such overt narrators and narratees," Esen suggests, "in order to generate a mimesis of belief in his readers. It is as if he believes that he can influence and educate his readers only if they accept as plausible that he is talking about real events and people" (145). For a postmodernist reading of the novel, see Demir, *Zaman Zaman İçinde/Roman Roman İçinde*. For a reading of *Müşahedat* as a metanovel about "a harmonious multi-ethnic empire striving to become a member of the modern world without losing its virtuous character shaped by Islam" (46), see Saraçoğlu, "Reality with a Moral Twist."

But shall we interfere in the conversation? . . . Who is this ruthless man? . . . Shall we ask them?

But can one do this? Apparently, according to Christian ethics, a third person should not overhear a private conversation between two people. With what introduction . . . could we participate in the ladies' private conversation?

Yes, yes! Not possible. Indeed, ill-mannered [*terbiyesizlik*]! Even immoral [*edepsizlik*]!

But does it make sense to kick away a naturalist novel that landed at our feet? Whatever it costs, one should participate in this conversation. (28)

The novel will follow Midhat as he traces the life-stories of these two women. But it is less the content of this story than the construction of the author function that I am interested in, here. This scene of *overhearing,* we might say, constructs the author, from the outset, as the mediator of a language operating like a telecommunications technology, with messages traveling in all directions within its network. These perfect French speakers, who stand in for (a gendered) Europe, do not realize it, but the "clumsy" "Turkish" man is listening to them: he listens, reads the books and newspapers they are carrying, and he translates. When this man writes down what he hears, he moves freely in and out of his own text as a character, because he has identified—in the mode of the "we"—with the language he's transcribing. The differentiation between language and the events it describes is, in other words, yet to be demarcated, here.

These French-speaking women also, however, stand for religious and ethnic difference: specifically, the difference of Armenian Christians. We should recall here that *meddah* stories commonly treated the subject of relations (primarily love affairs) between different ethnic segments of the population, in a kind of staging of imperial urban cosmopolitanism. *Meddah*s also displayed their talent for mimicry, by imitating accents and speech patterns of their characters.[56] In Midhat's novel, however, religious and ethnic difference assumes a special status. First of all, because Istanbul Greeks, Armenians, and Levantines function as metonyms for Europe and its enchanting foreignness, and they can "pass" as French more easily than can Turks. This "competition" of appearances is a major motif in Midhat's novel, with "French-looking" Armenian or Greek characters revealing their true ethnicity only when they open their mouths to speak in either accented French, or in their own native vernaculars (44).[57] The narrator-character listening from within

---

[56] See Evin 32.

[57] In his introduction, Midhat differentiates "local" ("yerli") novels involving non-Muslim characters from "national" ("millî") novels restricted to the Muslim community (6). The former are more "colorful," Midhat tells us, whereas the latter employ hackneyed themes (6). After his novel *Yeryüzünde Bir Melek* ("An Angel on Earth," 1879) was criticized for depicting an illicit love affair between a married Muslim woman and her former lover, Midhat never again wrote stories with unfaithful Muslim heroines (Esen, "Narrator" 140).

Turkish does register these differences. Secondly, because the translatability of
Turkish into and out of other languages of the empire is a primary concern for
Midhat, explored in the novel in scenes of intersection between Armenian and
Turkish. When Midhat follows the two women and introduces himself to one of
them (44), she recognizes his name, because his novels were being published in
"Turkish in the Armenian script" ("Ermeni hurufuyla Türkçe") at this time (50).[58]
For Midhat, who sought to combine Ottoman multinationalism with Turkish-
Islamic political and cultural hegemony, this translatability and traversal of Turkish
reinforces its function as a kind of imperial vernacular. In the conversation of Mid-
hat with the Armenian women, the language is described as "Türkçe" ("Turkish"),
"Osmanlıca" ("Ottoman")," and "lisan-ı Osmanî" ("the Ottoman language") (51)
interchangeably.[59]

The novel unfolds with Midhat traveling across the city, interviewing the two
Armenian women, as well as other characters, to gather information for the
story yet to be written. This mobility of the author is a figure of the linguistic
power of translative language, traveling into all corners, absorbing like a sponge
all that is spoken. While the irreducible difference of French and Armenian—or
even the internal difference of Ottoman Turkish, registered in Armeno-Turkish—may seem appropriable, here, this does not also mean that translation is
understood to pose no threat at all, in this novel. The authorial "I," who so easily
slips in and out of the text while traveling in translative language, can indeed be
tempted by what he hears. Such "total" travel is after all nothing but constantly
crossing borders—and in translation, there is always the possibility of radical
loss in self-forgetting.

The passage cited earlier registers the first instance of a social transgression
when Midhat self-consciously and comically acknowledges that inserting himself
into the women's conversation is "rude" and "immoral," though he decides the
writing of the novel is worth this risk (28). As he follows the women in order to find
out where they live, both the driver of his own carriage and the doorman of the
women's lodging house assume him a flirtatious lech—though he is confident that
his readers will know he is the well-known writer Ahmed Midhat, a respectable man

[58] Armeno-Turkish is Ottoman Turkish written in Armenian script. There is a significant body of literature published in Armeno-Turkish, from the early eighteenth century onward. The oldest periodicals date from
1840, and the most recent from 1947. Midhat's *Filatun Bey ile Rakim Efendi* was published in 1879 by Aramyan
in Armeno-Turkish (Stepanyan 192). For a detailed bibliography of publications in Armeno-Turkish, see Stepanyan, *Ermeni Harfli Türkçe Kitaplar ve Süreli Yayınlar Bibliyografyası (1727–1968)* (in Turkish, French, and
Armenian).
[59] Historically, the vernacular named "Turkish" was distinguished as such from other vernaculars of the
empire. But Midhat used "Ottoman" interchangeably to mark the composite nature of the language, as well as
to instrumentalize it as a bulwark of his own Ottomanist ideology. For Midhat's views on the language question, see his article "Osmanlıcanın Islahı" ("The Reform of Ottoman," 1872). In *Elifbeden Alfabeye*, Ertem
quotes from an 1874 newspaper article published in *Kırk Anbar*, in which Midhat offers a comparative analysis
of the Greek, Latin, Armenian, and Ottoman ("elifbe-i Osmani") alphabets, praising the Armenian alphabet
as the most perfect (qtd. in Ertem 122). Midhat writes that the deficiencies of "the Ottoman alphabet" itself
could be remedied by borrowing necessary missing letters, such as the *w* and *x* of the Latin alphabet.

of values (42; 61). When Midhat leaves the company of Siranuş (one of the women) in a state of "sweet dreaminess" and "absentmindedness," however, we witness a rare instance of authorial self-forgetfulness:

> Instead of turning right upon my arrival at the tunnel square, I apparently just walked towards the Mevlevihane. I must have just gone down the hill from top to bottom, I don't know. Once I regained my state of consciousness by the Bridge as I was about to pay, I almost became afraid. Where am I, what's my state, I looked around for answers. (59)

Here, we are transported back to the bridge connecting the two sides of the Golden Horn, where we first encountered our "chic" novelist. Both here and in the scene described earlier, we might say that it is the public gaze, met on the bridge, which awakens the enchanted novelist. Where in his earlier appearance, the novelist associated his self-foreignization with a relatively straightforwardly enjoyable freedom, on this (rarer) occasion, he admits to its fundamental uncanniness, the defamiliarization of the familiar producing that fearful helplessness Freud called *das Unheimliche*.[60] Anticipating the possibility of total self-loss, the "I" of *Müşahedat* retreats, here, in fear of the foreign self (selves) he might assume, as a subject of the Ottoman communications revolution. The incipiently split self, here, turns to literature as an instrument for domesticating his double's transgression:

> I know myself. I'm not in love. I am not an old geezer [*kartlık*] either! Not even in my youth were victorious lovers able to enslave me so easily. I'm not talking about coarse [*âdi*] desires and wishes. Those kinds of defeats are mostly voluntary. What puts me in this state is my contentment concerning my art. Writing novels [*Romancılık*]! (59)

The authorial "I" emerges precisely where the author-narrator separates from the "we" of language in fear, *after* his recognition of self-forgetfulness in the pleasures of translation. Indeed, one can find the subtext of a quite different and much more perverse novel within *Müşahedat*, the lecherous protagonist of which is Midhat himself. This subtextual novel manifests itself, we could say, in the spaces of misunderstanding or mistaken appearance, the zone of the "as if" opened up by transgressive language. One magically doubles, triples in this freed zone, transforming from a respectable writer to a potential womanizer. The radical disjuncture between appearance and identity, signifier and signified, induces an intense pleasure, a "heartthrob," in Midhat's phrasing, like that of "falling in love" ("dil düşürmek") (49).

Within the novel, however, these subtextual drives are neutralized and recoded into morally permissible narrative—the excitement for the "novel," for "art" or a "father-daughter" relation (307). One such sublimated climax occurs when Siranuş

---

[60] On the uncanny as "that class of the frightening which leads back to what is known of old and long familiar," see Freud, "The 'Uncanny'" 220; "Das Unheimliche" 231.

"puts her lips burning like fire on [his] hand" in recognition of Midhat's symbolic paternity (302). For Midhat, the "spiritual pleasure" ("ezvak-ı ruhaniye") of having a daughter like Siranuş would not even be comparable to the "physical pleasure" ("ezvak-ı maddiye") of "having a thousand Siranuşes combined as [his] mistress" (306). Midhat withdraws in fear of what the revolutionary freedom of language makes him see he *could* do. The enchanting transformative power of language takes on the dimensions of what James T. Siegel has called the fetish of modernity (*Fetish* 93)—and it must be controlled. A schism between world and text, reality and representation, author and story begins to appear, here, as the author becomes aware of the subversive powers of language and seeks to control its "freedom" by appealing to moral discourse. No longer an extension of the vernacular, writing is now the secondary representation of an externalized truth, marking the ascendance of phonocentrism. Modern literature, which meant the mediation of the enchanting news of a translative vernacular, is now abstracted and distanced in normatively functioning fiction, inhabiting and habitualizing the temporal gap opened by a terribly seductive language.[61] The normativity of literature, here, is unquestionably determined by the mores that historically constitute its social grammar—but the modern author now (and belatedly) upholds its values with an awareness of their inherent arbitrariness.

The author figure is doubled, in *Müşahedat,* by a figure representing the moral merchant. Many critical readers of *Müşahedat* have remarked its celebration of ethical capitalism, embodied in the persona of an Egyptian merchant, Seyyit Numan Efendi, who represents a capitalism generating wealth for the general good,

---

[61] This detachment is also the very condition of possibility of Midhat's theoretical writings on the novel. I have already mentioned "Romancı ve Hayat" and "Roman ve Romancılık Hakkında Mütaalamız." See also his 1873 article "Hikâye Tasvir ve Tahriri" ("The Depiction and the Writing of a Story") and his 1890 critical study of the novel, entitled *Ahbar-ı Asara Tamim-i Enzar* ("A General View of Literary Works"). The latter work needs to be read in the context of the debates over realism and Romanticism, during the late nineteenth century. The Ottoman materialist Beşir Fuad (1852–1887) initiated a well-known public debate on Romanticism and realism (*hayaliyun* and *hakikiyun*) with the publication of his 1885 critical study *Victor Hugo,* which defended Zola's scientific approach to literature against Hugo's Romanticism. For an account of these exchanges, see Okay, *Beşir Fuad* 138–181. For an account in English, see Evin 96–98.

Midhat's *Ahbar-ı Asara Tamim-i Enzar* joined this debate, resisting the categorical opposition between the real and the imaginary. Midhat began by defining *hikaye* (story), via Daniel Huet, as the depiction of something real or imaginary in a captivating fashion—naming the first register "history" ("tarih") and the second "tale" ("masal") or "novel" ("roman"), used interchangeably. Midhat suggested that although these two registers are initially distinguishable from each other only in terms of content—the former as the thematization of the world of humans, the latter of gods (38)—in time, as states begin chronicling events in a plain, orderly ("muntazaman") manner, history and novel diverge qualitatively from each other (43). While the novel assumes historically different forms, including the chivalric, political, and love novel, among others, for Midhat its function remains in many ways the same: to narrate the extraordinary ("harik-i ade") (31) or the marvelous ("havarık") (35) in an enchanting ("cazibiyet") fashion. For Midhat, then, the "realism" and the "imaginariness" of a story are entirely secondary elements. Even realists like Zola "search after seemingly impossible and strange truths, which evoke surprise [*hayret*] and joy [*lezzet*] in their readers once their truthfulness is established" (35). Reality and fiction are not to be opposed (at least initially), because the writer necessarily makes amendments, anyway, in rendering his story attractive and moral. While Midhat's novels thus need to be read in the context of the debates over realism and Romanticism, as his work demonstrates to us, the abstractions "realism" and "imagination" become meaningful only through the communicative force of translative language. Midhat's attempt to have it both ways (his enjoyment of the pleasures of a seductive language, on the one hand, and his suppression of it, on the other) does not last long—though its breakdown is *itself* visible, of course, only in translative language.

rather than for individual self-interest (200).[62] But the complexity of the displacement through which *Müşahedat* links author and merchant, as each other's doubles, cautions us against reading for merely archetypal analogy, here. The author is at work mediating the exchange of words through which the merchant figure is represented overseeing the exchange of commodities, and less than "capitalism" (ethical or not) as such, what Seyyit Numan really stands for is nothing less than the transnational generalization of the commodity form, in his trade in soap, cotton, rice, oil, and textiles in a territory from Egypt through Marseilles to Trieste and London, on the one side, and on the other, from Russia through the Aegean islands to the Mediterranean (187). The analogue of translative language, in the world of trade, is money circulating in all directions, permitting, and indeed enforcing contact with the as yet unseen and unheard. Excruciatingly aware of the translative-transformative power of language as money and money as language, Midhat continuously attempts to recontrol its "freeing" in his fictional not-to-dos, sending his characters enchanted by its promises to their doom. As a meticulous money-counter and bookkeeper, the ethical capitalist merchant knows—and shows us—how to suppress the temptation to expenditure and serve the social good.[63]

Most blatantly, the figure Seyyit Numan serves to legitimize the author figure as a trader of stories; and it is in this respect that they complement each other most intimately. Seyyit Numan agrees to prepare clean copies of Midhat's manuscripts for publication (244), while the author in turn watches over the merchant's business accounts during his subsequent illness (422). Seyyit Numan's ethical-capitalist "greatness" generates surplus (*fazl*) through buying and selling of goods (188), while the author generates his own surplus in the exchange of the stories of *Müşahedat,* itself. "Don't worry, my brother!" Midhat says to his publisher, who has complained about his reduced rate of production, "we'll make up for the twenty five percent loss [*ziyan*] once we finish the novel" (471). Various characters are enlisted in story-writing, and in making corrections to the manuscript of *Müşahedat*

---

[62] On Midhat's economic views, see Georgeon, "L'Économie politique selon Ahmed Midhat." For a comparison with the institutionalization of authorship in Indonesia, see Siegel, *Fetish* 60–68.

[63] Midhat's novel *Felâtun Bey ile Râkım Efendi* ("Felâtun Bey and Râkım Efendi," 1876) must also be read in this context. Contrasting the success story of the industrious Ottoman bureaucrat, translator, and language instructor Râkım with the downfall of the lazy, wasteful dandy Felâtun, this novel is regarded as the first substantial Ottoman literary exploration of the cultural effects of Westernization. Although critics including Tanpınar, Moran, and Mehmet Kaplan have correctly registered the moral "message" of *Felâtun Bey ile Râkım Efendi*—be industrious, be financially prudent—they have tended to overlook the importance of the object of labor and exchange, here: the Ottoman Turkish language itself. Râkım is described as a "work machine" ("iş makinası"), translating books from French, composing commissioned legal documents in Turkish on behalf of his "Frank" friends (18), and giving Turkish language lessons. Unlike Felâtun, Râkım has a strong command of the orthography and lexicon of the language, described interchangeably as Ottoman and (more frequently) Turkish. In the accented Turkish of Râkım's female Circassian and English pupils, whom Râkım finds attractive, there can be something of the seductive power of a language and transit and inflected by the "foreign." In *Felâtun Bey ile Râkım Efendi*, as in *Müşahedat*, the successful realization of conservative modernity is contingent on the establishment of moral linguistic exchange, in both translation and instruction. To read this novel as thus foregrounding the question of language in transit, would be productively to recontextualize it in relation to *Araba Sevdası*, independently of the question of "super-westernization."

(133), occasionally objecting to Midhat's appropriation therein of a public commodity. This dramatic emergence of the author as a talented retailer of circulating stories reaches a kind of climax when the Armenian women begin to weep on hearing their life-stories narrated to them by Midhat (152), who has appropriated the technique of the *meddah*-author as his own, in a bid for originality (127). As a doubled paragon of the good capitalist, the author serves the social good, here, by distinguishing permissible from impermissible stories, and by marking the impermissible with a warning sign.

In many of his works, *Müşahedat* included, Midhat notes the hastiness of his own writing, complaining frequently about never having had time to complete or properly proofread his manuscripts. Located at the leading edge of a language in movement and acceleration, the "I" of his authorial alter egos is always on the chase and constantly out of breath. This is the breathless "I" we've encountered earlier in "Romancı ve Hayat," in the figure of the novelist chasing the novel: "Of course, there is something very important ahead: There is the novel in that direction; he's running towards . . . that novel. How can we dare to stop him?" (66). I have earlier mentioned that Midhat was also compared to a "writing machine." In his encyclopedic *Ondokuzuncu Asır Türk Edebiyatı Tarihi* ("History of Nineteenth-Century Turkish Literature," 1942; rev. in 1956), Tanpınar (perhaps unsatisfied with this relatively simplistic metaphor) offers us two other analogies for Midhat's prolific productivity: "[Midhat] has the appetite of a giant. Quantity always beats quality in his work. His reading, writing, and speaking . . . demonstrate his measureless consumption. A giant eats without thinking about digestion. Midhat Efendi reads and writes in the same fashion. Like a water tower [*su terazisi*], he releases what he collects shortly after" (452).[64]

Even metaphors split and reproduce more metaphors, in describing Midhat. The voracious giant devouring words and, like a siphon, releasing the remains, is a terrifyingly apt figure for Midhat's ravenous *generalization*. The seduction of all that one reads and hears, as such an author, is too strong—the "giant" overeats, yet the *author,* paralyzed by fear of what he has done, defecates his excessive representation in the form of moral messages. Midhat has often been read as cultivating the persona of an omnisciently didactic father-teacher, restrictively borrowing from the West while emphasizing the dangers of modernization, in the attempt to produce an Ottoman synthesis of Western modernity under the sign of Turkic-Islamic values. And while it is certainly the case that Midhat strove for just such an Ottoman synthesis of Western modernity, we might say that the motor of such a project, in this case, was the productivism leading the gluttony of "overeating" words to the emission of moral messages. In *Babalar ve Oğullar,* Parla has read Midhat as just such a father figure embodying an absolutist idealist Ottoman-Islamic epistemology, and

---

[64] *Su terazisi* were towers built to maintain pressure for an efficient distribution of water.

we might supplement this valuable reading of *Müşahedat* by thinking that epistemology, itself, as a cancellation of other, illicit acts that Midhat *might have* committed, on the verge of seduction by language. As a popular cultural translator
working between Ottoman Turkish and French, Midhat did in one sense reproduce
the social authority of the teachers of recitational logocentrism. Just as the classical
teachers had established their authority by putting Turkish speakers in contact with
an unknown power announced in Arabic, Midhat established his own authority by
putting Turkish speakers in contact with an enchanting foreign element in the extra-
Turkish outside—with one important difference. In mimicking the moralizing voice
of this older mode of authority, Midhat was only obscuring his own agency in
transmitting a competing source of power capable of uprooting the Ottoman-
Islamic order of things.

Midhat was not alone in this deep and intractable fear of a "freed" writing. In
a commentary on Ekrem's *Tâlim-i Edebiyat* ("The Teaching of Literature") discovered posthumously among his papers, Midhat's contemporary Namık Kemal also
emphasized the necessity for control of writing in deeply and determinatively gendered terms: "A microscope can show a fly as if it were an elephant. A telescope can
display the moon for a whole night. It can put a sixty-year old woman into a twenty-
eight-year old girl's outfit. [. . .] But literary judgment never diminishes the large,
nor does it enlarge the small" ("Ta'lim-i Edebiyat Üzerine" 282). For these writers,
modernity's magical translational-transformative power to disjoin appearance and
identity, signifier and signified *must* be controlled, and we might say that literary-
fictional not-to-dos serve this end, above all else. We can hear echoes, here, of the
terror expressed by the theologian and philosopher Friedrich Schleiermacher, over
the border in Europe, in the 1813 lecture to the Berlin Academy of Sciences we
know by the title "Über die verschiedenen Methoden des Übersetzens" ("On the
Different Methods of Translating"). Remarkable in its conflicted embrace of what
Lawrence Venuti calls "foreignizing" translation, "Über die verschiedenen Methoden des Übersetzens" is a call for the enlistment of translation in the enrichment
of the German language and its literature by precisely that displacement through
which the translator can "impart to the reader the same image . . . that he himself
received thanks to his knowledge of the original language of the work as it was
written, thus moving the reader to his own position, one in fact foreign to him"
("On the Different" 49; "Über die Verschiedenen" 74–75). The direct service of the
translator to German culture in this project is necessarily offset, Schleiermacher
realizes, by the possibility and indeed, the likelihood that the "freeing" transvaluation of all values will generate unexpected and possibly unwanted effects for *any*
such project. In translation, the seduction of the foreign may drive one to "turn
against nature and custom and desert . . . mother tongue . . . subvert all hierarchies
[*Ordnung*] and laws," ending by "walking about doubled like a ghost [*doppelt geht
wie ein Gespenst*]" (59; 88).

Modernity's communications revolution has not delivered on its promise of
democracy—then or now, in the European or in the Ottoman context. Where the

work of Edward W. Said and Aamir R. Mufti, as critics of Orientalism, have provided us with important accounts of this failure from a perspective exterior to the Ottoman Empire, Midhat's *Müşahedat* can serve as its supplement in so far as it narrates that failure from within. It is without doubt that the ascendance of Ottoman and Turkish identitarianisms, in the late nineteenth and early twentieth centuries, was profoundly overdetermined by the history of European imperialism, and indeed *Müşahedat* shows us how the "othering" of Armenian difference in Ottoman Turkish turned on its (mis)perceived cultural and religious approximation of Frenchness. But alongside this external determination, *Müşahedat* also shows us the effect of an equally significant internal determination: that through which the internal difference of Armenian became a "minority problem," with and *in* the discovery of the "native" vernacular, itself, as an uncanny technology with fundamentally indeterminate origins. In *Müşahedat*, this "problem" is resolved by Siranuş's conversion to Islam, in a legitimating compensation for the Muslim masculine transgression of an uprooting and generalizing modernization itself. Chapter 2 will focus on the catastrophic consequences of the identitarian foreclosure on the communications revolution. But before we reach that point, we should attend to Midhat's contemporary, Ekrem, in his historical registration of a politically unrealized, yet fully and substantively imagined possibility of non-identitarian writing, in the silhouette of a non-identitarian social that animates *Araba Sevdası*.

3. Overcoming Phonocentrism

As a translator, poet, critic, and novelist, Ekrem (1847–1914) also registered the communications revolution in different ways in his works and professional activities. Ekrem was known best for his poetry, and his most substantial contribution to the literature of his time was a transformation of Ottoman lyric poetic practice through the introduction of French Romantic imagery. As a literature teacher at the School of Civil Service (Mekteb-i Mülkiye) and the Galatasaray Lycée, Ekrem is considered an important *birleştirici,* or literary-historical link, between the first generation of the reformist intelligentsia and the literary modernists of the early twentieth century.[65] As just such a literary-historical copula, Ekrem's work stands as much for a form of continuity as for the break that it *also* marks. The introduction of authorial talent as a critical category, the psychologizing of literature, and the conceptualization of a disinterested aesthetic sphere ("art for art's sake") emerge in Ottoman Turkish literary criticism with Ekrem's rhetoric textbook *Tâlim-i Edebiyat* ("The Teaching of Literature," 1882), a production that shaped the institutionalization of modern literature as an autonomous field distinct from Islamic ethics.[66]

---

[65] See Tanpınar, *Ondokuzuncu* 467. For a short biography in English, see İz, "Ekrem Bey."

[66] The first lithographic copy of *Tâlim-i Edebiyat* was printed in 1879. For a detailed study of Ekrem's *Tâlim-i Edebiyat*, see Yetiş, *Tâlim-i Edebiyatın Retorik ve Edebiyat Nazariyâtı Sahasında Getirdiği Yenilikler.*

While Ekrem set the tone of many polemical debates of the period, his early poetry had been criticized for its sentimentalism.[67] In *Ondokuzuncu Asır Türk Edebiyatı Tarihi*, Tanpınar writes: "His poetry, lacking any kind of arrangement, employing arbitrary rhymes, made of words neither used by the people nor found in the literary tradition—merely picked from a dictionary—could only give birth to crippled children" (475). Desiring to write like the French Romantics, Rousseau and Lamartine, Ekrem might have failed to invoke an authentic language of interiority in his "barren" love poems and elegies (*mersiye*) (475). Nevertheless, he surfaces as one of the most crucial figures of the late Ottoman period, having "discovered" the first Ottoman Turkish realist novel (in the European sense) in the space of this poetic failure. A sensitive reading of *Araba Sevdası* will reduce it to neither a sui generis production of autonomous literary genius in its own context, nor a derivation through time and space from an archetypal European genre. Rather, it will find in Ekrem's novel the registration of historical vernacularization and translational exchange-ability *as conditions of its own possibility* as realist fiction—and in this, a kind of signaling of the multiple "origins" of the Ottoman Turkish novel in diglossia. If like Midhat's *Müşahedat*, it also thematizes the danger of self-loss in translation, *Araba Sevdası* parts company with Midhat's work in laying radically bare the fundamental arbitrariness of the modern. It is with *Araba Sevdası* that Ottoman Turkish literature takes as its task not the fabrication of national representations but the figuration of a non-identitarian social *despite and with* modern alienated self-consciousness.

Araba Sevdası too begins in translation, opening with a description of the new Çamlıca Garden, a famous gathering place for the members of a society in decay and in thrall to French (and Francophone) commodification:

> Going from Üsküdar to Çamlıca via the Bağlarbaşı road, if one looks from the Tophanelioğlu intersection approximately one hundred paces ahead to the end of the wide road, one would see a grove enclosed by a wall of less than one-meter [*arşın*] height. Upon reaching the grove, the road separates into two continuing to the right and to the left. Enclosed by a wall, the grove has a rather large gate exactly at the point where the two roads separate. . . . This place, called the Çamlıca Garden, is the first arranged, opened garden in Istanbul. (3–4; 209–210)[68]

It is a critical commonplace, in reading *Araba Sevdası,* to emphasize the narrator's meticulous, camera-like documentation and scene setting. Like the space it describes,

---

[67] Ekrem's first book of poetry was *Nağme-i Seher* (1871); later works included *Zemzeme* 1, 2, and 3 (1882, 1883, and 1884, respectively), and *Nijad Ekrem* (1900; 2nd ed., 1910), a collection of poems and other writings about his beloved son Nijad, whom he survived.

[68] The first page numeral here references the original, in Ottoman Turkish script; the second, the transliterated version prepared by İsmail Parlatır et al. In the original Ottoman Turkish, borrowed French words are written in boldface Ottoman Turkish letters; occasionally, they are also distinguished from the bulk of the text with brackets. No translations are provided anywhere in the text for readers lacking knowledge of French. Tanpınar argued that the novel would have received more attention if the French words had been typeset in Latin letters, with translations provided in footnotes (489).

however, the *language* of this description is also a product of translation, self-consciously self-differentiating from the symbology of an Ottoman lyric tradition in which the garden, as an informal religio-mystical space for gathering and poetry recitation,[69] was itself a recurring metaphor in divan poetry. Andrews has described this symbolic spatialization as embodying three principles: "(1) every object of this world has an otherworldly counterpart; (2) otherworldly truths are accessible insofar as one can perceive the essence of this-worldly objects (or this-worldly objects stripped of the accidental qualities that veil their essences); (3) this-worldly objects have meaning only by virtue of their analogues in the other world" (*Poetry's Voice* 70).[70]

As such critics as Güzin Dino, Robert P. Finn, and Ahmet Evin have observed, Ekrem's contemporary Namık Kemal also began his 1876 novel *İntibah* ("Awakening") with a description of the Çamlıca Garden,[71] composed in the language of a classical ode (*kaside*) and comparing the garden, "a part of the revered paradise [that has] descended to earth" (7), to the beauties of a newly arrived spring (5).[72] This description includes a passage about the pleasures of watching the cityscape from Çamlıca, which we might say reveals more about the logic of poetic writing during its historical displacement than about the view itself:

> Çamlıca is such a viewpoint that if one goes up near its fountain during spring and looks out, one will see another world before one's eyes composed of a hundred thousand natural, artistic [*sınaî*], and scientific grand beauties. The eyeball turns into a map of this world of beauty, compressed into a single point [*nokta-i vâhide*] with exceptional talent. (7)

Like the lyric poets of the past, Kemal regards the garden as a religio-mystical space. Even though what Kemal is describing here is an actual garden, in a particular city, the worldly attributes of the garden are constructed to reflect an otherworldly reality. Of even more importance, here, is the position of the observer as imbricated in the world (and in language), rather than alienated from it. Between the viewer and his object of contemplation, here, there is a form of unity; the vision recorded is the abstract representation of a "map," but it is also an infusion of the observer, himself.

Freed of the conventions of classical logocentrist rhetoric and no longer the symbol of an other-worldly space, the garden in *Araba Sevdası* serves in contrast as a merely descriptive label for the Çamlıca Garden. Composed in a simplified phonocentric Ottoman Turkish, Ekrem's language (though significantly more formal than the vernacular used in *Müşahedat*), echoes its historical situation in its register. And yet rather than the influence of a European literary current, we might say that Ekrem's realist description marks the reign of a new phonocentric representational writing, in

[69] On the social significance of Ottoman gardens as informal leisure spaces, see Necipoğlu, "The Suburban Landscape of Sixteenth-Century Istanbul as a Mirror of Classical Ottoman Garden Culture" 43.

[70] On the symbolism of the garden in divan poetry, also see Tanpınar, *Ondokuzuncu* xxiii.

[71] See Dino 63–69; Finn 71–73; and Evin 161–163.

[72] For more on this poetic form, see Krenkow.

which the outside as an arbitrary externalized space is first encountered. The histo-ricity of discovery, as Kojin Karatani has written in another context, is immediately forgotten: "In the very moment when we become capable of perceiving landscape [as such], it appears to us as if it had been there, outside of us, from the start" (29). For-getful of this "discovery," we posit words as secondary transparent labels for things located "outside," even though things are first discovered as such only as an effect of this writing. We construe evaluative literary histories, of the final "triumph of re-alism" in Ekrem's work, for example, when his predecessors must be understood to have had their own, equally legitimate, but meaningfully different conceptions of realism—as the mediation of the speech of a community, for example, or of the figuration of an imperio-religious representational space. Only under the effect of an historical metalepsis substituting effect for cause do we experience writing as the secondary, one-to-one reproduction of a material world prior and external to it.[73]

There is more to be said about the opening description. Unlike the narrator of Kemal's *İntibah*, who stands imbricated in the world (and in language), the narrator of *Araba Sevdası* is an individualized viewer, observing the world at a distance. The alienated subject of the modern age experiences the world as a scene held in reserve, at a distance. In narratological terms, this marks the emergence of Ekrem's narrator as a focalizing agent, besides its function as a storyteller. More significantly, however, it registers the emergence of interiority. Just as the modern subject encounters the out-side first in phonocentric representational writing, he "discovers" (to borrow Karatani's term) "his" interiority as an effect of this writing. The discovery of the outside is simultaneously the discovery of a subjective inner "voice which is most im-mediate to the self, and which constitutes self-consciousness" (69)—although one may certainly forget this original discovery. Phonocentrism is, in other words, the condition of possibility of a privileged inner voice, understood as a gateway to consciousness.[74]

Araba Sevdası then archives the operation of a new writing practice, as a condition of its own possibility as a work of literature. Against the critical impulse to read this novel as a performance of failed representation, *Araba Sevdası* demonstrates from the start a masterful command of the new conventions of phonocentric-representational

---

[73] The first edition of *Araba Sevdası* reinforced this effect by prefacing the text's description of the Çamlıca Garden with a photograph of its gated entrance (3). The novel makes use of illustrations, as well as a photograph, in reinforcing the effect of verisimilitude; according to İsmail Parlatır, the novel is the first illus-trated novel of Ottoman Turkish literary modernity (230). Though criticism of the novel has largely neglected these visual materials, it could be said that the juxtaposition of the textual description of the Çamlıca Garden with a photograph of its gated entrance is not without its own significance. In a sense, the photograph serves to certify the text's representational realism, while establishing an identification of the narrator's point of view with that of the camera capturing or generating the image. The content of this embedded image could be said to reinforce a linguistic interiority, as well, enframing the interior as a *gated* entrance.

[74] See Cemal Kafadar's introduction to Asiye Hatun's *Rüya Mektupları* and "Self and Others," as exam-ples of autobiographical literature from the seventeenth century. My goal here is not, of course, to discount the importance of this literature—but only to emphasize the *difference* of the modern relation between the self and language. Subjectivity, in modern literature, is staged as a scene of listening to one's own voice, as registered in Bihruz's internal monologues. If, as Moran notes, this technique is first used in *Tanzimat* literature in *Araba Sevdası* (84), that is because the development of the novel is accompanied by the practice of a new phonocen-tric writing (84).

writing, which it employs in proposing a comprehensive *Weltbild* or "world-picture"[75] of Ottoman modernity. This is not to say that *Araba Sevdası*'s narrator is content with the things he discovers in this world scene. In the "free" garden of modernity, lovers are no longer the beloveds of the Ottoman lyric tradition; nor are they replaceable by equivalent tropes from the literary store of French Romanticism. Instead, they are mere prostitutes; the public is a mannerless crowd; and the pool is no longer either the *havuz* of Ottoman poetry, or the *lac* of French Romanticism, but a "muddy and yellowish pool" (20; 229). Modernity's translation has already pinned up the world in the form of substitutable representations, the content of which is their exchangeability, itself.

Tracking the comical adventures of Bihruz, the "super-westernized" dandy, Ekrem's narrator, like Midhat's "awakened" novelist, seeks in part to demonstrate the dangers of self-loss in a freed language. The spoiled son of a former vizier with no proper education in French or Ottoman Turkish (here, called "Türkçe")[76], Bihruz has spent the significant sum of wealth he has inherited in cash, to adorn himself with "shiny shoes from *Herald*" or "a silver cane with the inscribed French initials of the brand M. B." (7; 214).[77] Bihruz is so enchanted by the seductions of translative language that he develops as a speech affectation his own version of a hybrid "Franco-Turkish," incomprehensible to others. In many ways, *Araba Sevdası* is a masterful parody and irony of Bihruz's hyperboles, which ensure that every sign Bihruz encounters is taken for something it is not: a liar, Keşfî, for a friend; a prostitute, Perîveş, for an elegant beloved; and a muddy pool for a *lac*. The novel follows Bihruz as he (mis)composes a love letter to Perîveş through a chain of mistranslations, misreadings, and misunderstandings, which begin when Bihruz realizes that he has included in his love letter a quotation from a poem that was originally addressed to a man, not a woman. Bihruz then composes a second letter, apologizing for the inappropriateness of the quotation, and when he is unable to deliver this second letter (he does not see Perîveş again at the Çamlıca Garden), he is persuaded by Keşfî's lie that Perîveş has passed away. (Just as Bihruz begins searching for the cemetery in which Perîveş is buried, he unexpectedly runs into her in the street.)

In an invaluable analysis of Ekrem's use of parody and irony, Parla has read Bihruz's "poorly composed, incomplete, and unread epistle" as a staging of "the fruitlessness of *Tanzimat* writers's labors to represent and communicate" at a time of "clash between the empirical, realistic epistemology of the Western novel and the aprioristic and idealistic" epistemology of Ottoman classical forms ("Car" 538).

---

[75] See Heidegger, "Die Zeit des Weltbildes" ("The Age of the World Picture" or "The Time of the World Image").

[76] At the conclusion of his 1882 rhetoric textbook entitled *Tâlim-i Edebiyat*, Ekrem writes that he has referred to the language as Ottoman (*Osmanlıca*) and not Turkish precisely because it is a composite language incorporating Arabic and Persian words and grammatical constructions (386). Criticized by the Turkist Süleyman Pasha, Ekrem published an article in *Hürriyet-i Fikriye* that same year concurring with the Pasha and stating that "the phrase, the Ottoman language, is meaningless" (qtd. in Levend 137). On this exchange, see Levend 135–137.

[77] In the original, "*Herald*" is bracketed, to indicate the Ottoman Turkish orthography of a foreign word; "M. B." appears in Latin lettering.

Nurdan Gürbilek has extended this line of interpretation, suggesting that we read Bihruz's snobbism as a "constitutive element of the 'original Turkish spirit' itself" ("Dandies and Originals" 623) and as an iteration of translation without any "outside." Without conflating Bihruz himself with the narrator of *Araba Sevdası*, we might accept these assessments of *Araba Sevdası*'s final judgment on modernity, as asserting modernity's fundamental arbitrariness. At the same time, we might supplement these assessments by considering the extent to which Bihruz's letter-writing *exceeds* the failure to represent. *Araba Sevdası* does not stage the failure of the *Tanzimat* writer "to represent and communicate" so much as it explores the revolutionary possibility of overcoming representation.

Araba Sevdası lays radically bare the arbitrariness of a modern writing freed of classical logocentrist rhetoric, and we might say that what is ultimately at stake, in this novel, is an anticipation of the possibility of a modern writer operating beyond phonocentric representation altogether. Bihruz is incessantly ironized by the realist narrator, but he is also the narrator's double who doggedly collects emptied signs emitted by the narrator's representation and tries, in his failed poetry, to move them beyond exchange. In parody and irony, Bihruz seeks to produce a counter-text canceling the narrator's representations. We know from the beginning that there can be no retreat to the past, in this mad writing lost in translation, and reading *Araba Sevdası,* we wait in vain for the transformation of the madman into a *modern* poet: the figure from whom he is so removed, yet to whom he distantly aspires. However negatively constructed, Bihruz does register *another* hope embodied in *Araba Sevdası:* the hope for a new writing, in a foreignized Turkish, that will somehow interrupt the logic of modern phonocentrism. Where we might say Midhat instrumentalizes literature as a device for suppressing the arbitrariness of modern identity, Ekrem, *despite and with* self-consciousness of modern arbitrariness, practices literature as uncanny writing, in the faintest promise of a new social order grounded in difference.

During one of his outings to the Çamlıca Garden, Bihruz has spotted two women riding in an elegant carriage, promptly falling in love with one of them—or at least he believes that he has fallen in love with one of them. His first encounter with Perîveş occurs by the pool in the garden, in the company of her older friend, Çengi. The narrator's scene-setting begins with an extensive description of the two women:

> [H]er eyes were not blue like a beautiful-looking, corrected mistake of nature's decorator [*nakkaş-i tabîat*] but dark yellow; . . . her face was comparatively rounder in relation to her delicate body . . . and her mouth was five, ten thousand times bigger than the measure of the point [*nokta-i mevhûme*] that the poets imagined, yet still ordinarily small. (18; 226)

In describing Perîveş's every facial feature, the narrator makes allusion to the conventions of the ghazal of divan poetry. But rather than affirming such conventions, the allusion appears to be made as part of the performance of failure, here:

the failure of poetry itself, and its registers, within representational writing, as Perîveş is pictured in and by a sequence of descriptive *negations.* Her eyes are neither hazel nor black, as they would be in divan literature; they are not even blue (which would indeed be a "corrected mistake" of nature, in this context), but "dark yellow." A sub-sequence of cancellations is deployed in the description of Perîveş's mouth, rejecting the standard metaphor (*mazmun*) of divan poetry for describing the beloved's mouth.[78] The economy of poetic similes (*teşbihat*) collapses, here, in a "freeing" of language in which words no longer "weigh" as they should—or at all. As arbitrary, worn-out metaphors—"coins which have lost their image and now can be used only as metal, and no longer as coins," in Nietzsche's words[79]—they can be inverted, crossed out, or hyperbolized, and they can be *spent,* profusely.

And they are. Here, the narrator does more than describe these two women from a distance; he actively mediates their conversation by "the calm waters of the pool [*havuz*] [which] did not yet acquire the green color that is . . . sometimes more pleasurable than its transparency, though still muddy and yellowish enough to reflect the trees, plants, and other surrounding shapes" (20; 229). As Perîveş gazes at the reflective surface of the muddy water, watching herself, we overhear the following exchange between the two women:

> "Look look Çengi Hanım, it is an earth mirror [*yer aynası*]! Do you see yourself?"
>
> "An earth mirror? What's that? I know of earth apple[80] [*yer elması*], but have not heard of earth mirror!"
>
> "If you lift your yashmak, you'll even see two earth diamonds [*yer elması*] in the earth mirror . . ."
>
> "What shall I look at? The water is muddy. Those red things must be Amasya apples [*Amasya elması*] . . ."
>
> "What? [The city of] Amasya has diamonds [*elmas*]? I did not know that."
>
> "Apple [*elma*], my dear, apple! Not diamond [*elmas*]! Who wouldn't know that diamonds come from England?" (21; 229)

Traditional popular vernacular performances, such as the shadow theater and the *ortaoyunu,* commonly staged such linguistic misunderstandings to comic effect. In the vernacularized world of the modern novel, constructed from substitutable

---

[78] While describing Perîveş's clothes (in another such chain of cancellations), the narrator makes critical use of a series of clichés: "(If we were sure that our category of similes [*teşbihat*] would not turn into clichés [*ibtizale düşmek*], we would liken her light blue bonnet and her hair to a sunny sky)" (19; 227). As if negation had not completed the expiration of poetic writing, the narrator cannot help but launch an attack from the side, in parenthesis, deploying a reserve army of clichés to finish the job. This side attack is seconded by the next parenthetical remark, comparing the beloved's umbrella to a dark cloud: "(If expert readers would like, they could liken this umbrella to a dark cloud in that sunny sky. However, then a contrasting image invoked by this simile is revealed. Instead of the cloud being inside the sky, the sky gets inside the cloud)" (19; 227). Obviously, when inverted in this way, the poetic art of similitude borders on absurdity.

[79] See Nietzsche, "On Truth and Lying in an Extra-Moral Sense" 250.

[80] The reference here is to the vegetable called in English "Jerusalem artichoke" ("earth apple" in Turkish).

representations, poetic possibility is not merely comic, because it is no longer merely correctible; instead, it collapses into nonsense. In a way, we know from the outset that the pool, described in Perîveş's vernacular, will not meet its equivalent in the *havuz* of divan poetry; nor will it by transferred to the French Romantic substitute-value of the *lac*. Perîveş's *literalizing* metaphor instead leaves it a simple "earth mirror." This short moment of minimal poetic creativity is itself immediately annulled, as Çengi conflates the compound metaphor with the vegetable "earth apple." This metonymic substitution sets off a new chain of misunderstandings around the referent of *elması*: is it *elması* (of the apple, *elma* in third-person possessive form) or *elması* (of the diamond, *elmas* in third-person possessive form)?

There is confusion here, we might say, only to the extent that these emptied selves try too strenuously to see *through* representations. For Perîveş and Çengi, this undecidability is a temporary frustration, one forgotten when they leave the scene of the pool. Bihruz, however, who feels himself something of an awakened, yet empty sign, wants to walk *into* the scene, inhabit it from the inside, and to supplement an interiority he understands as fundamentally *lacking*. The more masterfully the narrator ironizes the evacuated French and Ottoman poetic registers, the more plundered and wasted metaphors his double, Bihruz, collects and tries to transform beyond exchange value. Approaching the women, whose conversation he has (mis)interpreted, he informs us that "the metaphor [*teşbih*] of the earth mirror" and "the allusion [*telmih*] to the earth diamond in the earth mirror" demonstrate Perîveş's "*poetik* [French *poétique,* in Ottoman Turkish orthography in the original]" elegance, in her role as his beloved. Bihruz presents Perîveş with "a white *jeraniyum* [French *géranium,* in Ottoman Turkish orthography in the original], that is, a *sardalya çiçeği* in vulgar Turkish," and delivers this speech:

> Even if this *fane* [*fanée*] flower cannot reciprocate your brilliance, whose worth would buy all England, France, and even Europe, I consider myself delighted to have asked you to accept it. I cannot tell you how *örö* [*heureux*] your praise has made your *admiratör* [*admirateur*]. (21; 230)

Although Perîveş accepts the geranium, during this encounter, we learn subsequently that Bihruz's hybrid language is incomprehensible to her, for what *she* hears in *fane* (the French *fanée,* or faded, in Bihruz's Franco-Turkish) is in fact the Arabic loanword *fâni* (transitory). Her response is to decide that Bihruz is "mad," "foolish," and "unaware of what he's doing" (29; 240).

Bihruz alone, in *Araba Sevdası,* is unreconciled to the alienation of modernity; Bihruz alone experiences the law of representation as a *problem.* Perîveş and Çengi, Bihruz's French instructor Monsieur Pierre, and Bihruz's friend Keşfî, by contrast, all appear to enjoy the novel's various scenes of modernity from the critical distance of a settled "reason." Approaching the muddy interior depth of the *lac* and what it does (rather than represents), they tend to retreat, laughing at the madman who, in the words of the Foucault of *The Order of Things,* "takes things for what they are not, and people one for another" and gets lost in arbitrariness (*Order* 49; *Mots* 63).

Bihruz, we might say, further interpolating Foucault, "fulfills the function of *homosemanticism*: he groups all signs together and leads them with a resemblance that never ceases to proliferate"—and indeed, *Araba Sevdası* follows Bihruz to its end as he wanders, mishearing and misreading signs in a broken language, aspiring to be a poet without even really being aware of what it is he aspires to. We wait in vain for the madman become a poet. "The poet fulfills the opposite function [than the madman]: his is the *allegorical* role; beneath the language of signs and beneath the interplay of their precisely delineated distinction, he strains his ears to catch that 'other language' . . . of resemblance" (*Order*, 49–50; *Mots* 63). Finding himself unable to comprehend Rousseau's *Julie, ou la nouvelle Héloïse*, Bihruz turns to *Le secrétaire des amants* and finally to a sonnet by Vâsıf-ı Enderunî, weaving Perîveş a love letter through the translating mediation of Ottoman Turkish and French dictionaries. Misreading the Ottoman Turkish script of the first line of Vâsıf's sonnet, "He is a youth with a dark complexion," he transposes this image into a "young, blonde woman" (88–89; 320–322). From page to page of *Araba Sevdası*, we follow Bihruz translating as mistranslating, reading as misreading, understanding as misunderstanding, and writing as miswriting. One might well imagine *Araba Sevdası* as two texts crossing each other out, in the figure of a chiasmus. Bihruz registers the *unfulfilled* hope of *Araba Sevdası* for a revolutionary new writing, which will somehow cancel phonocentric representational prose and overcome the modern.[81]

Araba Sevdası begins and ends, as it were, in its own middle. In the novel's closing scene, Bihruz unexpectedly encounters Perîveş in the street and realizes that Perîveş is not the idealized beloved of his fantasies, after all; here, the perspective of Bihruz the "madman" converges with that of the ironic narrator, in a confluence or contiguity that is not an opposition or a cancellation of either of its terms:

> All of a sudden he was taken over [*istilâ*] by a strange emotion [*hiss-i garîb*] that was like surprise, hate, and longing but really none of them—an emotion impossible to describe and analyze. . . . He did not know his existence. He was moving his body without thinking where he was, what he was doing, and what he would do.
>
> He felt a strong emotion of hate when he looked at the unpleasant form of the truth [*şekl-i nâpesend-i hakîkat*] he was following against his will. But he did not have the power to separate from the red umbrella. (170; 444)

When Bihruz recognizes himself, as he does here, as the effect of an arbitrary order, there can no longer be any figure of the beloved. Perîveş has become an arbitrary sign, an "unpleasant form of the truth" fixed temporarily by an exchangeable commodity (the red umbrella). Bihruz is able to tear himself out from the spell of such

---

[81] For a treatement of this question in the Japanese context, see the proceedings of the 1942 Tokyo symposium "Overcoming Modernity," in Calichman, *Overcoming Modernity.*

lifeless, machinic signification only because he sees that he is about to be run over by a carriage—a response that clinches the novel's conclusion as foreclosing on the imagination of any other future.

Bihruz's retreat, here—from the carriage, from Perîveş—signs *Araba Sevdası* with an apology in a borrowed word: "*Pardon!*" (170; 445). Whose forgiveness is asked by this "*Pardon,*" we might ask—and what sense of responsibility or guilt does it mark? In so many ways, it is an apology for a "survival" irreducibly contingent on a minimal reconciliation to the representational writing of modernity—and it is through this apology that Ekrem leaves us hanging, at the close of *Araba Sevdası,* in modern resignation to the closure of poetic possibility in freed language. "*Pardon,*" here, is the mark of a helpless, genre-less, always already borrowed text, which registers profound skepticism about the possibility of another future.

We must recognize that each "texting" of a freed language, in this way, is necessarily singular. If we can say that something in the simultaneously entwined and disparate histories of Ottoman and Western European modernities has pushed Ekrem to mourn *both* poetic traditions, at the same time, one cannot exactly say this mourning is reciprocated in the literature of European modernity, itself. In bringing this discussion to a close, we might nonetheless briefly turn to Mallarmé, whose "Crise de vers" ("Crisis in Poetry," 1896; trans. 1956), published concurrently with *Araba Sevdası,* also confronts the closure of the Romantic poetic tradition—even if for Mallarmé the collapse of that tradition does not consume *all* of literature, as it does for Ekrem. For Mallarmé, in an exchange society in which "language, in the hands of the mob, leads to the same facility and directness [*représentatif*] as does money" ("Crisis" 43; "Crise" 213), the revolutionary writing of modern literature is the medium through which the mysterious voice of language speaks. And if in the modern present, literary magic cannot compete with the magic of money and with the phonetic sign, repressing mediation in the "easy and direct" circulation and availability of objects or meanings, the modern writer still can upset this order, by exposing the deceit involved in any immediate "presencing." "When I say: 'a flower!,'" as Mallarmé put it, "then from that forgetfulness to which my voice consigns all floral forms, something different from the usual calyces arises, something all music, essence, and softness: the flower which is absent from all bouquets" (42; 213).

The Mallarméan performative begins by reminding one of what has been forgotten: the arbitrariness of the relation between the sign "flower" and its abstract signified. But it does not stop there. The "flower" invoked by the utterance is neither an arbitrary sign, nor a typical particularity (calyces) with which it might be equated. One would be foolish to take the "flower" for the material object of the flower itself. Beyond annulling the illusion of immediacy or unity that might be offered in different ways by classical logocentrism and modern phonocentrism, the performative utterance generates "something" so powerful that it even turns the plenitude of the physical object into a lack. Where the representational order of modernity has flattened out the poetic irreversibly, here, in the "plain sheet of paper" of the newspaper and the novel ("Book" 25; "Livre" 225), Mallarmé responds by stealing back, as it were, the surplus materiality of "the twenty-four letters of the alphabet" (26; 225).

Ekrem, too, made a home in this zone of a radically freed writing—but *Araba Sevdası* is finally ambivalent about the value of its suspensions, and Bihruz's mad nonsense is explicitly *not* affirmed as a possibility for new beginnings. We can explain this as a measure of Ekrem's recognition of the resolute power of commodity fetishism—but also as a recognition of the structural condition of *uneven translatability* that marked French as a culturally hegemonic language in the Ottoman Empire. And while the deep skepticism with which Ekrem treated his "super-westernized dandy" is entirely justified, we might also observe that Ekrem has built a literary world too entirely and unilaterally absorbed in and by French and Francophone commodification. *Araba Sevdası*'s deeply Francocentric world-view negates other unrealized, extant possibilities in the raw historical material of mid-nineteenth century vernacularization and phonocentrism. Where the mid-nineteenth century saw the rise of the hybrid "Franco-Turkish" of a Bihruz, it *also* generalized a practice of writing and publication in Ottoman Turkish using non-Turkish writing systems including the Armenian and Greek alphabets.[82] This is to say that the communications revolution created many other hybrid possibilities and practices of writing—and that the unfulfilled promise of a non-identitarian, egalitarian writing, to which *Araba Sevdası* can gesture only indirectly, is not an elimination of the promise itself.

Araba Sevdası is nevertheless one of the most important meta-novels of the late nineteenth century, in its ability to pose the question of literature in a historically novel way. When the narrator momentarily focuses on the liar, Keşfî, as an embodiment of the literary displacement of *Araba Sevdası* itself, he relates how Keşfî's friends have advised him not to waste his talent in lying—to "become a novelist [*romancı*] or at the very least a poet [*şair*]," instead (157; 346). Indeed, in *Araba Sevdası*, Ekrem remains visibly ambivalent about the stakes and value of his own novel. It is nevertheless the case that in Bihruz's writing, Ekrem *does* take us most of the way, as it were, to the unmarked, unhomely zone of bare signification exceeding all personal, national, humanist, or other appropriations. Only at this frontier, where the letters of the alphabet are let loose again, "thinking . . . takes on new figures: drawing out particular features; linking events; and on each occasion inventing the series that move from the neighborhood of one particular feature to the next."[83] Like the aphasic who "create[s] a multiplicity of tiny, fragmented regions in which nameless resemblances agglutinate things into unconnected islets," thought "continues to infinity, creating groups then dispersing them again, heaping

---

[82] According to Rekin Ertem, an 1883 newspaper article published in *Vakit* mentioned a proposal by Macid Pasha for the adoption of Armenian lettering for Ottoman Turkish (125). Even if the actuality of such a proposal is disputable—Macid Pasha strongly denied ever having made one—the discursive conceivability of such a change, and its brief debating in *Vakit,* is noteworthy.

[83] Deleuze, *Foucault* 117; for the French original, see *Foucault* 125.

up diverse similarities, destroying those that seem clearest, splitting up things that are identical, superimposing different criteria, frenziedly beginning all over again" (Foucault, *Order xviii*; *Mots* 10). At this frontier, fiction can assume, for the first time, the task of imagining a heteronomous, non-identitarian social, despite and with the self-consciousness marking the ground of such ethics as necessarily indeterminate. As the return of the ineradicable in the modern episteme, this aphasic writing harbors the promise of new social possibilities.

My goal in this chapter has been to approach *Müşahedat* and *Araba Sevdası* as a special archive of phonocentrism and its contradictions. I use the word "archive" here in a distinct sense. As a "system of statements" (128), as Foucault has it in *The Archaeology of Knowledge*, modern literature is an archive marking the *limits* of what is sayable. Localized "outside in" the episteme of phonocentrism, literature is at once "inside," its form and content profoundly shaped by overarching changes in writing practices: just as in Foucault's work, the institutions of confinement expose the workings of the larger social as a whole, the domain of modern Turkish literature registers the historical conditions of its possibility, as well as its own limits. At the same time, literature is manifest "outside," for as *fiction*, literature is distinguished from other discourses by its free use of language independent of phonocentric truth. "At the moment when language . . . becomes an object of knowledge, we see it reappearing in a strictly opposite modality" in its full indiscipline in literature, where it "has no other law than that affirming—in opposition to all other forms of discourse—its own precipitous existence" (Foucault, *Order* 300; *Mots* 313). This "exterior interiority" of modern literature is often taken for granted, though it bears crucial ethico-political implications. Where the suppression of literature's freedom is almost always accompanied by a politics of closed identitarianism, as in Midhat, its affirmation in and for itself might point to the possibility of revolutionary beginnings beyond the phonocentric modern.

In his search for a radical revolutionary writing, Ekrem refused to cathect an emerging nationalism. Many of the writers for the literary journal *Servet-i Fünun* ("The Riches of Science"), including Halid Ziya [Uşaklıgil] (1866–1945), Cenab Şahabeddin (1870–1934), and Mehmed Rauf (1875–1931), were criticized along with Ekrem (who acted as an advisor for the journal) for their aestheticism and their "incomprehensible" Bihruz-like language.[84] Still, the "hearing," so to speak, of novel nationalist representations within a translative language undoubtedly had captivating effects on other listeners. The next chapter will explore how the discourse

---

[84] Founded in 1891 by Ahmed İhsan [Tokgöz] (1868–1942), one of Ekrem's students at the School of Civil Service, *Servet-i Fünun* was particularly influential on the Ottoman Turkish literary scene from 1896 to 1901 as the initiator of the *Edebiyat-ı Cedide* movement. The new generation of novelists and poets that gathered around this journal developed a unique linguistic style of their own, incorporating outmoded Arabic and Persian words and using them to construct neologisms and unusual compounds in an attempt to produce, in Ottoman Turkish, something of the effect of the French realist fiction and Parnassian poetry they took as their models. Produced in translation, this "heavy" linguistic register was vilified by many of their contemporaries (including Midhat) as incomprehensible. On the language of the *Servet-i Fünun* writers and the debates surrounding it, see Levend 169–240.

on phonocentrism took an explicitly nationalist turn during the early twentieth century, and how that nationalism turned in part on a profound hatred for literature in and of itself. Following that, Part II of this book will examine exceptions to this dynamic, which affirm the madness of what we might call bare writing, in a manner that once again invokes Ekrem.[85]

---

[85] Chapter 3 will propose a comparison of Ekrem's *Araba Sevdası* with Tanpınar's *The Time Regulation Institute*. I do want to be clear, here, that it was not only the inheritance of a written culture of diglossia, embodied in the works of Ekrem and Tanpınar, that permitted the conceptualizing of an alternative practice of literature. Where Midhat foreclosed that possibility from within the anonymous popular culture of the vernacular, Nâzım Hikmet (as we will see in Chapter 5) reconceptualized a new "literary common" by tapping other sources.

2

The Grammatology of Nationalism

> Türkiye'de bir harf katliami olduğunu tahayyül ettiğim,
> geri dönüşü olmayan bir yolculuk olduğunu düşündüğüm
> şeyi üstlenmeye ve yanıma almaya, sanki içimdeymiş gibi
> onu kavramaya ve yeniden yaşamaya çalışıyorum.
>
> —Derrida, "İstanbul Mektubu"

In a 1911 journal article entitled "Yeni Lisan" ("The New Language") and signed with a large question mark, the journalist and short story writer Ömer Seyfeddin (1884–1920) called on his younger contemporaries to take on the challenge of writing in a "new language." What Seyfeddin meant by "new language" was not a newly invented language, but rather a new practice of Turkish writing based on the Istanbul vernacular and freed of all Arabic and Persian particles, plural forms, and compound phrases (*terkib*), with the exception of those already assimilated into ordinary speech.[1] Seyfeddin suggested that the borrowing of words from other languages was inevitable and at times necessary in any practice of writing, but rejected as unacceptably unnatural "the disruption of the mechanism of Turkish by the adoption of Arabic and Persian grammatical principles," as in the "old" ("eski") written language of the imperial past (109). Since it will be impossible, Seyfeddin noted, to expect an older generation to support changes that will "erect monuments of oblivion on their graves" (109), it was up to young people to "cure this hereditary disease" and produce a new "national literature" ("millî edebiyat") in "the natural [*tabiî*] and national [*millî*] language" (110).

Seyfeddin knew he was writing for a readership receptive to proposals for the simplification as well as the Turkification of the written language. The late nineteenth century had already seen the rise of new and influential histories of the

---

[1] It would not be accurate to describe the supporters of this "new language" as purists. While Seyfeddin did explicitly oppose the adoption of the "Christian" "Latin letters," in "Yeni Lisan," he left the question of orthography open, as something to be dealt with in the future (109). Until that question could be resolved, Seyfeddin advocated spelling Arabic and Persian loanwords as they were spelled in Arabic and Persian, and Turkish words with vowelization marks and letters.

Turkish people and the Turkish language dating back to the pre-Ottoman period.[2] The second constitutional revolution of July 1908, in which the Western-educated soldiers and bureaucrats known as the Young Turks restored the constitutional sultanate, ending the absolutist reign of Sultan Abdülhamid II,[3] marked an important turning point in the history of Turkism. Although the vanguard İttihad ve Terakki Cemiyeti (Committee of Union and Progress; hereafter CUP), which organized the revolution and remained the most important political actor in the empire until 1918, professed Ottomanism as official state ideology, it also advanced policies favoring Muslim Turks. The CUP also actively supported newly established journals and societies devoted to the propagation of Turkish national consciousness,[4] including the influential Salonica journal *Genç Kalemler* ("Young Pens"), in which Seyfeddin had made his challenge.[5] Described as "the Christopher Columbus of our contemporary literary Turkish" in a 1922 commemoration,[6] Seyfeddin distinguished himself in this vibrant post-revolutionary scene by offering not only theoretical prescriptions, but a visible practice of such "new language." In many ways, we can say that it was Seyfeddin's vehement rejection of the *Servet-i Fünun*

---

[2] Where Süleyman Pasha's history textbook *Tarih-i Âlem* ("World History," 1876), informed by the French Orientalist Joseph de Guignes's *Histoire générale des Huns, des Turcs, des Mogols, et des autres Tartares occidentaux* (1756–1758), had helped integrate pre-Islamic Turkish history into Ottoman school curricula, Şemseddin Sami's writings had revalued the kinship of the Ottoman Turkish language with the languages of Central Asia. In his 1881 article "Lisân-ı Türkî-i (Osmanî)" ("The [Ottoman] Turkish Language"), Sami criticized the use of "Ottoman" and "Chagatai" to describe the respective languages spoken by the Turkish peoples of the Turkey (*Türkiye*) and Turkestan (*Türkistan*), arguing for the renaming of these languages "Western" and "Eastern Turkish," respectively. The Greco-Turkish War of 1897 produced the first distinct efforts at a national poetry in the vernacular, Mehmed Emin [Yurdakul]'s *Türkçe Şiirler* ("Turkish Poems"). Newspapers published in major cities such as Salonica, Istanbul, and Izmir at the turn of the twentieth century also provided forums for debating the language question. On the Turkism of the late nineteenth century, see Kushner, *The Rise of Turkish Nationalism 1876–1908*.
[3] The first Ottoman imperial constitution was introduced in 1876. The parliament which had met for the first time in March 1877 was closed by Sultan Abdülhamid II in February 1878. The second constitutional revolution is often described as the "Young Turk Revolution"; 1908–1918 is commonly described as the Young Turk period. For a historical overview of this period in modern Turkish history, see Zürcher 93–132. For an intellectual genealogy of Young Turk political thought, see Mardin, *Continuity and Change in the Ideas of the Young Turks*. Hanioğlu's two-volume *The Young Turks in Opposition* and *Preparation for a Revolution* is a pioneering study of Young Turk activities between 1895 and 1908.
[4] One must not underemphasize the heterogeneity of the various Turkist discourses of the time. In his analysis of journals published by various Turkist organizations during the Young Turk era, Masami Arai identifies two different major strains of Turkism. The first was promulgated by Ottoman Turkish intellectuals, as a route to Turkish national consciousness for the protection and perpetuation of the Ottoman state. For these intellectuals, a Turkified Ottoman state was to be a building block for a territorially expanded future pan-Turkist state incorporating all peoples of Turkic origin. The second strain, which had more support among Russian Turkic émigré intellectuals, did not consider the Ottoman state essential in itself. This second strain advocated the founding of a pan-Turkist state centered in Central Asia and incorporating the Turkic peoples of both the Ottoman and the Russian Empires. Arai argues that the Young Pens collective distanced itself from the Russian émigrés' strain of Turkism. See Arai, *Turkish Nationalism in the Young Turk Era*.
[5] On the history of *Genç Kalemler* and its relation to the CUP, see Arai 44–47. See also Alangu 427—431.
[6] Signed with the name of the journal (*Küçük Mecmua*) that published it, this commemorative notice was most likely written by Ziya Gökalp, the CUP's leading ideologue, who was also *Küçük Mecmua*'s editor and Seyfeddin's close friend. It served as a supplement to a longer memorial article written by Ali Nüzhet and published in the first issue of *Küçük Mecmua* on 5 June 1922. See "Ömer Seyfettin İçin."

literature of the late nineteenth century, as much as the divan poetry of the past, that put modern Turkish literature on a path of divergence from the vision of Recâizâde Mahmud Ekrem.

This chapter will explore the nationalization of the Ottoman Turkish language during the Young Turk period and the Republican periods that followed. Seyfeddin is of central importance in this history, because of the way that his literary writings shaped what I will call a national grammatology—one deriving its legitimacy, I will argue, from links it established between the Turkish vernacular and death. The work of Benedict Anderson has taught us that a discourse focused on the control of death is at the center of many, indeed possibly all, surviving formations of nationalism (the image of the tombs of unknown soldiers with which Anderson opened *Imagined Communities* powerfully underscores his suggestion that "the magic of nationalism" in modernity consists in its "transformation of fatality into continuity, contingency into meaning" [11]). Still, we might say that death as the radically unknown, as the *most* foreign element of life or experience imaginable, is for that reason radically and fundamentally unstable in itself, as a "signifier"—and that nationalism rules us not only by promising meaning, but also by tapping our terror of death's inscrutable and unstable illegibility. My reading of Seyfeddin's novellas along with Republican state documents concerning the language reforms suggests that the historical specificity of Turkish national grammatology lies in the nationalization of language through the identification of the speech of the extra-Turkish "outside" with nothing less than death itself. Where the nationalists of the early twentieth century, like their predecessor Midhat, were profoundly self-conscious of the possibility of self-loss in translative language, what that self-consciousness produced was the reduction of *all* communicability and translatability to an all-or-nothing choice between life in a national language and unmourned death in a banished outside.

The "national literature" practiced by Seyfeddin played a crucial role in establishing this deadly discourse. Yet either despite, or perhaps because of his prolific work on these questions, we should note that Seyfeddin's relationship to literature was deeply ambivalent from the very start. In a letter dated 28 January 1910, paving the way for Seyfeddin's membership in the *Genç Kalemler* cadre, Seyfeddin wrote to Ali Canib [Yöntem] (who was later to become *Genç Kalemler*'s *sermuharrir* or editor-in-chief), "I am writing before having received your reply. . . . I had written to you that I hated literature [*edebiyat*] and that this hatred was of a disgusting and repulsive kind" ("Ali Canip'e Mektuplar" 329). Writing in a rush, to clarify the nature of this revulsion, Seyfeddin goes on to explain that his "hatred is directed more towards the language than to literature."

On the one hand, "literature" here is thus merely a proxy for the hated "old language and literature" of the past. But his hatred of literature will haunt Seyfeddin even as he moves into his project for the right kind of *national* literature. Implying the irreconcilability of literary and socially purposive writing, he begins his novella *Ashab-ı Kehfimiz: İçtimaî Roman* ("Our Seven Sleepers: A Social Novel," 1918), with a short preface stating that his goal had not been to produce "a literary work" ("edebî bir eser": 6; 111).[7] Prefacing another novella entitled *Efruz Bey: Fantazi Roman* ("Efruz Bey: A Fantasy Novel," 1919), Seyfeddin describes his method therein as "the stating of the truth as it appears without doing literature [*edebiyat yapmadan*]" (3; 47).[8] It is figuration (*mecaz*), itself, as the very condition of possibility of Seyfeddin's writing of these works, that he must repudiate in these prefaces and introductions, as posing a threat to direct communicability of a national message.

One might say, then, that Seyfeddin produced literature in fear of literature. Yet posthumously published portions of Seyfeddin's diaries reveal that a profound malaise accompanied the ontological project of fabricating a "national writing." In an entry dated 7 December 1917, Seyfeddin mentions the unrealized project of a longer novel to have been entitled *Ararken* ("While Searching"), noting in disappointment that he lacks the inner "fervor" ("şevk") to write, even though all the characters of this "custom-made" ("ısmarlama") novel are ready in his imagination ("'Hatırat'" 253):

> I guess nobody feels the lust of reading as much as I. To lean against a couch and to read an enjoyable, curious novel. To smile calmly while glancing at poems that conceal in them the keenest excitements, the warmest tears. But to write? This is indeed difficult. I suffer a lot when I write. My nerves are shot. My right foot becomes ice cold. My mouth dries up. (254)

Where *reading* retains the possibility of seductive self-foreignization, the new national writing, from which the stakes of deviation are so high, produces an entirely joyless, perhaps even deathlike state. As a writer of national literature, Seyfeddin will leave behind a trail of enemy corpses and suicidal cosmopolitans (*kozmopolit*)—but not without consuming himself, as well.

If I foreground this backstage drama of a death-like writing, here, that is by way of suggesting that Turkish national grammatology was shaped in the void of what we might call a literature without literariness, during the first half of the twentieth century. If it was nationalist authors and intellectuals who controlled the

---

[7] The first page numeral here references the original, published in Ottoman Turkish script; the second numeral, the transliterated version prepared by Hülya Argunşah.

[8] *Efruz Bey* was first serialized in the newspaper *Vakit* between 10 December and 23 December 1919 under the title "Hürriyete Layık Bir Kahraman" ("A Hero Fit for Freedom"). It was immediately retitled *Efruz Bey* and reprinted as a book by the newspaper's own press. The first page numeral here references *Efruz Bey*, published in Ottoman Turkish script; the second numeral, the transliterated version prepared by Argunşah. Efruz, the dandy-hero of this novella, is modeled on Bihruz in *Araba Sevdası*. Seyfeddin intended *Efruz Bey* as a social critique of a Turkish society devoted to appearances, in the post-revolutionary period; but where Ekrem held at a distance the idea of an authentic and proper national order of things, Seyfeddin remained committed to it.

conditions of possibility of communicability and translatability during the Young Turk period, this authority was transferred during the Republican period to the state, with Mustafa Kemal, as head of state, inheriting the literary-nonliterary legacy of Seyfeddin. What both formations shared, on the other hand, was the articulation of a posture of national self-annihilation in the search for an uncontaminated identity. As we will see, linguistic nationalism found it unable to stop at the final abstraction and expulsion from the Ottoman of all extra-Turkish difference, as a figure of death; its momentum was carried, during the second quarter of the twentieth century, into the seeking and destruction of an irreducible deadly difference in the "self." If the project of Turkish national grammatology is indeed a "modernist" project, I will suggest, its modernism lies not in its superficial mimicry of an Occidental modernity, but in the conservative identitarian vehemence of the pursuit of an impossibly pure self, as such.

1. The Language of Death

We should begin by distinguishing the language politics of the Young Turk period from those that followed during the second half of the nineteenth century. It would not be entirely incorrect to say that despite the claims they made for, and on behalf of, a new language, early twentieth-century partisans of phonocentrism were by and large playing out their predecessors' end game. As early as 1872, in an article entitled "Osmanlıcanın Islahı" ("The Reform of Ottoman"), Midhat himself, for example, had proposed some of the same measures Seyfeddin would echo later (the elimination of Arabic and Persian grammatical rules for compounds and plurals; the vernacular substitution of Turkish for Arabic and Persian loanwords). However, while there is thus an important continuity between the Young Turk measures and those that followed, we must highlight some important differences as well. The novelty of "new language," in this context, lay not in an unprecedented style; rather, novelty here marks the complete freeing of the vernacular, *as* national language, from the outmoded and evacuated authority of an old logocentrism.[9] As I suggested in my discussion of Midhat's work during the second half of the nineteenth century, Midhat was both

---

[9] For my purposes in this book, it might be useful to think the phrase "new language" well outside and beyond the specific semantic range given to it by Seyfeddin, as a designator capturing the linguistic "structure of feeling" in all the many and varied projects of vernacularization advanced by the different formations of linguistic nationalism in this period. I will have more to say about the diversity of Young Turk engagement with language reform later in this chapter; for the moment, let me underscore here that the production of an extensive discourse on the history and characteristics of a "Turkish" language, during this period, itself marks an important shift. For a comprehensive overview of the language debates carried on in Turkist journals, see Arai, *Turkish Nationalism*.

typically and profoundly self-conscious of the translative vernacular as a kind of new language, and he sought to contain its novelty by resubjugating it to the hegemony of Ottoman-Islamic values. And in precisely this gesture, Midhat's aggressively domesticating translation practice announced what we would have to call a discursive rupture, for in tapping a competing source of communicative power, his writings helped to accelerate the breakdown of the Ottoman-Islamic hierarchy he sought to retain.

Midhat could nonetheless claim to have reproduced classical values, as it were in their passing—a reproduction marked by Midhat's mixed nomenclature in *Müşahedat*, referring now to "Ottoman," now to "Turkish," interchangeably. For Seyfeddin and the early twentieth-century nationalists educated in reformed imperial schools, on the other hand, the authority of Arabic and Persian, and of the high Ottoman Turkish saturated with Arabic and Persian borrowings, had been evacuated from public discourse.[10] If "new language" in this general sense thus registers, as I have said, the complete freeing of a translative vernacular from the dominance of an old hierarchy, we would be mistaken if we were to take this liberation as a realization of that revolutionary writing sought by Ekrem. The novelty of new language, here, is not the novelty of an unprecedented egalitarianism embodied and practiced in open communicability; it lies rather in the reterritorializing establishment of new linguistic hierarchies and communicative controls welding vernacular to *millet,* or nation.

The word *millet,* in Seyfeddin's "Yeni Lisan" and generally during this period, is itself another, doubly domesticating translation. Borrowed from Arabic, and long used to name the Ottoman administrative system of semiautonomous religious communities, *millet* was by the turn of the twentieth century being used by Ottoman intellectuals in a new sense, denoting the exclusive community of the Turks.[11] The resignification of *millet* was accompanied by a profound shift in the way the word "Turk" itself was used. Prior to the nineteenth century, variants of the word "Turk" in European languages denoted the Ottoman state or the Muslims of the Ottoman Empire, while within the Ottoman Empire itself, "Turk" was either a general differential term distinguishing Turkish-speaking Ottomans from other population groups, or a pejorative term for the "ignorant" Anatolian peasant (Kushner 8; 21). At the fin de siècle, the new national sense of *millet,* denoting the nation of Turks, emerged from the translation of foundational works of the newly established Orientalist discipline of Turcology in Europe, on

[10] In articles entitled "Türkçeye Karşı Enderunca" ("Turkish against the Language of the Palace School") and "Osmanlıca Değil Türkçe" ("Turkish, Not Ottoman"), Seyfeddin explicitly objected to the use of the descriptor "Ottoman."

[11] In his preface to *Müşahedat,* Midhat suggested that his novel could not be described as "millî." "If it were such," he noted, "it would have been set only among the Islamic community [*cemaat-i islâmiye*]" (6).

the one hand, and the dissemination of the writings of Russian Turkic nationalists, on the other.[12] It is noteworthy that despite these doubly foreign origins of the discourse of Turkish nationalism, then, its domestication in the writings of the Turkish nationalists insistently presented nationality as a natural condition. In "Yeni Lisan," for example, Seyfeddin's use of the adjective *millî*, national, is followed immediately by a qualification marking *millî* as *tabiî*, or natural. The circuit of such domesticating translation is completed by Seyfeddin's use of this domesticated signifier, *millî*, as a supplement guaranteeing the propriety of translative vernacular itself. According to the oxymoronic logic implied here, translative language, in which one hears the foreign news, as it were, of one's national self, is identically self-same despite its undeniable origin in, and opening to, a foreign "outside."

The structural condition of possibility of such domestication had certainly already been established by Midhat and other mid-nineteenth-century writers, who we could say habituated their readers to translative modernity by enabling them, so to speak, to "wear" the foreign in the form of a "moral" novel, the system of "good" capitalism, or the mask of Islamicized Armenian Christian difference *while* guaranteeing identical self-sameness. But changing historical circumstances introduced other important determining factors. The appropriation of freed vernacular as a national language was contemporaneous with the codification of a new global linguistic hierarchy, in the discourse of Orientalism, and that codification's colonization of the communications revolution itself. Educated in the new reformed military and civic schools of the empire, the Ottoman intelligentsia deeply resented this global linguistic hierarchy, which subordinated Turkish to Western European languages and its cultural carriers; at the same time, they found in the discourse of nationalism an identitarian promise of Turkish recognition on a world stage. If in the classical episteme it was God, the third term, that legitimized the "inevitability" of borrowing words from Arabic, in its modern successor it was the discourse of *muasırlaşma* or modernization itself, as a universalizable condition, which legitimized the domesticating translation of the nation form from European languages into Turkish.[13] As Seyfeddin's "Yeni Lisan" also shows us, the rise of

---

[12] I have already mentioned de Guignes's *Histoire générale des Huns,* translated into Turkish by Hüseyin Cahid [Yalçın] between 1923 and 1925. Necib Âsım [Yazıksız] (1861–1935), who authored *Türk Tarihi* (1899), the first history of the "Turks," based his work on David-Léon Cahun's *Introduction à l'histoire de l'Asie* (1896). Other influential Orientalists of the period include Friedrich Wilhelm Radloff, who published extensively on the history and the grammar of the Turkish language; Vilhelm Thomsen, who deciphered the Orkhon inscriptions; and Elias John Wilkinson Gibb, who authored *A History of Ottoman Poetry* (1900–1909). Finally, the 1904 article of the pan-Turkist Tatar émigré Yusuf Akçura (1876–1935), entitled *Üç Tarz-ı Siyaset* ("The Three Ways of Politics") and advocating Turkism against Islamism and Ottomanism, is considered the first coherent formulation of Turkist ideology. On the influence of European Turcology and of Russian Turkic nationalism, see Kushner 9–14.

[13] See Ziya Gökalp, "Türkleşmek, İslamlaşmak, Muasırlaşmak 1" ("Turkification, Islamicization, and Modernization 1," 1913), marking the three ideological pillars of Turkish nationalism. The article was republished in modified form as "Üç Cereyan" ("Three Currents") in 1918, in a collection of Gökalp's work entitled *Türkleşmek, İslamlaşmak, Muasırlaşmak*; the 1913 version is the one I discuss here. This highly influential work

Greek, Bulgarian, Serbian, Montenegrin, and Albanian nationalisms played a key role in the mobilization of Turkish nationalism during this period.[14] And although the CUP continued to profess Ottomanism, Turkism seemed the only viable option for Ottoman intellectuals and bureaucrats trying to protect the remaining territory of the Ottoman state after the Balkan Wars of 1912–1913.[15]

My suggestion is that while Turkish nationalism found strong support among the intelligentsia, following the territorial losses of 1912–1913, the irreducible foreignness of the multiple sources of that nationalism "haunted" its discourse in translation, irrespective of the persistence of attempts at naturalizing it. In any case, national identification was very far from being either axiomatic or automatic, amid the multitudes of a multinational and multireligious empire. As Seyfeddin's stories show us, the domesticating translation of the nation found its limit not only with the "self-forgetful" Turkish elite, but also with the empire's commoners, who identified themselves as Muslims, not as Turks. Although identification with and by Islam was not a problem for the nationalists in and of itself (Gökalp had famously enumerated the ideological pillars of Turkish nationalism as "Turkification, Islamicization, and modernization"[16]), the unavailability of any spontaneous popular-national Turkism did pose a significant challenge to the nationalist ideological project during the empire's disintegration (arguably in part because the elite considered such an internally self-recognizing national public necessary for its *own* self-binding as national[17]). Vernacularization and phoneticization serve such a project not in so far as they open communicability and translatability, but in so far as they *close* it as a homogeneously national field of communication, within which the extra-national is

---

by the key ideologue of the CUP articulates a fascinating theory of nationalism in translation. Gökalp uses the word *muasırlaşmak*, deriving from the Arabic word *mu'āṣir,* contemporaneity (itself the derived active participle of the Arabic root *'aṣr,* epoch or period) as the Ottoman Turkish equivalent of the French *modernisation* (the French word, typeset in the Latin alphabet, is juxtaposed with the word *muasırlaşmak* in the article's second paragraph). Strictly speaking, "modernization" for Gökalp designated a catching-up with European technology (*âliyat* in the Ottoman Turkish original, provided along with the French equivalent *technique*) (336). Gökalp saw the modernizing nation as necessarily borrowing technique, but *not* borrowing culture, from Europeans (*Avrupalılar*): "The need for modernism [*asriyet* in the Ottoman Turkish original; elsewhere in the article equivalent to the French *modernisme*] mandates that we borrow only technology [*âletler*] and technique from Europe. We also have spiritual needs, which as in Europe, must be found in religion and nation, though it is not necessary to borrow [the content of] these from Europe" (336–337). Interestingly, Gökalp also appears to have conceived the nation *form* itself as a kind of universal "technology," in this article (a gesture that underscores a certain unresolved tension or ambivalence, in his thought).

[14] Addressing his contemporaries, Seyfeddin writes that "the Bulgarian, Serbian, Montenegrin, and Greek governments do not conceal their waiting for our agony. The schools of the Greeks, Bulgarians, and Serbs are out in the open, in the Ottoman homeland . . . They teach a strong anti-Turkism, and the whole world knows this . . ." (111).

[15] In this context, we must not neglect to note the internal heterogeneity of the discourse of Turkism, itself. See footnote 4.

[16] See Ziya Gökalp, "Türkleşmek, İslamlaşmak, Muasırlaşmak."

[17] Compare Adorno and Horkheimer's discussion of the Western bourgeoisie's "self-binding," in the first chapter of *Dialectic of Enlightenment.* Adorno and Horkheimer do not extend their dialectical analysis of enlightenment "identitarianism" beyond the scope of European modernity, but a "dialectical" comparison with the Turkish case would open up their work to a deeper exploration of the relation between nationalism and the enlightenment domination of nature.

coded as death. This "fixing," as death, of the inherently foreignizing communicative power of vernacular, so as to transform a sporadic, heterogeneous, and nonnational social collective into a unified nation, is the most important legacy of Young Turk phonocentrism.

Let me begin with Seyfeddin's 1918 short story entitled "Nakarat" ("Refrain"), subtitled "An Excerpt from the Journal of an Old Officer Who Spent His Youth in Macedonia" and set in 1903 in the Bulgarian town of Pirbeliçe.[18] As a military officer, Seyfeddin had served with a border patrol unit in Macedonia from 1909 to 1911 and subsequently (1912–13) on the Balkan War front[19] (Seyfeddin's biographer Tahir Alangu has suggested that "Nakarat" draws relatively directly on Seyfeddin's service in Macedonia [119–124]). Composed as a series of journal entries, the story opens with the Ottoman Turkish military officer-narrator reflecting that he had chosen a career in the military under the spell of the novels of Georges Courteline, hoping to lead a "chic" ("şık"), "lecherous, joyful, carefree life" (50). Failing in his bid for promotion to the military General Staff (*erkânıharb*), the narrator has served his time as a lower-ranking officer, fighting nationalist revolutionaries in a land where, he tells us, "reality" is "poverty," "dirt," and "wretchedness" (51, 53).

During a stay at an inn in Pirbeliçe, the narrator, highly susceptible to the enchantment of the foreign, is bewitched by a female voice coming from behind a

---

[18] For a friend and colleague's account of Seyfeddin's life and work, see Ali Canib Yöntem, *Ömer Seyfeddin*. Alangu's *Ömer Seyfettin* is an influential biography. On Seyfeddin as "a link between the Ottoman modernizing thought of the nineteenth and early twentieth centuries, and the Republic," see Karpat, "Ömer Seyfeddin and the Transformation of Turkish Thought" 680. Seyfeddin published more than one hundred short stories on a wide range of topics, including autobiographical stories based on his childhood, realist stories depicting the loosening of social mores, and satires of the Westernized elite. In 1917, he wrote approximately twenty stories for the weekly *Yeni Mecmua*, commissioned by the Ministry of War and edited by Ziya Gökalp. These stories, published in a series entitled "Old Heroes," restage heroic tales from the Ottoman past; another series, entitled "New Heroes," takes as its theme the heroic sacrifices made in battle at Gallipoli. "Nakarat" and "Tuhaf Bir Zulüm," the stories I discuss here, are among the last ones he published in *Yeni Mecmua*. Seyfeddin had published stories prior to 1917 and continued doing so in several other venues from 1918 to 1920.

It should be noted that Seyfeddin uses the term "nation" with more clarity and precision in the articles and booklets he published following the Balkan Wars. In the booklet *Mektep Çocuklarında Türklük Mefkûresi* ("The Ideal of Turkism in Schoolchildren," 1914), addressed to the schoolchildren of its title, Seyfeddin defines a nation as a "unity of religion and language" (353). Seyfeddin suggests that "Turk" names the Turkish nation and "Ottoman" the name of the state (*devlet*), and that the two entities should not be conflated. While the state is defined as "the establishment administer[ing] groups of people belonging to different nations and religions in one territory" (354), Seyfeddin does not attempt to explain how such administration actually works. For Seyfeddin, Turks, as the most numerous group in the territory in question, have a historical claim to the Ottoman state as its founders and builders (357). It is also important to remember that Seyfeddin's nationalism was linguistically and religiously conceived, not based on a concept of blood. *Mektep Çocuklarında Türklük Mefkûresi* states that a true Turkist "treats immigrants who learn Turkish and mix into the Turkish nation as if they are one's old blood brothers" (362). At the same time, of course, one must keep sight of the contradictions inherent in Seyfeddin's position, especially in the light of racism as "*a supplement internal to nationalism*" (emphasis in original), as Étienne Balibar has analyzed it ("Racism and Nationalism" 54).

[19] Seyfeddin's military service strongly influenced his linguistic and political views. One cannot overlook, for example, a published journal entry dated 30 October 1912, which finds Seyfeddin deploring the absence of a common language in his unit, which he likens to a "Tower of Babel," with more than half its soldiers unable to speak Turkish ("Balkan" 275). For a biographical account of Seyfeddin's military service, see Alangu 110–149 and 212–265.

wall, singing a song in Bulgarian. This "pleasant," "smooth," "affected," "female" voice, the narrator discovers, belongs to the "beautiful, burly, strong" Bulgarian peasant girl living next door (55). Though he knows no Bulgarian, the narrator writes in his journal a Turkish translation of the song "with certainty of its accuracy": "I love you, / I love you. / I crossed and came to you from the Balkans, from Şipka . . ." (59). At points during the story, the narrator repeats the refrain "Naş naş / Çarigrad naş," singing it back to the girl by "imitating her harmony" (60). He also inscribes this refrain using the Latin alphabet on the frame of his window (where other Turkish soldiers have written or carved messages in the past), in the hope that "perhaps a reader of Bulgarian will understand the dream of love I saw" (62). On the day of his departure, when the narrator approaches the Turkish-speaking Bulgarian innkeeper to inquire about the identity of the girl, he is told that she is the daughter of a priest and revolutionary (*komite*) killed in battle, and that the song's refrain in Bulgarian is "Ours ours / Istanbul will be ours" (66).

The contact of Turkish with other languages (French, Bulgarian, Italian, Armenian, Greek) is a theme in many of Seyfeddin's stories, as it was in the work of his predecessor Midhat. In "Nakarat," the narrator, acting as what we might call a misinterpreter, is able to travel to unseen and unheard-of places in a translative vernacular, fantasizing about deserting the army and escaping to the United States with the Bulgarian girl, Rada (56). Yet in Seyfeddin's work the stakes of such *uncontrolled* travel are much more violent. Where Midhat sees the worst of such self-forgetting as a confusion in which one might mistake oneself for, or even "become" a foreigner (a Francophone or Armenian Christian), Seyfeddin's work imagines it as extinction, with the narrator retreating, at the story's end, in fear of destruction by the impulse to exteriority to which his desire impels him. Seyfeddin's work thus *totalizes,* as a terminal condition, the annihilation that is certainly *one* inherent and undeniable possibility, in any radical self-forgetting.

Death, here, serves as a volatile and double-edged signifier. Anderson has suggested that as the discourse of a secular modernity of bureaucratic and mechanized "senseless" violence, nationalist discourse legitimizes itself by promising us *meaningful* and *mournable* death. "Nakarat" gives us just such a figure in the dead priest and revolutionary fighter, of whom the narrator (who has fallen ill after discovering what the song's refrain really means) writes in his journal: "I've been lying for a week in the Velmefçe forest, thinking of the difference between myself and the brave daughter of the dead priest-revolutionary who died for a sacred idea of his own" (68). We might say that the narrator's admiration for an enemy who died meaningfully normalizes death as legible in national terms, "domesticated" as one of the self-destructive possibilities inherent in social contact in (and through) language— and no longer to be feared, in so far as *both* the nation itself (embodied in the narrator), and its extra-Turkish "outside" (in the priest-revolutionary) give it meaning.

But that also means that while the normalization of death is a constitutive element of Turkish nationalism as a domesticating discourse, it carries within itself its uncanny other. For the narrator of "Nakarat" also registers another, radically inassimilable death. If the narrator does not actually die, in the course of the story, the story continually signals the narrator's death as a possibility. To die as an anti-nationalist is marked as an undesirable death, here, because of the humiliating character of its irony: not only in mistaking the enemy for the beloved, but in unintentionally embracing the song of one's own self-destruction. Where war renders death ordinary, Seyfeddin renders it as uncanny, in the figure of an "awakened" narrator who understands that the cost of extra-national travel in language is a doubly ironic death at the hands of the misread and misunderstood other. We might say that irrespective of the level of Turkish patriotism of his implied readers, Seyfeddin counted in "Nakarat" on the force of this doubly self-negating, mortifying death, as something impossible to claim for oneself as a dignified human being.[20]

Linguistic nationalism thus entails the abstraction and recoding, as death, of the speech of the extra-Turkish outside, in a foreclosure on and suppression of non-national possibilities of being in a translative vernacular.[21] Following Derrida on this point, one might suggest that "all graphemes are of a testamentary essence" (*Of Grammatology* 69; *De la grammatologie* 100) in so far as death understood as the absence of the writing subject, the addressee, and the referent is a constitutive condition of the very possibility of linguistic signification, itself.[22] And yet where for Derrida such death's "meaning," as such, is fundamentally

---

[20] Seyfeddin is not staging a Hegelian death struggle, here. Composed at a historical moment when the Ottoman Muslim relation to death as administered by Islam had become partly fluid, "Nakarat" might productively be compared with Freud's "Zeitgemäßes über Krieg und Tod" ("Thoughts for the Times on War and Death," 1915), which reflects on the violence of the war on the other side of the Balkan border. Comparing modern man's unconscious attitude toward death with the attitude of premodern man, Freud suggested that the reality of death is comprehended primarily through the death of a loved one. The pain felt at the death of a beloved, who forms "a part of [one's] own beloved self," forces one to confront the reality of one's own death. And yet because "in each of the loved persons there was also something of the stranger" ("Thoughts" 293; "Zeitgemäßes" 346), the death of the loved one is *also* gratifying. For Freud, this *ambivalence* felt at the death of a loved one was itself the source of the ethical injunction not to kill. "It was acquired," as he put it, "in relation to dead people who were loved, as a reaction against the satisfaction of the hatred hidden behind the grief for them; and it was gradually extended to strangers who were not loved, and finally even to enemies" (295; 349). Modern man, who no longer experiences such extension, will "return home joyfully to his wife and children, unchecked and undisturbed by thoughts of the enemies he has killed whether at close quarters or at long range" (295; 349). If "Nakarat" does not stage any actual such killing, it certainly echoes Freud's supposition of the collapse of any distinction between loved one and enemy. In coding the loved one as a misrecognized enemy, "Nakarat" fully closes the space in which the ethical injunction not to kill is invoked.

[21] As I have noted, the only "messages" permitted to escape this communicative and translative closure are those directly serving the ends of Turkish nationalism. Seyfeddin's journal articles, as well as booklets such as *Vatan! Yalnız Vatan . . .* ("Homeland! Only Homeland . . ." 1911), are larded with quotations from Gustave Le Bon's *La psychologie politique*. Seyfeddin also translated the *Kalevala* and the *Iliad* from French editions into Turkish in 1918, presenting them as examples of "national epics" ("millî destan"). In a note prefacing his translation of the fifth song of the *Kalevala*, Seyfeddin writes that "the translation [*nakl*] of the names of epic characters with their Finnish endings [*terminezon*] is ponderous and disrupts the harmony of our language" (357). Noting that "[other] nations, which translate masterpieces into their own languages, adapt the names of heroes to their accents," he decides to "call 'Veynemöynen' [Väinämöinen] 'Vayna' and 'Yukaheynen' [Joukahainen] 'Yuka' henceforth" (357). Seyfeddin follows a similar domesticating strategy in his translation of the *Iliad*, rendering "Akhilleus" as "Aşil" and "Troia" as "Truva."

[22] To the extent that in the most general sense, writing, which as a supplement to memory must be able to circulate beyond the writer's bodily presence and control (and so beyond her "death," be it figurative or

indeterminate, it is the particularity of Turkish national phonocentrism to fix Derrida's "*spacing* (pause, blank, punctuation, interval in general, etc.)" (68; 99), understood as inherent in language as the final and *total* condition of an absolutely unacceptable annihilation.

Over and over, Seyfeddin's writings circle in the space of this uncanny death, marked and traversed by Turkish contact with Bulgarian, Armenian, and Italian and by the encounter of a translative vernacular with itself. In "Tuhaf Bir Zulüm" ("An Odd Cruelty," 1918), Seyfeddin shifts his implied address from the Turkish national elite of his own context to imagined Muslim commoners, as a Turkish *nasyonalist* narrator remediates the gossip of a Turkish-speaking Bulgarian local administrator. As a vernacular complement to the inward translation of the texts of Orientalist Turcology, this foreignizing speech of the Turkish-speaking internal neighbor threatens with mortifying death the Muslim implied reader reluctant to recognize himself as a Turkish national. Observing that "Turks have no other quality than their religious bigotry" (73), the *gospodin* tells the narrator that he transformed a Turkish village into a Bulgarian one by releasing pigs in the Turkish quarter, compelling the Turkish villagers to leave.

We might well describe Seyfeddin as hijacking the modern institution of literature, for the dissemination of these deadly messages. What we call fiction, I have already suggested, is something more than merely descriptive usage of language: it is an *act* of speaking otherwise, unbound by the conventions of everyday communication. If as "the Christopher Columbus of our contemporary literary Turkish," Seyfeddin is indeed the central linguistic nationalist of this period, this is because his work achieves something more than the dissemination of descriptive and representational messages. Rather, as an author of fiction, he *actively* colonized the one domain in which modern language speaks unconditionally in and for itself, beyond the nation.

Subtitled "the journal of an Armenian youth," *Ashab-ı Kehfimiz* is perhaps Seyfeddin's most comprehensive performance of internal linguistic colonization. In contrast with other stories narrated by characters of Turkish origin, this meta-novella of a national literature employs an Armenian narrator as a figure of the

---

literal), we can say it anticipates the death of both the sender of a message, and the intended receiver, by *managing their absence*. Emerging in the space of an irreducible unknown, against the blank of a page, writing opens onto the substantive disappearance of the writing subject. As Derrida has put it:

> Spacing as writing is the becoming-absent and the becoming-unconscious of the subject. By the movement of its drift/derivation [*dérive*] the emancipation of the sign constitutes in return the desire of presence. That becoming—or that drift/derivation—does not befall the subject which would choose it or would passively let itself be drawn along by it. As the subject's relationship with its own death, this becoming is the constitution of subjectivity. On all levels of life's organization, that is to say, of *the economy of death*. All graphemes are of a testamentary essence. And the original absence of the subject of writing is also the absence of the thing or the referent. (*Of Grammatology* 69; *De la grammatologie* 100–101)

intimate internal other *par excellence*. Such willful self-foreignization might of course have served the possibility of a non-identitarianism; but *Ashab-ı Kehfimiz,* which Seyfeddin describes in his preface as a "non-literary" novel, turns the act of speaking otherwise into the fixture of the Turkish-speaking Armenian as death, legitimizing his destruction in the institution of the nationally self-same.

Set in Istanbul in the wake of the Young Turk revolution, *Ashab-ı Kehfimiz* narrates events taking place from 1908 to 1925.[23] In the first journal entry, dated 30 August 1908, Dikran Hayikyan, the narrator, describes the Young Turk restoration of the Ottoman constitution as the beginning of a new epoch. This coming of "freedom" ("hürriyet"), Hayikyan suggests, opens the possibility of a mixed egalitarian "Ottoman society," prompting him to abandon his Armenian nationalism and remain an "Ottoman" (16; 115). The narrative advances through the next two journal entries, containing Hayikyan's descriptions of his own encounters with lower and upper-class Turks who are living in denial of their own national identities. The fourth journal entry, dated 17 May 1909, reports on the "counter-revolution" of April 1909 organized by Islamists and other supporters of the former regime.[24] Interviewing, in the guise of a journalist, a counterrevolutionary who denies that he is Turkish and identifies himself as a Muslim, Hayikyan comments on the "oddness" of these self-denying Turks, so different in their self-conception from Armenian nationalists (25; 119).

The bulk of *Ashab-ı Kehfimiz* narrates Hayikyan's involvement with a newly established Ottomanist cultural society called the Ottoman Mixing Club ("Osmanlı Kaynaşma Kulübü"). Founded by a Western-educated Turk in 1909, the society initially brings together "Greek, Jewish, Levantine, Arab, Bulgarian" members (41; 128). With the goal of establishing a common cultural identity, the society promulgates its vision of Ottomanism in an official weekly newspaper entitled *İnsanlık* ("Humanity"),[25] whose first issue proposes a new Ottoman language as "a mixture of Arabic, Persian, Greek, Albanian, Serbian, Bulgarian, Spanish" and a new Abrahamic religion synchronizing Sabianism, Judaism, Christianity, and Islam (79; 145). In one journal entry, Hayikyan provides a summary of an article he wrote for this first issue of *İnsanlık,* arguing that the Muslims of the Ottoman state were Greeks and Armenians who had been forcibly converted to Islam and concluding

---

[23] Although *Ashab-ı Kehfimiz* was published in 1918, Seyfeddin claims in his preface to have composed it in 1913. Though this is far from implausible, Seyfeddin's back-dating of the book is also strategic (see footnote 30).

[24] On the counterrevolution of April 1909, see Zürcher 95–99. The uprising was swiftly suppressed by an Action Army (Hareket Ordusu) composed of military forces assembled by the CUP (Seyfeddin himself had served in this unit).

[25] *Vatan! Yalnız Vatan . . .* ("Homeland! Only Homeland . . ." 1911) presents Seyfeddin's critique of humanism. Rejecting internationalism (*beynelmileliyet*) and humanism (*insanlık*) as "attractive" "empty dreams" (144), Seyfeddin insists that nationalism is the most viable modern politics. Interestingly enough, however, in this booklet published before the outbreak of the Balkan Wars, Seyfeddin defends "Ottoman" patriotism, associating it with the unity of a Turkish-speaking Muslim population.

that "In the land of the Ottomans, there is no racial [*ırken*] or any other kind [*cins*] of Turk" (80; 146).

Seyfeddin tells us in his preface that *Ashab-ı Kehfimiz* is intended as a hyperbolic ridicule ("mübalağa") of proposals for such a syncretic Ottomanism (6; 112). Despite his general impatience with figurative language, Seyfeddin deems hyberbole necessary, he tells us, in so far as even after the Balkan Wars and the First World War, there are still those who conflate Ottoman state subjection with national identity proper (6; 111). Seyfeddin's strategy in *Ashab-ı Kehfimiz* is to radicalize communicability as what Derrida called "a tremor, a shock, a displacement of *force*,"[26] demanding the attention of a distracted implied readership including the Western-educated elite *as well as* Muslim commoners excessively receptive to the omnidirectional possibilities opened by translative vernacular.

If hyperbole is a rhetorical means of production of this radicalization, in *Ashab-ı Kehfimiz*, its structural complement is Seyfeddin's *staging* of an Armenian narrator. Very much unlike the narrator of *Müşahedat*, who retreats in fear of losing himself in the speech of the Armenian women, Hayikyan is a voice assumed, by *Ashab-ı Kehfimiz*, with all of Seyfeddin's confidence in his own invulnerability, because from the very start, the purpose of assuming an Armenian voice is nothing less than to fix Armenian speech as the speech of death. Following the description of the society's newspaper, the narrative jumps to the year 1925, with Hayikyan reporting retrospectively on the protests organized by Turkists in response to its publication. Hayikyan quotes extensively from an anonymous article published by one such Turkist, which effectively brings what we might call an absent nation into presence, in the act of responding to Hayikyan's claim that "In the land of the Ottomans, there is no racial or any other kind of Turk." "To tell a nation, especially the Turks," goes this rebuttal, "'You are nonexistent!' ['*Sen yoksun!*'] is a fiery curse. In Turkey [*Türkiye*], the national spirit [*millî ruh*], awakened by recent catastrophes, has flourished, flamed, and spread everywhere" (94; 153).[27]

It is undeniable that, as both the novelist Elif Shafak and the historian Halil Berktay have suggested, the most problematic legacy of Seyfeddin's nationalism is what Shafak calls the fabrication of a "distinction between 'Us/Turks' and 'them/Others'" (24). Where "Nakarat" produced this bifurcation through control of the external translatability of Turkish in contact with the Bulgarian and French languages and their cultural carriers, *Ashab-ı Kehfimiz* more directly and violently expels the Turkish-speaking Armenian into a linguistic outside. Still, what is at stake, in this project for a national literature, is not only or merely this externalization and negation of difference, as such, in a way that might be said to presume the distinction that it reifies and enforces. In the end, such externalization and negation

---

[26] See Derrida, "Signature Event" 309; "Signature événement" 367.
[27] At the novella's conclusion, it is revealed that the self-denying Turkish members of the Ottomanist Society either go insane or commit suicide (98; 155).

does not constitute merely a gesture of segregation, of two presumptively existent, if different fields or ways of being. Rather, it is an explicit identification of one of those presumptive existents with nothing less than death itself. And it is not, then, that contaminative contact with such a negated other is in any way *denied* by Seyfeddin's writings, in their constructed bifurcation of Us from Them and Turk from Other. The point is rather that one relates to that negated other *as if she or he were the embodiment* of death itself, as the common sign—the *only* common sign—with which Seyfeddin seems to have felt he could mobilize his distracted implied Turkish reader.[28] If we think of death as that finally and terminally "foreign" to which each of us relates without knowing the meaning of that relation, we might say that Seyfeddin appropriates the power of death, in his work, by giving it the face of the familiar-yet-foreign internal other. In the telegraphy of these compact, serial writings, we hear a foreign element speaking a familiar vernacular so as to communicate a terrorizing annihilation. *Ashab-ı Kehfimiz* shows us a Turkish national common embodied in the institution of Young Turk-era national literature, not because the speakers of the vernacular share an internally connected world, but because they find themselves in contact with a commonly recognized deadly outside.[29]

Thus grounded in what we might call the legible illegibility of death, nationalization has obviously and extremely violent social and linguistic consequences for the mixed social that it embodies itself against. In many ways, the "peaceful" national uprising staged by *Ashab-ı Kehfimiz* attempts to obscure the extreme violence of nation-building manifest in the bringing of a hitherto "absent" Turkish nation into present being by killing the internal other. If Seyfeddin's novella thus elides entirely the 1915 deportation (*tehcir*) and mass killing of Ottoman Armenians, we might say that it is precisely in and with this deadly historical absence that *Ashab-ı Kehfimiz* testifies to the substantive *limitlessness* of nationalist violence.[30] In 2007, one century after *Ashab-ı Kehfimiz*'s publication, it was manifest in the assassination by a Turkish teenager of Hrant Dink, editor-in-chief of the bilingual Turkish-Armenian daily *Agos*, for the thought-crime of insulting Turkishness.[31]

---

[28] My goal here is merely to describe the logic of this national discourse; it was, of course, only partly effective in actually mobilizing a nation. Section 3 of this chapter takes up the actual effects of Turkish national grammatology.

[29] Compare Anderson, *Imagined Communities* 22–36. The scenes of reading staged in *Ashab-ı Kehfimiz* are not merely mimetic; rather, they are performative. We might say that for Seyfeddin it is not the circulation of legible messages that institutes the nation, but the mediation of this "legible illegibility" of death as terrifying self-annihilation. Compare also Rafael, *The Promise of the Foreign* 82–95.

[30] Commenting on the journal entry dated 20 August 1912, in which Hayikyan describes Greek and Armenian hopes of seizing and annexing western and eastern Anatolia, respectively, Berktay argues that Seyfeddin intended *Ashab-ı Kehfimiz* as a justification of the 1915 mass killing of Ottoman Armenians. Berktay believes it unlikely that the novella was composed in 1913, as Seyfeddin claimed.

[31] After publishing in *Agos* an article dated 6 February 2004 suggesting that Sabiha Gökçen, Atatürk's adopted daughter, might have been Armenian, Dink was vilified by the nationalist media as an enemy of the Turks. In October 2005, Dink was convicted by the Istanbul Şişli Criminal Court under Article 301 of the penal code for insulting Turkishness and was given a six-month prison sentence. Although Dink appealed, the Ninth

Seyfeddin's project for a Turkish national literature is nothing less than the serial "othering" of all extra-Turkish linguistic difference as death, in the mad attempt to murder the very possibility of the non-national. As we shall see, Republican linguistic nationalism marks the extension of this seriation, as the "successful" consolidation of a pure self, in a language welded to death, becomes an autoimmunity of self-consumption. It is this extreme internal violence that *Ashab-ı Kehfimiz,* as a "mad" meta-novel of national literature, figures and anticipates in its conclusion. Set in a future 1925 (Seyfeddin died in 1920) by which time each Ottoman nationality has been promised its own nation, *Ashab-ı Kehfimiz*'s conclusion presents Hayikyan, now married and a fully-fledged Armenian nationalist (and possibly writing from his home in a newly autonomous Armenia), concludes his journal entries by relating his wife's objections to his writing them in Turkish. Refusing his wife's request "to rip up and get rid of" of his Turkish journal, Hayikyan reflects on what he perceives as her motives:

> Oh, poor Turkish notebook! Shall I rip you up now! But, no, no . . . I'm not a woman. I can't be as sensitive a nationalist as Hayganoş. I'm going to throw you into a corner, where she won't be able to see you. Sleep there as if you were a clump of weeds in the Cave of the Seven Sleepers [*Ashab-ı Kehf*]. But stay out of my lover's sight with your Turkish lines . . . Do not be jealous of her and make her cry . . . (101; 157)

Despite the pointedness and the aggression of Seyfeddin's profound ironizing of his Armenian narrator, throughout *Ashab-ı Kehfimiz,* one might say that this conclusion ironizes Seyfeddin's own linguistic nationalism itself, instead—or as well. As echoed in the attempt to unify these final fragments of Hayikyan's Turkish journal, Seyfeddin's attempt to master the temporal and figurative difference of writing goes off the rails in this ironic letter to the future—as it would subsequently misfire in the hands of the Turkish Republican nationalists. For if *Ashab-ı Kehfimiz* literally disappeared from view after 1928, that was not an achievement of the Armenian nationalism Seyfeddin had ironized in his work, but rather of the Turkish Republican alphabet reform itself.[32] The mad desire to externalize and erase the inherent difference of writing, in the name of uncontaminated national life, leads only to more death in writing, in time producing the confinement of even Seyfeddin's "new language," itself.

We can say that in this closing scene, Seyfeddin sought to mark the domestication of an omni-directionally libidinous translative language, in the figure of

---

Criminal Chamber of the Supreme Court upheld the verdict. In the meantime, additional charges were filed, for "attempting to influence the judiciary" and insulting Turkishness. See *Dink Cinayeti ve İstihbarat Yalanları* ("Dink Murder and Intelligence Lies," 2009), by Nedim Şener, a reporter for the daily *Milliyet*, regarding events leading up to Dink's murder and its aftermath.

[32] Bilgi Yayınevi published the first Latin-alphabetic transliteration of *Ashab-ı Kehfimiz* in 1970.

Hayganoş, Hayikyan's wife, as a figure here of national heterosexual reproductive femininity.[33] We can also say that this domestication fails in so far as the Cave of the Seven Sleepers, as a figure for the womb and man's universal home, assumes a contrary significance as the uncanny grave of the "meta-novel" of national literature itself.[34]

Although the radical position advocating the wholesale purging of Arabisms and Persianisms from the new Turkish did find support during the Young Turk period, for the most part the Young Turks advocated a milder program of linguistic simplification, proposing the elimination only of Arabic and Persian grammatical structures and the most complex and least utilized loanwords.[35] While such prominent figures as Hüseyin Cahid [Yalçın], Kılıçzade Hakkı, and Celal Nuri [İleri] had called for the adoption of the Latin alphabet, during the Young Turk period, the majority of Turkists opposed the measure, at that point, on grounds that it would weaken cultural ties to the rest of the Islamic world.[36] The most widely held position during the period was probably that of Milâslı İsmail Hakkı, who recommended that Turkish be written discretely or disjointedly (*huruf-ı munfasıla*), with separated letters rather than in joined letterforms.[37] The most noteworthy development of the period was the adoption of the reformed *ordu elifbası* or "army alphabet," also called *hatt-ı cedid* (new writing) and *Enverpaşa yazısı* (Enver Pasha writing), devised by Minister of War Enver Pasha (1881–1922)

---

[33] Continuing the Young Pens' modeling of "new language" on the vernacular of Istanbul women, Seyfeddin's writings often gender national language explicitly (as female). Women appear in a variety of different and conflicting roles in Seyfeddin's arguably misogynistic short stories and novellas. "Fon Sadriştayn'ın Karısı" ("The Wife of Von Sadristein"), for example, concerns the rarity or nonbeing of any nationally ideal Turkish woman; after receiving much criticism for this story, Seyfeddin produced an argument that contradicted it in a sequel entitled "Fon Sadriştayn'ın Oğlu" ("The Son of Von Sadristein"). Seyfeddin's 1918 novella *Harem*, meanwhile, depicting the relationship of a married couple with conflicting modernist and traditionalist world views, is focused on the lack of unconditional trust in its protagonists' marriage. In so far as it suggests that the gap between appearance and reality simply cannot be overcome, *Harem* makes for interesting reading alongside *Ashab-ı Kehfimiz*.

[34] On the womb as uncanny home, see Freud, "Das Unheimliche" 259; "The 'Uncanny'" 244.

[35] Fuad Köseraif (1872–1949), who served as the president of Türk Derneği, or the Turkish Association (established in 1908 in Istanbul as the first private cultural center), was a notable advocate of linguistic purification (*tasfiyecilik*). While most of the members of this eclectic institution in fact supported the more moderate position of linguistic simplification (*sadeleştirme*), the association was nevertheless attacked by its critics, including the Young Pens, for its radical purist agenda. The Turkish Association was succeeded by the Türk Yurdu Cemiyeti (Turkish Homeland Society) in 1911 and superseded by the Türk Ocakları (Turkish Hearths) in 1912. For more on the language debates of the Young Turk period, see Levend 300–370.

[36] In the journal *Hürriyet-i Fikriyye* ("Freedom of Thinking") edited by Kılıçzade Hakkı, a series of anonymous articles were published in 1914, supporting the adoption of the Latin alphabet for writing in Ottoman Turkish. Debate over alphabets was reinvigorated by the outbreak of a series of uprisings in Ottoman Albania. Fifteen thousand people demonstrated in the city of Korçe in 1910 to protest the Ottoman government's opposition of the Latin alphabet used for writing in the Albanian vernacular since 1879 (Trix 264). See Hüseyin Cahid [Yalçın], "Arnavut Hurufatı" ("Albanian Lettering"), which defends the use of the Latin alphabet for Albanian. On debates specifically concerning alphabets, during the Young Turk period, see Ertem 135–172.

[37] See Milâslı İsmail Hakkı, *Yeni Yazı ve Elifbası* ("The New Writing and Its Alphabet"). Milâslı İsmail Hakkı, who devised a simplified phonetic Ottoman Turkish writing system as an alternative to adoption of the Latin alphabet, was a founding member of the semi-private Islah-ı Huruf Cemiyeti (Society for the Reformation of Writing) established in 1911.

in 1913 for use in wartime correspondence. Although Enver resisted critics' objections that the *ordu elifbası* actually slowed, rather than speeding military communications, it was soon abandoned.[38]

Nevertheless, and despite the relative moderacy of Young Turk reform initiatives for vernacularization and phoneticization, one might suggest, without implying simplistic causal relation (much less any tele-historical inevitability) that Young Turk phonocentrism really did pave the way for the extremism of the Republican period. If modernity, as Siegel has put it, "is associated with the ability to achieve an identity as opposed to being always defined by identity given by birth,"[39] then we might say that modern nationalism, in the Turkish context as elsewhere, is prone to destructive violence precisely in its suspicion of its own origin in a translative vernacular. In what follows, I will suggest that the new linguistic hierarchy we see established and indeed, *instituted* in Seyfeddin's work prevailed through the Republican period, as elite national regulators, now in control of the state structure, implemented ever more extreme devices and measures for codifying the internal difference of language as death. As anticipated by Seyfeddin, one of the founding fathers of Turkish national grammatology, this intensified and excessive mode of linguistic and literary colonization was to generate its own both predictable and surprising contradictions.

2. The Letter Coup

In the formation of the modern nation-states of the world we still inhabit today, the nineteenth and twentieth centuries each generated many and various projects of linguistic modernization. Among these, the Turkish Republican language reforms might be said to have earned the singularly uneasy and intense fascination of a contemporary Western liberal public. Such deep attention marks the very extremity and excess of the Turkish project, which distinguished itself from other linguistic nationalisms of the period as something much more than a mere language *reform*. If "fashion[ing] a 'modern' national culture that is nevertheless not Western"[40] was unquestionably a challenge taken up by many of the non-European nation formations of the age, it is equally unquestionable that Turkish Republican linguistic

---

[38] Based on the principle of *huruf-ı munfasıla*, this "army alphabet" should be understood as an important early trial of phonetic writing in the Turkish context, in its employment of varied forms of *elif, vav,* and *ye* for the individual representation of each vowel, and in its requirement that all the consonants and vowels pronounced in Turkish be represented discretely on the written line. On *Enverpaşa yazısı,* see Levend 360.

[39] See *Fetish* 93.

[40] Chatterjee, *Nation* 6. Modern Turkish nationalism, at least in its initial phase, fits quite well Chatterjee's paradigm of Third World nationalism, with its early ideologues (most famously, Ziya Gökalp) demarcating an inner national-cultural domain as distinct from the technological-material realm of the "outside," where the superiority of the West is unequivocally accepted. By claiming to have *confined* the West to such an outside, nationalism, we might say, attempts first of all to obscure its own origin in *global translation*. My own suggestion here is that Kemalist Republican nationalism diverges from Chatterjee's model to the extent that it empties out the "inner-cultural" domain.

nationalism, belonging purely neither to the imperial nor the anti-colonial nationalisms of the twentieth century, is marked by what we might call extreme self-
surgery, in the reconstitution of a modern inner cultural domain.

Although one cannot discount the element of Occidentalist mimicry (of European institutions) in the Republican language reforms, it is equally important to
understand these projects as driven by a fear of the inherent and uncontrollable
internal difference of language itself. That a less radical and entirely plausible set of
proposals for a phoneticized Ottoman Turkish writing, as devised by Young Turk
intellectuals, were superseded by more radical Republican measures reflects the
extent to which death, established as the negative limit of translative language, was
no longer confined to the extra-Turkish linguistic outside of Young Turk linguistic
nationalism. Fear of internal difference reached such heights during the Republican
period that along with the speech of non-Muslims and ethnic minorities, the spoken
Turkish of Anatolian Muslims themselves was seen as a harbinger of death in so far
as it carried and offered "impure" alternative identifications with Islam. Against the
wish and desire of the ideologues of nationalism, the acts of phoneticization and
vernacularization are never really anything like acts of transcription of an authentic
national speech. Rather, in a heterogeneous social context of mixed allegiances,
they serve precisely to enact the generalization of *one* specific variant of *one* vernacular, as a standard, for the total control of both written and oral communicability.

As outlined in this book's Introduction, the language reforms were contemporaneous with such other Republican measures as the abolishment of the caliphate
(1924), the banning of traditional attire and encouraging the wearing of European-
style clothing (1925), and the closure of religious orders (1925). We might say that
the semiotic reorganization of the mid-nineteenth century had already prefigured
the displacement—*not* the disappearance—of an Islamic episteme as the organizing
principle of the social and political everyday in the Ottoman Empire, and that the
first measures of the Republican state, in abolishing the sultanate and the caliphate
and adopting the Swiss civil code and Italian penal code (1926), formalized the
withdrawal of religion from most domains of public life.[41] Debates around alphabet
reform were in many ways contemporaneous with debates around the abolishing of
Arabic as the language of religious worship, and the language reforms were of
essential importance in consolidating state control of religious worship.[42]

---

[41] See Bernard Lewis 262–274. See also Zürcher 186–188.

[42] With the goal of Turkicizing the language of prayer, the Republican parliament in 1925 commissioned
the poet, politician, and critic Mehmed Âkif [Ersoy] (1873–1936) to translate the Quran into Turkish (con-
vinced it would be appropriated by the state for a secularist agenda, Âkif refused to publish the translation).
The first official Turkish translation and exegesis of the Quran, by the influential scholar and theologian
Elmalılı Hamdi Yazır (1878–1942), were published between 1935 and 1938. 1927 marked the first delivery of
sermons (*hutbe*) in Turkish, rather than Arabic. The Ramadan of 1932 was a crucial turning point, with the
Quran being recited for the first time in Turkish in the mosques, and a new law being passed, the following year,
regulating the muezzin's call to prayer (*ezan*) in Turkish (a stricture that persisted through 1950). On the history of the Turkification of the language of worship in Turkey, see Cündioğlu, *Meşrutiyet'ten Cumhuriyet'e
Din ve Siyaset*.

But the "disestablishment" of Islam in Republican Turkey had deeper social roots and ambitions than the privatization and state control of religious activity.[43] To understand what they are, one must consider the function of what Michael E. Meeker calls a "discipline of Islamic sociability" (*Nation* 44) for the Muslim majority. Meeker has observed that the language of "local and oral Islam" provided a social grammar of interpersonal subjectivity, in villages and towns ("Oral" 37), and that even when the power of Islam's institutions was attenuated, there remained the heterogeneity of a Turkish vernacular governed by an "ethic of face-to-face exchanges"—"seeing others and showing oneself, speaking and listening in turn, gestures of respect and tokens of affection"—and underwritten by Islamic belief and prescription (Meeker *Nation* 44).[44] We might say that the final goal of the language reforms was to evacuate this Islamic interpersonal "grammar" itself, replacing it with a new phonocentric writing institutionalizing *national* solidarity among anonymous others.

İlker Aytürk notes that the first notable language debate took place in the Turkish Grand National Assembly (Türkiye Büyük Millet Meclisi) on 1 September 1923 ("First" 278).[45] Occasioned by the "draft bill, the so-called Law on Turkish Language" submitted by MP Tunalı Hilmi Bey on 23 August 1923, this debate concluded with rejection of the bill.[46] On 20 March 1926, the Dil Heyeti, also known as the Dil Encümeni, or Language Council, was officially authorized, with the appointment of a nine-member council to "'study the method for adoption of Latin letters in [*Turkish*] and their applicability'" following two years later, on 23 May 1928

---

[43] "The disestablishment of Islam" is Bernard Lewis's phrase. See *The Emergence of Modern Turkey* 276.

[44] For a detailed historical account of the workings of Islamic interpersonal association, see Meeker, *A Nation of Empire*. Countering arguments positing an absolute break between the Ottoman imperial and the Turkish Republican periods, Meeker offers an alternative narrative. "Sometime during the seventeenth century," Meeker writes, "under the direct pressure of internal instability and external competition, the Ottomans took more radical steps to widen the circle of participation in imperial institutions in the core provinces of the Empire," leading to the emergence of regional social oligarchies with the power to administer the local populations (xix–xx). This decentralization of the imperial state system meant the dissemination of "the exercise of sovereign power by means of a discipline of interpersonal association" (xx) and the emergence of a state society. For Meeker, the emergence of the new Kemalist Republican state is not so much a rupture as a reorganization of the older state society. Just as local elites accepted the new conventions of national public life in order to retain their connection to the center of power, state officials sought out the provincial oligarchs as "their assistants and intermediaries" (80). "Kemalist on the surface and Islamist below the surface," such local elites relied on older networks of Islamic sociability for control over local populations; here, the interlocking of "Kemalo-Islamism" did not in the least bring an end to networks of Islamic interpersonal association (80–81).

[45] On the history of the Turkish language reforms, see Heyd, *Language Reform in Modern Turkey* (1954); Steuerwald, *Untersuchungen zur türkischen Sprache der Gegenwart* vol 1 (1963); Geoffrey Lewis, *The Turkish Language Reform* (1999); and Laut, *Das Türkische als Ursprache?* (2000). An early account of the reforms in Turkish is Levend, *Türk Dilinde Gelişme ve Sadeleşme Evreleri* (1949; 2nd ed. 1960; 3rd ed. 1972). Important histories focused on the alphabet reform are Ülkütaşır, *Atatürk ve Harf Devrimi* (1973), Ertem, *Elifbeden Alfabeye* (1991), and Şimşir, *Türk Yazı Devrimi* (1992). A more recent critical and theoretical account, informed by the perspective of the nationalism debates, is Sadoğlu, *Türkiye'de Ulusçuluk ve Dil Politikaları* (2003). Aytürk's articles (as cited) incorporate some of the most recently unearthed archival material. Other useful sources include Korkmaz, *Atatürk ve Türk Dili: Belgeler* (1992), an anthology of primary sources related to the language reforms; and Yetiş, *Atatürk ve Türk Dili* (2005), a three-volume collection of articles from Republican newspapers concerning the language question.

[46] The full content of the bill is unknown (Aytürk 278).

(280).[47] In this period between 1926 and 1928, debate over the proposed adoption of Latin orthography went public, with such prominent intellectuals as Avram Galanti [Bodrumlu] (1873–1961) and Mehmed Fuad [Köprülü] (1890–1966) publishing articles opposing the measure.[48] This public debate was instigated in part by the First Turcology Congress, held at the end of February 1926 in Baku, Azerbaijan, which saw a decisive vote for the adoption of the Latin alphabet in the Turkic republics of the Soviet Union.[49] The Turkish Jewish historian Avram Galanti, who objected to the congress's "unscientific" decisions (Galanti was dismissed from his faculty position at the Istanbul University during the 1933 university reforms), emphasized the example of Japan, whose cultural and scientific advancement was indisputable, despite the complexity of its writing system and the writing and printing machines associated with it.[50]

In August 1928, a forty-one-page report entitled "Elifba Raporu" ("Alphabet Report"), outlining principles for the adoption of a new alphabet, was submitted to Mustafa Kemal by the Language Council. Primary among the concerns expressed in this document was that "the new letters do not generate any ambiguity [*iltibas*] among the sounds they represent and that there be a one-to-one correspondence between each letter and sound" (İbrahim 34). Consonant with the theories of Ziya Gökalp and the program of *Genç Kalemler*, the report made the Istanbul dialect the standard for a "national phonetics" ("millî fonetika"), calling for "the spelling of all words as they are pronounced" (34). Equally noteworthy is the report's emphasis on the individualized representation of each sound. Instead of adopting digraphs such as *ch* and *sh* for Turkish sounds, the council recommended the use of *ç* and *ş*, respectively (30). The international provenance of Latin letters and letter diacritics selected for the new Turkish (including the characters *â*, *î*, and *û* and the consonants *j* and *y* borrowed from French, *ö* and *ü* from German and Hungarian, *ş* from Romanian, and *ñ* from Spanish) did not seem to present an obstacle to the commission, who deemed them consonant with "our national phonetic" ("millî fonetiğimiz [savtiyatımız]")[51] (34).

---

[47] Aytürk suggests that we might ascribe the delay to "the role of the Prime Minister İsmet Paşa (İnönü) in arresting the course of the events" (280). Although İsmet Paşa supported the Latinization of the alphabet, he wanted to ensure that it would not meet the fate of *Enverpaşa yazısı*.

[48] See [Bodrumlu], *Arabî* and [Köprülü], "Harf." The public debate around Latin orthography began in the pages of the newspaper *Akşam* on 28 March 1926, with the question "Should we accept the Latin letters or not?"

[49] On the history of Soviet language reforms, see Grenoble, *Language Policy in the Soviet Union*. Publication in Latin lettering in Azerbaijan dates to 1924, with 1929 marking the compulsory adoption of a newly devised Latin alphabet and the ceasing of all publication in Arabic script in the Turkic republics. To enforce centralization, and to prevent the possible revival of pan-Turkism (especially after Turkey's 1928 script change), Stalin ordered the adoption of Cyrillic as the new alphabet in 1939. To the best of my knowledge, a comparative study of the Soviet and Turkish reforms has yet to be undertaken.

[50] For Avram Galanti's views on the Baku Congress, see his "Bakü Türkoloji Kongresi'nin Gayr-ı İlmî bir Kararı," dated 24 March 1926 and republished in *Arabî* 7–12. For his comparison of Arabic and Japanese writings, see his "Arab ve Japon Yazıları," dated 29–30 April 1926, republished in *Arabî* 29–34. These articles were originally published in *Akşam*.

[51] As I have reproduced it here, the word *savtiyat,* derived from the Arabic loanword *savt,* sound, appears in the text in parentheses following the French loanword *fonetik.*

It is interesting to note how the report negotiated the transliteration of script lettering used in words of Arabic and Persian origin. On the one hand, the report refused equivalents for such letters as "se ث, sad ص, tı ط, zı ظ, and dat ض," "which are not part of our phonetic system" (35).[52] The council also refused equivalents for the individualized representation of the hard and the soft *k* (the letters *kaf* ق and *kef* ك), as well as the hard and soft *g* (*gayın* غ and *gef* گ). It ran a middle course, on the other other hand, in seeking a way to accommodate the orthographic retention of Arabic and Persian words, "which are currently part of the language but are to disappear in time" (36). To represent the palatalized sounds of *k* and *g* preceding back vowels in Arabic and Persian borrowings, for example, it advises inclusion of a letter *h* following the consonant, on the model of Portugese (36).[53] And while the report recommended the inclusion of the Latin letters *q*, *w*, and *x* in the new phonetic alphabet, the version approved by the assembly a few months later was to omit them.[54]

After having made alterations to the council's report, Mustafa Kemal first introduced the new alphabet to the public in a speech given in the Sarayburnu Park in Istanbul on 9 August 1928, as part of an event organized by the Republican People's Party. (The setting is strategic: Sarayburnu Park, which overlooks the entrance of the Golden Horn at the Sea of Marmara, forms part of the outer garden of the Topkapı Palace, which housed the Ottoman sultans from the fifteenth to the mid-nineteenth centuries.) Expressing his personal feelings of excitement and pleasure at this historic moment, Kemal indulged in a bit of public theater, requesting that a volunteer citizen (*vatandaş*) read aloud Kemal's own notes for the speech (Atatürk 272). When the volunteer proved unable to perform this task, Kemal once more addressed his audience: "Citizens, my notes are written in true [*asıl*], real [*hakikî*] Turkish words and Turkish letters. Your brother attempted to read them, but was unable to. Undoubtedly, however, he might be able to. I'd like that you all learn to do so in five to ten days" (272). Demonstratively marking the old Perso-Arabic script of Ottoman Turkish as illegible, and henceforth to be marked as alien, by modern Republican Turkey, Kemal in the same stroke identified the Latin alphabet adopted by legislative fiat as a newly "native" element of national Turkish culture:

> The richness and the harmony of our language will become manifest in the new Turkish letters [*yeni Türk harfleri*]. You must understand the necessity of saving ourselves from the incomprehensible [*anlaşılmayan*] signs

---

[52] *Se* (a voiceless alveolar plosive) and the other four emphatic consonants were used in spelling Arabic loanwords. *Tı* and *sad* were used in the spelling of Turkish words only if the initial *t* and *s* were succeeded by a back vowel (*a*, *ı*, *o*, *u*).

[53] For example, the word *kâtip* (scribe) would be written as *khâtip* and *dergâh* (convent) as *derghâh* (İbrahim 36).

[54] Other differences included the incorporation into the official alphabet of the letterforms *ö*, *ü*, and *ğ*. In the council's report, these letters were described as spelling conventions, and not assigned places in the alphabet itself (İbrahim 40).

we cannot understand, and which have imprisoned our minds in iron for centuries. The whole world will soon become a witness to the proofs [*âsar*] of your understanding. (272)

Like Midhat and Seyfeddin before him, and with other members of the modernizing elite supporting him, Kemal here appropriates the foreignizing communicative powers of the Turkish language to bring *in* the European *outside,* at the same time promising it an impossible self-sameness. Kemal does not once describe the new alphabet, in this address, as "Latin" lettering, as it was often described in debates of the period. Unlike those of his predecessors who had opposed the adoption of the Latin alphabet, Kemal does not even invoke the concept of translation in this speech; rather, he *directly* borrows a foreign element with mixed origins (incorporating diacritical marks used in German, Romanian, French, and Hungarian)—and in such a way that obscures doubly its inherent mediacy. This foreign element is then presented as immediately expressive of "the feelings, desires, excitements, and goals rising from the hearts of the esteemed people constitutive of Turkish society" (273).

At one level, the alphabet reform is thus merely an extraordinarily vivid illustration of Rafael's counterintuitive definition of nationhood as "the condition of being endowed with the power to incorporate that which lies outside the nation, and to do so without any loss" (2). That it requires a kind of staged dialogue, in the form of an epistemically violent "writing lesson" featuring Kemal, the volunteer citizen, and an anonymous public assembled in Sarayburnu Park, is one index of the real complexity of this imagined transaction. Kemal knew he could count on at least one of his implied addressees here, the "civilized world" ("âlem-i medeniyet") (274), to receive the "message" embodied in a new "polyglot" Turkish alphabet, as validating Republican Turkey's struggle for recognition on an uneven global stage.[55] But he was visibly less assured of the *internal* comprehensibility of the national message, as demonstrated by the urgency he attached, in this speech, to its local audience's coming to "understand" what was happening, and its urgency.[56]

More than the mere shock of change from one "old" system of writing to another, newer one, we see in the citizen's "failure" to read that serves as the speech's gambit a perseverance of the modern welding of language to death. Kemal's

---

[55] The European and U.S. press reported promptly on the alphabet change. See, for example, W. G. Tinckom-Fernandez's *New York Times* article dated 2 September 1928, entitled "Changing Alphabet Obsesses Kemal."

[56] Kemal's rhetorical imperatives do not merely express the necessity for Turks to "save ourselves" from the old script; the sentence in question, in his speech, ends with a supplementary clause emphasizing the *obligation* (*mecburiyet*) of his audience to understand what he is saying, *in* making this point. Here is the Turkish original of the sentence cited earlier in English translation: "Asırlardan beri kafalarımızı demir çerçeve içinde bulundurarak, anlaşılmayan ve anlayamadığımız işaretlerden kendimizi kurtarmak, bunu anlamak mecburiyetindesiniz" (272). The final section of Kemal's speech foregrounds once again such a collective "duty" of understanding: "Many words, long words are said for one thing: To take to truth those who don't understand the truth [*anlamıyanları*]. . . I passed these stages" [Çok söz, uzun söz bir şey için söylenir: Hakikati anlamıyanları hakikate getirmek için. . . Ben bu devirleri geçirdim.] (273). The explicitly exhortatory self-awareness of these gestures suggest something of Kemal's anxiety about how ideally communicable his message *really* is.

implied internal audience, for this speech, might not *all* be aware of the gaze of the "civilized world" compelling the adoption of a modern alphabet—but it does recognize itself as members of an internal social community, and Mustafa Kemal as its savior and head of state. This staged "writing lesson," a lesson in what we might call phonocentric deliverance, marks the "distracted" audience as exposed to *social death* as the consequence of failing to read Turkish in Latin letters.

Henceforth, to travel in the Ottoman Turkish lettering, or to inhabit an orality underwritten by the social grammar of Islam, is to be a *dead* outcast. Like the letterforms of the obsolete script, the volunteer citizen becomes an incomprehensible sign, spectacularly unrecognizable in the appeal to a new legibility. Again, it is not merely novelty, in the alphabet reform, that produces such estrangement and self-estrangement: rather—and this is precisely the power of Kemal's address—that alienation is produced by and from the conjunction of the illiteracy of "Latin writing" with this social death performed before the crowd.[57] As a *negative* limit, in this sense, the Latin alphabet is then re-rendered as proper and proprietary, in the repetition of this scene that saw Kemal pass his notes to the Language Council member Falih Rıfkı [Atay], who performed a "successful" reading of most of the rest of Kemal's speech. Finally, in a concluding section that Kemal delivered himself, describing the low level of literacy in Turkey as "shameful," Kemal tells his audience that the ability to read and write is the necessary condition for any social recognition, at all (274).[58]

We observe here the extension, into the Republican reforms, of Seyfeddin's "fixing" of the non-national non-Turkish in the form of death, in a form of intensification that makes *oneself* the foreignized "messenger" of one's own death, in the internal communicative travel of the Turkish language. To the extent that this inaugural scene of Turkish Republican phonocentrism turns on the symbolic slashing of the tongue, as it were, of the volunteer citizen, it shows us how reformed writing becomes legible, for the internal audience, by what we might call *differentiation against a deadly difference.*[59] And at some level, then, we might see this historical scene as a kind of recapitulation and reenactment of an originary entry into language, in so far as the volunteer citizen, rendered an absent presence on stage,

---

[57] Writing in wartime and in the midst of war, Seyfeddin appropriated the imagination of actual bodily death and ostracizing "social" death simultaneously. By contrast, in *this* particular speech, at least, Kemal could be said to making use only of the latter. See also notes 90 and 91.

[58] This scene, we might say, marks the official emergence of a new public relationship with sovereign power: a relationship founded on written, rather than oral communication. Where Ottoman administrators had relied primarily on the oral transmission of written directives, Kemal made writing the new administrative norm. A famous photograph taken on 28 August 1928 in Sivas, depicting Kemal standing in front of a blackboard covered with writing in the new Latin alphabet, is explicit about the very means of communication with the new ruler. For an analysis of the oral authority of the Ottoman state, see Aymes, "The Voice-Over of Administration." On the logic of social recognition as the discipline of personal and interpersonal subjectivity in Turkey, see Meeker, "Once There Was, Once There Wasn't" and *A Nation of Empire.*

[59] It is noteworthy that Kemal's writing lesson itself is *structured* as writing, understood as difference and repetition. The "necessity" of Latin letters is registered by the difference in the repetition of Falih Rıfkı's successful performance.

(doubly) spectralized by the new alphabet that he cannot read, is a figure for the "forgetting" of one's own birth and receipt of a mother tongue—a "forgetting" which is of course really a not remembering, in the nonmemory of having been born and first attempting speech. Republican self-emptying is in one sense the effect and realization of a radical abstraction inherent in language. Yet if the originary entry into language is an opening to infinite possibilities (including death), here, the "gift" of the Latin alphabet reduces all such written and oral communicative possibility to a single choice between national phonocentric life-writing and totalized death.

The Law Concerning the Adoption and the Application of Turkish Letters (Türk Harflerinin Kabul ve Tatbiki Hakkındaki Kanun) was passed unanimously by the National Assembly on 1 November 1928. As of 1 December 1928, all public signs, newspapers, and magazines were required to be printed using the new alphabet, and beginning on 1 January 1929, all state institutions, banks, societies, and corporations had to conduct their administrative business using it, as well. Ordinary citizens could submit documents to the government using the old script up until 1 June 1929, but by 1 June 1930, all public and private correspondence was to be conducted in the new alphabet, without exception.[60] In a dispatch dated 24 October 1928, Ernest L. Ives, the first secretary of the U.S. Embassy in Turkey, reported that "The removal of these characteristic and decorative letters now lends to the streets of [Constantinople] a very peculiar aspect reminiscent of Balkan cities, a few foreign signs being the only ones visible now as those in Arabic characters have been either scratched out, painted over, or covered up pending their replacement by signs with the new Turkish letters" (75). Perhaps most drastic was the law passed on 11 November 1928, requiring all male and female citizens between the ages of sixteen and forty to complete an alphabetic literacy course at the Millet Mektepleri or public schools then being created nationwide.[61] During the first year of the alphabet reform, approximately six hundred thousand people learned how to read and write in these courses.[62]

Marshall McLuhan, who wrote of phonetic alphabetization as "the greatest processor of men for homogenized military life" (72), made creative use of the myth of Cadmus to link phonetic writing to organized and monopolized violence:

> The Greek myth about the alphabet was that Cadmus, reputedly the king who introduced the phonetic letters into Greece, sowed the dragon's teeth,

---

[60] The complete text of this legislation can be found in "Türk Harflerinin" 71–72.

[61] The complete text of this legislation can be found in "Millet" 84–102.

[62] Başvekalet İstatistik Umum Müdürlüğü, *Maarif 1928–1933: Millet Mektepleri Faaliyeti İstatistiği* 45, qtd. in Şimşir, *Türk Yazı Devrimi* 244. The literacy rate, at 8 percent (about one million and one hundred people) according to the 1927 census, increased to 19.2 percent by the 1935 census. The work of Foucault, among others, on schooling as a "disciplinary technology" ought to leave us suspicious of such promotion of mass literacy in and of itself.

and they sprang up as armed men. . . . Languages are filled with testimony to the grasping, devouring power and precision of teeth. That the power of letters as agents of aggressive order and precision should be expressed as extensions of the dragon's teeth is natural and fitting. Teeth are emphatically visual in their lineal order. Letters are not only like teeth visually, but their power to put teeth into the business of empire building is manifest in our Western history. (82–83)

For McLuhan, the introductions of phonetic alphabets, separating the sign from the signified and establishing the visual domain as an arbitrary carrier of meaning, mark crucial turning points in the history of media and the modern rationalization of the world, through which the universal translatability of phonetic writing is empowered to absorb *all* difference. Ottoman classical logocentrism demonstrates that all historical writing systems may certainly be said to be "armed," in this sense, for the violent introduction of hierarchy. And yet the Republican adoption of the Latin alphabet, paving the way for similarly radical lexical reforms, shows us something of the iterative *intensification* of violence that is phonetic writing as a foundation of modernity. Endorsing the Turkish nationalist Sadri Maksudi [Arsal]'s influential *Türk Dili İçin* ("For the Turkish Language," 1930), an early text of systematic linguistic planning for a purified or *öz* Turkish with the subtitle "Reflections on the Collection, Arrangement, and Selection of Turkish Words and on the Invention of Scientific Words from Turkish Roots," Kemal laid the grounds for an "armed" policy of purification that decisively superseded the violence of classical logocentrism, as a violence itself to be violently overcome. In a commentary on Maksudi's book explicitly comparing the language reforms with the War of Independence, whose slogan was "Freedom or Death" (*Ya İstiklâl Ya Ölüm*), Kemal demanded: "The Turkish nation, which knows how to protect its [country] and its sublime freedom must save its language from the yoke of foreign languages."[63] This defense of language reform as liberation warfare would become an integral part of the discourse of Turkish national grammatology during the first half of the 1930s.

Historians of the Republican language reforms generally agree that the replacement of the Language Council by the Türk Dili Tetkik Cemiyeti (Society for the Study of Turkish Language, later Türk Dil Kurumu), on 12 July 1932, marks

---

[63] An émigré from Soviet Russia, Sadri Maksudi sought to "purify" Turkish, within a pan-Turkist agenda for linguistic unity across the Turkic regions of Central and West Asia.

[64] In "The First Episode," Aytürk suggests that the struggle between radical purists and the supporters of a more moderate program continued within official circles until the 1931 closure of the Language Council. For an analysis of the role of the Language Society in the language reforms, see Aytürk, "Politics" 13–23. Unlike the Language Council, the Language Society was privately administered by a central governing committee (Umumi Merkez Heyeti) whose members were selected internally. The society's legally private status, however, did not protect it entirely from state interference, especially given that Mustafa Kemal served as its *hâmi reis*, or guardian chairman, and that the Turkish state was the main contributor of society funds. For a description of the society's approved organizational structure, see "Türk Dili Tetkik Cemiyeti Nizamnamesi."

the victory of a radical purist agenda that held sway between 1932 and 1936.[64] The Language Society's program, as finalized at its First Congress (Birinci Türk Dili Kurultayı) held between 26 September and 5 October 1932, had among its goals the creation of new comprehensive modern Turkish dictionaries, as well as the promotion of comparative study of the Turkish language with Sumerian and Hittite, as well as Indo-European and Semitic languages.[65] This first goal produced the nationwide "word-collection mobilization" (*söz derleme seferberliği*) of 1932, undertaken to compile words from Anatolian dialects. Assigned the task of compiling lists of words, the army officers, teachers, and doctors conscripted for the task were transformed into linguistic ethnographers, required to send their gathered data to "collection committees" established in the capital of each province. Approximately 126,000 documents were collected by August 1933.[66] Supplemented by terms gathered from manuscripts and books published in other Turkic languages, the collected results were published in *Osmanlıcadan Türkçeye Söz Karşılıkları: Tarama Dergisi* ("Word Synonyms from Ottoman to Turkish: The Collection Journal") in 1934. To take two of Lewis's examples of the heterogeneity of actually existing language at the time, in all its linguistic "confusion," the *Tarama Dergisi* listed twenty-two possible Turkish substitutes for the Arabic loanword *hikâye* (story), and seventy-seven for *hediye* (gift).[67]

One might say that Arabic and Persian borrowings, in the vernacular, had already been "spectralized" by the mere institution of the new alphabet. Caught in its "teeth," these words that could "not find their sounds on the keyboard of the new alphabet," wrote the poet Ahmet Haşim in an article dated 3 December 1928 ("Lisan" 317), "sound[ed] like the muffled and ugly screams of people whose voices are becoming hoarse."[68] In a way, the real goal of the linguistic mobilization of the early 1930s was to eliminate these agonizing signs of death, in the institution of an impossibly self-same nation. And yet, rather than bridging the divide between the language of the intelligentsia and the common people, as intended, the purifications of the early 1930 produced a new, abstract Turkish that was in many ways unintelligible to both groups. Newspaper columnists required to use the new language first wrote their articles privately in Ottoman Turkish, employing an intermediary group of "substitutors" (*ikameci*) to "translate" their articles into "officialese."[69] These substitutors would choose from *Tarama Dergisi,* often more or less arbitrarily, the

---

[65] For a description of the society's official agenda, see "Türk Dili Birinci Kurultayınca Kabul Edilen Çalışma Programı."

[66] See *Osmanlıcadan Türkçeye Söz Karşılıkları 1*, 6.

[67] The entry for *hikâye* appears in *Osmanlıcadan Türkçeye Söz Karşılıkları 1,* 315–316; the entry for *hediye* on 303–305 in the same volume. See Geoffrey Lewis 50, for his discussion of these two examples. The second volume of *Osmanlıcadan Türkçeye Söz Karşılıkları* consists of an "index" (*indeks*) of "pure Turkish" (*öz Türkçe*) and "Ottoman" (*Osmanlıca*) equivalents. This appears to have been intended to accommodate readers unfamiliar with "pure Turkish" words.

[68] "Teeth," here, refers my reader to McLuhan, as cited above.

[69] "Officialese" is Aytürk's term. See Aytürk, "Politics" 17.

new equivalents they liked best. Even Mustafa Kemal, self-constrained to deliver a speech full of neologisms at a 1934 banquet in honor of the Swedish Crown prince and princess, grew irritated with the haphazard course of the reforms. (Kemal delivered his remarks "with the awkwardness of schoolchildren who have just begun to read" [Tankut, qtd. in Geoffrey Lewis 56].)[70]

The final solution to the linguistic chaos of the Republican period was embodied in the promulgation of the famous Güneş-Dil Teorisi, or Sun-Language Theory, which identified Turkish as the original source of all other human languages. First announced at the Third Language Congress (Üçüncü Türk Dil Kurultayı) in 1936, the Sun-Language Theory marked an important shift, in the new Turkish national grammatology, away from its grounding in death. Where the negation of difference as death had produced only *more* death, the Sun-Language Theory might be said to have sought to master the negativity of that ineffaceable and infinitely extensible difference, by appropriating and incorporating it into mimetic identity. On the one hand, the very foundationalism of the theory legitimized the retention of those Arabic and Persian borrowings that had become a focus of deadly struggle, implicitly acknowledging that the purification of Turkish was an impossible task. At the very same time, that foundationalism was a violent act of the denial of such alterity as was embodied in Arabic and Persian precisely as "problems" for Turkish.

Efforts to promote the notion of Turkish as *Ursprache* had already been made by Samih Rıfat (1874–1932), the first director of the Language Society. In his *Türkçede Tasrif-i Huruf Kanunları ve Tekellümün Menşei* ("The Rules of Declension of Letters in Turkish and the Origin of Speech"), published in 1922, Rıfat, who proclaimed that Turkish was the primal language of humanity, suggested that root-based philological typology be discarded for the analysis of sound units as the basis of articulation (Aytürk "Turkish" 13–15).[71] With the development of the Turkish Historical Thesis (Türk Tarih Tezi) by the Turkish Historical Association in the 1930s, the question of the philological kinship of Turkish with unclassified languages such as Sumerian and Etruscan, as well as with Indo-European lan-

---

[70] *Osmanlıcadan Türkçeye Cep Kılavuzu* ("Pocket Guide from Ottoman to Turkish"), a compendium of proposed Turkish equivalents published in 1935, represents the Language Society's belated attempt to control the chaos generated by the *Tarama Dergisi*. The pocket guide included neologisms derived from Turkic words as replacements for purged Ottoman Turkish words. For example, the proposed replacement for the Arabic loanword *hikâye* (story) is *öykü* (117), a neologism most likely derived from the words *öykme* and *öykünme*, according to the *Tarama Dergisi* used in Denizli (in southwest Anatolia) as equivalents of *hikâye* (316). On the methods (or lack thereof) used in the invention of neologisms before and after the 1950s, along with specific examples, see Lewis 75–123. Some of the same tensions observed in adopting the Latin alphabet animated the process of inventing neologisms. Lewis writes that the Serbo-Croatian loanwords *kıraliçe* (queen), *çariçe* (tsarina), and *imparatoriçe* (empress) provided the feminine suffix *–çelça*. "Added to *tanrı* 'god,' it made *tanrıça*" the *öz Türkçe* or "pure Turkish" replacement for the Arabic loanword *ilâhe* (95). Also noteworthy is the suffix *–sell sal*, derived from "the French *culturel* and *principal*" as a "substitute for the Arabic and Persian adjectival suffix *–î* as in *tarihî* 'historical' and *siyasî* 'political'" (101).

[71] For an overview of nineteenth-century European philological debates regarding Turkic languages, see Aytürk, "Turkish." In many ways, such assertions carried forward late nineteenth century Ottoman resistance to the European view of Turkic languages as nomadic and therefore uncivilized, a resistance that often took the form of incorporation.

guages, assumed renewed importance. (The thesis held that the Turks of Central
Asia who had migrated to China, India, the Near East, North Africa, and Europe
were the founders of the world's oldest civilizations.[72]) The monogenist theory of
Japhetology, developed by the Soviet linguist Nikolai Y. Marr (1865–1934), who
lectured in Turkey in 1933 on the origin of languages, was influential in this context. Marr questioned the Eurocentric premise of comparative philology, arguing
that Indo-European languages had evolved from those he designated as Japhetic,
including Georgian, the Turkic languages, Basque, Etruscan, and the ancient languages of Asia Minor.[73]

But it was a Viennese linguist, Hermann F. Kvergić, who furnished some of the
more useful material in promulgating the Sun-Language Theory. In January 1935, on
his own initiative, Kvergić had sent Atatürk a copy of a study entitled "La psychologie
de quelques éléments des langues turques." In this paper, Kvergić tied the experience
of phenomenological proximity and distance to phonemic signification, with the
closest interval being represented by a phonemic "m," as in *men*, the ancient form of
the Turkish *ben* (I). "N," Kvergić explained, indicated proximity to the self, as in the
Turkish *sen* (you). "Z," finally, broadens that proximity, as in the Turkish *biz* (we) and
siz (you).[74] Kvergić argued that this elemental phenomenological signification of
Turkish pronouns had remained the same since the language's genesis. Although
Kvergić has often been credited as the first source of the Sun-Language Theory, recent
archival scholarship has demonstrated that the fundamentals of the Sun-Language
Theory had already been drafted by the time of Kvergić's official enlistment by the
Language Society in late 1935.[75] While the creative origin of the theory thus remains
indeterminate, its dissemination certainly required more than one such mastermind,[76]
with the final version incorporating elements of these various contributions.

The Sun-Language Theory was presented at the Third Language Congress on
25 August 1936 by İbrahim Necmi [Dilmen], general secretary of the Turkish
Language Society. Dilmen argued that all human language had originated in the
exclamation "Aa!" (in Turkish, *ağ*), ostensibly uttered when the first human
language speaker first gazed at the sun. In its elongated form, "Aa" was represented

---

[72] For an outline of the Turkish Historical Thesis, see [İnan] et al., *Türk Tarihinin Ana Hatları*.

[73] Regarding Marr's influence on the etymological method of the Sun-Language Theory, see Shaw,
"Whose Hittites" 140–144. For a more comprehensive account of Marr's theories, see Lähteenmäki, "Nikolai."
In Marr's schema, all the world's languages derived from four basic "tribal" particles that he designated SAL,
BER, JON, and ROŠ. Marr opposed the conventional understanding of language families altogether, explain-
ing the difference of languages as reflecting differing stages of a universal glottogenetic evolution.

[74] For a personal account of the development of the Sun-Language Theory, see Emre, "Güneş." For the
Turkish translation of Kvergić's paper, see "Türkoloji İncelemeleri." For Kvergić's presentation at the Third
Language Congress, see *Üçüncü* 439–445.

[75] See Aytürk, "H. F. Kvergić." The booklet, published anonymously in 1935 and entitled *Etimoloji,
Morfoloji ve Fonetik Bakımından Türk Dili* ("Etymology, Morphology, and Phonetics in the Turkish Language"),
includes the first sketches of the Sun-Language Theory. It was sent to Kvergić as a guide for his research. Aytürk
suggests that Kvergić's involvement was solicited to provide external credibility.

[76] While Atatürk's involvement cannot be denied—he is credited as the author of *Etimoloji, Morfoloji ve
Fonetik Bakımından Türk Dili*—it is unlikely that all or even many of the theory's specifics originated with him.

by the silent guttural consonant *ğ*—a Latin equivalent for the Ottoman Turkish letters *gayın* and *gef*—and produced the radical phoneme *ağ* (60). New historical and linguistic evidence proved, Dilmen argued, that "the long sought primitive roots of the Indo-European" and of "Semitic languages" are to be found in "primitive, pure Turkish" (*Üçüncü* 64–65). In combination, the eight vowels and twenty-one consonants used in Turkish produced 168 phonemes (each the combination of one vowel with one consonant), and the combination of these phonemes into monosyllabic words produced the roots ("racine") of classical linguistics. Dilmen suggested that "seemingly basic monosyllabic roots, such as 'ka, la, me, and ne' are, in actuality, biphonemic sound constructions—*akağ, alağ, emeğ, eneğ* [emphasis added]—whose initial vowels and final consonants are dropped" (63). With each phoneme corresponding to a psychological unit of meaning, and agglutinative suffixes having evolved for the purpose of phenomenological orientation, the linguistic methodology of the Sun-Language Theory demanded and proved Turkish as the origin of all human language. Dilmen suggested, for example, that the Turkic word *idi*, meaning God or ruler, and purportedly related to the Greek *theos*, the Latin *deus*, and the French *dieu*, was formed by the combination of the phonemes *iğ* + *id* + *iğ* (74–75). When *iğ*, meaning power or sovereignty, was combined with *id*, marking possession, it formed *id*, signifying the possessor of power, with the third phoneme serving the function of iterative reinforcement (77–78). Once discredited (primarily by foreign academics attending the Third Congress), the Sun-Language Theory was abandoned shortly before Atatürk's death in 1938 and was not mentioned at all at the Fourth Language Congress of 1942.[77]

The Sun-Language Theory may be understood, at least in part, as an attempt to overcome the alienating effects of the semantic arbitrariness embodied in the new phonetic alphabet. As phonetic writing established an entirely abstract "gap" between writing and speech, the revolutionary etymological method of the Sun-Language Theory refashioned the Turkish language as ideo-phonographic, effectively naturalizing each phonemic unit. The psychological dimensions of the theory, which were of special interest to Atatürk,[78] are captured by Meeker's suggestion, apropos the architecture of Kemal's tomb in Ankara, that "there is nothing left for interior desire save its extinction in the name of the nation" (Meeker, "Once" 175). In a diagram published in the proceedings of the Third Language Congress, Dilmen represented the human ego at the center of six concentric circles marking the phenomenological spatialities of the self (*ben*), the singular other (*sen*), and the plural self and other (*biz/siz*) (*Üçüncü* 362). (An earlier version of the diagram published in the daily *Cumhuriyet* on 24 February 1936 included the sun—frequently, a symbol

---

[77] Atatürk himself never officially disowned the Sun-Language Theory. Regarding Atatürk's position on the language question at the time of his death, see Geoffrey Lewis 67–74.

[78] See Emre, "Güneş" 323, quoting Kemal: "The psychological analyses seem important to me."

[79] For a reproduction of the *Cumhuriyet* diagram, see Shaw 148.

for Atatürk himself—centrally positioned above and outside the outermost circle.[79])
Following Meeker, one might suggest that such diagrams graph nothing less than
the total appropriation of the subjective and intersubjective, for the nation's needs
and ends.[80] (See Figures 2.1 and 2.2)

It has been noted that in profound ways, the invention of the Sun-Language
Theory involved the production of national subjects at once severed from the
Ottoman-Islamic past and autochthonous to an irreducibly heterogeneous Anatolia, and the very same time, figured in kinship with Europe.[81] To the extent that
a fundamentally *typographic* ambition aimed to produce what Phillippe Lacoue-
Labarthe has called an "onto-typology," in the Turkish case, it conforms to his
stylized definition as "imprint[ing] or impress[ing] a *hexis*, in general, or a *hab-
itus*, a style of existence, if you like, or an *ethos*" (*Heidegger* 10). The ethos of
typography in the theory, along these lines, is a refashioning of Turkish as the
original language "type" or *Ursprache* of humanity. In many ways, the assimila-
tive racism of the Republican period in Turkey, denying alterity in precisely the
universalization of Turkishness, can be distinguished from the discriminating
and exclusive European racisms of the same period.[82] Its orientation tended over
time to slow the elimination of loanwords—a way of asserting the Turkish revolution in relation to Europe, by denying that it was in any way derivative *from*
Europe.

One might observe, as well, that it is the Sun-Language Theory that grounded
the Turkish state's totalizing claim for *license to fiction* in a now-universalized
Turkish language—and not only in the "fixation" of a fictional account of origin
as the truth. Where Seyfeddin, coding literature as the speech of a deadly linguistic outside, had sought to efface its alterity, the Sun-Language Theory, which
posits the undifferentiated mimetic speech of a new Self as the very *source* of all
fictional other-speaking, is a refusal of and foreclosure on the possibility of any
literature at all—even a deadly literature.[83] Here, all conceivable communicative
and translative paths lead back to the primal phoneme *ağ*, capable of reproducing itself infinitely, without doubling or splitting.[84] As a presentation given by

---

[80] In a comparative analysis of the architecture of the Atatürk Memorial Tomb (Anıtkabir) and that of
Topkapı Palace, Meeker discusses Republican agents' appropriation of an older idiom of interpersonal intimacy. See "Once" 168–174.

[81] See Shaw 135. On the pseudo-positivism of the theory in the context of Turkish ethnic nationalism, see
Ersanlı, *İktidar* 205–213. See also Ersanlı, "Naming."

[82] Here I mean not, of course, to imply an evaluative distinction between "good" Turkish and "bad"
European racisms (such a position is neither moral, nor logical). I would, however, insist on a *descriptive* ac-
knowledgment of this discursive peculiarity of Turkish racism.

[83] To the extent that literariness was equivalent to death, for Seyfeddin, his relationship to literature was
of course a relationship of *non*relation. My point here is that even in this negative form, Seyfeddin's work
contains a *recognition* of alterity; the Sun-Language Theory does not.

[84] In many ways, one might think the Sun-Language Theory as the product of a paradoxically anti-
mimetic desire to "conquer" mimesis, as Lacoue-Labarthe has described it:

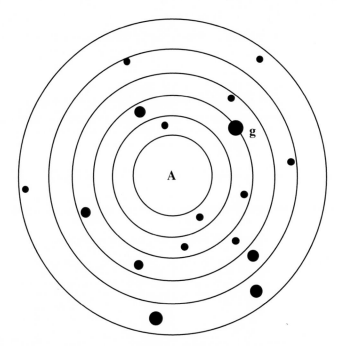

FIGURE 2.1 Diagram entitled "The First Object of Consciousness," used by İbrahim Necmi Dilmen during his presentation to the Third Language Congress, illustrating "first" man's first consciousness of surrounding objects. The capital letter "A" represents first man, the lower-case letter "g" the sun.

Source: From İbrahim Necmi Dilmen, *Üçüncü Türk Dil Kurultayı 1936-Tezler Müzakere Zabıtlar* (Türk Dil Kurumu/Istanbul: Devlet Basımevi, 1937), 360.

the parliamentarian Naim Onat at the Third Language Congress suggests, even the blurring of boundaries between absence and presence, loss and plenitude, and darkness and light is not to be taken as disconcerting, in self-same "sun-writing":

> Some of the words we use to describe a place of shelter derive from the idea of darkness, and others from that of light and illumination. It is quite

---

This is why the only recourse, with mimesis, is to differentiate it and to appropriate it, to iden-tify it. In short, to *verify* it. Which would without fail betray the essence or property of mime-sis, if there were an essence of mimesis or if what is "proper" to mimesis did not lie precisely in the fact that mimesis has no "proper" to it, ever (so that mimesis does not consist in the improper, either, or in who knows what "negative" essence, but *eksists*, or better yet, "de-sists" in this appropriation of everything supposedly proper that necessarily jeopardizes property "itself"). ("Typography" 116)

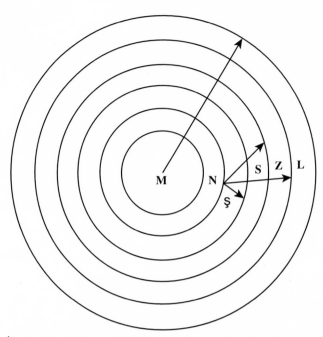

FIGURE 2.2 İbrahim Necmi Dilmen argued that man "invented vowels and consonants to mark the differences of objects and their zones of position, as well as to represent the relation of these zones to one another and in relation to the self." The capital letter "M" here stands for the self, while "N" marks the zone of objects closest to the self, and "Z" a zone of objects at a distance.

Source: From İbrahim Necmi Dilmen, *Üçüncü Türk Dil Kurultayı 1936-Tezler Müzakere Zabıtlar* (Türk Dil Kurumu/Istanbul: Devlet Basımevi, 1937), 362.

common to see words originating from the same thought assume in time opposite meanings, and words with opposite meanings coming to denote the same thing. (*Üçüncü* 187)[85]

Where for Freud, the deeply disconcerting convergence of *heimlich* with its "opposite," *unheimlich,* indicated something of humanity's psychic inability to reconcile with originary unhomeliness, for Onat and the architects of the Sun-Language Theory, the convergence of light and darkness achieves the denial of originary self-differentiation. And yet one might—indeed, must—suggest, against the intentions of this national grammatology, that all that the "overcoming of the long distances between the meanings of words" (*Üçüncü* 188) can offer us, in the end, is the stasis and death of a *sealed* language—something

---

[85] Onat's presentation, entitled "Comparing Turkish and Arabic on the Basis of the Sun-Language Theory," sought to demonstrate the relationship of Arabic and Turkish words denoting darkness, evening, and death, among others. See *Üçüncü* 151–189.

we might not want to call language any more, at all. As Freud merely hinted in "The 'Uncanny,'" and developed in *Beyond the Pleasure Principle*, the repetition of the desire to overcome death, constitutive of and inherent in the self as such, can only end in total and absolute noncommunication.

3. The "Hauntology" of Turkish Literary Modernity

Although the Sun-Language Theory was discarded following Atatürk's death in 1938, İsmet İnönü, who succeeded him as Republican Turkey's second leader, pursued the purism of the language reforms through the period of the Second World War. The Turkification of the language of the 1924 Constitution (Teşkilât-ı Esasiye Kanunu) was one notable project of the first years of the 1940s. In terms of their legacy for Republican Turkey, we can say that the language reforms did succeed in producing what in effect was an amnesiac majority of modern Turkish speakers and writers. This is the state of affairs lamented by Erich Auerbach, the German Jewish émigré who taught at Istanbul University from 1936 to 1947, in a letter to Walter Benjamin dated 3 January 1937: "No one under 25 can any longer understand any sort of religious, literary, or philosophical text more than ten years old and . . . the specific properties of the language are rapidly decaying."

On the other hand, we cannot say, either, that the Republican construction of a nationalized language, from a radically heterogeneous context, was an unqualified success. For all its totalizing ambition to reconstitute an ontology of immediacy and self-presence, in a nationalized language, the new reality produced by the Turkish grammatology of nationalism can only be described as *spectral*. Observing the gap between the ideality and the reality of the Republican reforms, the sociologist Meltem Ahıska has schematized this "spectralization" as a bifurcation of the Republican everyday into two orders of things, one comprising the formal authority of a pure national society of appearances, the other, the externalized interiority of the disavowed "Ottoman," along with the Republic's women, peasants, fundamentalists, criminals, communists, and ethnolinguistic others, the remainders of the Kemalist revolution.[86] The pedagogue, academic, and calligrapher Ismayil Hakkı Baltacıoğlu's (1886–1978) charts of Ottoman Turkish letterforms transvisualized as partly limbless, substantively evacuated human forms can be read as a powerful visual registration of this spectrality. (See Figure 2.3).

Published with *Türklerde Yazı Sanatı* (1958), a "socio-psychological essay on the graphology and the aesthetics of Turkish script arts," these charts transvisualize each letter of the Ottoman Turkish alphabet as a scriptural paradox: what we might call a

---

[86] Ahıska, "Türkiye'de İktidar ve Gerçeklik." I thank Özge Serin for referring me to this essay, and for her valuable insights concerning it.

[87] See *Türklerde Yazı Sanatı* 91, 92.

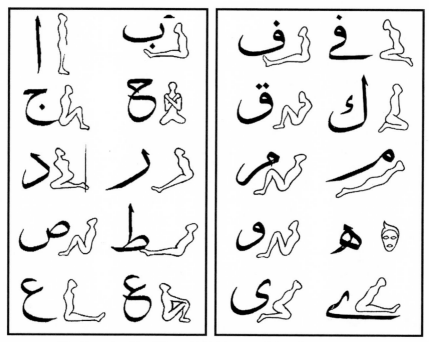

FIGURE 2.3 Chart transvisualizing Ottoman Turkish letters as human figures. *Source:* From Ismayil Hakkı Baltacıoğlu, *Türklerde Yazı Sanatı* (Ankara: Mars T. ve S. A. S. Matbaası, 1958), 91–92.

non-figurative representation of the human body, arranged in an expressive pose.[87] Baltacıoğlu pursued this project in various forms throughout a lengthy career, beginning with the publication of his first articles on "Islamic writing" in 1910.[88] With these charts at its center, and integrating portions of earlier essays published during the Young Turk and early Republican periods, *Türklerde Yazı Sanatı* might best be described as a layered mosaic of Turkish writing's temporalities, its disembodied letterforms serving as visual indexes of a Turkish national grammatology, as I have traced it here[89]—a "trace" or deferred interval between a voided interiority and a new exteriority produced in the cleansing of heterogeneous possibilities "outside in" a translative language.

Without doubt, any individual subject's experience of a "spooked" national language, in this sense, will be both profoundly singular and profoundly overdeter-

---

[88] Among others, Baltacıoğlu's articles on the history of calligraphy include "İslâm Yazıları" (1910); "İslâm Yazılarının Tarihçesi" (1911); "İslâm Yazılarının Tarihçesi 3- Sülüs Nevi" (1912); and "Türk Yazılarının Tetkikine Methal" (1927). Selections from these were also republished in Baltacıoğlu's 1934 book *Sanat* ("Art").

[89] Although elements of Baltacıoğlu's analysis do draw on an Islamic philosophy of writing and poetics, one must attend to the substantive nuances and modifications he introduced to it. It is spectralized, genderless, calisthenically "exercising" *modern* bodies that Baltacıoğlu sees in his humanized letters, for example—*not* the traditional figure(s) of a beloved. For more on *Türklerde Yazı Sanatı*, see my "Surrealism and Turkish Script Arts."

mined by the particularities of his or her gendered, ethnic, religious, and social identity. In the Turkish case, a Western-oriented elite of bureaucrats, military officials, and teachers reconciled itself with the foreignness of the new writing by embracing the discourse of official nationalism. At least for some, it was possible to *produce* an interiority within a fictively indigenous, always already Europeanized Turkishness. For the Muslim majority in the provinces, meanwhile, the resilient local and interpersonal grammar of Islam, which the politics of phonocentrism could not destroy, became the means for the reconstruction of an alternative identitarianism.[90] Coerced to acquire Turkish for participation in legally public life, ethnolinguistic and religious minorities retained their own languages in the private domain.[91] Though as Ahıska has put it, this "illicit," "surplus" interiority of provincial Muslims and ethnolinguistic and religious minorities has been ostentatiously discarded as the

---

[90] A good example is *Risale-i Nur* ("The Treatise of Light"), by Bediüzzaman Said Nursî (1873–1960), an Islamic philosopher of Kurdish descent who spent the later part of his life under state surveillance, either in prison or in forced exile in central and western Anatolia, after being charged with involvement in the 1925 Kurdish-Islamic rebellion led by the Nakşibendi Kurdish Sheik Said. Opposing the Kemalist "disestablishment of Islam," Nursî developed a new cultural-religious belief system for the Republic's alienated Muslim subjects, disseminated in his writings composed in Turkish using the Ottoman Turkish script. Breaking with classical Islamic scholarship as well as from the Sufist orders (both of which relied on the oral transmission of texts), Nursî used primarily written means of communication, eliminating the chain of authoritative reading in the recitational logocentrism of classical scholarship, while encouraging the study of his texts in small, intimate communities. Because the publication of his writings was forbidden, Nursî's manuscripts, produced during a long period of imprisonment and forced exile, were handcopied and distributed secretly by his followers, known as the *Nur postacıları*, or the "Nur postmen." Nursî's writings, which revealed a hybrid local and national, Islamic and phonocentric culture of writing, could be said to have served to restore a sense of normality to a disjointed present. Objectifying the *Risale*, by referring to it by its own title in the main body of his text and by identifying God as its ultimate source, Nursî constructed his own "authorship" as mere mediumship, displacing the textual authority of his own writing. Where Republican phonocentrism estranged and externalized the inner voice, then, the belief system of Islam can be said to have made possible the reunification of a fragmented self, in the reidentification of a linguistic outside as God. For an intellectual biography of Said Nursî, see Mardin's seminal *Religion and Social Change in Modern Turkey.* For an analysis of the Nur movement in the context of Turkish print culture throughout the twentieth century, see Yavuz, "Print-Based Islamic Discourse: The Nur Movement."

[91] For a useful introduction to the status of minorities in Turkey, see Oran, *Türkiye'de Azınlıklar.* The Lausanne Treaty of 1924, recognizing only non-Muslims (*gayrimüslimler*) as minorities (*ekalliyetler*), protects language, education, and religious rights. While it does not specify ethno-religious and language groups, it does include a clause granting "those of Turkish descent who speak other first languages than Turkish" the right to use their languages "orally in courts" (70). The language rights of all minorities in Turkey have been violated in different ways and degrees during the twentieth century. While traditionally recognized non-Muslim minorities (Armenians, Greeks, and Jews) were permitted to administer their own schools, many such schools closed during the Republican period in the face of constant interference by the Turkish state (69). Such other Christian communities as the Syriacs, Nasturians, and Yezidis were never recognized as minorities to begin with. Ethnolinguistic communities of Arabs, Kurds, Zaza, Circassians, Georgians, Laz, Romani, Albanians, Bosnians, and Bulgarians were all subjected to Turkification policies, adopting Turkish names, attending Turkish schools, and relinquishing all languages other than Turkish in the public domain. While Turkishness and the rights and privileges of full citizenship were open to non-Turkish Muslims willing to assimilate, those who resisted were targets of policies designed to assimilate them by force. After the 1925 and 1930 Kurdish rebellions, the state passed the 1927 Law Regarding the Transfer of Certain Individuals from Eastern Districts to Western Provinces (Bazı Eşhasın Şark Menatıkından Garp Vilayetlerine Nakillerine Dair Kanun), along with the Settlement Law (İskan Kanunu) of 1934 forcing selected Kurds to migrate to designated Turkish-populated areas for the sake of Turkish "linguistic, cultural, and racial unity" (Yıldız 252). I will return to the question of language rights in Chapter 4 and in my conclusion. On the Turkification policies of the Republican period, see Ahmet Yıldız, "*Ne Mutlu Türküm Diyebilene.*"

"garbage of history," it was in fact the very domain of the Republican everyday in which power struggles took place ("Türkiye'de" 23).[92] Unable, in the end, to destroy this illicit externalized interiority, Kemalism ruled Turkey by coding the extra-national as death, on the one hand, and negotiating with it, on the other. The reforms' most dangerous legacy lay in this continuous abstraction and bifurcation of the Republican everyday, an immense structural violence within which no prospect for the legal recognition of difference, in and for itself, could be imagined.

We might ask ourselves, then, where we can locate the institution of literature itself, on the Turkish Republican social landscape partitioned by the fetishism of appearances of a national language and the reciprocal identitarianism of a plurilingually divided social. Seyfeddin's writings show us that literature can quite easily and efficiently be colonized, instrumentalized, and incorporated into a regressive identitarianism; indeed, one might say that such "death" in colonization and instrumentalization is a possibility inherent in literature itself, understood as an internally *heterogeneous* institution. As the "institution of fiction which gives *in principle* the power to say everything, to break free of the rules, displace them, and thereby to institute, to invent" (Derrida, "This Strange" 37), however, literature is also that power to open a space of mediation between the abstract reality of a hollowed-out Turkish national legality and its ghostly remainders. With its legal illegality, it is literature that serves as a recognized and legitimate platform, "outside in" the social field of phonocentrism, for the spectralized Turkish subject to speak and respond in his own idiom to the "writing lessons" of the state. And literature teaches us that to the extent that in a heterogeneous social, such responses are countless and, indeed, irrepressible, the literature of the Republican period exhibits a linguistic and idiomatic plurality that exceeds and unbinds any totalizing frame. Ahmet Hamdi Tanpınar's Ottomanesque style, the polylingual Turkish of Peyami Safa, and the idiomatic, ventriloquial vernacular of Nâzım Hikmet Ran are elements of its substrate.

But as the works of the next authors I will discuss teach us, literature also offers another, equally important and absolutely singular promise, which must be affirmed as well. That is literature's power to reopen the translative and communicative travel of language, *without* appropriating the unknown origin of what "travels" in it. By convention, we assume that the voice of literature is an "author," forgetting that in writing fiction, an author willfully abstracts the authorial "I," assuming the voice of a narrator (or characters) who merely exist in language—who are *not* presences in an actual speaking situation. What speaks in fiction is an anonymous language "possessed" by no person and traceable to no fixed source. Literature is in this sense the practice of a non-possessive relation to language and the

---

[92] See also Meeker, *A Nation of Empire* 80–81. See also note 44. For a psychoanalytic analysis (oriented by the work of Žižek) of the production of the state in the Turkish public life of the 1990s, see Navaro-Yashin, *Faces of the State*.

promise of an alternative, non-identitarian connection to a "mother tongue." No doubt, the work that awaits to be done, in a divided Turkish context, is to rigorously conceptualize, and to then implement and institutionalize, a new *legal* framework for multilingualism, which might reverse a national grammatology drawing its power from death. And yet it is just as important to know that the very condition of possibility of such a heteronomous social common is, first and foremost, an affirmation of the otherness of language that does not demand its origin—in death, one's own death, or any other fixed "supplement."

PART TWO

Other Writings

Writing, the exigency of writing: no longer the writing that has always (through a necessity in no way avoidable) been in the service of the speech or thought that is called idealist (that is to say, moralizing), but rather the writing that through its own slowly liberated force (the aleatory force of absence) seems to devote itself solely to itself as something that remains without identity, and little by little brings forth possibilities that are entirely other: an anonymous, distracted, deferred, and dispersed way of being in relation, by which everything is brought into question—and first of all, the idea of God, of the Self, of the Subject, then of Truth, and the One, then finally the idea of the Book and the Work—so that this writing (understood in its enigmatic rigor), far from having the Book as its goal rather signals its end: a writing that could be said to be outside discourse, outside language.

—Maurice Blanchot, *The Infinite Conversation*

3

The Time Regulation Institute: Dwelling in a Mechanized Language

1. Tanpınar's Three Voices

A professor of nineteenth-century Turkish literature who also served as a member of the Turkish parliament from 1942 to 1946,[1] Ahmet Hamdi Tanpınar regarded the Republican language reforms as the most recent episode of a longer history of Westernization rooted in the nineteenth century. Critical of the diglossia of the "old civilization," in *Ondokuzuncu Asır Türk Edebiyatı Tarihi* as much as in individual articles such as "Türk Edebiyatı'nda Cereyanlar" (1959), Tanpınar took an affirmative position on mid-nineteenth-century simplification measures, as efforts to overcome a linguistically structured social divide between elite and common subjects of the empire. If as a self-identified "veteran Occidentalist,"[2] he considered such "renewal" a necessity, Tanpınar was also critical of *Tanzimat* reformers for introducing a cultural "duality" (*ikilik*) into Turkish spiritual life. For Tanpınar, the impossibility of catching up quickly with a "twenty-five-century [literary] inheritance of the Occidental civilization," combined with the weight of an "Oriental inheritance," had produced an unresolved "identity crisis" ("benlik buhranı") ("Türk Edebiyatı'nda" 105–106). Tanpınar saw the "unnecessary and extreme [*müfrit*] movements" of a "very young generation" as intensifying this identity crisis, pushing "renewal in language and nationalization to a level that could be considered a danger to the continuity that is the essence of national life [*millî hayat*] itself" (105).[3]

---

[1] For a brief biography of Tanpınar, see Enginün, *Günlüklerin* 19–48. The son of a *kadı* (judge), Tanpınar was born in 1901 in Istanbul, but passed his childhood and youth in Sinop, Kirkuk, and Mosul, among other cities. He lost his mother when he was thirteen. Studying literature at the Istanbul Darülfünun (University) between 1919 and 1923, Tanpınar was strongly influenced by the work and views of his mentor Yahya Kemal. After teaching high school in Erzurum, Konya, Ankara, and Istanbul between 1923 and 1933, he was appointed first to an instructorship at the Istanbul Fine Arts Academy (1933) and subsequently as professor of nineteenth-century Turkish literature at Istanbul University (1939). After failing in his bid for reelection as a Republican People's Party MP in 1946, Tanpınar was reappointed in 1949 as professor of "new Turkish literature" (*yeni Türk edebiyatı*) at Istanbul University, where he remained until his death in 1962.

[2] See Tanpınar's introduction to the second edition of *Beş Şehir* xii.

[3] Regarding Tanpınar's critique of the extremism of Republican language reforms, in his posthumously published diaries, see also Enginün, *Günlüklerin* 326.

Situated in literary-historical terms at the crossroads marked by Bergson, Valéry, and Mallarmé, on the one hand, and by Ottoman and modern Turkish poets such as Şeyh Galip, Ahmet Haşim, and Yahya Kemal,[4] on the other, Tanpınar's body of work can be read as an effort to overcome what he frequently called a "crisis" (*kriz*) in language. Tanpınar's model in this effort was his mentor Yahya Kemal [Beyatlı] (1884–1958), the most influential Turkish poet of the early twentieth century.[5] Kemal, whose poetic formation has been described as a "homecoming through the Frank," had lived in Paris between 1903 and 1912, absorbing the influence of a long line of European cultural figures including Mallarmé and José-Maria de Heredia.[6] The result of Kemal's engagement with Heredia's neoclassicism and Mallarmé's sound poetics was to have been taken back "home," in the composition of a new poetry in simplified Turkish using classical Ottoman poetic forms and meter (*aruz*). For Tanpınar, Kemal's work, its "purified language and the complete newness of its themes"[7] notwithstanding, represented the final "reunification of Turkish poetry with its great and authentic [*esaslı*] trajectories, after a fifty-year rupture" ("Türk Edebiyatı'nda" 112).

In elaborating his teacher's view that "national life is a synthesis . . . whose natural development should not be interfered with" (111), Tanpınar too pursued a project of articulating change *within* continuity. Where such influential early twentieth-century Turkists as Seyfeddin and Ziya Gökalp disowned the eclectic Ottomanism of the *Tanzimat* reforms, Tanpınar's *Ondokuzuncu Asır Türk Edebiyatı Tarihi* reclaimed this negated history, with all of its successes and failures, as part of a continuous historical development. Tanpınar's analysis of the language modes and techniques of nineteenth-century poets and prose writers is still an invaluable guide for new generations of readers ever further alienated from the history of Ottoman Turkish writing. The literary register Tanpınar developed for himself, meanwhile, which was fiercely criticized by his contemporaries for its "archaic" lexicon, ornate poeticisms, and Ottoman themes, stands today as a vital word-archive of a modern Turkish language in continually accelerating transition, during the second quarter of the twentieth century.

Celebrated today as an important articulation of "conservative modernism" in Turkey,[8] Tanpınar's writings reveal that suturing the Ottoman linguistic and literary-

---

[4]On Tanpınar's literary influences, see Tanpınar, "Antalyalı Genç Kıza Mektup" (often read as a literary-aesthetic manifesto).

[5]On Yahya Kemal, see my "Modernism Disfigured," in *The Oxford Handbook of Global Modernisms*, ed. Mark Wollaeger with Matt Eatough (Oxford University Press, 2012), 529–550.

[6]See Eyüboğlu, "Yeni Türk San'atkârı yahut Frenkten Türke Dönüş" ("The New Turkish Artist or the Return from the Frank to the Turk"). On Kemal's literary influences, see Yahya Kemal, *Çoçukluğum, Gençliğim, Siyâsî ve Edebî Hatıralarım* ("My Childhood, My Youth, My Literary and Political Memories," 1999) 108.

[7]"Purified language" here does *not* refer to the "pure Turkish" (*öz Türkçe*) of the reformers. Although when measured against the divan poetry of the past, Kemal's poetic register was considerably simplified, it included borrowings and compounds considered deviant from the official standard.

[8]The phrase "conservative modernism" describes the work and activities of Turkish Republican intellectuals "known for their 'conservatism' in politics," as Nazım İrem has put it, "and 'modernism' in their philosophical inspirations." While supportive of Turkish national independence, these intellectuals, including

historical past to the Republican present was no easy task. Nurdan Gürbilek's reading of *Beş Şehir* ("Five Cities," 1946), a book-length sequence of essays that Tanpınar dedicated to Yahya Kemal in the effort to "settle accounts and come to a mutual understanding with" the past (*Beş Şehir*, 2nd ed. x), has shown us that there is more than one Ahmet Hamdi Tanpınar, as it were, in Turkish literary history.[9] The modern Turkish writer who drew on the mythic modes common to German Romanticism used them to elicit, from the Seljuk and Ottoman imperial past, a vision of Turkish history as the evolution of a Turkish national spirit.[10] But the typically hybrid text of *Beş Şehir*[11] is nothing, in the end, if not what we might, following Gürbilek, call a staging of failed traditionalism. Here is this "other" Tanpınar, speaking in *Beş Şehir*'s Istanbul segment:

> I am running from one mirage to another. At every spring I run toward, mysterious faces reach out to me; lips I do not know, voices I do not recognize speak to me endlessly, in signals that I do not understand. When my soul moves away from their lips, I see that nothing has changed. Perhaps they are telling me about . . . their own hardships. "We were like you," they say, "you will not find the answers to your questions. The only real is the longing [*hasret*] inside you . . ." And to stoke this fire of longing, they make me encounter the overture of Ferahfeza, the song of Acemaşîran, Süleymaniye's white ship in twilight, or the cypress groves of Karacaahmed. They give me a pile [*yığın*] of names that resemble the broken marble pieces of Şerefâbâd's pools, these ready-made forms [*kalıp*] that I can fill with the longing inside me.[12] (*Beş Şehir* 215–216; *Beş Şehir* 2nd ed. 331–332)

Baltacıoğlu, Safa, and the philosopher and translator of Bergson Mustafa Şekip [Tunç] (1886–1958), turned to the "other West" of Romanticism, spiritualism, and Bergsonism in a critique of the materialism of the Turkish modernization project. İrem, who focuses mostly on intellectuals who offered explicitly theoretical interpretations of the Republican revolution, does not include Tanpınar among them—but my invocation of the phrase here is intended to include Tanpınar as well. See İrem, "Undercurrents of European Modernity and the Foundations of Modern Turkish Conservatism"; İrem, "Turkish Conservative Modernism"; and my "Modernism Disfigured." On Tanpınar's conservatism, see also the essays by Atay, Altınyıldız, Gürbilek, Ayvazoğlu, and Türkeş in the fifth volume of *Modern Türkiye'de Siyasî Düşünce*, devoted to Turkish conservatism (*muhafazakârlık*).

[9] See Gürbilek, "Kurumuş Pınar, Kör Ayna, Kayıp Şark." For an earlier Benjaminian reading of Tanpınar, see also Gürbilek, *Yer Değiştiren Gölge* 11–23.

[10] In Tanpınar's teleology, which inverts the mythical historicism of official nationalism, the Seljuk past is understood as comparable to the Gothic period of Europe, whereas the Ottoman period is a kind of golden age, the Turkish "Renaissance" (v). For an analysis of Tanpınar's concept of history, see Demiralp 59–74.

[11] As a sequence of essays combining the aesthetic modes of public historiography, private memoir, and fiction, into which cited verse (in one instance, one of Tanpınar's own poems) is periodically interpolated, *Beş Şehir* defies any straightforward generic classification. As a composite of the many different modes in which Tanpınar worked, during a long writing career, it is also in many ways a composite of Tanpınar's body of work at large.

[12] For an extended analysis of this passage and of what one might call the "soundscapes" of *Beş Şehir*, see my "Modernity and Its Fallen Languages." "Ferahfeza" and "Acemaşîran" are classical *makam* (modal) musical compositions; the allusion here is almost certainly to the renowned Ottoman classical composer İsmail Dede Efendi (1778–1846), whose work virtually becomes a protagonist in Tanpınar's novel *Huzur* (*A Mind at Peace*, 1949). The Süleymaniye Mosque, completed in 1558 for Sultan Suleiman I by the architect Mimar

Embodied in these mysterious faces, the historical past is overtly anthropomor-
phized here, acquiring human form and asserting the human behavior of speech.
But to read this passage carefully is to see that these faces are not in fact embodied,
but rather *dis*embodied, preceding or exceeding any settled and stable approximation of human form. The "faces" are mysterious: their lips are visible as they speak,
but their voices are strange, and what they say cannot be understood. Tanpınar's
self-conscious performance of a *failed* anthropomorphization, here, suggests something of the fundamental ambiguity of relating to the past, juxtaposing the past's
proximity and natural familiarity with its irreducible distance and difference.

It might be said that beginning from the interjection "Perhaps," the second
half of the passage develops this ambiguity even further. This drama of fictive
speaking can serve as something of an index to the special role played by the idea
of fiction in Tanpınar's work. Where we might say that writing in general, for
Tanpınar, consists in the reception (or receivership) of expelled "foreignized"
signs of the past, the interdiction, through which the faces "Perhaps" declare "We
were like you," conjures fiction as a *mediation* of such foreignized signs that is *not*
their "decoding." Throughout *Beş Şehir* and indeed, throughout Tanpınar's
body of work at large, proper names, those most talismanic of words, are invoked
as the carriers of the last remaining recognizable traces of the past, within a
language in transformation. If Tanpınar's historical and historiographic writing
can be said to seek to restore to these proper names their proper referents, his
fictions, which make proper names their very protagonists, testify to the futility of
any hope for a final settling of accounts with the past. We might say that "the
overture of Ferahfeza, the song of Acemaşîran, Süleymaniye's white ship in twilight, or the cypress groves of Karacaahmed" are markers of an indeterminate
excess that haunt Tanpınar's literary writing, doubling and assuming *improper*
lives in his poems and short stories, and perhaps especially in his novel *Huzur*
(1949; trans. *A Mind at Peace*, 2008).[13] Literature as such then serves not only to
interrupt official national grammatology, in Tanpınar's body of work as a whole,
but also to suspend the traditionalist identitarian agenda of Tanpınar's own literary criticism. Where it burns with desire for redemption in the modern present,
Tanpınar's work, partly despite and against that desire, simultaneously stages its
perpetual disappointment. It is in this sense that Tanpınar does indeed use more
than one voice.

Sinan, is prominently situated on a hill on the Golden Horn. Karacaahmed Cemetery is located in the Üsküdar
district of Istanbul; it is known for its centuries-old cypress groves. Şerefâbâd Palace, also in Üsküdar, was
constructed by Murad IV (1612–1640), demolished in 1794, and rebuilt several times subsequently.

[13] Set in 1939 on the eve of the Second World War, *A Mind at Peace* follows the relationships between four
characters: the protagonist Mümtaz, who is undergoing a spiritual crisis; his older cousin and mentor İhsan, a
figure for Tanpınar's own mentor Yahya Kemal; Mümtaz's former lover Nuran, trained in Ottoman classical
music; and the nihilist Suad, who stands for the moral bankruptcy of the Westernized Republican elite. That
portion of the novel focused on the relationship between Mümtaz and Nuran is particularly rich in the imagery
of the Ottoman past.

But even this second, non- or anti-identitarian fictive "other" voice tends to crack, at times, in Tanpınar's work. In place of the melancholic mediation of the foreignized signs of the past characterizing so much of Tanpınar's early literary work, his final novel *Saatleri Ayarlama Enstitüsü* (*The Time Regulation Institute*, trans. 2002), serialized in 1954 and published in book form in 1961, offers a comic-ironic pastiche, vastly different in tone and style from that earlier work, of scenes of writing that do not and cannot fill the "gaps" in language. Constructed as the autobiography of an anti-hero who introduces himself on the first page as an uneducated writer and reader, "a skipper of Arabic and Persian words" (9), *The Time Regulation Institute* capaciously records the deadly alienation of speech in a reformed language. Let me suggest that we cannot fully and most productively assess Tanpınar's engagement with the question of language without attending to the difference of this third, ironic voice. *The Time Regulation Institute,* I will argue here, is not only Tanpınar's most ambitious and comprehensive thematization of what I have called the "spectraliz-ing" Turkish language reforms; it also represents Tanpınar's fully coming to terms with the impossibility of overcoming an "inalienable alienation"[14] in language. This third ironic voice, in his work, might be said to countersign Tanpınar's oeuvre, re-nouncing such desire and affirming the uncanniness inherent in language.

The Time Regulation Institute records its protagonist's absurd and arbitrary entanglement in a project to create an official clock-setting institute charged with synchronizing all public and private time measurement in Turkey: a project whose doomed grandiosity is echoed in both the publication history and the critical recep-tion of *The Time Regulation Institute* itself, as a literary artifact. The transliteration to Latin orthography of Tanpınar's manuscript, handwritten in Ottoman Turkish script, for its 1954 serialization in the newspaper *Yeni İstanbul* was apparently such a daunting task that according to Tanpınar's student Turan Alptekin, *Yeni İstanbul*'s editor announced a proofreading competition to reward whoever tabulated the most errors in typesetting (70–71). The fact this competition ultimately produced no winner, because there proved to be too many undecidable cases (71), is some-thing of an echo of the strained comedy through which *The Time Regulation Insti-tute* enacts and embodies the irreducible difference inherent in writing. Like the books he reads by skipping its Arabic and Persian words, the life-text of Hayri İrdal, its protagonist, is written in a "cut" language of deadly mechanization, which fails to cohere in a sensible whole. And like the elements and ornaments modeled on Ottoman mosques and palaces designed for the institute's "new" building, at the novel's end, these "skipped" foreign words and proper names continually return to interrupt the modern present—not as symbols of the past with cult value, but as new use values by means of which Hayri İrdal finally forges an alternate future. If the alienated autobiographical narrator of *The Time Regulation Institute* serves as

---

[14] The phrase is Derrida's, in Derrida, *Monolingualism* 25; *Monolinguisme* 48.

a kind of guardian of the difference of the past, in this sense, it is not, in the end, for the sake of an impossible redemption, but for a new, "unhomely" way of dwelling in the arbitrary modern.[15] In the end, in programmatically reenacting such "other-writing" against its negation and suppression, *Time Regulation Institute* suggests that the break with a terrorizing grammatology comes in learning to affirm the irreducibly indeterminate otherness of one's own language.

If I foreground this embodiment of illegible writing, in *The Time Regulation Institute,* it is by way of suggesting that this novel is an important episode in the Republican settling of accounts with the history of nineteenth century Ottoman Turkish language and literature—a settling that is also an *un*settling of those accounts. Tanpınar fails to acknowledge Ekrem among his many literary and intellectual influences, assigning him in *Ondokuzuncu Asır Türk Edebiyatı Tarihi*—which is critical of Ekrem's "crippled poems" as failing to "enliven any of the fancies swarming in one's depth" (475)—a merely transitional role between the more significant generations of writers born in the 1840s and 1860s, respectively. Yet one might say that in many ways, in thus re-collecting the "crippled children" of the father figure of phonocentric Turkish writing, the Tanpınar of *The Time Regulation Institute* achieves the composition of a text left importantly unfinished, by Ekrem's Bihruz. If as Tanpınar was always careful to emphasize, we are *always* in debt to the past, it is arguable that the greatest debt of his own is not to his mentor Yahya Kemal, but to his own uncanny double in Ekrem, the "failed" or failing poet.

2. Autobiography as Thanatography

Divided into four segments, *The Time Regulation Institute* begins with the narrator's childhood years, during the final decade of the nineteenth century. (Hayri's birth date is given as 16 Rajab 1310, or 3 February 1893 in the Gregorian calendar.) In this section, entitled "Great Expectations," we meet the four figures who shape Hayri's character: the Istanbulite Abdüsselâm Bey, of Tunisian descent, patriarch of a Babelian Ottoman household including individuals from the four corners of the empire; the dervish-like watchmaker Nuri Efendi, who first instills in the narrator a love of clocks; the fabulist Seyit Lûtfullah, who first awakens the narrator's interest in occult and magic; and the Greek alchemist and pharmacist Aristidi Efendi, who dies in 1912 in a fire during an attempt to make gold. For the narrator, this cast of characters comprises an Ottoman past which he "can neither completely escape nor become fully part of" (55).[16]

---

[15] In this light, one might say that *The Time Regulation Institute* performs the double gesture of deconstruction as such: overturning the hierarchy between absence and presence, writing and speech, *and* displacing the ground of such opposition in a finally ironic counter-signature.

[16] In referring to this novel, I use the title of the English translation by Ender Gürol. However, all passages cited here are in my own translation, with citations corresponding to the 1961 Turkish edition.

The second segment, "Little Truths," tells the story of Hayri's adulthood, beginning with his integration, along with his first wife, into Abdüsselâm's household upon his return from fighting in the First World War in 1918. Following Abdüsselâm's death, a number of misunderstandings arise concerning the details of household property ownership, and Hayri is charged by Abdüsselâm's children with having stolen a diamond that belonged to their father. Diagnosed as mentally ill after a breakdown at his court hearing, Hayri is remanded to the judicial psychiatrist Doctor Ramiz for treatment. Following his release, Hayri takes a position as the secretary of the Spiritualism Society, whose members participate in séances together, as well as attending Dr. Ramiz's public lectures on psychoanalysis.

In the novel's third and longest segment, entitled "Towards Dawn," Hayri meets Halit Ayarcı (the surname means "setter"), who, impressed with Hayri's knowledge of clocks and of the Islamic philosophy of time, proposes the establishment in Istanbul of a Time Regulation or Clock-Setting Institute, which Hayri will serve as its assistant director.[17] Modeled on the *muvakkithane* or clock-rooms of mosque complexes devoted to the marking of prayer intervals by the transit of the sun, the Clock-Setting Institute will initially open its bureaus throughout Turkey. The ironic account given of all these plans, as the novel unfolds, points to the gap separating the ideality from the actuality of Republican reforms, in the staged dysfunctionality of an institution devoted to accelerating the modernization of a new nation and the modern automatization of its new national subjects.

In "Each Season Has Its End," the novel's final segment, a foreign delegation visits the institute, leaving unimpressed and puzzled. Three days later, Hayri and Halit Ayarcı receive a government order to dissolve the institute. *The Time Regulation Institute* concludes with the appointment of the institute's dismissed affiliates to a newly founded "Permanent Liquidation Committee" tasked with overseeing its dissolution.[18]

In Turkish criticism, this fourfold structure has served as a scaffold for reading *The Time Regulation Institute* as a satirical allegory of the transformation of modern Turkish society from the late nineteenth century to the mid-twentieth century.[19] While both considerable and useful in its own right, such critical consensus might be said to have developed partly at the expense of close attention to matters of language and modes of close or clos*er* reading. Right from the start, *The Time*

---

[17] From this point on, I will use the phrase "the Clock-Setting Institute," in my opinion a more accurate translation than "the Time Regulation Institute." No such institution existed during the Republican period. Note, however, that Islamic timekeeping was replaced in 1925 by the international European time and calendar measurement system.

[18] I discuss the novel's unpublished postscript later in this chapter.

[19] Kaplan read the novel's first section as an allegory of the absolutist reign of Abdülhamid II, its second section as an allegory of the end of the Young Turk period, and its third and fourth sections as allegories of the Republican period. See Kaplan, "Saatleri Ayarlama Enstitüsü." Moran's reading is similar, albeit with some modifications (297). Yet another allegorical reading of the novel is that of Ayvazoğlu; see Ayvazoğlu, "Saatleri."

Regulation Institute demands that we consider the discursive implications of Turkish linguistic modernization alongside, and in interaction with, their social facticity and historicity:

> Those who are acquainted with me know that I don't have much interest in the business of reading and writing. In fact, all that I have read—if we exclude the Jules Verne and Nick Carter stories I read in my childhood—consists of a few history books, which I glanced through while skipping over the Arabic and Persian words, and *The Tales of a Parrot* [*Tutinâme*], *The Thousand and One Nights*, and *The Tales of Abu Ali Sinâ*. Later, during my years of unemployment before the foundation of our institute, I also ran my eyes over the children's school books at home, and sometimes read brief articles and serial pieces at the Edirnekapı and Şehzadebaşı coffee-houses, where I was compelled to read [*hatme mecbur kaldığım*] the newspapers from cover to cover. (9)

We are introduced from the very start to a narrator who describes himself as a detached reader and writer with limited control over his own language. Unlike the melancholic narrator of *Beş Şehir,* who strives to resurrect the purged words of the linguistic and literary past, the narrator of *The Time Regulation Institute* has been conditioned (or conditioned himself) to "skip" them.[20] This is, in part, a reflection of the narrator's low level of education, limited to the popular tales of the Arabic, Persian, and Indian Islamic world. But in many ways, the "cut" language with which the novel thus opens is also a liminal figure for Turkish modernization, in its displacement of the Ottoman-Islamic discourse network preceding it. And it is a "cut" text that marks the fragmentation of Ottoman imperial culture in a later scene, when Abdüsselâm experiences the departure of his Bosnian, Bulgarian, and North African relatives after the Balkan Wars as the reading of "a text whose meaning is incomprehensible because its essential sentences were erased from its midst" (41). While this metaphor can be found in various forms throughout Tanpınar's work, its development in this instance is arguably something of a culmination, in so far as in the final analysis, *The Time Regulation Institute* must be said to preserve such "cut" text *in its incomprehensibility,* without filling in its missing parts in the end (or along the way).

We might say that this opening passage serves as a synecdoche for the body of *The Time Regulation Institute* as an iterative series of arbitrary metonymic structural signifiers. As the narrator moves us along, the marvelous mode of folktale narration

---

[20] The narrator's Turkish diction is constructed to mark him as more "old-fashioned" than *The Time Regulation Institute*'s other "super-westernized" figures. For example, in the passage just cited, he uses the Arabic loanword *mektep* instead of the *öz Türkçe* neologism *okul*. Other Arabic loanwords used in the passage include *hikâye* (story), *hattâ* (even, as in "in fact"), and *mütalâa* (reading). At the same time, however, the novel's writing plainly and purposefully abjures the signature Ottomanesque poeticisms of Tanpınar's principal literary style.

becomes progressively saturated with the absurd, and Abdüsselâm experiences the vanishing of the Ottoman world the way a reader approaches a fragmented text that seems to be missing sentences. First, Abdüsselâm, following an old household tradition, names Hayri's newborn daughter—but, while meaning to name her Zahide (the name of Hayri's mother), in fact mis-names her Zehra (Abdüsselâm's mother's name); of this slip in the signifying chain, Hayri observes that "the chain of disasters that followed one another began with this meaningless error" (89). Having thus mis-named the baby girl, an aging Abdüsselâm comes to confuse her with his dead mother and arranges to leave his inheritance to Zehra instead of his own children. In narrative time, the episodes encapsulating this inversion of the apparently natural reproductive order run parallel to events marking the establishment of the Turkish Republic. Implicitly, at least, this juxtaposition satirizes the revolutionary claim to historical priority, recoding that priority as a foundation of the absurd.

Momentarily interrupted by Hayri's corrective renunciation of Abdüsselâm's inheritance, the "chain of disasters" picks up again with an innocent lie Hayri tells one drunken evening, meaning to tease a friend who has been asking curious questions about Abdüsselâm's possessions (94). "All of a sudden, the vision of Seyit Lûtfullah passed in front of my eyes" (93), reminding Hayri of the tale of a "Şerbetçi diamond" Seyit Lûtfullah had told him when Hayri was a child. Hayri tells his friend that while he does not know for sure, it is possible that Abdüsselâm might have owned the "Şerbetçi diamond." Just as in glancing through the old history books and the children's books, Hayri consumes them indiscriminately and arbitrarily, when it comes to telling stories of his own, he mechanistically assembles elements of truth and fiction as they occur to him, virtually ensuring that his own stories will entrap him. Accused by Abdüsselâm's children of the theft of the (non-existent) diamond, he observes:

> I told you earlier that I'm an ignorant man. I spent my life learning words. In each phase of my life, I remade my own dictionary, by living it in my own life, in body and soul. The story of the Şerbetçi diamond taught me what we call the "absurd" [*abes*]. Until then, I had only known this absurd outside my life. Now it had become part of it. (176)

Other characters in *The Time Regulation Institute* tend either unselfconsciously to channel this absurdity, or to remain entirely unaffected by it. Nermin, one of the institute's appointed secretaries, is depicted as forgetful of what she says in every third sentence, jumping like a "sparrow" from one thought to another without any self-awareness (229). Hayri's second wife Pakize, meanwhile, forgetting the word "hammock" (*hamak*), invents a comical lie—that her husband sleeps naked on the floor—in order to cover it up (287). Hayri, by contrast, recognizes as "senseless" the chain of arbitrary signifiers that confront him; unable to cathect his own life-text, he experiences it as a radical split and division.

That the absurd is the only non-self-negating concept manipulated by Tanpınar, in *The Time Regulation Institute,* perhaps represents in itself the novel's final judgment on Turkish modernization. Still, we might say that what is also exposed, by Tanpınar's novel, is our own natural and unavoidable presumptuousness as its readers, in believing that language can be or might have been *dictated* in the very first place. Against the Republican fantasy that "cutting" a few words here and there is an act at once unavoidable and inconsequential, the autobiographical narrative of *The Time Regulation Institute* shows us how to live (and that it is impossible to live) in a thoroughly metonymic language in which "either nothing jibed, or everything was connected in the most surprising way" (140). For Hayri, this is no light human comedy, social or antisocial, but rather a being thrown into, and being caught in the cogs of, a deadly machine: "No matter what I did, I was caught up in its claws. I couldn't save myself from it. Wound up from the outside, the machine was following orders from the outside, now accelerating its speed, then decelerating, sometimes pausing. Once it stopped, neither its saw nor its knife operated. Fear quickly replaced agitation and torment at such a time" (176–177).

The machine is not another *thing,* here, so much as it is a metaphor for writing in the "cut" text of an arbitrarily ontological-reproductive national grammatology. For the reader of Arabic grammar books, the new language destroys any imagination of writing as human, exposing an arbitrary chain of signification that operates (if it "operates" at all) according to formal laws beyond human nature.[21] Unable to recognize himself in this inhuman writing, Hayri worries that he might be (or might have been) "beheaded" by it. Where a national grammatology, enacting the cathexis of life in the nation, recoded the old language as death, *The Time Regulation Institute* might be said to record the radical lifelessness of the compensation of the modern nation itself. Autobiography, here, becomes thanatography, and Hayri is really a recording device for an uninterruptible chain of mechanized language.

If as Zeynep Bayramoğlu has recently argued, *The Time Regulation Institute* is to be read as a novel of the uncanny, this is perhaps not (as she implies) because a catalog of the novel's thematic episodes and token objects (animate clocks, the magic of Seyit Lûtfullah, Hayri's dead aunt's resurrection, the visitations of Afroditi's aunt's spirit) can be mapped to Freud's catalog of tokens of the uncanny.[22] (Freud makes it clear that none of these tokens are sources of

---

[21] At the start of the novel, the narrator describes the introductory Arabic morphology and grammar texbooks *el-Emsile* and *el-Avamil* as the only books his father had approved him to read. Tanpınar's suggestion here evokes de Man's observation in "Excuses (*Confessions*)" that

> The machine is like the grammar of the text when it is isolated from its rhetoric, the merely formal element without which no text can be generated. There can be no use of language which is not, within a certain perspective thus radically formal, i.e. mechanical, no matter how deeply this aspect may be concealed by aesthetic, formalistic delusions. (294)

[22] See Bayramoğlu, *Huzursuz Huzur ve Tekinsiz Saatler* ("Discontent Contentedness and Uncanny Clocks," 2007).

uncanniness in themselves.) The uncanny, here, is best thought not as an object or a relation between objects, but rather as that death in mechanized language that annihilates Hayri as autobiographical narrator, unable to break the *repetition* of being caught in its "cogs."[23] In this mediation of a mechanized writing uncanny and out of bounds, Hayri's autobiographical narrative and the institutional history (such as it is) of the Clock-Setting Institute are entwined, with Hayri's "life" overflowing its autobiographical-narratorial frame and disseminating in the nation. Of the institute's founding moment, Hayri tells us, "It was born out of a few words. It resembled a fairy tale. I had told Halit Bey some things. Halit Bey had looked at the unsynchronized clocks around and remembered that he was unemployed. And others believed in him" (227). Naturally, when the institute is audited by the mayor of Istanbul, in Halit Ayarcı's "magical notebook" there is nothing to be found but "a series of numbers and a few majuscule letters" (239). The absence of any mimetic relationship between the institute's founding "text" and its referent marks its radical groundlessness as an institution—a groundlessness that spreads, like a cancer, to the institutional life of the nation at large and eventually, the entire world.[24] (After it is replicated first in six South American cities, and later in countries in the far and near East and Europe, the Clock-Setting Institute will provide a pretext for the establishment of an International Society of Clock Lovers [345]).

In planning the training of the institute's bureau employees, who will dress in uniform, "act like set clocks," and speak, smile, and pause at set intervals while delivering memorized speeches, Halit Ayarcı and Hayri speak of automatization as the "greatest strength and dependence [*zaaf*] of this century" (251). The task of the institute's employees is to extend and consolidate a new temporality, a series of atomized, isolate present moments as pure and exact repetitions, absent any historicity linking each to its antecedent:[25] a goal articulated by the vision of the one hundred secretaries of the institute working together in one room, "hitting the

---

[23] Hayri twice compares his life to "riding on a carousel" (291; 342), its dazzling spin describing the hyperbolic curve of language thrown *beyond* and at the same time, the parabolic curve of a language thrown *beside*.

[24] While Halit Ayarcı is marked as "the puppeteer who directs all in the direction he likes" (324), we need not reify him as the "origin" of the novel's absurdity, as some critical readers have done. It is not the puppeteer as a persona who in and of himself generates the dystopian bureaucratic anomie associated with the institute, but the textual machine that *animates* it. As de Man has put it, in "Aesthetic Formalization: Kleist's *Über das Marionettentheater*":

> The puppets have no motion by themselves but only in relation to the motions of the puppeteer, to whom they are connected by a system of lines and threads. All their aesthetic charm stems from the transformations undergone by the linear motion of the puppeteer as it becomes a dazzling display of curves and arabesques. By itself, the motion is devoid of any aesthetic interest or effect. The aesthetic power is located neither in the puppet nor in the puppeteer but in the text that spins itself between them. This text is the transformational system, the anamorphosis of the line as it twists and turns into the tropes of ellipses, parabola and hyperbole. Tropes are quantified systems of motion. (285)

[25] On the automatization of the subject and mechanization of time in Western Europe, see Benjamin, "On Some Motifs" 170–180; "Über einige Motive" 201–214.

same A and B keys on their typewriters simultaneously," under the leadership of a conductor (321). In describing this synchronized unity of a centralized secretariat, Halit Ayarcı uses the Persian loanword *yekpare*, meaning "of one piece." This is a word that Tanpınar used elsewhere to mark the indivisible time of the past, notably in the poem "Bursa'da Zaman" ("Time in Bursa"), included in the Bursa segment of *Beş Şehir* (1946): "The promise of victory, each name here / Day, hour, and season in a unified moment [*yekpare anda*] / Lives the magic of the past time" (105).[26] We can say that this Ottoman Turkish word, with its special significance in Tanpınar's poetic lexicon, endures in the disenchanted "dictionary" of *The Time Regulation Institute*, where it denotes the mere unity of the nation's perpetual present. Emptied of all interiority, capable only of reflex actions, the novel's spectralized automatons have liquidated their memories in this present. Hayri's second wife Pakize, an admirer of Hollywood actresses, is figured as the very type of the individual automaton (*otomat*), whose human sensibility has been thoroughly hollowed out by the new discipline: "Her face was taut, as at tense moments. It was the utter absence of humanity!" (290).

To be sure, Tanpınar holds no monopoly on the figuration of modern language as machine language. We have seen how at the conclusion of *Araba Sevdası,* an awakened Bihruz, who represents in himself the only glimmer of hope for a different future Ekrem seemed willing to grant, describes the way Bihruz has followed Perîveş, an "unpleasant form of the truth," as something done "against his will" (170; 444). We might say that the machine as an *implied* metaphor, in Ekrem's concluding vision of automatization, at the end of the nineteenth century, is rendered explicit and recurrent in the writings of the Republican intellectuals who lived through the language reforms. In *The Time Regulation Institute, everyone* is a Bihruz (or Bihruz is everyone), lacking any control over language whatsoever; in this respect, Tanpınar's novel can be said to significantly intensify the level of diagnostic abstraction Ekrem was able to bring to bear. In Tanpınar, we might say, mechanization has run its full course, and assumes modernity in its fullest aspect, in the deathlike subjective and social alienation of the modern national subject.[27]

---

[26] Bursa, the first capital of the Ottoman Empire, houses some of its earliest monuments. In *Beş Şehir*, Tanpınar describes Bursa as the place where he "learned what made the second, deeper time that is adjacent to the actual time" we live in (105). "Bursa'da Zaman" was published in 1941, 1943, 1944, and 1961, each time with minor revisions. Tanpınar omitted "Bursa'da Zaman" from the revised second edition of *Beş Şehir,* while the poem's 1961 edition substitutes the vernacular Turkish word *tek* (single) for *yekpare*. The line "*Yekpare, geniş bir anın*" ("Of a unified, vast moment") is a signature phrase of the poem "Ne İçindeyim Zamanın" ("Neither inside Time"), first published in 1933 in the literary journal *Varlık* and later republished as part of Tanpınar's 1961 collection *Şiirler* ("Poems"). "I'm neither inside time /" Tanpınar wrote, "Nor completely in its outside / In the indivisible flow / Of a unified, vast moment" (*Bütün Şiirleri* 19).

[27] Where as Derrida has put it in *Specters of Marx*, "the specter is a paradoxical incorporation, the becoming-body, a certain phenomenal and carnal form of the spirit" (*Specters* 5; *Spectres* 25), the automaton here stands for the emptying-out of life. While there is an ontological difference between spectrality and mechanicity, it is not a difference we can essentialize: automata can appear to be "alive," and each is a powerful metaphor of abstraction in any case.

3. The Language Politics of Irony

For a solution to the crisis of inauthenticity endemic to this modern Republican present, Tanpınar might have looked again to the Ottoman cultural past, as he had done in his earlier work. Instead, the Tanpınar of *The Time Regulation Institute* permits his novel to question the very *possibility* of cultural memory, in a new writing "reformed" with the goal precisely of foreclosing on memory. In this sense, the textual cut that launches *The Time Regulation Institute* on its way can be read as a symbolic registration of the problem of the "missing archive," as Meltem Ahıska has analyzed it.[28] Ahıska uses this phrase primarily to mark what she calls "the social insignificance of archives for [Turkish] national history" (11), made manifest in the neglectful mismanagement and careless destruction of archives; but we might well extend the range of the "missing archive" to mark that social indifference to the "archive" of cultural memory, in the broadest sense, that was programmatically *produced* by the language reforms. The register of truth effaced in the destruction of public archives is marked by "dark holes . . . that can only be apprehended as lifeless and meaningless signs of an absent past" (24), and that *other* register of truth, in the private narratives of memory confined to "the intimacy of private places" (24), can only partially make up for this loss. Unrecognized by and discordant with official history, the private register cannot free the imprisoned specters of the past, cannot license the imagination and construction of another future.

In marked contrast with Tanpınar's earlier work, *The Time Regulation Institute* refuses the possibility of communicating with the specters of the past even in this private register. Throughout the novel's second segment, during which Hayri works as the secretary and treasurer of the Spiritualism Society, the Genoese-Greek character Afroditi receives messages from her dead Italian aunt in a mixture of Italian, Greek, French, and Turkish (159), urging her to claim her inheritance in Italy. We might say that a mechanized language produces its own occultism here, in "possessing" a multilingual-multiethnic subject, dictating to her the effaced signs of her own past, embodied in an inheritance.[29] The narrative momentum of this episode seems crafted to mark the *closure* of the communication channel between spirit and the medium: after Afroditi and her mother, having returned to Italy to claim the inheritance, return to Istanbul, their adopted home, against the spectral aunt's wishes, the Italian aunt ceases appearing to Afroditi altogether (161). Another medium named Sabriye, meanwhile, regards "the other world . . . merely [as] an extension of this one" (167). "The spirits who spoke through her mouth," Hayri observes of Sabriye, "preferred to be occupied with ordinary worldly business" (169). According to Hayri, "if a caller [*operatör*] were to listen to Sabriye Hanım respond to the

---

[28] See Ahıska, "Occidentalism and Registers of Truth."
[29] This scene effectively thematizes the "loss" of Ottoman multireligious and multilingual heterogeneity outside a Turkish Muslim context. In Safa's *Matmazel Noraliya'nın Koltuğu* (as we will see in the following chapter), the legacy of this multilingual past moves to the center of literary concern.

question of the purification [*tasfiye*] of spirits, instead of the medium Hüsnü Bey, the son of an old Kadiri dervish," he'd hear about the dissolution [*tasfiye*] of a company instead of the metaphysics of spiritual cleansing (169).

To the extent that *The Time Regulation Institute* posits an emptied temporality, absent the weight of any history, when questions of origin do disrupt this "perpetual present," the response is to promptly and unceremoniously reconstruct a "past" by substituting arbitrary new truths for all missing originals. During the novel's third segment, Halit Ayarcı conscripts a reluctant Hayri for the composition of a fictional biography of a seventeenth-century clockmaker, to be entitled *The Life and Work of Sheik Ahmet Zamanî*.[30] In due course Hayri overcomes his initial resistance to this project, eventually pursuing it to the point of altering the public archives housed at the Nuruosmaniye Library, interpolating into the description of manuscript collections the name and works of Sheik Ahmet Zamanî as an invented personality (297). Though we might certainly read this episode, among many others, as part of the novel's satirical critique of the Republican effacement and fabrication of public memory, the truth is that the relationship between putative fact and verifiable or unverifiable fiction, here, is in fact far more volatile than such a reflective critical approach can permit. Reporting on criticism of the biography upon its completion, Hayri observes:

> Unfortunately, despite the friendly enthusiasm of the environment, a few scholars sought to discredit the proposition. . . . If I were in the same mindset as I was when I had first started writing this work, I would have been pleased with all the criticism. "My God! I would have said, thank you. . . . They are not accepting the lie. . . ." Unfortunately, I had changed. During the six months of working on this book, I had internalized Halit Ayarcı's discipline in a way that made it hard for me to accept every objection easily. . . . Besides which, I grew to like Ahmet Zamanî Efendi. . . . In one word, I was living what Halit Ayarcı called relativism [*izafîlik*], if that is the right word, as truth [*hakikat*] in my very own life. (298)

Above and beyond accepting that which he initially resisted, Hayri exceeds it in the *irony* of a reluctant fiction-writing through which he "even grew to like Ahmet Zamanî Efendi."

Frustrated as he was by such doublings or splittings and other inconsistencies, Moran faced the difficulty of classifying *The Time Regulation Institute* as social satire, the effects of which depend on normative values held in common by writer and reader (320). Rather than taking such confusion of critical designation as a

---

[30] For another reading of this scene, see Feldman, "Time" 56. Feldman suggests that the fabrication of Ahmet Zamanî's life serves as a metaphor for a contemporary Islamist historical discourse denying or deemphasizing "the lack of congruence between the intellectual development of Ottoman Turkey and contemporaneous Europe, so evident to the generation who had lived through the 1908 Constitution or the Republican revolution" (56). This conclusion strikes one as somewhat tendentious: neither science nor clock-making were unknown to the Ottomans, and *The Time Regulation Institute* explicitly affirms an older practice of time-keeping, through the nonironized figure of Nuri Efendi, the inspiration for Hayri's love of clocks.

lamentable index of "confusion" in the artifact itself, we might well see that disruption as the source of *The Time Regulation Institute*'s literary subtlety and strength.[31] *The Time Regulation Institute* teaches us that modernity is indifferent to its own discrediting or disestablishment as what Hayri calls "a serialized [*tefrika*] lie" (264). Like his predecessor Ekrem, Tanpınar is profoundly self-conscious of the impossibility of closing or overcoming a false order of appearance merely by diagnosing the fetishism of appearances in the modern nation. In Hayri's contiguously reluctant *and* excessive investment in the fictional life and work of Sheik Ahmet Zamanî, and in the refraction of that investment in a critical discourse devoted to eliciting satirical or otherwise reflective meaning from the literary artifact, questions of truth and lie, authenticity and inauthenticity are irresolvable by appeal to misperceptions of reality correctible by changes of perspective, or similar means. Rather, they index the structural determination of reality *produced* as appearance, within the frame of, and by means of, a radically arbitrary writing.[32] As what might be called a critique of "the constitution of the *appearance in objectivity*,"[33] *The Time Regulation Institute* demands a critical reading fully informed by the history and theory of the logic of modern representation, in the broadest sense of that term.

Nor can the revelation of the arbitrary logic of a modern society of appearance in itself overcome the facticity of linguistic mediation. As I argued in this book's Introduction, *all* writing practices, including those of Ottoman Turkish institutions and social formations, are necessarily mediated and mediating, and therefore "inauthentic" in relation to any ideal of immediacy. If Hayri is to be taken as an internally split narrator who thus doubly negates and ironizes his own writing, that is best understood not as a characterological inconsistency producing unwarrantable confusion in the reading experience, but as a statement, embodied in narrative, of the impossibility of *ever* assuming in language the indivisible voice implied by solicitous criticism. If there is a strategy embodied in the deployment of irony, here, it is one guided by that non-assimilating verisimilitude through which, as Paul de Man put it, "irony comes closer to the pattern of factual experience and recaptures some of the factitiousness of human existence as a succession of isolated moments lived by a divided self" ("The Rhetoric of Temporality" 226).

There is perhaps no claim for and of the self in language that is not inherently ironic, posited and claimed with the pronoun and designation "I," yet legible (to

---

[31] In "Unset *Saat*s, Upset *Sıhhat*s: A Fatherless Approach to *The Clock-Setting Institute*" (discussed below), Süha Oğuzertem makes a similar point.

[32] On the production of reality as appearance, see Marx, *Capital* 1 163–177; for a reading of "the necessity of appearances" in Marx, see Balibar, *The Philosophy of Marx* 60–62. If I foreground language as a constitutive medium, here, that is because I believe *The Time Regulation Institute* itself asks us to do precisely that. This is not to imply, however, that the linguistic organization of reality operates independently of the formation of economic value.

[33] See Balibar, *Philosophy* 61.

oneself, as much as to others) only in so far as it is already a repetition of itself. Only that which is the same, and repeatable *as* the same, can be recognized. At the same time, repetition itself ensures that such a self never in fact fully coincides with itself, in a repetition producing a pure, continuous self-presence; rather, because each repetition is separated from its own "past" and "future" iterations by a temporal gap—by a gap that "is" temporality, if temporality "is" anything—repetition is *also* variation. The interval of temporality in repetition is at once the very condition of possibility of repeatability of any "I" *as* the repeated same, and its ironizing as unavoidable variation.

Where writing understood as "self-presencing" must suppress the divisibility marked by this interval, in positing (by power of sheer fiat) a continuous and self-succeeding self, ironic writing is that writing *foregrounding* temporality as interruption—staging a duel, as it were, between irreconcilable selves.[34] In *The Time Regulation Institute*, these two selves are marked by the Hayri who remarks and resists the absurdity of the perpetual present in which he lives, and the Hayri who is automatically incorporated into it—not in the least "against his will," but with a will that pushes its logic to its limit (in addition to the biography of Ahmet Zamanî Efendi, Hayri fabricates official histories of the Clock-Setting Institute, devises a system of punishment to be applied to the owners of unsynchronized clocks, and cheats on his wife). In each of the clashes between these two selves through which Tanpınar's novel drives itself forward, the Hayri demanded by writing understood as "self-presencing" dies a little death. And while this "staging," in writing, of Hayri's internal divisibility does *not* in fact demand that we relinquish all hope of exit, so to speak, from a modernity of complete and total automation, it *does* tell us that the vehicle for any such exit cannot be an immortal authenticity. *The Time Regulation Institute* shows us that no intervention into a deadly grammatology is possible if we do not first fully come to terms with the *inherent* inauthenticity of writing.

By recourse to the de Man of "The Rhetoric of Temporality" (one with motives that diverge from my own appeals to that essay, here) Süha Oğuzertem has

---

[34] As de Man put it, in "The Rhetoric of Temporality":

> The ironic, twofold self . . . seems able to come into being only at the expense of his empirical self, falling (or rising) from a state of mystified adjustment into the knowledge of his mystification. The ironic language splits the subject into an empirical self that exists in a state of inauthenticity and a self that exists only in the form of a language that asserts the knowledge of this inauthenticity. (214)

In "The Concept of Irony," originally delivered as a lecture at Ohio State University on 4 April 1977, de Man publicly corrected his thought in "The Rhetoric of Temporality," resisting its reduction of irony to a dialectic of the self (170). "There is no narration without reflection," he observed self-critically, "no narrative without dialectic, and what irony disrupts (according to Friedrich Schlegel) is precisely that dialectic and that reflexivity, the tropes" (181). Still, rather than straightforwardly accepting de Man's imputation of a schism to his own work here, we might read that gesture itself as one of a continuity in self-interruption and its own critical mode. The impossibility of reconciling the fictional with the real, in the first essay, implies that the subject, continuously facing self-dissolution, is trapped in a language that is "a text machine, an implacable determination and a total arbitrariness," as de Man put it later ("Concept" 181).

suggested the futility of any critical reading of *The Time Regulation Institute* that insists on its divergence from Tanpınar's earlier lyrical works. Such assumptions are perhaps one driver of a brief, yet clustered critical history of receiving *The Time Regulation Institute* as a break with the poetic thematizations of the past in Tanpınar's earlier work.[35] For we might say that while the melancholic allegories of *Beş Şehir* and the presentist ironies of *The Time Regulation Institute* certainly differ (as de Man put it) in "mood and structure," together they register something of the same "fundamental experience" of time in mechanized writing (de Man, "Rhetoric" 226). Where the narrator of *Beş Şehir* narrativized the gap between sign and signified as an allegorical fall from an idealized anteriority, Hayri as the narrator of *The Time Regulation Institute* experiences that gap as an instantaneous fall. In both of these configurations, we witness the modern subject confronting the inauthenticity that is endemic to modernity.

Following de Man still further, one might add that if the genre of the novel is in some ways defined by a "truly perverse" temporal-historical schism, in "using both the narrative duration of the diachronic allegory and the instantaneity of the narrative present" (226–227), this itself serves to articulate both the taxonomic problem in criticism of *The Time Regulation Institute* and a reason to fall back on "the novel" as its designated class descriptor. To dwell on the taxonomic problem is to consider the extent to which mechanized writing, in serving as a structure of repetition undermining the *same* in the event of repeating it, gives us the paradox of what de Man named the "allegory of irony," in the "permanent parabasis" of a "novel of novels": that which disables the unavoidably determinatively stabilizing critical impulse itself, even as it rearticulates it again (228). The characterological "duel" that unfolds between Hayri and his benefactor Halit Ayarcı, in *The Time Regulation Institute,* is in this sense not a critically stabilized version of the schismatic duel between Hayri's two selves, as I have described it, so much as it is an (is *another*) iteration. Halit's orchestration of an automatized society and Hayri's resistance to that automatization are not clarified opposites, that is to say, so much as they are mirror images of each other (at one point, Halit tells Hayri, "You are my most beautiful mirror!" [341]). In the entirely iterative, rather than critical distance between these two distinct protagonists, we find an *ironic* distance between temporally iterated selves in general (something that was echoed in Tanpınar's own multiple *authorial* personae[36]).

---

[35] Bayramoğlu reads this "cacophonous" text as an expression of Tanpınar's despair, contrasting it with *A Mind at Peace*, in which a synthesis of the cultural schism of the new Turkish nation is still possible. Bayramoğlu suggests that the structural organization of *A Mind at Peace* reflects the sequencing of Beethoven's String Quartet Opus 132 in A Minor, balanced by the form of the Ottoman composer Dede Efendi's Ferahfeza hymn (183).

[36] The recent publication of Tanpınar's diaries, recording his critique of Ottoman culture (Enginün 274) and his resentment of his mentor Yahya Kemal (280, 308) have done much to discredit the prevailing myth of Tanpınar as a traditionalist, while his support of the violent 1960 military coup (213–214, 305) made it difficult for liberal readers to grapple with his politics. In this light, one might well read Tanpınar's final novel as a kind

Oğuzertem's reading of *The Time Regulation Institute* turns on the novel's
unpublished postscript (omitted from the original edition, as well as subsequent
editions), in which Hayri is marked as a paranoiac and, we are told, dies in the
course of treatment at Dr. Ramiz's clinic. Oğuzertem argues that far from representing a break with Tanpınar's earlier work, the "existential intrapsychic drama"
of *The Time Regulation Institute,* indexed by this postscript but ignored in much of
the Turkish criticism on Tanpınar to date (by 1995), marks its continuity with
Tanpınar's earlier treatments of "themes of imaginary and disillusioned love"
(3–4). Oğuzertem goes so far as to suggest that a properly psychoanalytic reading
of the "symbols and doubles" (6) constituting what he calls *The Time Regulation
Institute*'s "private language" will reveal its utter inhospitability to the schism
between an implicitly or self-evidently true world and a world of deception and
falsity, on which social satire relies. In Oğuzertem's decoding of this "private
language," *The Time Regulation Institute* is really the allegory of an "impossible,
ill-fated, narcissistic love" (14), and the novel's *ironies* "attack" not a concealed
truth or a remediable injustice, but "versions of the narrator-protagonist's self"
(15), in a dynamic preventing the conclusive judgment of narrator by reader (critical or otherwise). "When both self and other are alternately and similarly negated,"
Oğuzertem concludes, "what needs to be abandoned, together with satire and the
ethical universe it implies, is the model that requires separate selves to be in relationships. That model will not help us comprehend . . . the specific nature of its
irony that has chaotic effects" (16).

One can recognize and affirm the value of this sensitive reading of *The Time
Regulation Institute* (and of its intervention into Tanpınar criticism) without obscuring the risk taken with the psychoanalytic approach, which might be said to
reproduce, at another level, the very segregation of aesthetico-philosophical from
socio-historical interpretive critical modes that it problematizes and seeks to
deconstruct. The reverse reification of the literary text, in this reading, as an aesthetic object situated at a psychoanalytically determined remove from a nonetheless quite specific Turkish historical context might be said to leave unanswered the
important question begged by the conclusion of Oğuzertem's reading, concerning
the *unmodified* application of the concepts of European psychoanalysis to Turkish
literature.[37] On the one hand, for better or for worse, Tanpınar's novel is anchored
and focused by particular episodes and events in a very specific history; on the other
hand, emerging both "actually" and fictively in the interval opened by a "cut"

---

of parabasis of the narration of his diaries. For a review of the diaries in their published form, see İğrek,
"Hangi Tanpınar?" ("Which Tanpınar?"). For statements (both affirmative and dismissive) by prominent Turk-
ish intellectuals regarding the significance of these diaries in Tanpınar's oeuvre, see "Günlüklerin Işığında
Tanpınar'ı Değerlendirdiler."

[37] Freud has a definite place as an influence in Tanpınar's work, and I am not in the least rejecting the value
of psychoanalytic discourse and concepts, for any sensitive reading of *The Time Regulation Institute* in particular. My point here is that such a reading must *also* integrate some of the depth of Tanpınar's unmistakable
ironization of psychoanalysis itself. The relation between Hayri, sent to Ramiz for treatment by a judge at Hayri's

writing, *The Time Regulation Institute* erases the typological and taxonomic contour segregating aesthetic fiction from historical reality. Where a programmatically reformed language must confine a freely communicable and translatable *fiction* in a separate domain, to guard against its contamination of the invented real, Tanpınar's novel takes its own license to fiction, exposing the stakes of such control and repeating the work of freedom.

If as Oğuzertem persuasively suggests, the unpublished postscript is cardinal to a truly thoughtful reading of *The Time Regulation Institute,* that importance lies perhaps not in the postscript's "revelation" of Hayri's mental illness (a literary fact of which we cannot be certain, in any case), in itself, but in its demonstration of the utter irreconcilability of the gap between the fictive and the real, the literary-aesthetic and the socio-historical. Presented in the form of a letter from Halit Ayarcı to Dr. Ramiz, the postscript represents on the one hand a kind of terminal irony, discreditably resituating the entire "novel" preceding it as the unreliable narrative of a paranoiac (Hayri), a mad text that Halit Ayarcı receives by mail from Dr. Ramiz. And it is on the other hand an *interminable* irony, an irony that necessarily ironizes itself, in so far as irony's resituation of the conditions and terms of discourse, as much as its effects, never in fact *settles* anything. "I'm not suggesting," Halit Ayarcı writes to Dr. Ramiz in his letter, "that I have been unaffected by the reflection of my radically transformed personality in this mirror. I might go even further and say that I've gradually begun to suspect myself. Who knows, if I had the opportunity . . ."[38] (Alptekin 69).

For reasons that are unclear, Tanpınar dictated the postscript to his student and assistant Turan Alptekin, who subsequently published it in his 1975 book *Bir Kültür, Bir İnsan.*[39] Moran suggested that dictation may have been hoped to provide plausible deniability of its implied critique of the Republican reforms, in the event that Tanpınar were to face trouble with the authorities (321).[40] Given that *The Time Regulation Institute* contains allusions to such prominent members of Tanpınar's

---

trial for the "theft" of the Şerbetçi diamond, is the mark of an epistemic divide: Ramiz, the European-educated Freudian, treats his patient in an ultra-orthodox fashion, in what we might call a translation-in-mistranslation of psychoanalytic practice as a temporizing contemporary form of European modernity. (At its extreme, Ramiz's militant Freudianism drives him to *order* Hayri to have a dream manifesting the codified symptoms of the Oedipus complex [117].) It is hard to miss the chain of effects (including such tics as cleaning his nails obsessively with a pocket knife, wiping his hands with alcohol, and incessantly locking and unlocking his briefcase) that recast the *analyst,* here, as the neurotic (116). At this level, *The Time Regulation Institute* quite plainly asks us to ask ourselves a larger critical question regarding the direct "translatability" of European psychoanalysis, in this particular historical form, into a Turkish context, without any historical mediation. The writings of Frantz Fanon serve as just one guide to such critical engagement, in an extra-European theater of operations.

[38] Ellipsis as in the original.

[39] *Bir Kültür, Bir İnsan: Ahmet Hamdi Tanpınar ve Edebiyatımıza Bakışlar* was revised and republished in 2001 under the title *Ahmet Hamdi Tanpınar: Bir Kültür, Bir İnsan.*

[40] According to Enginün and Kerman, Tanpınar composed the postscript while revising the serialized version for book publication (269). A diary entry on 19 March 1961 indicates that Tanpınar wished to revise the serialized version (268), but the plan for doing so never fully materialized. Tanpınar nowhere states clearly why he dictated the postscript.

circle as Peyami Safa and the poet and psychologist Sabri Esat Siyavuşgil (Alptekin 71), it is also possible that the postscript was conceived as a way of neutralizing the force of parody. Either way, one might well read this highly ambiguous and ambivalent "disclaimer" of a postscript not as negating or resolving, but as extending the "duel" between Hayri's two selves—and taking them as it were beyond the covers of the book. The imputation of "necessity" to this thoroughly supplemental document serves in any case only to underscore the struggle of ironic knowledge against mechanized writing: its discrediting of Hayri as "mad" is nothing if not a rearticulation and reinforcement of the madness of the social "real," itself, which like the novel's innumerable automatons, cannot see itself critically in its fictional double. In preventing the distinction between reality and fiction, truth and lie, politics and aesthetics, irony itself prevents us from successfully reading Tanpınar's novel, either critically or uncritically, as a self-enclosed literary object or "self."

4. Dwelling in a Mechanized Language

If I have described *The Time Regulation Institute*'s self-representation as fiction, that is not by way of marking it as a kind of "play," but rather as directly engaged with the problem of linguistic and literary modernity. Writing, in *The Time Regulation Institute,* is never a merely and universally neutral and value-free tool for communication; rather, in the specific historicity of its historical context, it is profoundly constitutive of a new reality programmatically organized as a modern national Turkish order of appearance. Though this novel's thoroughgoing irony provides us with a continuous reregistration and rerepresentation of the *emptiness* of that order of appearance, we find in it no entertainment of illusions about the resolution of inauthenticity, either through modernist ideology critique or Ottomanist nostalgia. In this section, I will suggest that it is only *after* Hayri reconciles with writing's inherent inauthenticity that the novel offers a figure for an impure, yet critically interruptive alternative writing. At this level, Tanpınar's enactment of an uncanny writing also offers something of a commentary on, and lesson for, the comparative literary-critical methodology engaging *The Time Regulation Institute* itself.

We might take note, to start, of the final textual affirmation contained in the last chapter of *The Time Regulation Institute,* as Hayri and his estranged son Ahmet, who normally keeps his distance from the Clock-Setting Institute, collaboratively design the institute's new building. This project is, in one sense, another manifestation of the absurdity of machine writing. When Hayri, charged by Halit Ayarcı with overseeing the design of the Clock-Setting Institute's new building, opens a national competition inviting new, "original" designs, he ironizes Halit Ayarcı's own wishes, amending the competition announcement to demand models "representative of the name and function of the institution" on both the interior and exterior of the building (346). Unable to find anyone able or willing to undertake the challenge of designing a building whose interior *and* exterior both resemble a clock, Hayri decides to design the new building himself with the help of Ahmet.

This endeavor is narrated in a discrete episode (346–357). "Work," Hayri tells us, "cleanses and beautifies humans, makes one oneself, relates one in many different ways to one's surroundings . . . However meaningless and absurd it may be, a man who takes the responsibility of a job cannot escape it, becomes its prisoner" (353). What we might call the active cathexis of the absurd, here, in full "knowledge" of its absurdity, does not necessarily entail unquestioning submission to the "fatality" of mechanized writing; fatality, in this instance, does not *oppose* the chance at play in the absurd, so much as it signals the very possibility of difference.[41] Each absurd "throw" of oneself into the machine of modernity and mechanized writing is *also* an ironic fall in which there inheres the possibility of a break with the order of appearance and the possibility of a different future, despite and against all failures of precedent (a possibility figured, for example, in the reunion of Hayri with his estranged son[42]).

As a figure of an alternative practice of writing, in this sense, the imagined building stands for the possibility of *active dwelling* in the uncanny and unhomely modern. Where the narrator of *Beş Şehir* wants, impossibly, to reconstruct the lost Şerefâbâd Palace from its broken fragments, the narrator of *The Time Regulation Institute* articulates the broken pieces of the past in and toward something we might want to call assemblage. In the end, Hayri decides to model the building on the shape and structure of an old wall clock inherited from his own father and named "Mübarek" (351); in hope of inspiration as to where to place the hour and minute hands, in his design, he visits the major mosques of Istanbul, Bursa, and Konya, finding what he is looking for only in a small, unidentified Istanbul mosque (352). Confronting the problem posed by an exceptionally long hallway, he decides to divide it with a railing resembling one marking the graveyard of a demolished Kahvecibaşı Mosque (354). This ruin of a railing, which Hayri had stolen from the site to sell during his years of unemployment (and later bought back after seeing it by chance in an antique shop), finds its place in the new building of the Clock-Setting Institute (55–56). He models the four glass pillars representing morning, noon, evening, and night on the minarets of the Üç Şerefeli Mosque in Edirne, built in the fifteenth century and named for its unique minaret embellished with three galleries (355). However, where separate staircases leading to each of these three galleries would make it difficult for a muezzin ascending to one gallery to see another, in the Clock-Setting Institute's building, the pillars' glass-windowed exterior permits complete visibility (355).

As a figure of writing, this aggregative incorporation of heterogeneous elements from different sources must be distinguished from the composition of the

---

[41] On repetition as difference, see Deleuze, *Nietzsche and Philosophy.*

[42] Noting that Ahmet is one of the only nonironized characters in *The Time Regulation Institute,* Moran reads this father-son collaboration as a figure for a new ethics of work (and as such, as Tanpınar's solution to the crises of modernization) (321–322).

invented biography of Sheik Ahmet Zamanî, on the one hand, and the melancholic writing of *Beş Şehir,* on the other. While this "text" is also inauthentic, in its citational reconstruction of the past, it is not a *complete* fabrication, as is *The Life and Work of Sheik Ahmet Zamanî.* Here, we might say that the names of the past *do* return to "haunt" the modern writing of the present, as forms of indigestible or unincorporable difference. No longer invested with the desire to force or to reconstitute a "lost" totality, however, the apparently stiff and lifeless fragments composing the nontotality of the building's design in fact mark the possibility of a new future—one come from the past, yet no longer captivated strictly by a fantasy of redemption. One might say that here Hayri acts as a "foreignizing" translator, in the sense defined by Carol Jacobs's interpretive translation of a canonical passage from Walter Benjamin's essay "Die Aufgabe des Übersetzers" ("The Task of the Translator," 1923):

> Just as fragments of a vessel, in order to be articulated together, must follow one another in the smallest detail but need not resemble one another, so, instead of making itself similar to the meaning [*Sinn*] of the original, the translation must rather, lovingly and in detail, in its own language, form itself according to the manner of meaning [*Art des Meinens*] of the original, to make both recognizable as the broken parts of a greater language, just as fragments are the broken parts of a vessel. (Benjamin, qtd. and trans. by Jacobs, in "The Monstrosity of Translation" 762)[43]

For Benjamin, in Jacobs's interlinguistic translation, the *Bruchstücke* of the vessel are isolate "broken parts" of a nonwhole, rather than fragments of a preexisting, potentially restorable whole—intervals in an interminable and interminably discontinuous and discordant "monstrous" translation. In like manner, we might say, the nonintegrably heterogeneous design of the building for the Clock-Setting Institute stands for a monstrous translative writing, reassembling the broken parts of the

---

[43] For the German original, see Benjamin, "Aufgabe" 59. Jacobs is revising and correcting Harry Zohn's translation of the same passage in Benjamin's essay. Jacobs suggests that the more literal translation makes it plainer that for Benjamin, "the final outcome of translation is still a 'broken part'," a *Bruchstück* (Jacobs 763), rather than any "organic growth, kinship, sameness, and fidelity" (762), and that this distinction turns on Benjamin's distinction of "what is meant [*das Gemeinte*] from the manner of meaning [*die Art des Meinens*] in the intention" (Benjamin, qtd. in Jacobs 760). "The manner of meaning," here, refers to the logic of differentiation constitutive of meaning, which makes *what* is meant by the German "Brot" and the French "pain" the same, while their "manners" of meaning remain distinct. The task of the translator, for Jacobs's Benjamin, is to point, from within the repetitious difference of the target language, to the differential interval or spacing that is the very condition of possibility for meaning in the source. As de Man put it in "Conclusions: Walter Benjamin's 'The Task of the Translator'," in a commentary on and elaboration of Jacobs's argument:

> Zohn said, "fragments of a vessel which are to be glued together must match one another in the smallest detail." Benjamin said, translated by Carol Jacobs word by word: "fragments of a vessel, in order to be *articulated* together," which is much better than *glued* together, which has a totally irrelevant concreteness—"must *follow* one another in the smallest detail"—which is not at all the same as *match* one another. What is already present in this difference is that we have *folgen,* not *gleichen,* not to match. We have a metonymic, a successive pattern, in which things follow, rather than a metaphorical unifying pattern in which things become one by resemblance. (43)

foreignized past, in the modern present, without erasing their singularly heterological difference as such. The future that *The Time Regulation Institute* risks affirming, in this heterology, is a future offering no transcendental assurance, no stable ground of any kind whatsoever: a future of neither cult value, nor exchange value as such, but of *new use values* to be used in "building" a future. Tanpınar shows us how to construct a dwelling, so to speak, in a language doubly foreignized, without simultaneously masking or suppressing its originary "unhomeliness."

The building's interior represents Hayri's final affirmation of the nonsubjective interiority, nonrecuperable by analogy to the consciousness of a self, that is opened up by an arbitrary metonymic writing. Responding to Doctor Ramiz, who worries about Hayri's lack of experience in architectural design, Hayri observes that the idea of a stairless floor really originated from Ramiz's own descriptions of the psyche as such (362). Absurd and unnatural in the architecturally pragmatic sense marked by a normative "dwelling," such assemblage, Hayri insists, nevertheless "makes one oneself" (353). Counterposed with the total evacuation of organic interiority from such automaton-figures as Pakize, the "depth" of the clock building is simultaneously a depth without bottom and a perfectly superficial exteriority. The stratification of different floors, each of which is merely a form of exterior, points to both the endless production of meaning, and the lack of any absolute foundation in a mechanized writing.[44] The final affirmation of *The Time Regulation Institute,* as I suggest it asks to be read, unravels the very binary opposition it sets up between living human and dead machine. As a figurative institution housed in a figured building, the Clock-Setting Institute is finally also a figure for a kind of subjective interiority produced *within* and *by* a machine.

Reacting to what are, in the end, externally placed stairs connecting the floors from the outside, one newspaper commentator on the building's design invokes the inverted word order of a transposed sentence (*devrik cümle*): "Precisely at a time when the practice of new syntax began in Turkish, the new architecture also bore its fruits. What will the enemies of transposed sentences do in the face of Hayri İrdal's success?" (361). We might say that Tanpınar's transposed writing completes the text left unfinished by Bihruz, interrupting a phonocentric-representational order of appearances without simultaneously generating a competing logocentric-identitarian agenda. We are offered an alternative "dictionary" in the new syntax of this transposed life-writing, comprised of the cut symbols of the Ottoman past and affirmed

---

[44] In "A Note Upon the 'Mystic Writing Pad'," Freud proposed a children's writing toy (a wax slab with two cover sheets made of transparent celluloid and translucent waxed paper, respectively), as a model for the double system of memory as "an ever-ready receptive surface" retaining "permanent traces of the inscriptions that have been made on it" (228). Freud likens the removable cover sheets to the psychic layer of consciousness, which receives stimuli without itself retaining them, and the wax slab to an unconscious psychic layer behind or beneath it. Derrida observed that this analogy "joins the two empirical certainties by which we are constituted: infinite depth in the implication of meaning, in the unlimited envelopment of the present, and, simultaneously, the pellicular essence of being, the absolute absence of any foundation" ("Freud and the Scene of Writing" 224).

as inauthentic. In the palimpsest of this dictionary, Tanpınar's beloved *yekpare*, the Persian word meaning "of a single piece," neither denotes only a unified past, nor only a disenchanted perpetual present. Rather, it stands for the aggregation of different temporal fragments in anticipation of a new future.

To be sure, the novel's conclusion signals a deep uncertainty regarding the real distribution of the will required for such an affirmation. Hayri and Ahmet form a minority in relation to the thoughtless majority membership of the Clock-Setting Institute, who are in it for financial and other material gain, and who form the core of its "Permanent Liquidation Committee," in the end. It is clear that Tanpınar distrusted his contemporaries, whom he did not expect to engage the challenge of modernity in any depth, or even to face it openly. My reading of affirmation from self-alienation in writing, in *The Time Regulation Institute,* is also shaped and limited by the ethnically homogeneous masculine social continuity marked by Hayri and Ahmet's reunion as estranged father and son, *as* the very pretext of unhomely dwelling in the modern. Contemporary critical treatment of this novel nonetheless continues to ignore the challenge it poses to those who make Tanpınar's name a token of Turkish identitarianism, today, in the attempt to carve a home out of globalization.[45] If the "message" of what I have called Tanpınar's other-writing is in fact lost, in a space between the Westernizing and traditionalist Turkish identitarianisms organizing his place in literary history, then we might also imagine the inevitable disintegration of such literary-critical interiorities, as much as the social interiorities the novel contests and conditionally reconstructs, as holding open the possibility of an alternative reading.

---

[45] One symptom of this development is the resurgence of critical and popular interest in Tanpınar that followed the recent republication of many of his works by Yapı Kredi Yayınları, a publishing house owned and controlled by Yapı Kredi, the oldest private bank in Turkey. In 2000, YKY approached the Dergâh publishing house, which has a traditionalist academic focus and retains publishing rights to Tanpınar's works on the basis of a contract with Tanpınar's brother and executor Kenan Tanpınar, with a proposal for republishing a selection of Tanpınar's work that Dergâh refused. YKY meanwhile offered a separate rights contract to Kenan Tanpınar's adopted daughter and legal heir Meliha Büyükçelebi, which she signed. The suit subsequently filed by Dergâh against YKY, which had already begun printing the new editions, eventually went to the Turkish Supreme Court, which ruled in Dergâh's favor in 2005. For a more detailed account of this episode, see Öztürk.

4

Safa's Translation and Its Remainders

"If I were to lay end to end all the lines I've written for the defense of Turkish since the day I took a pen in my hands, it would be longer than the railway line between Istanbul and Ankara," observed the journalist, novelist, and critic Peyami Safa (1899–1961) in an article in the daily *Cumhuriyet* entitled "İlk Basamak" ("First Step") and dated 30 March 1940 (55).[1] Despite his highly regarded literary talent, Safa was a consistently controversial figure among his contemporaries on both the political right and the political left. After flirting with socialism in his bohemian youth and dedicating his 1930 novel *Dokuzuncu Hariciye Koğuşu* ("The Ninth Surgical Ward") to his friend Nâzım Hikmet, Safa had by the mid-1930s embraced a political conservatism that decisively severed all links to the left. The arguably over-studied 1931 novel *Fatih-Harbiye* frames Turkish modernization as an East-West conflict and reconciles it in favor of what Safa considered the East (its title links the traditional Istanbul neighborhood of Fatih to the more gentrified Harbiye). Safa's *Türk İnkılâbına Bakışlar* (*Reflections on the Turkish Revolution*, trans. 1999), published in 1938 following travel in Europe during 1936, is a theoretical treatise offering a conservative culturalist interpretation of the Turkish Republican revolution. In this book, Safa amended his general position in *Fatih-Harbiye*, coming out in favor of the Kemalist modernization measures. At the same time, he warned his Turkish readers of the spiritual crisis that had been generated by extreme rationalization in Europe, suggesting a synthesis of "European science" with "Oriental intuition" (177).[2] Concurrent with the rise of fascist sympathies in Turkey, the 1940s

---

[1] For a biography of Safa, see Ayvazoğlu, *Peyami*.

[2] In his 1958 introduction to the second edition of *Türk İnkılâbına Bakışlar*, Safa revealed that the "writing discipline" of 1938 had forced him to "restrain his thought" in some ways (5). While he stood behind his earlier arguments, Safa edited out from the first edition his praise of Atatürk and the passages outlining a program for the Republican People's Party. For a useful differentiation of Safa's "traditionalist conservatism" from "religious reactionism" and "modernist radicalism," see İrem, "Kemalist Modernizm ve Türk Gelenekçi-Muhafazakârlığın Kökenleri." İrem argues that Safa's *Türk İnkılâbına Bakışlar* does not oppose the Kemalist

produced a move further to the political right, with Safa defending a corporate nationalism against liberal individualism on the one hand and against socialist internationalism on the other.[3] Known for his interest in spiritualism and parapsychology during this decade, Safa was ironized in Tanpınar's *The Time Regulation Institute* as a "social hygienist" advocating a program of spirit mediumship (to be administered by the novel's Spiritualism Society) as moral cleansing (*Saatleri* 172).[4]

If Tanpınar found his former friend too "ill-tempered," "calculating," and "egoistical to let any belief system take root in himself," he was willing to affirm Safa's "struggle with the new language" (Enginün 306). As the author of more than 120 newspaper articles on the language question, posthumously collected in a book entitled *Osmanlıca Türkçe Uydurmaca* ("Ottoman, Turkish, and Fake-ish," 1970), Safa shared Tanpınar's critique of the Republican break with the Ottoman literary past, arguing for parallel instruction of the "Latin-letter generation" in "Arabic letters" for the sake of cultural continuity.[5] Safa repeatedly emphasized that the complete linguistic purification of Turkish was a practical impossibility, and while he welcomed those Turkish neologisms of which he approved—*oy* (vote) in place of the Arabic *rey*, *bölge* (district) in place of the Arabic *mıntaka* (*Osmanlıca* 134), *iyimser* in place of the Persian *nikbin* (optimist) and *kötümser* in place of the Persian *bedbin* (pessimist) (227)—he defended the retention of other Arabic and Persian loanwords (*hâtıra*, memory; *medeniyet*, civilization; *rüya*, dream) that he saw as *mots justes*, superior to the neologisms proposed to replace them (228). If Safa reserved for the state the right to intervene in language to assist its development (116), he thought that such intervention ought to be guided by the literati, who approached language spiritually rather than mechanically (125). In the words Safa used as the title of an article dated 25 September 1943, "language is not made but created" (123). The gradual cultivation of language by proper literary judgment, Safa argued, would also limit the vulgarization of the written register by colloquial idiom—the goal of linguistic nationalism being to elevate, not to sink to the cultural level of the commoner (27, 148).

---

revolution, but rather reinterprets and legitimizes it, in an alternative traditionalist-modernist idiom. For further development of this argument, see İrem, "Undercurrents of European Modernity."

[3] Turkey remained neutral during the Second World War, officially declaring war on Germany on 23 February 1945 in order (as Zürcher puts it) "to qualify as a founding member of the United Nations" (Zürcher 205). Pan-Turkism regained some of its popularity in Turkey during the German invasion of the Soviet Union. On Safa's corporate nationalism, see his 1943 *Millet ve İnsan*. While Safa clearly distinguished Turkish nationalism from German and Italian nationalism, respectively, his corporate nationalism has a symmetrically authoritarian cast.

[4] See Alptekin 71. In a journal entry dated 16 June 1961 following Safa's death, Tanpınar expressed a clearly personal dislike for Safa (Enginün 306–307). Alptekin notes that following Safa's son's death in February 1961, Tanpınar cut from the book extensive material ridiculing Safa (29).

[5] Articles critical of the alphabet reform include "Arap Harfleri" ("Arabic Letters"), published in *Cumhuriyet* on 24 January 1940 and "Arap ve Lâtin Harfleri" ("Arabic and Latin Letters"), published in *Tercüman* on 9 July 1959. In the course of his career, Safa was consistently critical of the alphabet reform, with the notable exception of a remark in *Türk İnkılâbına Bakışlar* affirming the "nationalist" and "modernist" pedigree of the reforms in general (91–94). For Safa's privately critical reaction to the alphabet reform as relayed by the friends in his inner circle, see Ayvazoğlu, *Peyami* 96–97.

If Safa, like Tanpınar, had strong reservations regarding the intentions as well as the execution of the language reforms, he was a more vocal participant in the lexicon, orthography, grammar, and terminology debates of the mid-1930s and 1940s.[6] Describing grammar as "the sole police force against the murders committed in the language of a country" (78), Safa served as a member of the Grammar Commission that met in July 1941 under the supervision of the Ministry of Education to settle the principles of Turkish grammar for school instruction.[7] Along with the newspaper and the grammar textbook, Safa used the novel as a medium for the safeguarding of Turkish against "bandits shooting at" its body (78). One of his less-studied works, *Matmazel Noraliya'nın Koltuğu* ("Mademoiselle Noralia's Armchair"), first conceived in 1944[8] and published in 1949, is especially noteworthy in this respect.

Constructed as a *Bildungsroman* tracking the development of its protagonist from modern nihilist to corporate spiritualist-nationalist, *Matmazel Noraliya'nın Koltuğu* is a strong literary representation of Safa's interests in parapsychology and mysticism during the 1940s, and much of the criticism dealing with this particular novel addresses itself to that theme. For this or for other reasons, the novel's highly ambitious thematization of what Safa elsewhere called "language anarchy" has been neglected.[9] But we can hardly take this as a sublimated element of *Matmazel Noraliya'nın Koltuğu,* given the remarkable scene of breakdown of meaning with which the novel begins:

> Ferit, Ferid, **it, id, t, d**, not **t** but **d**, phonetic, phonetic, and his father's laughter; then his mother, indistinguishable behind whichever tree hid her in the darkness of a forest, was screaming painfully with a sound of green, orange, and then red flame, a sound that was coming from the wide mouth of a lute [*saz*] in the shape of a trumpet [*borazan*] into which a shadow

---

[6] As an attendee of the First Language Congress in 1932, Safa also participated in the fifth and the sixth congresses, held in November 1945 and December 1949 respectively. Elected to the governing committee at the seventh congress in July 1954, he was expelled from the Language Society after the 1960 military coup (Ayvazoğlu, *Peyami* 98).

[7] 1940 marks the publication of the first official comprehensive grammar handbook of the Republican period, prepared by Tahsin Banguoğlu and entitled *Ana Hatlarile Türk Grameri* ("Outlines of the Turkish Grammar"). Because in the 1930s the Language Society had prioritized purifying the lexicon, the first grammar studies undertaken by the society had focused on defining rules for the invention of neologisms and the compilation of a more comprehensive handbook was deferred (Levend 418). At the July 1941 meeting, Banguoğlu's handbook was approved with recommendations for revision. Safa's account of this meeting can be found in his "Türk Gramerinin Esasları." Grammar books Safa authored include *Okul Grameri Elkitabı* ("Handbook of School Grammar," 1941–1942) and *Türkçe İzahlı Fransız Grameri* ("French Grammar with Turkish Explanations," 1948).

[8] On 1944 as the novel's starting date, see Ayvazoğlu 414.

[9] The phrase "language anarchy" appears a number of times in Safa's work. See, for example, "Allahım, Bu Ne Anarşidir!" (My God, What Anarchy!"). On the skillful manipulation of free indirect discourse in *Matmazel Noraliya'nın Koltuğu*, see Moran 237–258. For a study placing this novel in context of Safa's body of literary work at large, see Tekin, *Romancı Yönüyle Peyami Safa* 221–249. Tekin notes each character's identification in the novel with a distinct speaking style and lexicon, arguing that this stylization is an element of the novel's realism (39–40). For a study comparing *Matmazel Noraliya'nın Koltuğu* to Herman Hesse's *Der Steppenwolf*, see Kınış. Kınış briefly discusses linguistic alienation in the case of super-westernized Turkish characters (104–105), though the primary focus of his comparative study is the novel's embrace of spirituality and mysticism as antidotes to modern alienation.

resembling a monkey was blowing. The trumpet and the monkey disappeared. Then as the forest disappeared along with the maternity of the sound, a shadow resembling a train passed speedily without generating any mechanical noise, and the scream this time ascended from the chimney of the locomotive as yellow-black smoke.

With the violent shaking of his feet, everything went dark. Only the scream, unconnected to any shape, lasted through the foggy depth filled with light spots. (7)[10]

Narrating part of a dream, this passage finds the protagonist Ferit, a medical school drop-out and later a drop-out from a university philosophy department, taking up residence at an inexpensive lodging house in Istanbul, sometime during the 1940s. As much as anything else, we might say that the sentence "Ferit, Ferid, **it, id, t, d**, not **t** but **d**, phonetic, phonetic" registers from the very outset, here, the extreme linguistic chaos generated by the reforms. When Ferit's father calls out to his son, Ferit's name begins to disintegrate and double: the Arabic "Ferid" (meaning "unique" or "incomparable") yielding to the reformed Turkish "Ferit." This transformation from "Feri*d*" to "Feri*t*" may seem a small thing, but the fact is that in thus sounding out Ferit's new name, breaking it apart into atomized syllables, the father's voice creates an ugly new association: "it," the particle split off from Ferit's name, is in Turkish a pejorative colloquialism meaning "dog."[11] "There is no phonetic in today's spelling" (17), Ferit recalls his father saying later in the novel, to emphasize that the new, reformed orthography, intended to match the spoken Turkish language precisely, in truth distorts it profoundly.

But the breakdown of meaningful communication is not merely a semantic event in *Matmazel Noraliya'nın Koltuğu*. Rather, the failure to name, in a newly "lawless" language, is nothing less than a failure to reproduce the social order. Ferit's father, whose calling out to his son sets off this initial disintegration, is associated with the hedonism of a carefree lifestyle, taking the law lightly (for much of the novel, his whereabouts are unknown). Ferit's mother, introduced as a "half artistic, half mad, horny . . . cocaine addict" (56) who died from tuberculosis, appears in the dream-scene immediately after Ferit's father, not as a stabilizing or grounding maternal figure, but as an intensifier of linguistic alienation. An uncanny figure of a lost origin, Ferit's mother is consumed, in the dream-scene, by the leap into modernity spanning nature and civilization, her disappearance into the technological modernity of a "shadow resembling a train" leaving us with only a disowned scream "unconnected to any shape."

---

[10] Boldface text follows the formatting of the original text.
[11] Words of Turkish origin do not end with the voiced consonants *b, d, g,* and *c.* In spelling words of Arabic origin with terminal voiced consonants, final voiced consonants were replaced by the unvoiced consonants *p, t, k,* and *ç,* "to make orthography as phonetic as possible": thus *Mehmed* became *Mehmet, Ferid* became *Ferit, kitab* became *kitap,* and so on. See Dilaçar, "Atatürk ve Yazım" 315–316.

In beginning with this disembodied and indeterminate *cry* that is neither a human voice, nor a recognizable and categorizable nonhuman sound, Safa's novel begins with the failure of meaningful language to *originate*. Implicitly, it asks us if and how we can ever restore a meaningful order of signification, after such "originary" loss. Where Tanpınar had turned to the Ottoman past for the restoration of lost meaning, Safa here sets his sights on the renovated institution of unified national communicability. While this does not override Safa's genuine and general concern, in his work, about the consequences of the cultural amnesia produced by breaking with the past, it does seem that the resistance of a resilient linguistic heterogeneity, in the present, to the establishment of a working common language eventually posed a more urgent problem. We could say that *Matmazel Noraliya'nın Koltuğu* takes as its central literary problematic the fact that not only do the multiethnic and multireligious populations inherited from the Ottoman Empire speak languages other than Turkish, but vernacular Turkish itself differs from one region to another in pronunciation, vocabulary, and other aspects of both idiomatic and regionally common usage. In alarm, Safa's novel registers a real skepticism regarding the prospects for success of the project to homogenize this linguistic multiplicity by making the Istanbul vernacular the norm and standard of measure.[12]

Larded with French medical and psychoanalytic terminology, Arabic prayer words, archaic Ottoman Turkish grammatical constructions, and Kurdish borrowings, the linguistic texture of *Matmazel Noraliya'nın Koltuğu* is that of a fragmented and mechanized Turkish, neither fully generative nor fully able to circulate meaning. To describe this Turkish as "mechanized" is to emphasize the way Safa codes unregulated language as nonspiritual, lacking an indispensable "spirit." For Safa, no familial, social, or moral order can successfully be upheld in a state of linguistic anarchy, in which words as designators and enactors of bodily desire are able to circulate freely. The larger goal of *Matmazel Noraliya'nın Koltuğu* as a novel is in this respect profoundly restorative: to overcome linguistic fragmentation and mechanization in the constitution of a new transcendent order of signification. But this would be to sell Safa's ambition somewhat short: it would be more accurate to say that Safa's main concern, here, is not merely to recuperate the lost communicative function of language from fragmentation, but to positively *augment* it, in a new transcendence enacted in the nationalization and Islamicization of ethnic and religious difference. Here, normalizing the linguistic body means restoring it to divine potential, through the translative writing of gendered ethnic and religious minorities who willingly convert to Islam and assume a Turkish national identity.

In what follows, I will explore Safa's concerted effort to suppress the heteroglossia of Turkish in the literary construction of *Matmazel Noraliya'nın Koltuğu*.

---

[12] In a 1959 article entitled "Bölge Dilleri ve Ortak Dil" ("Regional Languages and Common Language"), Safa wrote that a "common language [*la langue commune*]" is established by the victory of one regional language over others (*Osmanlıca* 244). In the Turkish case, he suggests, the Istanbul dialect had won that battle. Published ten years earlier, *Matmazel Noraliya'nın Koltuğu* can be read as Safa's staging of such language "wars," then ongoing, in the attempt to help establish a "common" language.

Where my reading will emphasize the failures of Safa's various attempts at domesticating translation, that is by way of affirming them *as failures*, within which the incipient resilience of a heteronomous linguistic common can be glimpsed. The fact is that despite and against Safa's efforts to take linguistic control into his own hands, in this work, his translations always seem to leave behind remainders that evade any complete assimilation into a national common. *Matmazel Noraliya'nın Koltuğu* makes valuable reading, I would suggest, not only as a kind of account (or accounting) of the history of Turkish linguistic nationalization, but also as a record of the defiance of literary *author*ity by language itself. By the end of this novel, notwithstanding its author's intention, the uncanny language with which it opens and presents itself is every bit as *disowned* as ever.

1. Safa's Writing Machine

The protagonist Ferit, who describes himself as "désenchanté, démesuré, désorienté, déraciné, dégénéré," seeks a room at a lodging house (56). Having lost his mother, and with the whereabouts of his father unknown, Ferit maintains contact only with his younger sister, who lives with an aunt they despise. The lodging house clientele is composed of odd characters, and there seems always to be something mysterious going on. Ferit's next-door neighbors are a poor family with an aphonic daughter named Zehra, who can see into the future. The housemaid Fatma, an emigrant from rural eastern Turkey, continuously mourns the loss of her beloved in a traffic accident, imagining his ghost visiting her in her sleep. At night, a nude female sleepwalker, whose identity remains ambiguous, makes unexpected appearances to various guests, while the Armenian photographer Karnik cautiously follows her around, attempting to photograph her. The novel's first segment concludes with the intensification of Ferit's spiritual crisis as he and his lover Selma part ways after a fierce argument.

In the novel's second segment, Ferit and his sister receive an inheritance upon their aunt's death, moving into a summer home on the island of Büyükada in Istanbul that was once owned by the Mademoiselle Noralia of the novel's title.[13] At this point, it is a Greek Christian housekeeper, Fotika, who relates Noralia's life story. Born to a Muslim Turkish father and a Christian Italian mother sometime during the 1870s, Mademoiselle Noralia is a figure for the conflict of modernization structured by a binary opposition of East to West. By some accounts, we learn, she had

---

[13] Safa makes use of his experience as a writer of crime fiction, adding another important storyline. Tosun, who lives across from Ferit, turns out to be a serial killer. He kills Ferit's aunt Necmiye, who was withholding Ferit's and his sister's share of the money that they had inherited from their mother. While I will not discuss this narrative thread here, it would be worthwhile to note the institution of order in the novel through murder and theft. For further information, as well as a bibliography of Safa's crime fiction, see Üyepazarcı, *"Korkmayınız Mr. Sherlock Holmes": Türkiye'de Yayınlanmış Çeviri ve Telif Polisiye Romanlar Üzerine Bir İnceleme (1881–1928)* ("'Don't Be Afraid Mr. Sherlock Holmes': A Study of Translated and Original Crime Fiction Published in Turkey (1881–1928)").

changed her name from Noralia to Nuriye, upon converting to Islam. Noralia serves also as a double of Selma, Ferit's lover, who as the daughter of a *dönme* stands for ethnic and religious impurity.[14] At the summer home, Ferit's own mystical visions continue, but rather than evoking terror and paranoia, as before, his encounters with Noralia's spirit help him restore his faith in God and attain a state of spiritual enlightenment. *Matmazel Noraliya'nın Koltuğu* ends with Ferit's and Selma's reunion, in a scene invoking both the Turkish nationalization and the cultural and religious Islamicization of the non-Muslim. This closing scene gathers in all the sexual, spiritual, and social deviancy staged by the novel's first segment, incorporating and overcoming it, in the end, in the restitution of a reproductive heteronormativity.

The lodging house, in which most of the novel's first segment is set, is a microcosm of a mixed populace, rich in linguistic layers and a kind of continuous play with the formal qualities of words. Proper names are atomized into machinic nonsense: Vafi, the name of the housekeeper, moves through an arbitrary chain of rhyming associations—"Nafi, Safi, or more accurately Vafi" [12]—while Baha, who lives in the room next to Ferit, becomes "Babuş." Babuş's mother's Eda is called by the abbreviated form of her first name, "Adalet" (an Arabic loanword meaning justice) (31). It is not only Ferit who suffers a language disorder: Babuş's sister Zehra is aphonic, and Babuş himself has difficulties with reading. Attempting to read the newspaper out loud, he stutters, fragmenting words into syllables: "Ita . . . Italya . . . har . . . Harbe . . . gi. .girdi. .[. . .] an . . . angol. . anglo. . sa.sakson. basın. basınında . . . [. . .] tah . . . tahlili . . . tahlilinden. Amca, tahlil ne demek?" ("Ita . . . Italy . . . ent . . . entered . . . the . . . wa . . . War. . [. . .] in. . an . . . angol. . anglo. . sa.saxon. media . . . the. . ana. .analysis. . of. Uncle, what does analysis mean?" 49).[15] These word-globules, fairly oozing from Babuş's mouth, emphasize the estranging materiality of the language he is trying to read and speak.

One could cite many other examples of such atomized names and failures of reading. But the disassembling of proper names at the level of syllable and letter is far from the only manifestation of alienation through language in the novel. Employing a variety of different kinds of narrative discourse, Safa's novel registers

---

[14] *Dönme* is a word used by Muslim Turks to refer to the descendants of seventeenth-century Ottoman Jews who converted from Judaism to Islam, following the Messiah Rabbi Shabbatai Tzevi, who converted and became Aziz Mehmed Efendi. Until the 1924 population exchange between Turkey and Greece, which brought them to Republican Turkey, the *dönme* population was concentrated in the Ottoman city of Salonica. Considered apostates by orthodox Jews and crypto-Jews by Muslim Turks, the *dönme* are historical targets of Turkish hostility and discrimination. Marc David Baer notes that the early Republican period was for the most part a period of willing assimilation for Turkish *dönme*, to which the introduction of a discriminatory wealth tax (*Varlık Vergisi*) between 1942 and 1944 did significant damage (228). Justified as a tax on the wealth of war profiteers, it was applied as a tool of division, targeting Christians, Jews, and *dönme* with punitive rates. Muslims of *dönme* origin were charged a rate that was "twice as much as Muslims, yet half as much as Christians and Jews" (231). Quoting Turkish government figures, Baer observes that "Muslims were assessed 4.94 percent of their assets, Orthodox Christians 156 percent, Jews 179 percent, and Armenians 232 percent" (232). Many non-Muslims lost their businesses during this period, and those who failed to pay the tax were sent to labor camps in Aşkale in eastern Anatolia.

[15] I provide the Turkish original here, so as to emphasize its typographic play.

the negative social and moral consequences of mechanization in its manipulation of literary form. Much of *Matmazel Noraliya'nın Koltuğu* is focalized through Ferit, the protagonist, in free indirect discourse, with other characters entering the narrative only in so far as their speech is heard directly by Ferit. Since most of these characters are represented as having unique speech patterns of one sort of another, the novel's linguistic texture is really a capacious register of the heteroglossia of Turkish, what Bakhtin called "the social diversity of speech types," which exposes "the internal stratification of any national language into social dialects . . . professional jargons, languages of generations and age groups, tendentious languages, languages of the authorities . . ." (262–263). In Ferit's internal monologue, Latin and French medical and psychoanalytic terminology ("épidermophitie inginalis, or éczéma marginé de Hebra"; "choc"; "aphonie") marks the French influence on his education. Babuş and Zehra's uncle Tahir, who was an accountant with the Ottoman Public Debt Administration (Düyun-u Umumiye), is distinguished by his Ottoman Turkish lexicon (31), while the housekeeper Vafi is notable for his use of Arabic prayer words (131). Another, more subtle element is the parody of Turkish as spoken by *dönme* Anglophiles: the name "Haldun," for example, becoming "Haldn" when "pronounced with the English accent that thickens the *l*" (50). When Ferit's friend Suzy pronounces his name as "Feri*d*," we are told that "the letter *d* melts between her tongue [*dil*] and palate [*damak*] in a softness that would excite [Ferit's] father and [the housekeeper] Vafi. It is as if it will come out of her nostrils as smoke [*duman*]" (49).

In "Discourse in the Novel" ("Slovo v Romane," 1934–1935), Bakhtin suggested that the internal stratification present within a language at any moment in its history "is the indispensable prerequisite for the novel as a genre" (263). For Bakhtin, any given historical period is characterized by struggle between the linguistic effects of centralizing, homogenizing forces and those of other, decentralizing forces (272). Centralizing forces work toward homogenization and normativity: the composition and dissemination of dictionaries and grammar books, for example, as part of an effort to form heteroglossia into an official, unified literary language (270). Other social and historical forces meanwhile work to "disband" language, as in actual usage, words are accentuated and marked in varied ways in varied contexts (293). It follows from the diversification of *one* language into many that there are multiple ways of interpreting the world *in* language, and that multiple interpretations interact and compete with each other on a continuous basis. Bakhtin refers to this struggle between layers of language as "dialogized heteroglossia" (*dialogizovannoe raznorechie*) (273), emphasizing that dialogic language employs a variety of narrative discourses, from directly quoted speech to the mixture of several narrative voices within a single speech act (362).

Though Safa's novel delegitimizes the myth of a unified national language, opening it to heteroglossia, we cannot say that *Matmazel Noraliya'nın Koltuğu* in any way celebrates and affirms heteroglossia as liberation. The gendered "struggle among socio-linguistic points of view" (273), in this novel, is quite clearly violent and anarchic.[16] If the social discontinuity segregating Ferit from other characters is both reflected and staged by the manipulation of different speech patterns, we have to admit that linguistic diversity really assumes the form of noise, here, rather than sense, with the text operating as a kind of recording machine capturing sounds in word-forms devoid of any inherent meaning. The alterity of another is hardly expressible in such an inhuman machine language. Ferit is not only the *sole* focalizing agent of the novel's narrative: he fails ever to truly enter and inhabit another character's or persona's speech. Where readings of *Matmazel Noraliya'nın Koltuğu* have often praised its use of free indirect discourse as the skillful use of a European literary technique,[17] such treatments have often neglected to consider the implications of the confining focalization of free indirect discourse in and through Ferit. The language of others effectively freezes as they enter Ferit's linguistic world, becoming what Bakhtin called "naked corpses," devoid of life (Bakhtin 292).

Returning to the lodging house late at night, Ferit encounters a naked female figure on the dark staircase (36). While he fumbles for a light, the figure vanishes. Suspecting it was Fatma, the housemaid, Ferit goes to her room. This is how their first meeting is described:

> The first thing he saw on the pillow was a large nose. Then two thick black eyebrows as if painted with pitch. If it were not for the hair, it would have been easy to believe that this head with its big-boned chin, its black hair above the upper lip, and its thick and extremely dark facial skin . . . belonged to a porter instead of a woman. The difficult thing was to estimate the age of this confounding creature [*mübarek*]. There were parts on this face that would suggest thirty as well as fifty. Certainly, the breast that Ferit thought to have gripped downstairs could not belong to this dragon. If he were to remove the blanket, not a beautiful breast but the carcass of a mule [*katır leşi*] would be exposed with its long tail and legs covered with thick upright hair. (39)

The first two sentences here describe Fatma by fragmenting her into facial and bodily parts, listing these parts serially: first, she is a nose, then eyebrows, head hair, chin and upper lip hair, and only finally is she a head. Each of these parts serves as a synecdoche

---

[16] Generally speaking, Safa and Bakhtin's respective approaches to heteroglossia are diametrically opposed. Unlike Bakhtin, Safa very clearly regards linguistic diversity as a problem to be solved. Still, there are moments of convergence in their respective positions. Describing the phenomenology of dialogue between speaker and listener, Bakhtin suggested that the "speaker breaks through the alien conceptual horizon [*krugozor*] of the listener, constructs his own utterance on alien [*chuzhoj*] territory, against his, the listener's, apperceptive background" (282; 95). Borrowing Husserl's theory of perception, Paul de Man notes in "Dialogue and Dialogism," Bakhtin "uncritically assimilat[es] the structure of language to the structure of a secure perception" (112), risking the conflation of dialogism with "dialectical imperialism" (112). In this way of looking at it, dialogism is not a mark of the irreducible alterity of language so much as its territorialization in appropriation and defense, as well as forceful intrusion. Rather than suggesting a simple contradiction here, one might note that dialogism would necessarily be haunted from the outset by the risk of becoming merely a struggle for mastery. I thank David Goldfarb for his help with Bakhtin's original Russian.

[17] On this point, see Moran 238.

for Fatma's face, and then for her body. Not only is she broken down into pieces, in this way, but each atomized piece is as though zoomed in upon and enlarged, the eyebrows described hyperbolically and comically as "painted with pitch." Terms and phrases such as "confounding creature," "dragon," and "carcass of a mule," meanwhile, work to defeminize and dehumanize Fatma, attributing animal qualities to her.

This fragmentation and visual hyperbole of faces and bodies occurs elsewhere in *Matmazel Noraliya'nın Koltuğu,* as well. While Babuş's and Zehra's mother, Eda, narrates her family story, Ferit is focusing intently on her eyes, which are described as disconnected from each other: while the one, paralyzed eye evokes a detached spectator, the other evokes its animated counterpart, as if Eda "has filled herself into this eye" (23). The disfiguration of Eda's face by these observations is perhaps best not taken for a literary mode of physiognomic portraiture, so much as a metaphorization by, and as, the language of narrative itself. Like the surface of the face, the surface of the text, recording a community's variant speech patterns, is fragmented into many different layers, and while the physiological *and* spiritual signifiers of the human (the eyes and face) are reduced to a vulgar and vulgarly atomized corporeality, human speech is pared to a mutilated surface. Distorted, dehumanized, grotesque faces, lacking any coherence, are offered to us as nothing less than failures of signification.

Though *Matmazel Noraliya'nın Koltuğu* thus stages quite compellingly the heteroglossia of Turkish speech, it codes heteroglossia as a violent lawlessness, refusing any substantive encounter with the alterity of others and producing a "deviant" sexual desire unmarked by anything but violence. When Ferit first wakes her, Fatma tells him about the death of her beloved Hüseyin (40–47), asking Ferit if he thinks the "pıt pıt pıt" tiptoeing sounds she hears every night might be Hüseyin returning to visit her. At this point Ferit leaves her, but returns a few hours later, making tiptoe sounds of his own, and rapes her in the "guise" of her dead beloved (48). As the rape scene concludes, third-person narration yields to Ferit's internal monologue, which is a mash of paratactic fragments with little discursive or even merely grammatical coherence:

> Get up, kid, get up. Enough this morning chatter [*zevzeklik*] . . . Pıt, pıt, pıt, aha, behind that wood. It hit [*çaldı*] my head with the washing bowl. And you put [*çaldın*] your huge nose into my eye. Like a carrot, your nose entered into my eye. My lamb, what is *cendek*? Wish I had asked Fatma. (52)

After the rape, Ferit's inner voice manipulates idiomatic expressions and words from her dialect, absorbing them in the form of nonsense: as the mechanical senselessness of chaos, rather than as meaningful signs of Fatma's social and linguistic alterity. This linguistic chaos inverts even sexual identity, at one point reversing the positions of rapist and victim (Fatma's "huge nose" entering Ferit's eye). Recovering his senses, Ferit wonders: "Is it possible that in my sleep I have experienced a molestation [*sarkıntı*] that has brought down my aesthetic and epistemological structure from top to bottom?" (53).

A language surgically invaded has been permanently mutilated and can no longer be conceived as a reliable "keeper of secrets" (282). *Matmazel Noraliya'nın Koltuğu* records an inhuman machine language from which even the signs of an idealized truth have been banished. In Friedrich A. Kittler's media history of what he calls the writing system or "discourse network" of 1900, the work of Mallarmé, Nietzsche, and Freud heralds an epoch in which "culture [*Bildung*], the great unity in which speaking, hearing, writing, and reading would achieve mutual transparency and relation to meaning, breaks apart" (214). The typewriter transforms writing, substituting for the handwritten word a spatialized, abstract sign (193), while the phonograph and film provide ways to capture and store acoustic and optical data in parallel, "with superhuman precision" and as rapidly as it can be generated (245). Language now reverts to the category of the inorganic, and it can "form" only against a background of noise (nonsense), not sacred silence.[18] Like the "writing machines" of this historical "discourse network," *Matmazel Noraliya'nın Koltuğu* stages an "act of writing [that] is nothing beyond its materiality": a meaningless practice whose practitioners become "writing machines," or mere *effects* of technologies of inscription and storage (335). We might say that Safa's writing machine is indeed akin to a phonograph, in so far as in the melting of the letter *d* in Suzy's mouth, the nonsense-sounds ("ışş, uşş, vışş, huv") made by Fatma, and Babuş's oozing word-globules, "it registers real sounds rather than translating them into phonemic equivalencies as an alphabet does" (232).

For Kittler, "what the technological media record is their own opposition to the state and school" (240); for those who believe that "book language represents a never-spoken exception and impedes actual speech" (234), the writing machine permits and enables "undistorted oral presentations" (233). Quite unlike Kittler, Safa was unable or unwilling to *affirm* this "guerrilla warfare against disciplinary power" (240); in fact, we might say that in *Matmazel Noraliya'nın Koltuğu,* Safa deliberately took up the task left unaccomplished by the Turkish state. For Safa, the surface of the text *must* be restored as a meaningful medium of phonemic equivalence, through the suppression of the heteroglossia of Turkish and the plurilingualism of Turkey's national subjects. In the end, what *Matmazel Noraliya'nın Koltuğu* offers us is a new, nonverbal language, the language of "a meaningful sound, sigh, mimic, or gaze . . . a richer and deeper system of symbols . . . equivalent to pages of writing" (18–19), to be grasped as more immediate, more alive, than the order of words itself. Especially in its second segment, Safa's novel is really nothing less than a grand attempt to restore a representational economy of production and circulation of meaning to the failed mediumship of words.

---

[18] Note the resemblance between the primal scene of *Matmazel Noraliya'nın Koltuğu*, the dream scene quoted at the beginning of this chapter, and the primal scene of Nietzschean writing with which Kittler begins: "What I fear is not the horrible shape behind my chair but its voice: not the words, but the frighteningly inarticulate and inhuman tone of that shape. If only it would speak as people speak!" (Nietzsche, fragment of 1868–1869, in *Werke und Briefe* V: 205, qtd. in Kittler 183). Truly this is, as Kittler puts it, a "deafening noise in [the] still scene of writing" (183).

2. Scenes of Translation

This restitution of meaning is not merely a technical issue having to do with how signification is understood to "work." For it poses an ethico-political question regarding the process of assimilation of externalized gendered and religious difference into the nation. The image of Selma, Ferit's lover, as a *medium,* or a conduit for the experience of a new transcendence, is important precisely because she serves as a mark of ethnic and religious impurity, her mother being a *dönme,* while her father was a "pure [*halis*] Turk" (73).[19] Where the grotesque face of the rural migrant is a figure for the novel's mutilated linguistic surface, the eyes of Selma, as Ferit's beloved, operate as transparent signs for an idealized nonphenomenal realm. It must be emphasized here that when it comes to the question of assimilation of difference into the nation, what we mean by the ethics and politics of language cannot remain merely symbolic characterological functions. Rather, they must be understood as dynamics informing the novel's scenes of translation.

In one of many such scenes in *Matmazel Noraliya'nın Koltuğu,* Ferit recites to Selma in French the first lines of Rimbaud's "L'Éternité," translates and mistranslates them into Turkish, and finally rewrites the poem entirely. As an alien language itself, a fragmented national language here is restored, becoming habitable and native as a "mother tongue" only by violently incorporating words from foreign writing. The nonsignifying alien shapes of mechanized language become legible and familiar, once its internal division is healed in the act of appropriating external difference.

We saw earlier that in the act of raping Fatma, Ferit suffers a kind of linguistic breakdown. After the rape, Ferit has a violent argument with Selma that begins when Ferit forces Selma to kiss him, and the day after the separation that follows, Ferit runs into Selma unexpectedly on the street. Even though he has been out looking for her in order to apologize, Ferit is unable to speak when he sees Selma, and he walks away, obsessively replaying the details of this encounter in his mind (116). This in turn triggers the memory of reciting and translating Rimbaud's poem. As at other crisis points in the novel, narration flips unexpectedly back and forth, at this point, from the third person to the first person. Unlike the many lengthy, chaotic speeches of other characters, whose language Ferit's internal monologue merely records, Selma's casual remarks serve as a kind of direct hermeneutic challenge. Her greeting "How are you, Ferit? Where have you been? Are you always like that? [*Hep öyle misin?*]" (116) becomes the object of a lengthy exegesis,

---

[19] See note 14. Selma's mother is described as a "hystérique" who seduces and marries Selma's father Tahsin against her family's objections to her marrying a "Turk" (72). According to one of Ferit's friends, while Selma's mother is a woman of loose morals who cheats on Tahsin repeatedly, Tahsin refuses to divorce her, to protect their daughter from public scandal (73). After her father's death, Selma, resentful of her mother's side of the family, is raised by her paternal grandmother (74). With one (Francophile) exception, the *dönme* characters in the novel are for the most part cosmopolitan Anglophiles, associated with immorality and hatred of the "Turks."

with the ambiguity of the last question, in particular ("Are you always like that?") generating a proliferation of possible interpretations. In Ferit's "replay," Selma's eyes are imagined as media: "Ferit now saw Selma's eyes, abstracted from their scenery, in an emptied background . . . looking motionless as if they were frozen, yet at the same time spectacularly alive . . . In these eyes, there was a deep, pleasurable state that enveloped, pulled and transported one to a realm beyond spirit [*ruh*], beyond everything, to a motionlessness that we speculate belongs to eternity . . ." (120–121).

While we may note here once more the segmentation and hypertrophy of a single facial feature (Selma's eyes), the function of such segmentation is not to index the fragmentation of language as much as to imagine Ferit's lover's eyes as modes of transport and conduits to a nonphenomenal beyond. This is one way in which the transcendence of a higher meaning of language is restored precisely through and by means of a figure of religious and ethnic impurity. And yet we mustn't fail to note that Ferit's introspection here includes the remembrance of a *prior* experience of the transcendent, in Selma's eyes. This is, in fact, the occasion for reciting Rimbaud's poem:

I had read her Rimbaud's lines on the ferry last summer:
>On a retrouvé.
>Quoi?—L'éternité.
>C'est la mer allée
>Avec le soleil.[20]

And I translated them as something like this:
>It is found.
>What? Eternity.
>It is the course of the sea
>Under the sun.[21]

I wanted to say afterwards: "It is found. What? Eternity. It is your gaze, under my eyes." Because this rewriting [*nazire*] looked worse than my translation, I didn't recite it. (120)

I have already noted that the language of *Matmazel Noraliya'nın Koltuğu* is not only a heteroglossic modern Turkish, but includes sentences in English, French technical terms, and Arabic prayers. French medical and philosophical terms are marks of Ferit's education, of his fluency in professional speech, and

---

[20] Safa misquotes the first line here. For the original, see Rimbaud 186:
>Elle est retrouvée.
>Quoi?—L'Éternité.
>C'est la mer allée
>Avec le soleil.

[21] Here is the Turkish original of Ferit's translation:

for French cultural hegemony as the "source" of modernization in general. A Turkish speech larded with English and French words is also associated with the private language of the *dönme* household of Selma's uncle (62–65). We might say that in stark contrast with these other functions, Rimbaud's poem is here quoted in its original French to mark the intensity of a private encounter between Selma and Ferit.

It is in this scene that *Matmazel Noraliya'nın Koltuğu* points to an antinomy at the heart of linguistic modernization, illuminated by the debates regarding the language rights of minorities in Turkey. Even as efforts to purify and naturalize modern Turkish made it more deeply unfamiliar and artificial (indeed, chaotic), Turkey's ethnic and religious minorities were subject to ever stricter and more strenuous social and legal coercion to adopt Turkish as a primary language. Although the language rights of non-Muslim minorities were protected under the Lausanne Treaty of 1923, continuous state intervention throughout the Republican period shuttered many minority schools and ultimately attenuated existing minority educational privileges through incorporation into the national education system (Bali 185–196). Supporting the state's initiatives were civil movements such the "Vatandaş, Türkçe Konuş!" ("Citizen, Speak Turkish!") campaign, launched in 1928 by the student society of the Istanbul Darülfünun Law School. With sanction from the Republican government, the students placed signs commanding "Citizens, Speak Turkish!" around Istanbul, targeting non-Muslim minorities who spoke languages other than Turkish (especially French, Judeo-Spanish, and Greek) in public (135). Mimicking the authoritative voice of the state, these signs interpellated the neighbor as a national citizen and subject of an official state language. Though interethnic violence halted the "Citizen, Speak Turkish!" campaign after only a few months, heated debates over minority languages continued through the Second World War.[22]

Safa engaged these debates in his many newspaper pieces, actively supporting the assimilation of ethnic and religious minorities through the requirement to speak

---

Bulundu.
Ne? Ebedilik.
Bu, güneşin altında
Deniz yoluydur.

[22] The "Citizen, Speak Turkish!" campaign launched significant public debate within the Turkish Jewish community. In books entitled *Vatandaş: Türkçe Konuş! Yahud Türkçenin Ta'mîmi Meselesi* ("Citizen: Speak Turkish! On the Question of the Generalization of Turkish," 1928) and *Türkleştirme* ("Turkification," 1928), two prominent Jewish intellectuals of the period, Avram Galanti and Moiz Kohen, invited the Jewish community to learn Turkish and assimilate. Galanti explored the historical and sociological reasons for Turkish Jewish resistance to speaking Turkish, while Kohen published his book under the Turkic name "Tekin Alp," rewriting the Ten Commandments of the Torah as ten commandments to self-Turkify. Others, such as David Fresko and Max Bonnafous, strongly rejected Kohen's approach, emphasizing that Turkish hostility to the Jewish citizens of Turkey was the main obstacle to peaceful coexistence (Bali 149–156). Bali's *Cumhuriyet Yıllarında Türkiye Yahudileri: Bir Türkleştirme Serüveni (1923–1945)* ("Jews of Turkey during the Republican Period: A Story of Turkification [1923–1945]") provides a detailed history of the Republican politics of Turkification targeting the Jews of Turkey.

Turkish.[23] And yet in contemplating Ferit's quotation of Rimbaud in French, in *Matmazel Noraliya'nın Koltuğu,* we cannot rule out the possibility that the hierarchical distinction between foreign and national language is invoked precisely in order to suspend it, if only momentarily. Quoting Rimbaud in French is, after all, Ferit's response to what he experiences as Selma's "infinite" gaze, a response to the intimate experience of her alterity. Suddenly, here, it seems that *foreign* words (in French) are somehow more intimately "native," in some way, than the fragmented and yet seemingly unquestionably native language (Turkish) itself. At the same time, since thus relating to Selma *as* an other is at the very same time an experience of her "otherness" as finally insurmountable, it would seem that we are being asked to imagine that *no* language can mediate such a relation except in so far as it *is* a *foreign* language. Where Ferit's focalized recording of Fatma's Turkish dialect registers and preserves it as nonsense, then, quotation of French here momentarily affirms the possibility of relating to the other through the medium of alien language. We might describe this as a displacement of the exclusionary and purist categories of nationalism into an "unhomely" language.

However, this potentially radical gesture is soon recalled. Rimbaud's "avec le soleil," which might be read as suggesting the complementarity or mutual accompaniment of the sea and the sun, is translated into an image spatially subordinating one term to the other: "It is the course of the sea / Under the sun" (120). This translation is then rewritten as an image spatially subordinating Selma's gaze to Ferit's own: "[Eternity] is your gaze under my eyes" (121). Although Ferit does not actually share his rewriting of the poem with Selma, his mistranslation, transforming what is arguably an open relation of proximity and distance into a relationship of dominance and subordination, recodes alterity as hierarchy, effectively dictating the terms of their relationship.[24]

This scene of translation then dramatizes the appropriation of the foreign in the constitution of national language as "native" tongue. For Safa, a mechanized

[23] In "Kanunsuz Olmaz!" ("Not without Legislation!"), dated 22 December 1936, Safa addressed non-Muslim minorities (*ekalliyetler*), listing "nine principles" they should "pound into their heads," including Safa's own support for the imprisonment of Turkish non-Muslims speaking languages other than Turkish in public. Another article, entitled "Düetto" ("A Short Duet"), dated 8 April 1937, describes an exchange in French between two Turkish Jews, which Safa had ostensibly overheard on a tram. Noting that one of the Jews switched to Turkish on sensing Safa's "discontented gaze," Safa distinguished between two kinds of Turkish Jews: the "more Turkish Jews" like the speaker willing to switch to Turkish and the "less Turkish Jews" who refused to abandon French. In "Türk Olmak Şartı" ("The Condition of Being Turkish"), dated 21 December 1945, Safa described the experience of spending a summer with a *dönme* family. Criticizing cosmopolitan "Turks" who don't know any Turkish, or who know Turkish but refuse to speak it, Safa notes disapprovingly that the mother of the *dönme* family sang only American lullabies to her child. It is possible that *Matmazel Noraliya'nın Koltuğu*'s character Suzy has her source in this anecdote.
[24] Lawrence Venuti has observed that the act of translation is inherently violent, in its "reconstitution of the foreign text in accordance with values, beliefs, and representations that preexist it in the translating language and culture, always configured in hierarchies of dominance and marginality, always determining the production, circulation, and reception of texts" (Venuti 14). We might say that what we find in Safa's work here is *doubly* mistranslation. While it is impossible to deny the violence inherent in translation, one *might* embrace a practice of foreignizing translation that successfully moves a reader *toward* the foreign, rather than moving the foreign author toward the reader (14).

language can be restored to meaning, once its internal disunity—a specifically *gendered* disunity—has been suppressed and its differential exteriority domesticated and subordinated. Ferit's mistranslation is in some ways emblematic of the politics of the novel's second segment, which legitimize Ferit and Selma's union through the Turkification and Islamicization of a key figure of ethnic and religious impurity, the deceased Mademoiselle Noralia of the novel's title. In the summer house where she had once lived, Ferit has a series of mystical visions in which he encounters Noralia's spirit. Her life story, transmitted by the Greek Christian housekeeper Fotika as well as by the notebooks Noralia left behind, is the story of the Muslim mystic "Nuriye," born "Noralia" to an Italian mother and an Ottoman Turkish father (232). The many explicit analogies through which Noralia's and Selma's lives are linked, in this portion of the novel, suggestively construe Noralia as Selma's own prefiguration (259). We might say that if Safa thus makes the conversion or self-translation of a gendered foreign the very condition of possibility of an emerging nation, this very configuration itself also legitimizes the restoration of meaning in translation in the present.

In Noralia's life, language, explicitly gendered and sexualized, serves as a site of social, political, and moral contestation. But such tensions are resolved with her adoption of Turkish as a first tongue, in place of the Italian of her sexually promiscuous mother (232–233). "Have you ever heard of such a thing?" Fotika asks Ferit. "The mother speaks Italian and French, and the daughter responds in Turkish" (239). In a way, it is through Noralia's notebooks, embedded within the novel, that a meaningful Turkish writing emerges. "What do I still desire," Noralia writes, having cut ties with the outside world, "except not to desire?" (248). "My God!" she prays, willing her own sacrificial annihilation for the nation and for humanity. "Take me now. Scatter my pieces . . . Press my heart . . . Melt my mind . . . I ask you, my God, to distribute to the destitute my life, my soul, emotions, ideas and knowledge, all that I own" (257). The originary transgressive desire of the Ottoman Turkish man for the explicitly gendered and sexualized foreigner is purged, here, in this hybrid child's practice of self-annihilation under a Turkish-Islamic ethical code. Her act of writing literally serves as a means of melting, pressing, and disseminating the hybrid into thousands of "black signs" to be circulated and read as national redemption.

As repetitions of the scene of translation of Rimbaud, many passages from Noralia's notebooks include her translations of a variety of mystical texts, including *L'Imitation de Jésus-Christ* (251), the Tibetan "Book of the Dead" (253), and a fragment of Denys l'Aréopagite (254). Depropriated herself as a translator, Noralia, like Selma, serves as a medium of foreign messages, further purging herself in each act of mediation. Where Noralia's hybridity allows her to traffic in foreign words on behalf of an "indigenous" man, her self-translation ensures that no threat of deviant social contamination can come from such contact. Upon reading some of these notebooks, Ferit notes, "I think about reading all the notebooks and publishing them as a book. Such a spirit impresses the mark of her eternity here or there, as it wishes. It now blows in me like a wind. Once its book comes out, who knows how many more spirits it would fill" (259). No longer an archive of meaningless sounds, the surface of the text now stores traces of a domesticated foreign, and the mechanical reproduction of the notebooks is imagined not as a threat so much as a means for resolving a crisis of representation. Despite and against its material mediacy, the *restored* writing that resolves that crisis produces an illusion of the immediacy of the transcendent, filling Ferit with a kind of eternity (259), in the fleeting visual experience of "a great limitless brightness" beyond verbal language (214). This is nothing less than the realization of a logocentrism beyond the phonocentrism of official national grammatology: the institution of a radically transparent, self-annihilating writing capable of *transcending its own mediacy.*

There are several observations we can make about the novel's figuration of the foundation *and* restitution of the national and moral order through translative writing—"translation" being used here both literally and metaphorically, as the appropriation of the gendered and sexualized foreign. First, we can say that the novelistic account of nationalization, here, differs starkly from that to be found in conventional theories of nationalism, which explain the emergence of the national as the discovery and the reinvestment of a native Turkic identity by the Turkish-speaking Muslim population of a multiethnic empire, against other emergent ethnic-national groups, as well as against Europe. In *Matmazel Noraliya'nın Koltuğu,* the national order is *not* instituted by a people that differentiates itself from other peoples on the basis of shared identity and which separates from other peoples, forming an alliance on that basis. The dates recorded in Noralia's notebooks, running from 14 February 1314 AH (1896 AD) through 1924, coincide more or less with the last phase of Ottoman imperial disintegration, the Turkish War of Independence, and the establishment of the Turkish Republic. And yet Noralia's recorded entries mention no major national or world historical events apart from those associated with the First World War in Europe. In a way, it is the ethnically and religiously impure Noralia's "sacrificial" writing that stands in, in Safa's novel, for an account of the birth of the nation.

Secondly, we can say that Safa's account locates an explicitly *gendered* impurity at the very heart or kernel of the patriarchal nation. In *The Nation and Its Fragments,* Partha Chatterjee has argued that the production of a new woman, acting as the bearer and the guardian of an "inner" national culture, is essential to the success of patriarchal anti-colonial nationalism. Although anti-colonial nationalism acknowledges European superiority in economic, technological, and political matters, Chatterjee argues, it differentiates itself precisely by claiming its sovereignty over the "inner" cultural domain. The creation of a "national" language and literature "*outside* the purview of the state and the European missionaries" (7) was one such realization of this project, and the production of a new "national" woman, who acquires "the practical skills of literacy, accounting, hygiene, and the ability to run the household according to the new physical and economic conditions" (129–130), while "retain[ing] the inner spirituality of the indigenous social life" (126), was another. Deniz Kandiyoti, meanwhile, has traced the emergence of the "woman question" on the autonomous cultural terrain of the mid-nineteenth century Ottoman Empire.[25] Kandiyoti argues that it was only between the second half of the nineteenth century and the beginning of the twentieth that a "distancing from Islam as the only form of legitimate discourse on women's emancipation in favor of a cultural nationalism appropriating such emancipation as an indigenous pattern" could take place (23).

For Kandiyoti, the thought of Ziya Gökalp, a key ideologue of Turkish nationalism, manifests a crucial moment of the "transformation of the 'woman question' in Turkey" (23). Invoking a gendered conceptual distinction between "inside" and "outside," Gökalp argued in "Hars ve Medeniyet" ("Culture and Civilization," 1918) for the necessity of borrowing the "outside" (*haric*) of technique and form from Europe (9). Gökalp nonetheless emphasized that "the spirit must always be national [*milli*]—fitting to the [demands of] life and folk" (17). In *Türkçülüğün Esasları* (*Principles of Turkism*), women were ascribed a special importance as the vanguards of a new national Turkic community, at once modern and reconciled to Western liberalism, and at the same time ancient and unique, with its national-cultural mores rooted in pre-Islamic (Central Asian) Turkic practices (106–107).

Matmazel Noraliya'nın Koltuğu, by contrast, identifies precisely the *impure* woman as the agent of translative writing. Here, national culture is constituted not by the interiority of the "indigenous" woman, but rather by the mystical spirituality of the gendered hybrid. Such spirituality should not be imagined as either a closed (Central Asian) Turkic cultural nationalism, or as a strict Islamic traditionalism (the latter is, after all, explicitly crossed out with the murder of Ferit's religious aunt, Necmiye). The gendered hybrid is rather a complex site of translation of *foreign* texts of spirituality, into a Turkish-Islamic ethical code irreducible to either Gökalpian nationalism or Islamism—the latter being understood, here, as a political ideology aiming to organize the state, the economy, and the social by Quranic principles.[26] There is no question that the idealization of the gendered hybrid is an act of tremendous violence, in so far as it fails to affirm her difference, as it were, in and for herself. Noralia and Selma are accepted, in other words, only in so far as they gather in and incorporate the foreign outside *and* efface their own, "translative" difference in self-conversion. If this dynamic is not identical to that at play in Seyfeddin's coding of extra-Turkish difference as terrifying death, the end is the same each case: the nation itself as the actual and/or symbolic death of the other. Safa's imagination is in fact even more troubling than that of Seyfeddin, in so far as in the substitution of the personal diary of the self-sacrificing Noralia for any

---

[25] See Kandiyoti, "End of Empire."

[26] I am grateful to Özge Serin for her reading of an earlier draft of this chapter, which helped me to rethink Noralia's significance here.

"objective" history of the early twentieth century, Safa almost entirely obscures the social violence of Turkish nationalization.

While we can thus say that *Matmazel Noraliya'nın Koltuğu* is instructive, in its Midhat-like staging of an inherently seductive, omni-directional communicative and translative travel in the Turkish language, we must acknowledge that Safa falters dramatically in his moralizing religious, national-identitarian, and gendered attempt to *discipline* that traffic. The literariness, as literary *difference,* of Safa's novel is placed under conspicuous pressure in those passages in its second segment tracking Ferit's conversations about Noralia with the philosophy teacher Aziz. In these passages, the novel's third-person narration dissolves into something Ferit anxiously describes as hovering "between a Platonic dialogue and a newspaper opinion poll" (264). Aziz—into whose mouth are placed the key arguments of the newspaper articles collected in Safa's 1943 volume *Millet ve İnsan* ("Nation and Human")—serves as Safa's proxy for controlling the threat of "open" circulation of the literary work *Matmazel Noraliya'nın Koltuğu,* itself.

The nation, Aziz tells us in these passages, plays a mediating role between God and individual, as the first form of a higher ideal encouraging the subject's sacrifice to an otherness beyond selfhood (261–263). Opposing Marxist class struggle, on the one hand, and liberal individualism, on the other, Aziz ascribes "the contemporary world catastrophe" to "man's failure to rise from individuality to nation, and from nation to humanity and to God" (262). Aziz insists that "the movement of the Self [*Ben*] to annihilate [*yok etme*] itself in the name of God produces saints, to annihilate itself in the name of humanity produces geniuses, and to annihilate itself in the name of the nation produces heroes" (261). A chain of authority must be established, putting the individual under the command (*emir*) of the nation-state, and the nation-state under the command of humanity and of God (263).[27] And yet where the technicalization and objectivization of the world in such individual mastery simply refuses to conceive an irreducible alterity, Safa's negative sacrificial politics is nothing less than an active *fixture* of alterity *as* Turkish-Islamic. In this suicidally closed community, where death is "the infinite fulfillment of an immanent life" (Nancy 13), there is, quite simply, no otherness at all.[28]

---

[27] Safa believed that human societies would eventually demand the establishment of a world state. Rather than breaking down the nation-state, however, Safa thought that such an event might actually strengthen it (263).

[28] I will return to the question of sacrifice in Chapter 5. I want to emphasize here that the social bond must be understood as a structure of responsibility to the other. On this point, see Derrida, *The Gift of Death.* While Safa is *in part* correct in his critique of liberal individualism and the autonomous subject, he falters badly when he *fixes* the open and indeterminate relation to a unitary "essence." Safa's visionary community bears no little resemblance to the Hegelian community of the dead critiqued by Jean-Luc Nancy:

> In [the Hegelian] State, each member has his truth in the other, which is the State itself, whose reality is never more present than when its members give their lives in a war. . . . Doubtless such immolation for the sake of community—and by it, therefore—could and can be full of meaning, on the condition that this "meaning" be that of a community, and on the further condition that this community not be a "community of death" (as has been the case since at least the First World

We could say that following these explicitly didactic passages, Safa's novel moves back into a literary mode and back into explicit focalization through Ferit. In concluding *Matmazel Noraliya'nın Koltuğu* with an allegory of successful nationalist assimilation, Safa takes care to reconcile the various narrative threads involving different characters. In stark contrast with the "scream" of the novel's opening dream scene, its final pages imagine an assiduously and comprehensively restored state of orderly communicability. Zehra, the aphonic, resumes speaking, and Babuş's alexia is corrected with proper schooling, funded by Ferit himself (288–289). In a "resolution" of the problem of socioeconomic inequality and the restoration of justice, it is suggested that along with their mother Eda and uncle Tahir, Zehra and Babuş have been rescued from poverty by Ferit's benevolence (288). The symbolic restoration of *adalet* (justice) may be understood as the restoration of the mutilated proper name of Eda to its unmutilated form, "Adalet." At the novel's end, Ferit and Aziz, enlightened individuals in communion with the nation and with God, are seen walking together in silence in Noralia's garden, enjoying a telepathic mutual understanding in the fantastic immediacy of thought (295–296).

Only one character remains lost, here, evading this massive and comprehensive act of reconciliation redrawing a polyvocal text as a national act of literature. Notwithstanding Safa's clear intent to "redeem" all the major and minor personae of *Matmazel Noraliya'nın Koltuğu,* Fatma, the gendered migrant, is never mentioned again. The story of her geographic and social displacement, from Tatvan to Istanbul, remains an unresolved episode that lurks in the novel's narratological unconscious, as a potential discrepancy of its conclusive nationalism. Fatma's as-yet untranslated word *cendek* (which appears to be a Kurdish loanword for corpse[29]) remains an unresolved foreign element within the novel's reconciled Turkish, a small but resistant remainder of all its appropriations.

War, thereby justifying all refusals to "die for one's country"). Now, the community of human immanence, man made equal to himself or to God, to nature, and to his own works, is one such community of death—or of the dead. The fully realized person of individualistic or communistic humanism is the dead person. In other words, death, in such a community, is not the unmasterable excess of finitude, but the infinite fulfillment of an immanent life. . . . (*The Inoperative Community,* 12–13)

[29] The first volume of the six-volume *Türkiyede Halk Ağzından Söz Derleme Dergisi* ("Journal of Collected Words from the Vernacular in Turkey"), collecting the results of the word-collection mobilization of 1932–1934, was published in 1939 by the Turkish Language Society. It included an entry for *cendek* (253), noting three different patterns of usage. The first, in which *cendek* denoted "human or animal corpse," was noted in Tutak (Ağrı), Hınıs (Erzurum), and Kars in eastern Anatolia; Akalan (Samsun), Bayburt (Gümüşane), and Mecitözü (Çorum) in northern Anatolia; Konya in central Anatolia; and Kozan (Seyhan) in southern Anatolia. The second definition given for *cendek,* "body or corpse," had been noted in Kozan (Seyhan), Artvin (Çoruh), Erzurum and Ağrı. The third and final definition, "a long rod," was found in Yozgat. No information was provided regarding the etymology of these collected "Turkish" words, or regarding possible relations with other languages spoken in Turkey. Michael Chyet's *Kurdish-English Dictionary* (2003), which notes which of its Kurdish entries were absorbed from other languages, defines *cendek* as "corpse, dead body, cadaver; carrion" (87), with no indication that the word has passed into Kurdish from another language. Chyet also includes a list of earlier Kurdish dictionaries with entries for *cendek.*

Despite and against Safa's national ethics of transcendence, then, we can say that the death-touch, as it were, of this Kurmanji loanword, *cendek,* "survives" in precisely those gaps Safa hoped to have restored to an eternal, transmaterial immediacy.

We should recognize that Fatma's role is not an arbitrary one. The Selma/ Noralia dyad serves as a register of spiritual value, for Safa, first and foremost in their *not being* Fatma, in their insistently delineated difference from Fatma. It is no exaggeration to say that the very condition of possibility of Selma/Noralia's transcendently "eternal" intelligibility, *as* registers of spiritual value, is their differentiation from Fatma as dehumanized other and as a negative limit of language. *Matmazel Noraliya'nın Koltuğu's* final "forgetting" of Fatma as a *foundational other,* in this sense, is not to be overlooked.

Safa's novel very carefully specifies the ethnic identity markers of its many characters. And yet Fatma is not once explicitly marked or coded in any way as a Kurdish person, though she is clearly a migrant from a predominantly Kurdish-populated town.[30] As the enactment of a Republican discourse denying any distinct Kurdish identity, this negative act reminds us of Mesut Yeğen's thesis that "Turkish nationalism of the republican era has *principally* perceived Kurds as future-Turks" ("Turkish" 137). In fact, Fatma uses the word *cendek* in a story she tells about her mother's escape from a massacre of the Muslim population of her village by Armenians, telling us that her mother hid under the "corpse" (*cendek*) of an old woman (42). We might say that this subnarrative fails to produce its "intended" effect, in so far as the untranslated word *cendek* remains untranslated, haunting Safa's novel as a double register of the violence through which internalized Muslim Kurdish difference and externalized Christian Armenian difference alike were denied.[31] Taken together, rather than as constitutive opposites, the oral narration of Fatma and the written notebooks of Mademoiselle Noralia offer some of the missing bits of that bloody history of national warfare indexed by Noralia's "willed" self-conversion. And in its latent disruption of the suicidally closed and silent transcendent community that Safa himself willed to his novel, this persistent "noise" of an ineradicable linguistic heterogeneity certainly also points to an alternate form of communicability, cognizant of difference.

---

[30] In *Agha, Shaikh and State: The Social and Political Structures of Kurdistan* (1992), Martin van Bruinessen reports V. Cuinet's conclusion, in the late nineteenth century, that "forty per cent of the population within the boundaries of the former emirate of Bitlis" (to which Tatvan belonged) was Armenian—adding that the vast majority of the Muslims in the emirate were Kurdish (170).

[31] On Armenian uprisings in eastern Anatolia, see Akçam 196–204. Armenian attacks on Muslim villages did occur, during the First World War (197). As Akçam notes, because Ottoman authorities used these attacks to justify the deportations of 1915, the extent of Armenian organization during the period is still highly contested. Regardless of the level of Ottoman Armenian organization, there is no justification for the violence of 1915. Though Safa unsurprisingly omits any mention of the deportations, one might say that by including a (very) small fragment of this contested history, Safa is pointing to it, despite and against his own political agenda.

3. *Nazire* Comparison

In a newspaper article dated 13 August 1941 and entitled "Dost ve Düşman Kelimeler" ("Friend and Enemy Words"), Safa described the Turkish language as a "territory to be defended against foreign invasion." When "foreign words enter through the borders of the language," he continued, "one has to pick up arms and intern them" (96). Any language politics, Safa suggested, will be founded on the fundamental distinction between friend and enemy (97). In this respect, we can say that Safa's writings, as works and acts of literature, have left us a thoroughly *territorialized* language, and while we must attend to the fact that in *Matmazel Noraliya'nın Koltuğu,* not *all* foreign words take on the role of enemies, Safa unmistakably strove to neutralize the "dangerous supplement" he imagined as the embodiment of moral, spiritual, and social decay. And yet where Safa the author undertook to use literature to police a Turkish language he likened to a "mountaintop without any gendarme" (*Osmanlıca* 78), the anonymous third-person literary narrator of *Matmazel Noraliya'nın Koltuğu* in a way continually countersigns the novel, affirming language's ineradicable indiscipline.

I have dwelled on the word *cendek* as a remainder of Safa's domesticating translation. In concluding, I would like to highlight one other such translational failure, as discussed by the critic Berna Moran. In *Türk Romanına Eleştirel Bir Bakış* ("A Critical View of the Turkish Novel," 1983), Moran suggested that Safa was inspired by Aldous Huxley's *Time Must Have a Stop* (1944), pointing out striking plot similarities between the novels, noting the quotation of the very same lines of Rimbaud's "L'Éternité" in Huxley's novel, and identifying Huxley's *The Perennial Philosophy* (1945) as the source of Noralia's translations from *L'Imitation de Jésus-Christ,* the Tibetan "Book of the Dead", and a fragment of Denys l'Aréopagite.[32] While Moran certainly did not suggest that Safa "stole" from Huxley, he was highly critical of the "artificiality" of Ferit's mystical transformation, during the second segment of *Matmazel Noraliya'nın Koltuğu.* Safa might have created a more persuasively "authentic" and realistic story, Moran suggested, if he had dramatized Ferit's spiritual transformation by making use of the underground Islamic mystical sects in Turkey.

To the extent that Safa saw clearly the irreducible outside that language puts us in touch with, he must certainly be censured for reproducing a doubly violent Orientalist-Occidentalist discourse of national appropriation, through the ethical limits of the differential he employed to code exteriority. And yet if, as Moran

---

[32] A record of "the metaphysic that recognizes a divine Reality substantial to the world of things and lives and minds; the psychology that finds in the soul something similar to, or even identical with, divine reality; the ethic that places man's final end in the knowledge of the immanent and transcendent Ground of all being," *The Perennial Philosophy* describes the process through which an individual overcomes originary alienation through transformative contact with an ultimate reality (vii). Critical of the materialism of mass culture (as Martin Green has noted, the World Controller Mustapha Mond in *Brave New World* is modeled on Atatürk [vii]), Huxley retreated to a practice of "upward transcendence" during his émigré years in the United States.

suggested, there is in fact something finally, dismally leftover and inassimilable in Safa's literary appropriation of Huxley and Rimbaud, then we might resist the critical temptation to dismiss Safa's failures as mere failures of literary and literary-historical imitation. In this light, *Matmazel Noraliya'nın Koltuğu* is perhaps best read not merely as a text of Turkish inauthenticity, but as a novel of the foreignizing travel of the text of European literary modernism itself. We might say that *Matmazel Noraliya'nın Koltuğu* inscribes itself *and* makes an intervention into a *comparative* literary history precisely at that interstice, where it forces a sensitive reader to shift critical focus from the always implicit question of transnational mimicry, to the violence of uneven global capitalist modernity.

Returning to the scene of quoting, translating, and rewriting "L'Éternité," let us read it once more as a testament of the ethico-politics of the act of comparison. We may begin by noting that the figure of the non-Muslim and the text of the French poem also function as metonyms for Europe. One of Safa's goals in the novel is a kind of sublation of the East-West opposition in the Turkish nation, and the act of translating and rewriting "L'Éternité," mediated by the gendered minority, aims to realize this synthesis. In the novel, Ferit's rewritten text is identified as a *nazire,* an Ottoman genre in which the poet chose an admired poem (by another poet) and composed one similar in form, rhythm, and rhyme (Özkırımlı 899). *Nazire* is derived from the Arabic *nazir*, meaning alike, comparable, or equivalent, and this widely practiced form was a homage in which the *nazire* writer deliberately reproduced the textual practice of another poet. *Nazire* writing involved at once a claim for equality, in which the new artifact competed directly with the artifact it reproduced, and the risk of ending up with nothing more than a formal duplication of that original artifact. Accordingly, we might say that the measure of a successful *nazire* was its success in displacing the opposition between original and reproduction itself. As a practice of repetition with difference, successful *nazire* writing stripped the original of its exceptionality *as* an original, attributing both original and copy poem an originality *in* difference. As noted in the first chapter of this book (by reference to the work of Paker), the practice of *nazire* was instrumental in the formation of a composite written Ottoman Turkish.

There are, of course, meaningful limitations to the practice of perennial philosophy. The benefits of Huxley's anthological decontextualization, in the juxtaposition of a heterogeneous body of texts, come at the cost of a rigorous engagement with historical difference. Adorno has commented (in "Aldous Huxley and Utopia," 1955) on the "unconditional and atemporal opposition" of an immediate spirituality to reified materiality and on its perpetuation, rather than termination, of the "socially dictated separation of consciousness from the social realization its essence requires" (108). For Adorno, the Huxley of *Brave New World* "makes a fetish of the fetishism of commodities," attributing to it an irreversible ontic quality (113). In failing to read the contradictions immanent to a rationalizing modernity, he ends up defending cultural traditionalism (the bourgeois family, regulated sexuality, classical literature) and ahistorical individualism. Such tensions are manifest in *Time Must Have a Stop*, which locates the sole possibility of peace in individual spiritual awakening.

Moran observes that the first line of Noralia's notebook (Safa 247), an allusion to the medieval text *Theologia Germenica*, is quoted in *The Perennial Philosophy* (256). The quotation of *L'Imitation de Jésus* (Safa 251) may be found on page 297 of *The Perennial Philosophy*, that of the Tibetan "Book of the Dead" (Safa 253) on page 32, and that of Denys l'Aréopagite (Safa 254) on page 33–34.

One might argue that in Safa's novel, the function of this once commonly practiced and now obsolete Ottoman genre is to overturn and to displace an uneven comparative relationship with Europe. The Rimbaud to whom Ferit's *nazire* is addressed wrote in the course and the aftermath of the Paris Commune, when the internal expropriation of populations from the countryside to the cities was intensified, the atomization and serialization of work (*metiér*) consolidated, and French colonial expansion strengthened (Ross 20). Kristin Ross has suggested that even Rimbaud's most self-consciously "visionary" poems cannot be understood apart from their context in this French *crisis* of the modern. We might say that Ross is not pointing, here, to a historical "ethos" *expressed in* writing so much as to the nonexpressive registration, in poetic language, of the fragmentation and atomization of the subject in capitalist modernity. Rimbaud's "literal yet not . . . referential" (Ross 127) metaphors (the "blue wine" of "La Bateau ivre," the "green lips" of "Métropolitain") seem to enact a writing practice sabotaging the social status quo by juxtaposing "familiar parts to invent new functions" (131). The "gigantic and rational *de*rangement of all the senses [*dérèglement de tous les sens*]" (Rimbaud 376–377) is nothing less than a reassemblage of the French language for a perception exceeding all determined limits; writing, in the dialogics of "L'Éternité," is a means to a momentary experience of the transcendent, in the impossible image of "the sea gone off with the sun," in its disappearance on a receding horizon.

Read in this light, Rimbaud's Europe *no longer stands* as the telos of modernity (its own, or anyone else's). Rather, like Turkey itself, it stands only as a *site in crisis*. If Rimbaud was useful for Safa, we might say that was because Rimbaud, too, sought to restore transcendence to a broken language, in the face of modernity's inscrutable and unstoppable general rationalization. For the young Rimbaud, at least, poetic writing involved the possibility of an open revolutionary politics, while Safa's own form of such intuition eventually developed into the ground of a violently closed ethnic, religious, and sexual politics. There is nothing in the *comparability* of these two texts, I am suggesting, that can overwrite their finally deeper, more fundamental, and more obvious difference. And yet the uncanny Turkish travel of Rimbaud (and of Huxley) through Safa's work might be affirmed precisely for opening, however temporarily, a textual space in which literary-linguistic no less than world-historical continuities and discontinuities *can* be thought apart from the irresistibly hierarchical "question" of originality and derivation—a question haunting all normative and historicizing literary criticism alike.

5

Nâzım's Ghostwriting

The most controversial Turkish writer of the first half of the twentieth century was the communist poet Nâzım Hikmet [Ran] (1901–1963), whose life, work, and thought profoundly shaped modern Turkish poetry from the 1920s until his death in political exile in the Soviet Union in 1963.[1] As Yahya Kemal's student at the Istanbul Heybeliada Navy School in 1917, Nâzım began as a melancholic poet in Kemal's mode,[2] but his work changed dramatically after two stays in the Soviet Union during the 1920s, which exposed Nâzım to the vibrant energy of the Russian avant-gardes of the period (particularly in the work of Vladimir Mayakovsky and Vsevolod Meyerhold). The poetry collection published in 1929 entitled *835 Satır* ("835 Lines"), typeset in the Latin alphabet and blending free verse and typographic

---

[1] Nâzım was born in Salonica in 1901 to a socially prominent family, and his life took an important turn in 1921 with the decision to join in the Turkish War of Independence. Appointed as a Turkish language teacher in the northan Anatolian city of Bolu, Nâzım left that position after a short interval for travel to the Soviet Union in September of 1921. His stays in the Soviet Union from 1921 to 1924 and 1925 to 1928 had a profound impact on both his politics and his poetics. Between 1924 and 1938, Nâzım was periodically imprisoned in Turkey on various charges relating to his communist sympathies; this was followed by an uninterrupted twelve-year sentence served from 1938 to 1950, on a conviction for inciting the Turkish armed forces to revolt. In September 1949, after a public campaign for Nâzım's amnesty led by a liberal journalist was championed by the European and U.S. media, an international committee was established in Paris by Tristan Tzara to lobby the Turkish state for Nâzım's release, and a petition signed by Tzara, Louis Aragon, Jean-Paul Sartre, Albert Camus, Simone de Beauvoir, and Pablo Picasso, among other influential intellectuals and cultural figures, was promptly delivered to the Turkish prime minister. Although Nâzım was released in July 1950, he felt continually under threat, and fled in 1951 to Romania and subsequently the Soviet Union, an act that cost him his Turkish citizenship. He died in Moscow in 1963. For further biographical details, one may consult, in English, Saime Göksu and Edward Timms's *Romantic Communist,* and in Turkish, *Nâzım Hikmet,* authored by Nâzım's stepson Memet Fuat [Bengü].

[2] Yahya Kemal is reputed to have had an affair with Nâzım's mother from 1916 to 1919 (Göksu 12; Bengü 16). Nâzım's poem "Hâlâ Servilerde Ağlıyorlar mı?" ("Are the Cypresses Still Crying?"), published in the journal *Yeni Mecmua* on 3 October 1918, is a representative example of the work of this early phase. Nâzım's paternal grandfather Mehmed Nâzım Pasha, a member of the Mawlawi order founded by the followers of Rumi, was also an important influence on Nâzım's earliest poetry. Nâzım's early poems in the traditional style can be found in the posthumous collection entitled *İlk Şiirleri.* **159**

experimentation with Marxist literary themes, had a profound impact on the Turkish literary scene of the time. With Safa, Nâzım became the leading voice of an avant-garde waging a vanguardist campaign against the "idols" of the Turkish literary establishment in the pages of the journals *Hareket* ("Movement") and *Resimli Ay* ("Monthly Illustrated") during the late spring and summer of 1929.[3]

Rapidly developing irreconcilable political differences in the charged political climate of the 1930s, Safa and Nâzım parted ways with great drama, during a public exchange turning at least in part on a conflict over Nâzım's affirmation of national vernacularization. Like both Tanpınar and Safa, Nâzım engaged the language debates in many of the newspaper essays and other writings he published from the 1930s to the 1950s, with an approach clearly marked by his three years of study at the Communist University for the Workers of the East (KUTV) in Moscow, during the heady early 1920s. In *Toplumcu Gerçekçiliğin Kaynakları* ("Sources of Social Realism"), Ahmet Oktay has noted that despite the Republican regime's successful suppression of any independent communist platform, during the second half of the 1920s, the single-party regime's ideological commitment to "populism, peasantism, secularism, and statism" (294) had gained the support of many left-leaning intellectuals. Nâzım remained an outsider in relation to the Republican bureaucratic political and cultural establishment, but he joined other leftist intellectuals in a call for writing in "clean Turkish" in several essays published in the newspaper *Akşam* ("Evening") between 12 November and 18 November 1934. In one of these essays, entitled "Öz Türkçe Düşünceler" ("Thoughts in Pure Turkish"), Nâzım suggested that the difficulties of a transition period of vernacularization notwithstanding, "the deep separation between the spoken and the written languages will be overcome" in the end (51).[4] These articles generated the polemics pitting Safa and Nâzım against each other in a famously animated episode in modern Turkish literary history. Accusing Nâzım of hypocrisy for his open support of an official "national language" ("ulusal dil"), Safa wrote in a satire entitled "Cingöz Recai'den Nâzım Hikmet'e" ("From Cingöz Recai to Nâzım Hikmet"), "For two *papel*[5] every

---

[3] *Resimli Ay* was a literary magazine founded in 1924 by Zekeriya and Sabiha Sertel, two graduates of the Columbia University School of Journalism, which with Nâzım's support moved to the forefront of the Turkish avant-garde. For Safa's praise of Nâzım's work, including a declaration of "the coming of a new literature" that will "destroy the still living remnants of the divan literature," see Safa's "Varız Diyen Nesil!" ("The Generation that Says We're Here!"), dated 11 May 1929 and published in *Hareket*. The two anonymous articles published in *Resimli Ay* and attributed to Nâzım are "Putları Yıkıyoruz, No. 1: Abdülhak Hâmit" ("Demolishing the Idols, No. 1: Abdülhak Hâmit"), in June 1929, targeting Abdülhak Hâmit, an icon of Ottoman Turkish poetry, and "Putları Yıkıyoruz, No. 2: Mehmet Emin Beyefendi" ("Demolishing the Idols, No. 2: Mehmet Emin Beyefendi"), in July of the same year, targeting Mehmet Emin, an icon of Turkish national poetry. According to the author of these two articles, neither Abdülhak Hâmit nor Mehmet Emin has successfully given voice to the struggles of the people, and so neither deserves the esteemed status he holds. For a survey of the literary "wars" of this period, including an account of Safa and Nâzım's friendship, see Ayvazoğlu 169–187; for another account of their relationship, see Bengü *Nâzım Hikmet* 89–103 and 147–172.

[4] Although the difference should not be exaggerated, the linguistic style and register of the articles Nâzım published in *Akşam* between 12 November 1934 and 12 December 1936 is noticeably plainer than that of those published earlier in other newspapers. Nâzım's support for vernacularization never relapsed into a fanaticism of any kind whatsoever; he happily continued using "foreign" words that had their place in everyday speech. For an assessment of the articles published in *Akşam*, see Hilâv, "Nâzım Hikmet Üzerine Notlar" 57–59.

[5] *Papel* here is a slang word for the Turkish lira.

Evening [*Akşam*] / You write national language / . . . / Putting on the shirt of National-isma-Fascisma" [*Ulusalizma-Faşizma*] / you dig the grave of Bolshevism" (220).

If *835 Satır* can plausibly be read as a youthfully wholesale rejection of the Ottoman literary inheritance, the 1935 and 1936 long prose poems "Taranta-Babu'ya Mektuplar" ("Letters to Taranta-Babu") and "Simavne Kadısı Oğlu Şeyh Bedreddin Destanı" ("The Epic of Sheik Bedreddin"), along with Nâzım's master-work *Memleketimden İnsan Manzaraları* (*Human Landscapes from My Country*), the earliest passages of which were composed in the 1940s, suggest that Nâzım's youthful modernism was succeeded by a progressively more nuanced maturation of his engagement with the question of the Turkish language. Although Nâzım was throughout his life an unwavering supporter of the general project of vernacular-ization, his support diverged in very significant ways from the official agenda of the Turkish state and its reform institutions.

In this final chapter, I will argue that for Nâzım, vernacular writing in modern vernacular Turkish is nothing less than an opening up of the Turkish language to the difference of other historical registers and languages—Ottoman Turkish, Persian, Russian, German, Italian—that is *not* also a domesticating of that difference. As it was in different ways for Midhat and for Seyfeddin, writing for Nâzım was a *mediation* of the news and the message of a translative language. Where the institution of a national grammatology coded the foreignizing extra-national travel of language as death, I will suggest, Nâzım very explicitly counters that binding, openly, strongly, and consistently affirming the "othering" travel of language. In this respect, and despite their political differences, Nâzım's works complement those of his conservative modernist contem-poraries, Tanpınar and Safa, opening up the vernacular to the historical difference of Ottoman Turkish and affirming the internal heterogeneity of the Turkish language.

I have a second goal in this final chapter, as well, and that is to intervene in a popular critical discourse appropriating this communist poet as a national emblem, in a contemporary Turkey no friendlier to socialism than it was during the Cold War of Nâzım's late career. The first decade of the twenty-first century marked a major shift in the Turkish reception history of Nâzım's work, as the poet's outcast specter was allowed a sort of homecoming by the Turkish state. Following the national and inter-national celebration of the centennial of Nâzım's birth, in 2002, the Council of Min-isters of the governing AKP (Adalet ve Kalkınma Partisi) decided in 2009 to terminate a governmental decree originally issued in 1951, stripping Nâzım of his Turkish citi-zenship. At a time when the communist threat that the Soviet Union represented had vanished, and as the European Union was pressing Turkey to "democratize," these belated gestures of hospitality aimed at and through Nâzım can be said to have had two important effects. In the first place, for the world outside Turkey, they staged the political tolerance of a moderately developed nation, for a transnational audience of overdeveloped so-called liberal democracies. Secondly, on the national stage itself, they were part of a belated effort to appease and to reassure a Turkish national public anxious about the loss of cultural authenticity, in the neoliberal circuit of accelerated global travel and exchange. As one of the most frequently translated writers of modern Turkish literature, Nâzım was extended such an uncontroversial welcome because unlike other traitors and fugitives, he had always and unwaveringly foregrounded, indeed flaunted, his love of vernacular Turkish.[6] This "romantic son" may have been enchanted by the spells of a foreign common, but his global travels notwithstanding, Nâzım had remained true in his "Turkish" writings to his "Turkish" origin.

Or so the story goes. In the Turkish national imaginary, this amounts to a kind of cashing in of the symbolic capital of Nâzım's over-translated "Turkish" writings, against the loss of national cultural and linguistic purity in the global circuit of translation and exchange. In so far as Nâzım's specter thus returns home, in the promise of an impossible purity in translation, my purpose here is to place some pressure on a discourse reconstructing Nâzım's Turkish writing as an expression of Turkish national authenticity. For we might say that Nâzım's love for the Turkish language is a love for Turkish not as the self-identical medium of a closed community, but precisely as the deterritorializing communication that founds such a community in the *common* that it thereafter disavows, as the price of maintaining itself in continuity. To the claim for assimilation staked by contemporary Turkish cultural nationalism in celebrating his work, Nâzım's poetry reflects back an impure Self, inherently open to *alter*ation in translation and dissemination. To truly read Nâzım in the original, I will argue, is to bring his original Turkish, itself, under erasure: to cathect an othering writing in exchange for a non-identitarian form of revolutionary collectivism.

1. The "Futurist Moment" of 1929

835 Satır was published in Turkey in 1929, after Nâzım's return from a second visit to the Soviet Union. Described by Yakup Kadri [Karaosmanoğlu] (1889–1974), a member of the Language Council and an influential supporter of the Republican reforms, as "the first line of the revolution . . . in the Turkish language,"[7] the book is today considered a turning point in modern Turkish literary history. As the poem "San'at Telâkkisi" ("Regarding Art") made amply clear, Nâzım's literary futurism had found its opponent in Yahya Kemal and his circle, who, notwithstanding their engagement with simplified Turkish, were in Nâzım's eyes still too attached to the aura of the Ottoman poetic world. Against such old-wordly attachments, "Regarding Art" mercilessly pits a "cacophony" of the novel and new: "I don't pretend / the nightingale's lament / to the rose isn't easy on the ears . . . / But the language / that really speaks to me / are

---

[6] Here is a typical declaration of Nâzım's love for the Turkish language: "It is the greatest happiness and honor of my life to have occasioned the visibility of one of the world's kindest peoples, the Turkish people, and one of the world's most beautiful, and perhaps leading languages, the Turkish language, in foreign countries. I love the Turkish language in the same way as a peasant loves his land and ox, a carpenter loves his board and plane" (*Bursa Cezaevinden Vâ-Nû'lara Mektuplar* 84). Nâzım's supporters have commonly described him as a "citizen of the Turkish language."

[7] Yakup Kadri, qtd. in Memet Fuat [Bengü], "Nâzım Hikmet'in Türk Şiirindeki Yeri" 109. Bengü does not provide the source for this quotation.

Beethoven sonatas played / on copper, iron, wood, bone, and catgut . . ." ("San'at" 36; "Regarding" 4). *835 Satır* can be read as Nâzım's attempt to absorb and recode the Turkish revolutionary moment of 1928, by linking it to the language projects of the contemporary Italian and Russian avant-gardes. The poem "Makinalaşmak" ("Mechanization"), originally composed in Moscow in 1923, serves as a kind of a temporal *and* spatial copula in this respect: composed under the spell of Russian Futurism, but not published until *835 Satır*'s appearance in 1929, the poem in its Turkish context also serves as a register of the Turkish language reforms.[8]

In the poem's title, the noun "makina" (machine), a loanword from Italian, is transformed with the suffixes *–laş* and *–mak* into the infinitive "makinalaşmak," meaning "to become a machine," or "to mechanize." As a word generalized by the communications revolution of the nineteenth century, *makinalaşmak* is a carrier of its translational history. The creation of a new infinitive using suffixes is a movement mimicked in a figure at the end of the poem, a figure of the poet himself, who desires to "place a turbine on my belly and attach a pair of propellers to my tail" (23). Generally interpreted as a straightforwardly exuberant poetic declaration of revolutionary materialism (as the *content* of its poetic *form*),[9] "Makinalaşmak" is perhaps better read as a celebratory allegory of the mechanization of poetic language, itself, by modernity understood as a dynamic process of linguistic inflection, invention, and hybridization:

> trrrum,
>> trrrum,
>>> trrrum!
> trak tiki tak!
> Makinalaşmak
>> istiyorum! (22)

> trrrum,
>> trrrum,
>>> trrrum!
> trak tiki tak!
> I want to be
>> mechanized!

Set in type several points larger in face than what follows them, the poem's opening lines are at once evocatively onomatopoetic *and* visual, as the elongated and rolling "trrrum" is repeated in lines inset and stepping left to right, while the staccato "trak tiki tak" terminating the sequence contracts the poem back toward its spatial margin. Marked by neither syllabic nor the traditional *aruz* meter, this Turkish free verse, mimicking the "voice" of a machine in a novel pattern of human-voiced stress and

---

[8] No published English translation of this poem exists; translations here are my own.

[9] Mehmet Kaplan's reading, in *Şiir Tahlilleri II* (1965), is an exception to this exclusive focus on content. Critical of Nâzım's machine aesthetics, Kaplan argued that the poem performs a mechanization of the human voice and poetic language in the repetition of the consonants *k*, *r*, and *t*.

intonation, might be said to invoke for itself, as its auditor-reader, a new linguistic machine-human. In so far as "*trrrum*" is re-marked by the "*istiyorum*" ("I want") of the sixth line here, with which it is harmonized, and "t*rak* t*iki* t*ak*" is remarked by "m*ak*inalaşm*ak*," we can say that within this mixed or nondistinctive machine-human register, the best referent of "trrrum, / trrrum, / trrrum! / trak tiki tak!" is *not* in fact an external mechanical object ("the machine"), but the language of the poem itself *as* a machine. "Trrrum, / trrrum, / trrrum! / trak tiki tak!" *records* the mechanical sound of the utterance "Makinalaşmak / istiyorum!" and at the very same time, iterates a set of primary, elemental letters, the assemblage of which forms "meaningful" words. "Trrrum, trrrum, trrrum! trak tiki tak!" is iteratively echoed throughout the poem, in word choices such as "tükrüklü" (salivary), "bakır" (copper), "mutlak" (absolutely), "karnıma" (to my belly), "uskuru" (propeller), "geliyor" (it's coming), "çıldırıyorum" (I'm going insane), and "kovalıyor" (it's chasing).

To mechanize poetic language, in this way, is to affirm language as inhuman. At the very least, we can say that this poem of the era of language reform in Turkey determinedly chooses *not* to organicize the new Turkish language as a new national or otherwise socially "human" language. In fact, we might say that the poems of *835 Satır* are composed in a colloquial vernacular that defamiliarizes phonocentric vernacularism itself. Viewed in this light, the typographic play with the size and weight of typefaces, within the poem, is a very specific gesture: foregrounding the materiality of these new letters, it does not serve the expropriation of the expropriators as a gateway to some organic materiality of labor, so much as it offers a *textual* materialism staging the impossibility of ever effacing the inherent difference of writing. At the same time, it leaves us free to consider that figural or interpretive choice, itself, as nonexclusive, and to imagine that it is precisely in becoming aware of the mediation and mediacy of one's own language that the critical revolutionary subject first becomes possible at all. In the incorporation or even co-option of the Republican state's language project for its own ends, "Makinalaşmak" can be read as supplementing that state project with an aesthetic vanguardism paralleling it (and perhaps parasitic on it). And Nâzım's early work in *835 Satır* can thus be said to establish a kind of distant kinship between an aesthetic registration of the Turkish language reforms and the language projects of Italian and Russian Futurists at large.

In Italy, it was the artist, rather than the state, who launched Futurism as "parole in libertà." Composed and published after Marinetti's return from Libya, where he reported on the 1911–12 war between Italy and the Ottoman Empire for a French newspaper, Marinetti's 1912 "Manifesto tecnico della letteratura futurista" ("Technical Manifesto of Futurist Literature") registered the beginnings of the final dissolution of the Ottoman Empire as the liberation of the Italian language, in the military-technological innovations of Italian nationalist imperialism exalted subsequently in *La battaglia di Tripoli* and in *Zang Tum Tuuum*, composed as a Balkan war correspondent in Adrianople in 1912. (It was the Italo-Turkish or Tripolitan war that saw history's first aerial reconnaissance flight and first aerial bombardment, both carried out by Italy against Ottoman Turkish positions in

1911.) In place of an extant syntax no longer up to representing modern technology, Marinetti's freed language operates in what he called the "wireless imagination" (*l'immaginazione senza fili*) ("Technical" 97; "Manifesto" 46), at once the wireless telegraph syntax of war correspondents such as Marinetti himself, and that of "the . . . rapport . . . between two old friends" ("Distruzione della sintassi-Immaginazione senza fili-Parole in libertà" 62; "Destruction of Syntax-Imagination without Strings-Words-in-Freedom" [13 May 1913] 98). This entirely performative idiom eliminates adjectives and adverbs as unnecessary and interruptive ("Technical" 92; "Manifesto" 41); verbs, meanwhile, are only to be used as infinitives, which can "adapt themselves elastically to nouns and don't subordinate them to the writer's *I* that observes or imagines" (92; 41). In a language reduced to bare elements (nouns, plus verbs strictly in infinitive form) stripped of any connectives, analogy is the sole remaining basis of signification, generating meaning by juxtaposing "distant, seemingly diverse and hostile things" with each other: "man-torpedo-boat, woman-gulf, crowd-surf, piazza-funnel, door-faucet" (93; 41). Liberated words are to "capture the breath, the sensibility, and the instincts of metals, stones, wood, and so on" (95; 44) and to "penetrate the essence of matter and destroy the dumb hostility that separates it from us" (96; 46).

In Russia, David Burliuk, Aleksei Kruchenykh, Velimir Khlebnikov, and Vladimir Mayakovsky famously declared in the 1912 manifesto "Slap in the Face of Public Taste" (*Poshchechina obshchestvennomu vkusu*) their plan to throw "Pushkin, Dostoevksy, Tolstoy, etc., etc. overboard from the Ship of Modernity," replacing them with the language and literature of "the Self-sufficient (self-centered) Word" (Lawton 51–52).[10] But where Marinetti's imagination of a "wireless" language was very much a technocratic vision, the Cubo-Futurists of pre-revolutionary Russia imagined the poetic word as a primitive archaic object, instead (18). In the 1913 manifesto "New Ways of the Word" (*Novye puti slova*), Kruchenykh articulated a program for a free and universal, transrational language (*zaumnyi iazyk*) which would eliminate the modern subordination of language to technical reason. Structured by spontaneous phonetic analogy, rather than normative grammar and syntax, Kruchenykh's transrational language was to be a primordial expression of spontaneous and immediate ecstasy, revelation, and love, on the order of religious sectarians' speech in tongues or other articulations of religious ecstasy (71–72). Khlebnikov, as another practitioner of this "transrational" language, meanwhile uncovered the primordial sense of already existing words in the elemental consonantal root sounds from which he proposed to extrapolate "a single, universal, scientifically constructed language" (Khlebnikov 150).

By the time Nâzım arrived in the USSR in September 1921, the Futurists had split into Kruchenykh's Company 41°, which devoted itself to the poetics of transrational

---

[10] The Russian Futurists were a heterogeneous circle of small literary groups: Hylae, the Ego-Futurists, the Mezzanine of Poetry, and the Centrifuge, some of which converged. For a useful introduction to the history of the movement as well as for a selection of manifestoes in translation, see Lawton, *Russian Futurism through Its Manifestoes.*

language, and Mayakovsky's revolutionary Left Front of the Arts (LEF), which styled itself a representative of proletarian literature (Lawton 40). More than transrational language as such, it was Mayakovsky's poetics of *ostranenie* or defamiliarization that attracted Nâzım: in the estranging use of conventional words in unconventional ways, making ample use of internal and end rhyme and arranging the verse line in graphic stepladder form, Mayakovsky's work can be said to have suggested a poetics for the rapidly changing language in Turkey, and for the supplementary contestation, by an aesthetic vanguard, of the primary role taken by the state. To consider the dynamic of Mayakovsky's influence on Nâzım in this light is also to see Nâzım's own "contribution" to Futurism as definitively nonderivative *and* less than visible to Futurism's European historiography, in so far as it requires a historical grasp of the Turkish language reform as a *state*-led transmogrification of the very *medium* of written and printed literary production and transmission. In *The Theory of the Avant-Garde* (1962; trans. 1968), Renato Poggioli suggested that the obscure and hermetic language projects of the European avant-gardes had for the most part taken the form of "pure and simple protest" (38), with very little "cathartic" or "therapeutic" function "in respect to the degeneration afflicting common language through convention and habit" (37). Marjorie Perloff, in turn, has described the Italian and Russian "futurist moment" (a phrase borrowed from Poggioli) as "a short-lived but remarkable rapprochement between avant-garde aesthetic, radical politics, and popular culture" (*The Futurist Moment* xvii). Critical debate over the depth of influence of an aesthetic vanguard on the broader linguistic culture it assaults is turned inside out, in a way, by the Turkish futurist moment (if we would want to call it that), in so far as it is the state itself, in this case, that acts in the artist's place.

2. Literary Communism

This project to transformatively refract state language in a vanguard poetics can be said to have failed during the difficult 1930s in Turkey. Though this early "staging" of a mechanized language served as a kind of inheritance in Nâzım's later work, it would no longer be structured by the implicit binary opposition of a traditional organic human past to a modernist mechanized revolutionary future. Published in 1936, and most likely conceived during Nâzım's imprisonment in Bursa from March 1933 to August 1934, "The Epic of Sheik Bedreddin" is an important turning point in Nâzım's work, closing the door on *835 Satır* and the "Demolishing the Idols" campaign that had followed it.[11] The first in a series of extended prose

---

[11] The period of 1929–1933, Nâzım's most active and least politically constrained years in Turkey, came to an end in March of 1933 with his arrest on the charge of spreading communist propaganda (Göksu 111). Quoting Nail V, one of Nâzım's fellow prisoners, Göksu and Timms note that Nâzım began work on the "Epic" in 1933 in Bursa prison (128). Nâzım had published in 1929 a short poem entitled "Kablettarih" ("Pre-History") about the Bedreddin uprising, but the style of this poem in a modern vernacular diverges significantly from the "Epic."

poems articulating a historical materialist reinterpretation of Ottoman and modern Turkish history,[12] the "Epic" is a fourteen-canto narrative poem including a prose prologue, epilogue, and appendix, along with a separate prose postscript published subsequently.

As the "Epic" opens, the prologue's narrator (a poet and a prisoner in Bursa) is reading an account by the contemporary scholar and theology professor Mehemmed Şerefeddin of a fifteenth-century peasant uprising led by Börklüce Mustafa, a disciple of Sheik Bedreddin, in the western provinces of the Ottoman Empire (Karaburun, in western Anatolia, and Deliorman, in the Balkans).[13] Born sometime between 1359 and 1364, Bedreddin was an unorthodox Muslim scholar whose imagination of common property ownership was blamed for the uprising crushed in 1420 by Mehmed I, who sentenced Bedreddin to death afterward.[14] The account triggers a dreamlike vision in which the narrator feels he is directly witnessing the uprising, recounting various events in the fourteen cantos subsequent to the prologue and in this way "rescu[ing]" Bedreddin, as he puts it, "from this theology professor's Arabic script" ("Epic" 42; "Simavne" 223).[15] The "Epic" concludes, meanwhile, with an epilogue in which the narrator, waking from his vision, shares it with his fellow inmates. One of the prisoners, named Ahmed, asks the narrator to write an epic about Sheik Bedreddin and to add to it an appendix including a particular story that Ahmed will relate to him.

This supplement thematizing the writing, reproduction, and dissemination of the "Epic" itself may in some ways appear to constitute secondary material, but we might just as persuasively stipulate that it has an importance equal to that of the "unsupplemented" main body of the poem. What is proposed by the "Epic," I will suggest here, is not only the practice of a new form of national historiography, but a reclamation of the Turkish language understood as an uncanny technology. As such, it acts to open up, for the establishment of a new imagination of collectivity, the communicative and translative travel of the vernacular, at precisely that time marked by intensified efforts to control it.

The prologue begins with a frame narrative focused by a scene of reading, well worth quoting at length. "I was reading," the narrator recounts,

> "The Simavne Judge's Son Bedreddin," a treatise written by Mehemmed
> Sherefeddin Effendi, Professor [*müderris*] of Scripture at the University's
> School of Theology, and printed in 1925/1341 by the Evkafı İslamiye. I'd

---

[12] Other work from this period includes "La Gioconda and Si-Ya-U" (1929) and "Why Did Banerjee Kill Himself?" (1932), mentioned below.

[13] A professor in the Faculty of Theology at the Istanbul Darülfünun (University), Mehmed Şerefeddin [Yaltkaya] (1879–1947) did indeed publish such a study, entitled *Simavne Kadısı Oğlu Şeyh Bedreddin* ("The Son of the Simavne Judge Sheik Bedreddin"), in 1924.

[14] In scholarship of Ottoman social history, the historiography of the Bedreddin uprising is a contested issue. For an assessment of Nâzım's poem as historiography, see Gürsel, *Dünya Şairi Nâzım Hikmet* 217–299.

[15] Throughout, I refer to the English translation by Blasing and Konuk. Another translation of an excerpt from the poem may be found in Christie, McKane, and Halman, *Beyond the Walls* 51–67.

reached page sixty-five of this treatise. On this scripture professor's sixty-fifth page, Dukas, who had served as head scribe to the Genoese, was saying:

"At this time, a common Turkish peasant appeared in the mountainous region at the entrance to the Bay of Ionia, known by the people there as Stilaryum-Karaburun. Stilaryum is located across from the island of Chios. The said peasant, in preaching and giving counsel to the Turks, advised that—except for women—everything like food, clothing, livestock, and land should be considered the common property of all the people." (40, trans. slightly modified; 223)

There follows a description of the narrator's act of opening the partly faded crimson cover of the treatise, which likens the act to a linguistic border-crossing, an entry into the alien world of "Arabic script, antique pen-case, reed pen, and blotting powder" (42; 225). Quotation marks are used to demarcate the Turkish language of the treatise authored by Şerefeddin from the frame narrative composed in modern Turkish, implicitly contrasting the treatise's "archaic" register with the metonymic and paratactic colloquial language of its outside: "I closed the treatise. My eyes were burning, but I wasn't sleepy. I looked at the Chemin de Fer watch hanging on a nail over my bed. It's almost two. One cigarette. One more cigarette" (41, trans. modified; 224). In contrast with the substantive "permanence" of quoted archaic language, the series of descriptive statements in modern Turkish emphasize the transience of the narrator's own corporality.

It is not only the communist-vanguardist narrator's beginning with a traditionalist-conservative historiography that surprises, here, but the particular manner in which a quotation of Şerefeddin's citation of the Byzantine chronicler Dukas's *Historia Byzantina* (1465) is used. The text is quoted from a chapter in Şerefeddin's treatise entitled "Historical Sources on the Bedreddin Incident," comprised of excerpts from Ottoman and Byzantine chronicles on the Bedreddin uprising (52–67), and it is interpolated into the text in a manner that cedes authority to the quoted source, rather than assuming or manipulating it. This first act of writing staged in the "Epic" is then clearly marked as *not* being an act of original authorship, in the conventional sense. Rather, it is marked explicitly as a *mediation,* in translation, of the quoted words of a "foreign" fifteenth-century chronicler.

As we read the "Epic" we find, in fact, that not only this opening scene of writing, but the entire body of the prologue is a mosaic of quotations of different sources, from Şerefeddin's treatise, and the historical sources cited in Şerefeddin's treatise, to the modern Turkish translation of Marx and Engels's "Manifesto of the Communist Party." Şerefeddin's historical sources include Âşıkpaşazâde Derviş Ahmed's *Tevârîh-i Âl-i Osman* ("Chronicles of the House of Osman"), completed around 1478, and Mevlânâ Mehmed Neşrî's *Kitâb-ı Cihan-nümâ* ("The Chronicle of Neşrî"), completed between 1487 and 1493. Also referenced is the Ottoman Turkish translation of *Heşt Bihişt* ("Eight Paradises"), the commissioned history of the

Ottoman Empire, written in Persian by İdrîs-i Bitlîsî between 1502 and 1506. Whereas in the prologue's opening section, the narrator clearly identifies the author or speaker of each quotation, in its latter part, apparently overwhelmed by the urgency of the anecdotes he tells us he has "memorized from İbni Arabşah, Âşıkpaşazâde, Neşri, İdrisi Bitlisi, Dukas and even Şerefeddin Efendi,"[16] he merely lists a series of passages concerning the Bedreddin uprising. It is a list that continues for two pages without any authorial attribution or other specification of authorship (42–44; 225–227).

This two-page collage of text in different historical registers of Ottoman Turkish, set off by italics and quotation marks from the modern Turkish prose framing it, offers a chronological account of the Bedreddin uprising that does not follow the chronological sequencing of the sources themselves. It has been remarked that this textual amalgam serves primarily in the mode of historical contextualization: Talât Sait Halman and his collaborators, for example, have translated the "Epic" into English omitting the prologue and summarizing relevant background information in its place, in their own introduction to the English translation (*Beyond* 51). Selâhattin Hilâv and Nedim Gürsel, two prominent critics who have both focused on the general language politics of Nâzım's poem (if not this particular portion of the prologue), meanwhile suggest that the "Epic" marks a shift in Nâzım's oeuvre, away from an understanding of language as an instrument of narration and toward its use as an object in itself.[17]

And yet we could just as easily read the apparently arbitrary *serialization* of quotation, in this portion of the prologue, in another way altogether: as a staging of the decontextualizing power of language to break free of context and to graft itself into a new, unfamiliar context. What is being transmitted by this flood of quotation, in other words, is not the "story" of Bedreddin's life as such. Nor should it be understood as a merely passive, prop-like object. If the protagonist of the poem, in the way of reading it I wish to propose, is neither Bedreddin himself, nor the prologue's narrator and implied writer, Nâzım Hikmet, then it is language itself, as anonymous, reproducible, and traveling independently of the wills and intentions of its speakers *and* receivers—and in that travel, generative of unexpected consequences. At a time when official nationalism and socialist modernism alike sought to enclose modern Turkish, sealing it off from the Ottoman-Islamic past, Nâzım's "Epic" imagines the Ottoman Turkish language in an *intensified* character of communicability. Extending such power to the Persian, Greek, and German languages, as well (these are the original languages of some of the sources cited in translation), the poem continually interrupts the "national" vernacular with the traces of foreign languages.

Ottoman Turkish, here, is an unpredictable autonomous force that visits the narrator of the prologue from a foreign "outside." Images of "lighting a cigarette" (41, 44; 224, 227), of "palms burning" (41; 224), "head aching" (41, 44; 224, 227), and "eyes burning" (41, 224) accompany and frame the scenes of quotation, as somatic markers of the narrator's reception of the message of a foreign text. But

---

[16] "Epic" 42, trans. modified; "Simavne" 225.
[17] Hilâv 49, 51; Gürsel 280.

Nâzım does not code this linguistic outside (literally demarcated in the text by the italics and quotation marks) as the harbinger of a terrifying death, as Seyfeddin found it necessary to do. Here, bodily pain marks the narrator's transformation into a kind of translator, in time-travel back to the fifteenth century for the retelling of the Bedreddin uprising in a modern twentieth-century vernacular.

But it would be a mistake to imagine this "translation" as a process of substitution. It is rather something more like possession, as the communicative force of an intercepted language seizes the modern idiom of the narrator itself, as he translates it into that modern idiom. In the main body of the poem, the narrator "possessed" in this sense borrows phrases and sentences from these quotations, once again, but this time without demarcating the text that he borrows with quotation marks. This aspect of the narrative discourse of the "Epic" should *not* be read as a mark of the seamless blending of an exteriority with an interiority. Nor should it be read as the dialectical sublation of the past in the present: the relationship between the past and the present imagined here is too heterogeneous to be mediated solely by a dialectical structure of thought.[18] It might be more accurate to say that the ragged textual surface of the "Epic," composed primarily in free verse in mixed forms evoking those of the Ottoman Turkish divan and vernacular prose and poetic forms, opens itself to the foreignized lexical and stylistic registers of "archaic" language *without dissolving any of these registers into one another*. The main body of the "Epic" then emerges as an example of what Lawrence Venuti has called "foreignizing" translation, in which a "native" linguistic register is defamiliarized by the incorporation of a "foreignized" register (Venuti, "Invisibility" 16–17).[19] Vernacularization in the "Epic" is not to be understood as the recovery of a pure and essential linguistic idiom, as some readers of Nâzım's work have imagined it. Rather, it needs to be grasped as the mediation of an impure, uncanny language, absorptive of and disseminating an ineradicable foreignness.

A strong example of such foreignization can be observed in the poem's celebrated ninth canto, in which the narrator describes the battle between Bedreddin's disciple, Börklüce Mustafa, and the Ottoman army:

---

[18] On Nâzım's "organic" blending of the past with the present, see Gürsel 276–278. For a dialectical interpretation of the "Epic," see Hilâv 49.

[19] During his imprisonment in the 1940s, Nâzım worked on the Turkish translation of Tolstoy's *War and Peace* for the Translation Bureau (Tercüme Bürosu) founded by Minister of Education Hasan Âli Yücel for the translation of Western classics into Turkish. Describing his own foreignizing translation strategy in a letter to Kemal Tahir, Nâzım writes:

> This is what I understand of translation: not to Turkicize [*Türkçeleştirmek*] the translated work one hundred percent. I mean, while you're reading a translated novel, you're not to think a Turkish author has written it. On the contrary, you're to understand it in the same way as people read it in the epoch in which it was written. That is, in translation, the Russian or the French author is to speak in his own language and not in the language of a Turkish writer. . . If this principle is accepted, it's possible for different languages to enrich and open their borders to one another without being confined within their borders. (*Kemal Tahir'e* 252-253)

It was hot.

Hot.

The heat
    was a dull knife dripping blood.

It was hot.

The clouds were full.

The clouds were about
    to burst. (55; 243)

These truncated, repetitive lines of free verse register the intensity and the stress of the battle, and the style of this portion of the "Epic" recalls the compact, paratactic prose that conveys the narrator's restlessness in the poem's prologue. In the ninth canto, this lexical and formalistic colloquial modernism is followed by archaic language borrowed from a text previously cited in the prologue's two-page amalgam of unidentified and unattributed quotations from other texts. As it turns out, these lines appear in an Ottoman Turkish translation of the sixteenth-century court history *Heşt Bihişt*, composed by İdrîs-i Bitlîsî in a highly ornate Persian style.[20] Here is how the narrator rewrites İdrîs-i Bitlîsî's remarks on an "imperial edict" ("hükmü hümâyun") "handed down" ("sâdır olmuştu") to the son of Sultan Bayezid, Shahzadah Murad, to kill ("başına ine") "the heretic Mustafa" ("mülhid Mustafa"):[21]

Hükmü hümâyun sâdır olmuştu ki Şehzade Muradın
                                ismine
Aydın eline varıp
Bedreddin halifesi mülhid Mustafanın başına ine. (244)

An imperial edict had been handed down to Prince Murad
to hasten to Aydın
and descend on the heretic Mustafa, Bedreddin's caliph. (56, trans. slightly modified)

This rewriting simplifies the language of the Ottoman Turkish translation, which turns out to be one of the texts cited in the prologue. At the same time, it makes tactical use of word choice and phrasing to mark a real shift from the modern lexical and stylistic register of the text that frames it. It is as if the "Epic's" modern narrator has disappeared, for a moment, into the language of that which he

---

[20] For Şerefeddin's citation of *Heşt Bihişt* in Ottoman Turkish translation, see Şerefeddin [Yaltkaya] 61. It is likely that Şerefeddin is the translator of the excerpt cited. In 1733 *Heşt Bihişt* was translated into Ottoman Turkish by Abdülbakî Sa'di, at the request of Sultan Mahmud I (1696–1754). The translation found in Şerefeddin's study and cited by Nâzım in the poem's prologue is less ornate in style than Sa'di's version. For Sa'di's version, see Karataş et al., eds., *Heşt Bihişt* vol 2 277. It should be noted that the style of the Persian original exerted considerable influence on the development of *Türkî-i fasîh* (Karataş et al., *Heşt Bihişt* vol 1 50).

[21] The Turkish original of the passage cited in the prologue is "'Derhal Rumiyei suğra ve Amesye Padişahı olan Şehzade Sultan Muradın ismine hükmü hümayün sadır oldu ki Anadolu askerlerini cem ile mülhid Mustafanın def'ine kıyam eyliye. Ve mükemmel asker ve teçhizat ile Aydın elinde anın başına ine'" (226).

translates and has temporarily become a third-person narrator of a sixteenth-century imperial chronicle. The phrase *hükmü hümâyun,* or "imperial edict," is formed by the grammatical construction known as *izâfet,* borrowed from Persian and commonly used in Ottoman Turkish writing from the sixteenth century onwards, and arguably the cardinal mark of the turn in Ottoman Turkish writing from the plain style of the fifteenth century to the elaborate prose of the classical period.[22] Because in Turkish, in contrast with Persian, the complementing adjective regularly precedes the complemented noun, the Persian *izâfet* was viewed as an especially "alien" element and was a specific target of language reform initiatives dating back to the second half of the nineteenth century.[23]

The narrator's incorporation of this construction, in this way, could be described as largely ironic, in so far as the borrowed words of the imperial chronicler are necessarily read against themselves, in a historiography written in the interest of the subaltern "heretic Mustafa," rather than the state. On the other hand, as an instance of a kind of free indirect discourse, quotation without quotation marks here serves to interrupt, lexically and temporally, the modernist free verse that frames it. In the end, the "Epic" neither suppresses, nor undermines the narrator's emergence as an uncanny translative medium. Rather, emphasizing the necessity of a *critical* acceptance of the imperial past against its fanatical elimination, it counters the purged, self-identical vernacular of nationalism with another impure and foreignized vernacular.[24]

A second example of foreignizing translation, with a different effect, can be observed in the eleventh canto. Following the defeat and execution of Mustafa and his followers in Canto 10, Canto 11 opens with more quotation without quotation marks. The death of Torlak Kemal, Bedreddin's other disciple, is narrated in the style of a passage from Âşıkpaşazâde's *Tevârîh-i Âl-i Osmân,* another text cited in the poem's prologue.[25] Composed in plain Turkish, this fifteenth-century chronicle is the product of a milieu in which the written and the spoken registers of the language had not yet diverged from each other. Borrowing the compact, paratactic sentences of the original text, the narrator uncannily reappears in the guise of a

---

[22] On the *izâfet* construction, see Fleisch et al., "Iḍāfa." As generally used, it links a noun to a descriptive, appositional, or genitival determinant following it, with the enclitic *-i.* (Nâzım transliterates "hükm-i hümâyun" as "hükmü hümâyun," as the enclitic would be pronounced in this instance.) While Sa'di's and Şerefeddin's Ottoman Turkish translations of *Heşt Bihişt* both employ the *izâfet* construction liberally, it is infrequent in Âşıkpaşazâde's fifteenth-century chronicle.

[23] For an example, see Ahmed Midhat, "Osmanlıcanın Islahı." The repetition of the particle *ki* ("who, which, that") in Nâzım's rewriting is also noteworthy. Borrowed from Persian, and commonly used in Ottoman Turkish writing from the sixteenth-century onwards, the *ki* particle is another mark of the turn in Ottoman Turkish writing from the compact style of the fifteenth century to the lengthy sentences of the classical period.

[24] We might say that in this unhomely retention of the expelled traces of a high Ottoman culture, at least, Nâzım's "Epic" can be read as complementary and supplementary to Tanpınar's *The Time Regulation Institute.*

[25] The Turkish original of the passage quoted in the prologue is "'Ahir Börklüceyi paraladılar ve on vilây-eti teftiş ettiler, gideceklerin giderdiler bey kullarına timar verdiler. Bayezid Paşa yine Manisaya geldi Torlak Kemali anda buldu. Anı dahi anda astı'" (226). Rendered in English: "'Lastly, they tore Mustafa limb from limb and inspected the ten provinces; they killed those who had to be killed, returned the sovereign's servant lords their fiefs. Bayezid Pasha came to Manisa, there he found Torlak Kemal. He hanged him there also'" (44, trans. modified). For Şerefeddin's citation of Âşıkpaşazâde, see Şerefeddin [Yaltkaya] 56.

fifteenth-century storyteller, in Canto 11: "Bayezid Paşa Manisaya gelmiş, Torlak Kemâli anda bulup anı dahi anda asmış, on vilâyet teftiş edilerek gidecekler giderilmiş ve on vilâyet betekrar bey kullarına timar verilmişti" (252). ("Bayezid Pasha had come to Manisa, found Torlak Kemal there, and also hanged him there. The ten provinces were inspected, those who had to be killed were killed, and the ten provinces were then returned as fiefs to the sovereign's servant lords" [63, trans. modified].) Against the Republican nationalism of the period, which imagined an assimilated form of continuity between the fifteenth-century Anatolian Turkish and the reformed language of the modern present, the narrator here absorbs and redeploys the linguistic trace of plain Turkish *without domesticating its difference*. The archaic forms of the third-person singular pronoun "an" and the adverb "anda" (there) drift into the contemporary vernacular employed in the text that follows, "foreignizing" it.[26]

Where this rewriting of the Bedreddin uprising, in the "Epic," thus reclaims and affirms the modern vernacular as an open, uncanny translative medium, the poem's epilogue and appendix stage its dissemination as a foreignizing reproductive and telecommunicative technology. Entitled "The Lathe-Operator Shefik's Shirt," the poem's epilogue consists of a brief narrative of the narrator waking up in the prison and sharing with other inmates the story of his journey across the centuries. This episode foregrounds the importance of dissemination in print, as one of the inmates, Ahmed, asks the narrator to "write a 'Bedreddin epic'" and "stick at the end of [the book]" a story to be told by Ahmed (68; 260). Where the poem's prologue and main body have imagined Ottoman Turkish as a communicative force, its epilogue thus concludes with an affirmation of the disembodied, communicative travel of a foreignized modern Turkish, in print, into new contexts.

The "Epic's" appendix might be said to leave us with a compelling image of Nâzım's literary communism. Here the narrator, imagining himself an anonymous ghostwriter, dramatically exits his own "foreignizing" translation, ascribing it not to himself, but to an anonymous collective. The appendix, which takes the form of a legend Ahmed had heard as a child in Rumelia, advances the story of the epic beyond the frame of Bedreddin's public execution by imperial forces, telling of Bedreddin's secret burial by his supporters, who subsequently remove the buried body to prevent its confiscation. Presented as a *written* record of Ahmed's oral narration, without any active mediating intervention by the narrator, this appendix can be said to stage the narrator's willing self-effacement in the mediation of another's speech.

This final scene of ghostwriting, I want to argue, is a peculiar transaction, in which the singularity of the writerly self is willingly given up in exchange for the

---

[26] Nâzım is explicitly *not* indulging in the romantic peasantist (*köycülük*) discourse of his time, which assimilated popular oral literatures into the teleology of a national literary historiography. To the extent that he invokes the archetypes of the fairy tale (*masal*), in Canto 11, it is to defamiliarize them by juxtaposing them with the character of Karl Marx. The "Epic's" claim on a genealogy of popular oral literatures is made without effacing their historical difference. On the peasantist discourses of the Republican period, see Karaömerlioğlu, *Orada Bir Köy Var Uzakta.*

literary commons of an open, heterogeneous, extra-national collective.[27] In this light, we can say that not only does the "Epic" interrupt a national grammatology with foreignizing translation, it *also* refuses to embrace any other form of identitarianism as a compensating substitute. In the end, the poem affirms anonymity as a mark of the inherent foreignness of the self *to itself.* We must not conflate this final staging of a "ghostwriting" with what we might call the state-effect of Republican national spectralization, achieved in the official reforms. To the extent that one assumes a self in the generality of a language shared by and with others, every scene of entry into language, be it oral or written, is necessarily *inherently* abstracting, and yet where Turkish national grammatology appropriates this spectralizing power of language for the institution of what I have called an impossible self-sameness, Nâzım's "Epic" affirms it for the boundless dissemination of *difference.* The ghostwriter effectively gives up his name and his claim to authorship, so as to affirm a continuous "other-ing" in the messages of an open collective in continuous transformation.[28] The practice of literary communism I am describing here is a radical opening of the self to incessant alteration, in the etymologically marked "strict" sense of that English word.

As a figure for just such a radically deterritorialized language, the story of the lost, scattered body of Bedreddin is of fundamental importance. That there is to be no *proper* grave for the body, in the story, tells us that even Bedreddin's death cannot be made to territorialize that land the common ownership of which he fought for. Rather than leaving its signature on that land, the dead body "disappears," disseminating into the materiality of a translative language. Regarding the messianic belief of the villagers in Bedreddin's return, the peasant who has narrated this story to Ahmed observes:

> Jesus is to be reborn with his flesh, bones, and beard. That's a lie. Bedreddin will be reborn without his bones, beard, or moustache—in the look of an eye, the word of a tongue, the breath of a chest. This I know. We are Bed-reddin's people; since we don't believe in any afterlife or Day of Judgment, why should we believe that a dead, scattered body will gather together and

---

[27] One might also point to the association of writing with something like (potential) self-immolation, in the main body of the poem. In the third canto, we see Bedreddin vowing to himself:

The fire in my heart
has burst into flame
and is mounting daily.
Were my heart wrought iron, it could not resist
it would melt . . .
I will come out now and declare myself! (49; 232).

A subsequent scene has Bedreddin writing *Teshil* ("Foundations") and *Varidat* ("Illuminations") as his first revolutionary act.

[28] One might argue that Nâzım's use of abstraction toward the goals of socialism is a counter-intuitive lesson taken from *Capital* 1. For a remarkable reading of Marx's understanding of capitalist abstraction as *pharmakon,* see Spivak, "Ghostwriting." We might say that the "Epic" pursues this counter-intuition at the linguistic level, adapting it to its own context. My reading of Nâzım's ghostwriting has been informed by Morris's essay "Returning the Body without Haunting," which analyzes the legacy of the exiled Thai Marxist-communist poet Atsani Phonlacan, focusing on the poet's choice of pseudonyms and code names. As a mode of self-foreignization, "pseudonymy was a revolutionary gesture," Morris writes, "precisely because it entailed the transcending of the individual subjectivity that bourgeois ideology would have asked him to affirm" (40).

be revived? When we say Bedreddin will come again, we mean his look, word, and breath will come from among us. (71, trans. modified; 265)

We might well say that Nâzım's "Epic" thus concludes in and with a "messianicity without Messianism." Death is not feared as a terrifying abyss, or welcomed as a paradisiacal afterlife, here, but affirmed as an indeterminate unknown; if it "returns" into or as some *thing*, at most, that thing is the differed and deferred promise of a revolutionary politics.[29] In and as a deterritorialized, anonymous writing, Bedreddin's specter circulates through a "boundless" space and time in the anticipation of a different future.

As a literary artifact constructed through assemblage, the "Epic" has come to no closure, even following its publication. Under attack from the nationalist political right for his communist commitments, and charged by the internationalist political left with regressive nationalism, Nâzım in 1936 published an additional, separate postscript, entitled "Simavne Kadısı Oğlu Şeyh Bedreddin Destanı'na Zeyl Millî Gurur" ("Postscript to the Bedreddin Epic: National Pride"), responding to these charges (Bengü 201). Presenting a conversation between Ahmed and the narrator about the proper relationship of the national to the international, the episode becomes yet another staging of what I have been calling the "Epic's" *othering* politics of language. In response to the narrator's questioning his "national pride," Ahmed quotes at length from Lenin's "On the National Pride of the Great Russians" (1914), declaring that he "feels national pride because during a period of feudalism, the worker masses of this nation (that is, the nine-tenths of its population) gave rise to a movement that considered the Greek sailors of Rhodes and Jewish merchants as brothers" (272).[30] It is clear here that in Nâzım's vision, even the articulation of "national pride" is an effort to bring under effacement any cultural-ethnocentrist nationalism, cathecting a self-annihilating, translative writing in the embrace of a non-identitarian revolutionary collectivism.

3. Nâzım's World Republic of Letters

Published in 1935, "Letters to Taranta-Babu" further extends this staging of an open communicability in Nâzım's work of the period. Where the "Epic" foregrounds the opening of modern Turkish to the Ottoman Turkish of the past, as well as to the transnational languages of communism (chiefly, Russian and German),

---

[29] On "messianicity without Messianism" in Marx's writings, see Derrida, *Specters* 210–212; *Spectres* 265–267. With this phrase, Derrida means to suggest a different politics of temporality than those of religious "messianisms." One can never know, Derrida suggests, whether and when the revolutionary "event" of a just society will present itself; as there is no guarantee of such an event *ever* presenting itself, there is no real guarantee of justice, either. The political, in this way of thinking, is a continuous striving toward and preparation for revolutionary justice, despite and against the possibility that it may never in fact be possible.

[30] This page numeral refers to the Turkish original, and this translation is my own. Here is one of the three paragraphs cited in Turkish from Lenin, in English translation:

"Taranta-Babu" forges links between modern Turkish and the subaltern languages of Africa and Asia. Arguably the most theoretically driven of Nâzım's poems of the 1930s, the "Epic" and "Taranta-Babu" together spur us to reread such earlier works as "Jokond ile Si-Ya-U" (1929; "La Gioconda and Si-Ya-U") and "Benerci Kendini Niçin Öldürdü?" (1932; "Why Did Banerjee Kill Himself?"), as similarly motivated and like-minded acts of foreignizing translation.[31] At the same time, they anticipate the fully developed literary communism of Nâzım's magnum opus of the 1940s, *Human Landscapes from My Country*.[32]

Like the "Epic," "Taranta-Babu" is very much an assemblage of different textual units. Constructed as a narrative poem composed of thirteen letters written by an Abyssinian student living in Rome to his wife on the eve of Mussolini's invasion of Abyssinia in October 1935, this poem, too, includes a prose prologue.[33] The prologue opens with a short note composed by its anonymous Turkish narrator, regarding a letter and package that he has received from an unnamed Italian friend "unable to use his language freely in his own country" ("Taranta-Babu'ya Mektuplar" 181). While concealing the name of this friend to ensure his safety, the narrator reproduces a letter dated 5 August 1935, in which the friend writes that he has recently discovered a series of unmailed letters in his room at a lodging house

---

We are full of a sense of national pride, and for that very reason we *particularly* hate *our* slavish past (when the landed nobility led the peasants into war to stifle the freedom of Hungary, Poland, Persia and China), and our slavish present, when these selfsame landed proprietors, aided by the capitalists, are loading us into a war in order to throttle Poland and the Ukraine, crush the democratic movement in Persia and China, and strengthen the gang of Romanovs, Bobrinskys and Purishkeviches, who are a disgrace to our Great-Russian national dignity. Nobody is to be blamed for being born a slave; but a slave who not only eschews a striving for freedom but justifies and eulogises his slavery (e.g., calls the throttling of Poland and the Ukraine, etc., a "defence of the fatherland" of the Great Russians)—such a slave is a lickspittle and a boor, who arouses a legitimate feeling of indignation, contempt, and loathing. (Par 5)

While it is important to recognize the vitality of anti-colonial nationalism in Nâzım's writing and thinking, it is equally important to distinguish the specific historical form of this revolutionism from its popular cultural-ethnocentrist interpretations, today.

[31] For the former, in the Turkish original, see *835 Satır* 59–94; for a translated excerpt in English, see *Poetry* 6–31. For the latter in the Turkish original, see *Benerci* 7–90. A self-referential investigation of the role of art in revolution, "La Gioconda and Si-Ya-U" is a fantastic tale about a love affair between the Chinese revolutionary "Si-Ya-U" and the Gioconda of Leonardo da Vinci, which comes to life to join the revolutionary struggle in China. The poem, which bears the traces of *meddah* storytelling, might well be read as an opening up of the modern Turkish vernacular in relation to Chinese. As a fictional account of Nâzım's expulsion from the Turkish Communist Party, "Why Did Banerjee Kill Himself?" might meanwhile be read as contemplating a translative relation between Bengali and Turkish.

[32] Gürsel, for example, argues that the "Epic" is closer to *Human Landscapes* than to "Letters to Taranta-Babu" or to any of the other aforementioned work (221). In my own assessment, we cannot take for granted the relationship of the "Epic" with "Taranta-Babu"—a relationship that is in many ways key to understanding the larger project of Nâzım's work.

[33] Nâzım first attempted to publish the poem under the title "İtalya'da Habeşistanlı Genç" ("An Abyssinian Youth in Italy"), but succeeded in placing only parts of it in the literary magazines *Yedigün* and *Ayda Bir* (Göksu 123). Only after he changed the title to the relatively cryptic *Taranta-Babu'ya Mektuplar* did the entire poem appear in print, at the end of 1935, with a dedication to another specter of the anti-fascist struggle, Henri Barbusse (123). According to Göksu the "first of Hikmet's works to win a readership in the West," the poem appeared in French translation in 1936 in Louis Aragon's journal *Commune* (126). Page numerals throughout my discussion here refer to the Turkish original; all translations are my own unless noted otherwise. For an English translation of "Letters to Taranta-Babu" omitting the frame letter, see Nâzım Hikmet, *Selected Poems* 47–65. A translation of the sixth and the eighth letters can be found in Nâzım Hikmet, *Beyond the Walls* 49–50.

on the outskirts of Rome. These unsent letters were written by the previous occupant, a "Galla" man,[34] to his wife, named Taranta-Babu.

It appears that the author of these letters has been detained by the Italian police and possibly executed (184). The narrator's Italian friend, who speaks a number of Asian and African languages, translates the letters into Turkish, sending them along with their originals to the Turkish narrator so that the narrator might "publish and distribute" the letters as a book: something he thinks would be worthwhile even if neither the letters' author, nor their addressee Taranta-Babu were ever to see it, and even if the Italian friend and translator of the letters himself never sees it (186). The thirteen letters that follow, and which make up the body of "Taranta-Babu," are composed in free verse, juxtaposing lyrical images of an Abyssinian village with darker images of Italy under the black, bloody shadow of financial institutions (192) and reproaching D'Annunzio and Marinetti, the celebrities of fascist culture, along with the Pope and Mussolini (199). The thirteenth and final letter itself takes the form of a collage of press clippings about the Italian invasion of Abyssinia and high unemployment in Italy, pointing to imperial expansion as an attempt to compensate for the failures of the fascist social program (213–215).

Although it is unquestionably this critique of Italian imperialism and fascism that carries the primary "message" of "Taranta-Babu," the transmission of that message itself comes under meaningful scrutiny, in the poem. Like the "Epic," "Taranta-Babu" also foregrounds the Turkish vernacular as what I have called a telecommunications technology: authorship, in this poem, is imagined as the mediation of the news of a translative language that does not domesticate its difference. While we can say that "Taranta-Babu" does not thematize the translation *process* as extensively as does the "Epic," "Taranta-Babu" nevertheless clearly registers the "foreignization" of translation, in its focus on the transpositional dynamic through which the Italian friend renders the letters from their implied source (the Oromo language) into Turkish as a target language and the framing or terminal language of "Taranta-Babu" itself, with Italian as a possible intermediary. The impossibility of any flawlessly intact translation, in this dynamic, is emphasized, in the first and sixth letters, by translator's addenda noting missing sections of the original (188, 189, 202).

In "Taranta-Babu," reading, writing, translation, and print reproduction are all conceived as acts of opening up of the self to alteration. From the "Galla" student to the Italian translator to the Turkish publisher of the poems, each "messenger" in fact becomes an anonymous ghostwriter of these transposed letters. The absence of the letters' detained and possibly dead original author is mirrored by the invisibility of the translator, whose proper name never appears (181). The act of

---

[34] The author of the letters is described as coming from the "Galla" land, "a colony of Abyssinia, which is itself a semi-colony" (185). No other historical details are provided, in the prologue, but it is possible that Nâzım is referring here to the late nineteenth-century incorporation, by the Ethiopian Emperor Menelik II, of the territory of the Oromo people of southern Abyssinia (once called "Gallas"), into the Ethiopian state.

translating requires a transcendence of the self and submission to the text of the other, in an ethical gesture that the translator likens to both birth and death: "I did not see my mother's face. She died while giving birth to me. I don't know the face of this black man. He has been taken to death through this door. I entered through the same door. All of a sudden, I understood that he is as close to me as my mother" (185). The translator here embraces the double erasure of his own name: once in the act of translating and again in releasing the translation into circulation. We might say that such a *willful embrace* of anonymity offers an affirmation of the irreducible foreignness of the self as an originary ontological condition: a gesture repeated by the figure of the anonymous, absent-present Turkish narrator, who is merely an agent for the reproduction and circulation of letters, rather than a creator of unique impressions.

Once again, we must distinguish this kind of spectralization in anonymity from that effected by Republican national grammatology. Where the domesticating translation of the latter implicitly demands the self-annihilation of the subject in its name, Nâzım's ghostwriting affirms translatability "in all directions," as it were, without determining or privileging any single circuit. As I have read it here, Nâzım's work, far from obscuring foreignization in and with translation, rather embraces a perpetual "othering" of the self in translative language. The republic of letters in "Taranta-Babu" is nothing less than a dispersed, open collective of such anonymous ghostwriters.[35]

The five-volume epic novel in verse entitled *Human Landscapes from My Country*[36] comprises a massive assemblage of fragments composed during Nâzım's imprisonment during the 1940s. Starting with the life-stories of two groups of Turkish travelers on their way from Istanbul to Ankara on two separate first-class and third-class trains, *Human Landscapes* develops into an epic of the twentieth century, as the German invasion of the Soviet Union narrated in its fourth book dilates the action beyond Turkey. A massive work that quickly outgrew Nâzım's plans for it, *Human Landscapes* remains incomplete to this day, with many sections of the original manuscript having been dispersed and lost during Nâzım's imprisonment and exile. And yet it is in many ways clearly a development of the project declared by the Bedreddin epic and "Taranta-Babu." Its anonymous narrator, all the more spectralized for having no characterological role to play in the poem's plot, might best be described as a transcriptionist, who records the inner speech of the nation and its "beyond," now in direct testimonial quotation, now in free indirect discourse. In contrast with the works that preceded it, the most prominent source of the effect of

[35] One might add that in imagining such a dispersed alternative collective, "Taranta-Babu" inserts itself into a configuration alongside the society of outsiders in Virginia Woolf's *Three Guineas* and the "vagabond internationalism" of Claude McKay's *Banjo*.

[36] The history of composition and publication of *Human Landscapes* could make a study all its own. See Göksu and Timms 217–238 for a brief account. Nâzım first began work in 1939 on what he imagined as an "Encyclopedia of Famous People," chronicling the lives of ordinary citizens; by 1942, the work had taken on something close to its final form (such as it was). Distributed to friends for safekeeping, portions of the original manuscript were destroyed or lost at various points. The standard Turkish edition, edited by Memet Fuat, was published in 1966 and 1967.

foreignization in *Human Landscapes* is this use of impersonal third-person narration.[37] With no role to play in the poem's story, the narrator dissipates into the characters whose speech he transcribes and at the same time remains spectrally situated at this third-person narrative distance. If, as has been suggested, we ought to read *Human Landscapes* as purposefully mimicking cinematic montage, one might suggest that the poem's third-person narration functions as a kind of unassimilated voice-over, speaking in excess, as it were, of the poem's staged scenes. Quite different from the judiciously fixed voice of an authoritarian narrator, this impersonal third-person narration might be said to construct a strange exteriority within the epic, ascribing its own narration to the characters whose speech it transcribes, while at the same time refracting that speech as an unlocalizable, anonymous, mechanized language that seems to speak from nowhere and from everywhere.

Indeed, we might read *Human Landscapes* as a remarkable restitutional theft, or "stealing back" of the Turkish language from the controllers of its national grammatology, and as the reassignment of that language back to the common. While the epic stages the ordinary men and women of the twentieth century very much as voiced subjects, it refuses to reproduce a new phonocentrism, in that act.

---

[37] An example, from the poem's opening:

At the Haydar Pasha train station
in spring 1941,
   It is three p.m.
. . .
A man
   stands on the steps,
     thinking some things.
. . .
The man on the steps
  —Galip Usta—
   is famous for thinking strange things:
"If I could eat sugar wafers every day," he thought
   when he was five.
"If I could go to school at ten," he thought
   at ten.
. . .
"Will my wage go up?" he thought
   at twenty.
. . .
And now standing on the steps
   he's lost his mind
in the strangest of thoughts:
    "When will I die?
Will my blanket cover me when I die?"
   he thinks.
(*Human* 3–4, trans. modified; *Memleketimden* 11–12)

The third-person narrator speaks as a double of the focalized character Galip Usta, at once enjoying access to his private thoughts and at the same time partly remote from him. Here, third-person narration is *not* the omniscient narration of the nineteenth-century European novel, which, taking over from the epic, reconstructs in modernity a "lost" totality of premodern life. This ghostly narrator clearly knows something more about the poem's world than do the poem's characters—and yet the narrator is also clearly as at much of a loss about the final "purpose" of things in that world as are the characters. When the narrator speaks independently of a character's perspective, as here, the poem's fragmented, mechanized prose (trains, clocks, and radios all play a key role) tends to reveal little more than basic temporal and spatial coordinates.

Each scene of transcriptive quotation in *Human Landscapes* identifies cited language as intimately belonging to the subject specified and identified, and yet it is simultaneously estranged from final location *in* that speaking subject by textual interruptions and reframings of impersonal third-person narration. One might say that anonymous, ghostly narration, splitting each such speaking subject, serves to mark the inherent internal difference of language itself, permeating each and all in the common, without finally being possessed by any particular individual. It is in this sense that we can say that *Human Landscapes* "returns" language to the common, and never without foregrounding, once again, the irreducible *Unheimlichkeit* of the linguistically "native."[38]

Nâzım *did* genuinely love the Turkish vernacular, then: but only in its continuous foreignization as such, in its opening onto a boundless translation. As an interruption of the official national grammatology, as well as of other, competing practices of social identitarianism, Nâzım's literary communism nevertheless also finds its own limit in its gendered figures and its figuration of gender. If the ghostwriting of *Human Landscapes* does indeed open itself to the social difference of female or women's writing, we cannot necessarily say the same of the "Epic" and for "Taranta-Babu," both of which fail at some level to imagine the gendered subaltern as a *subject,* in the open collective of invisible messengers. Taranta-Babu herself, "the twenty-fifth daughter of her father / my third wife" (187), is imagined either as an exceptional, reified other, or else as a kind of generalization of the social type of "a" wife or daughter. A similar exclusion might be found in the "Epic," which is devoid of any imagination of foreignization by the difference of women's writing.

In opening this chapter, I remarked that the specter of a globally translated and disseminated Nâzım is openly welcomed in Turkey, today, as a symbol of uncontaminated national purity.[39] But no sensitive reading of his work, either inside or outside Turkey, can ignore the extent to which Nâzım's Turkish originality, as such, is constituted by and in nothing less than a radical linguistic impurity, within which what is conceived as native is imagined as already foreign in its inherent

---

[38] Like the "Epic" and "Taranta-Babu," *Human Landscapes* also includes embedded scenes of collective reading and listening. In Book 2, for example, the waiter Mustafa reads aloud (to the cook and the headwaiter of the first-class train) the "Legend of National Liberation War," a Leninist anti-colonial interpretation of the Turkish War of Independence composed by the imprisoned poet Cemâl (a figure for Nâzım himself). Göksu and Timms argue that the patriotism of this text is powerfully ironized by its being read aloud in a first-class train full of elite Turkish and European passengers who have built up their wealth in smuggling and other forms of war profiteering (225). If one part of Nâzım's goal here is to expose the manifest contradictions of Turkish nationalization, one might argue that another is to point to the formation of an alternative, non-national collective, in precisely this circulation of an imprisoned poet's work. This scene of reading should then also be thought in conjunction with the collective scene of radio-listening, in Book 4, where Shostakovich's "Leningrad Symphony" encourages the Turkish prisoner Halil to imagine the life of Ivan, a Russian soldier (*Human* 371–387; *Memleketimden* 433–442). In neither of these scenes is the imagined alternative community a closed, self-absorbed social.

[39] For a critical study of the translation of Nâzım's work from the 1930s to the present, and its circulation outside Turkey and the Turkish language, see Ergil, *The Image of Nâzım Hikmet and His Poetry in Anglo-American Literary Systems.*

openness to translation and to dissemination. If Nâzım understood quite clearly the threat posed by the appropriation of this translatability by the agents of global imperial capital, he also refused to endorse nationalist identitarianism as a strategy of resistance, seeking instead to counter the translating force of capitalist modernity with a reopening of modern Turkish to Ottoman Turkish, Persian, and Arabic, as well as Russian, Bengali, Chinese, and Italian. A renewed practice of literary communism, as Nâzım himself practiced it, might then begin right here and now—in decisively permitting ourselves, both properly and improperly, to be *haunted* by Nâzım's ghost.

Conclusion: On the Literary Common

"I have only one language; it is not mine." A maddening, even infuriating antinomy. If the history of Turkish phonocentrism is in some sense a "mad" attempt to overcome this maddening antinomy, then perhaps we can say that Tanpınar's, Safa's, and Nâzım's work recasts that history for the affirmation of the *impropriety* of the Turkish language. Whether in the form of the state, in and as its army and school, or of the body of the social itself, in and as its own complex of independent and intertwined practices of language, the field of national politics is perhaps nothing less than a deadly struggle for the containment of unlocalized and unlocalizable language within a demarcated interiority. Against such local linguistic colonization, which is always profoundly overdetermined by the global histories of Orientalism, the writings of Tanpınar, Safa, and Nâzım might be said to speak from within the innermost limit of language, in the loudest silence of writing: "I'm monolingual. . . . The monolingualism in which I draw my very breath, is, for me, my element. . . . Yet it will never be mine, this language, the only one I am thus detained to speak, as long as speech is possible for me in life and in death; you see, never will this language be mine."[1]

My intention in this book has been to translate and to mediate this "message" of literature's other-writing against its all too easy identification as self-same community. I have emphasized that the silent figurative language of literature does not *actively* resist its usurpation as prosthetic "heritage" by the community of the nation, of long-durational nationalism, or of any other simultaneously local and transnational social complex. In my reading of the work of Seyfeddin, I suggested that the performative power of literature itself can be appropriated as a communicative event for the purpose of instituting just such a closed community. In the hands of an elite controlling access to print and to translation, the anonymous

[1] Derrida, *Monolingualism* 1–2; *Monolinguisme* 13–14.

voice of fiction can survive as the deadly speech of a linguistic outside, dedicated to enclosing the vernacular despite and against all desire and will that it be otherwise. There is no *pure* literature free of the risk of such appropriation.

And yet I have tried to demonstrate the volatility of such appropriation, as well. The non-identitarian community of the Turkish of Tanpınar's, Safa's, and Nâzım's "other-writing" is not a territorially bounded community, and it is not a community strictly contemporaneous with itself. Rather, it is assembled in dispersion, sporadically and often unexpectedly, without entailing any guarantee of its own continuity. I have tried to suggest, as well, that the monolingualism-in-common of this literature in Turkish is not itself fixed as a kind of essence, but rather exceeds itself always and continually, in an indeterminate anonymity. As its origin is indeterminate, the free circulation of this language can never finally condense into internal hierarchy: no intermediary temporarily appropriating its communicative powers can enjoy a truly lasting claim to it, or on its behalf. The social promise of the "strange institution called literature" is not the promise of a dazzling spectacle of cultural diversity exhibited on a world stage, or that of a fetishistically rigorous "research" serving the ends of imperial conquest. The promise of literature is a *promise to learn to mean to say* "I have only one language and it is not mine; my 'own' language is, for me, a language that cannot be assimilated. My language, the only one I hear myself speak and agree to speak, is the language of the other."[2] The language wars of the first half of the twentieth century continue unabated today; in and from their midst, the literary common instituted outside, as it were, in literature's other-writing might be embraced as the practice of another social, open and tolerant of difference.[3]

At the same time, I have suggested that the generalization of literature will also entail the institution of a *plurilingual* common beyond the monolingualism-in-common of Tanpınar's, Safa's, and Nâzım's work. If these writers do not explicitly practice such a plurilingualism, in their work, they certainly point toward it in their

---

[2] Derrida, *Monolingualism* 25; *Monolinguisme* 47.

[3] Although there were meaningful shifts in the language policy of the Turkish state during the second half of the twentieth century, one might say that a *proprietary attitude* toward the Turkish language remained quite consistent through such changes. The Democratic Party (DP), whose rise to power in the 1950 elections ended Republican Turkey's twenty-seven years of single-party rule by the Republican People's Party (RPP), reversed some of the RPP's language policies, including reverting the official language of the call to prayer from Turkish to Arabic. The Turkish Language Society was reorganized under DP rule, with the removal of the provision making the Minister of Education President *ex officio*—effectively ending direct state financial and political support. The privilege of state support was restored by the National Unity Committee of military officers that took control after the coup of 1960. The 1980 coup marked yet another shift in language policies, with the reconstitution of the Language Society as part of a newly established Atatürk Kültür, Dil ve Tarih Yüksek Kurumu (Atatürk Cultural, Linguistic, and Historical Society) reporting—over the objections of its members at the time—to the office of the prime minister. Maintaining moderate policy positions in the face of a resilient Arabic and Persian lexical presence in Turkish usage, today's Turkish Language Society continues to sponsor research on the Turkish language and has focused lately on protecting Turkish from the influence of English. Since the collapse of the Soviet Union, the society has taken a special interest in the Turkic languages of Central Asia. For more detailed information on the evolution of language policies after the 1950s, see Lewis 153–168 and Aytürk, "Politics" 23–30.

respective articulations of a practice of foreignizing translation.[4] In the end, the affirmation of an improper Turkish suggests not only a new language politics for Turkish itself, but the hearing, as it were, of an indeterminate other, the very source of my speech, speaking *other* languages. In the Turkish case, this "hearing" itself marks and demands the free travel of languages—including among others Armenian, Greek, Judeo-Spanish, Kurdish, Romani, and Zazaki—in the Turkish legal public domain.

The year 2002 marked a turning point in Turkey, with the beginnings of legal protection for broadcasting and private education in the "different languages and dialects used traditionally by Turkish citizens in their daily lives."[5] Initiated along with other reforms for compliance with the objectives of the 2001 European Union Accession Partnership, these efforts codified a limited new framework for the language rights severely curtailed in the aftermath of the military coup of 1980. Although the directive of 1983, prohibiting publication and broadcasting in any non-Turkish language that is not the official first language of a state recognized by Turkey, had been repealed in 1991, Article 8 of the Anti-Terror Law (Terörle Mücadele Kanunu) prohibiting separatist propaganda, enacted in the same year amid war between the Turkish state and the guerrilla forces of the Kurdistan Workers' Party (PKK), was used to curtail free speech and language rights until its abrogation in 2003. The next year (2004) marked the opening of the first private courses of instruction in the Kurdish language, as well as the first broadcasts of the state-backed national public broadcasting agency Turkish Radio and Television Corporation (TRT) in Arabic, Bosnian, Circassian, Kurmanji, and Zazaki. By 2009, the TRT channel was offering a dedicated channel of 24-hour broadcasting in Kurdish, and by 2010 one in Arabic, as well.[6]

If for many supporters of multiple language rights in Turkey, such measures were as yet insufficient, that was because they did not by themselves ensure the extension of state recognition and protection into the national compulsory education, judicial, and electoral systems. Without a doubt, the work that remains to be done here entails a substantial augmentation of the legal structure of the national public domain. And yet alongside this forensic imperative, such work will certainly also entail what Gayatri Chakravorty Spivak has called supplementation of the discourse

---

[4] On the politics of literary multilingualism in Euro-Atlantic print culture after 1945, see Lennon, *In Babel's Shadow.*

[5] Article 8A of the Law Regarding Making Changes to Certain Laws (Çesitli Kanunlarda Değişiklik Yapılmasına İlişkin Kanun), which went into effect on 3 August 2008, amended the 1994 Law Regarding the Establishment and Broadcasting of Radio and Televisions (Radyo ve Televizyonların Kuruluş ve Yayınları Hakkında Kanun), adding the clause "broadcasting is permitted in different languages and dialects used traditionally by Turkish citizens in their daily lives." Article 11 of the same law amends the 1983 Law Regarding the Teaching and Learning of Foreign Languages (Yabancı Dil Eğitimi ve Öğretimi Kanunu), permitting the offering of private courses of instruction in "different languages and dialects used traditionally by Turkish citizens in their daily lives."

[6] Nesrin Uçarlar's *Between Majority Power and Minority Resistance* offers a useful account of the most recent developments in the evolution of language rights in Turkey, including interviews with Kurdish intellectuals in Turkey and in the Kurdish diaspora.

of rights with an "imperative to responsibility" (*Imperatives* 76). As important as the granting of language rights to communities whose first language is not Turkish will be the embrace of non-Turkish languages by Turkish speakers themselves—*as if* other languages *were also* their native language. To the extent that my language is irreducibly the language of the other, each and every one of us is responsible for the protection and the continuity of all the languages of a heteronomous common constitutive of ourselves. In and beyond Turkey, the "use" of literature lies in this continuous opening up of the self to those languages that are *confined outside.*

WORKS CITED

[Adıvar,] Halide Edib. *Memoirs of Halidé Edib*. New York: The Century Co., 1926.

Adorno, Theodor W. "Aldous Huxley and Utopia." *Prisms*. Trans. Samuel and Shierry Weber. Cambridge: MIT Press, 1981. 95–118.

Adorno, Theodor W. and Max Horkheimer. *Dialectic of Enlightenment*. Ed. Gunzelin Schmid Noerr. Trans. Edmund Jephcott. Stanford: Stanford UP, 2002.

Ahıska, Meltem. "Occidentalism: The Historical Fantasy of the Modern." Irzık and Güzeldere 351–379.

———. "Occidentalism and Registers of Truth: The Politics of Archives in Turkey." Ahıska and Kolluoğlu Kırlı 9–29.

———. *Radyonun Sihirli Kapısı: Garbiyatçılık ve Politik Öznellik*. Istanbul: Metis, 2005.

———. "Türkiye'de İktidar ve Gerçeklik." *Defter* 33 (Spring 1998): 19–40.

Ahıska, Meltem, and Biray Kolluoğlu Kırlı, eds. *Social Memory*. Spec. issue of *New Perspectives on Turkey* 34 (Spring 2006): 5–116. Istanbul: Homer Kitabevi, 2006.

Ahmed Cevdet Pasha. *Belâgat-ı Osmâniyye*. Istanbul: Matbaa-i Osmâniyye, 1298/1880.

———. *Medhal-i Kavâ'id*. 1268/1851. Ed. Nevzat Özkan. Ankara: Türk Dil Kurumu Yayınları, 2000.

Ahmet Haşim. "Lisan İmarı." *İkdam* 3 Dec. 1928. Rpt. in Yorulmaz 317–318.

———. "Sağdan Yazı." *İkdam* 13 Nov. 1928. Translit. in Yorulmaz 316.

Ahmed Midhat Efendi. *Ahbar-ı Asara Tamim-i Enzar*. 1307/1890. Ed. Nüket Esen. Istanbul: İletişim, 2003.

———. *Felâtun Bey ile Râkım Efendi*. 1292/1876. Ed. Tacettin Şimşek. Ankara: Akçağ Yayınları, 1998.

———. "Hikâye Tasvir ve Tahriri." *Kırk Anbar* cüz 2 1290/1873: 107–112. Translit. in Kaplan et al. 53–57.

———. *Müşahedat*. 1308/1891. Ed. Osman Gündüz. Ankara: Akçağ Yayınları, 2003.

———. "Osmanlıcanın Islahı." *Dağarcık* cüz 1 1288/1872: 20–25. Translit. in Kaplan et al. 70–74.

———. "Romancı ve Hayat." *Şark* cild 1, sene 1 1297/1880: 2–7. Translit. in Kaplan et al. 63–69.

———. "Roman ve Romancılık Hakkında Mütaalamız." *Tercüman-ı Hakikat*, no. 3547 21 Mar. 1306/2 Apr. 1890. Translit. in Kaplan et al. 58–62.

Akçam, Taner. *A Shameful Act: The Armenian Genocide and the Question of Turkish Responsibility*. New York: Metropolitan Books, 2006.

Akçura, Yusuf. *Üç Tarz-ı Siyaset*. 1904. Ankara: Türk Tarih Kurumu Basımevi, 1976.

Akyıldız, Ali. *Osmanlı Bürokrasisi ve Modernleşme*. Istanbul: İletişim, 2004.

Alangu, Tahir. *Ömer Seyfettin: Ülkücü Bir Yazarın Romanı*. Istanbul: May Yayınları, 1968.

Algar, Hamid. "Malkom Khān, Mīrzā, Nāzim al-Dawla." *Encyclopaedia of Islam, Second Edition*. Eds. P. Bearman et al. Brill, 2009. Brill Online. Pennsylvania State U. 05 June 2009. <http://www.brillonline.nl/subscriber/entry?entry=islam_SIM-4880>.

Alptekin, Turan. *Ahmet Hamdi Tanpınar: Bir Kültür, Bir İnsan*. Istanbul: İletişim, 2008.

And, Metin. *Türk Tiyatro Tarihi: Başlangıcından 1983'e*. Istanbul: İletişim, 1994.

Anderson, Benedict. *Imagined Communities: Reflections on the Origin and Spread of Nationalism*. Revised and extended 2nd ed. London: Verso, 1991.

———. *The Spectre of Comparisons: Nationalism, Southeast Asia, and the World*. New York: Verso, 1998.

Andrews, Walter G. *An Introduction to Ottoman Poetry*. Minneapolis: Bibliotheca Islamica, 1976.

———. *Poetry's Voice, Society's Song: Ottoman Lyric Poetry*. Seattle: U of Washington P, 1985.

Andrews, Walter G. et al., eds. and trans. *Ottoman Lyric Poetry: An Anthology*. Expanded ed. Seattle: U of Washington P, 2006.

Apter, Emily. *The Translation Zone: A New Comparative Literature*. Princeton: Princeton UP, 2006.

Arai, Masami. *Turkish Nationalism in the Young Turk Era*. Leiden: E. J. Brill, 1992.

Arnaldez, R. and H. Fleisch. "Ḥarakawa-Sukūn." *Encyclopaedia of Islam, Second Edition*. Eds. P. Bearman et al. Brill, 2008. Brill Online. Brown U. 10 Sept. 2008. <http://www.brillonline.nl/subscriber/entry?entry=islam_COM-0266>.

[Arsal,] Sadri Maksudi. *Türk Dili İçin*. İstanbul: Türk Ocakları İlim ve Sanat Heyeti, 1930.

Atatürk, Mustafa Kemal. "Türk Yazı İnkılâbı Hakkında Konuşma." *Atatürk'ün Söylev ve Demeçleri* I–III. Rpt. by Atatürk Araştırma Merkezi. Ankara: Türk Tarih Kurumu Basımevi, 1997. Vol. II, 272–274.

Auerbach, Erich. Letter to Walter Benjamin. 3 Jan. 1937. Letter 10 of "Scholarship in Times of Extremes: Letters of Erich Auerbach (1933–46), on the Fiftieth Anniversary of His Death." Introd. and trans. Martin Elsky, Martin Vialon, and Robert Stein. *PMLA* 122.3 (May 2007): 750–751.

Aymes, Marc. "The Voice-Over of Administration: Reading Ottoman Archives at the Risk of Ill-literacy." *European Journal of Turkish Studies*, Thematic Issue no. 6, Ill-literate Knowledge (2007): n. pag. Web. 16 July 2009. <http://ejts.revues.org/document1333.html>.

Aytürk, İlker. "The First Episode of Language Reform in Republican Turkey: The Language Council from 1926 to 1931." *Journal of the Royal Asiatic Society of Great Britain and Ireland*, Third Series 18.3 (2008): 275–293.

———. "H. F. Kvergić and the Sun-Language Theory." *Zeitschrift der deutschen morgenländischen Gesellschaft* 159.1 (2009): 23–44.

———. "Politics and Language Reform in Turkey: The 'Academy' Debate." *Wiener Zeitschrift für die Kunde des Morgenlandes* 98 (2008): 13–30.

———. "Turkish Linguists against the West: The Origins of Linguistic Nationalism in Atatürk's Turkey." *Middle Eastern Studies* 40.6 (2004): 1–25.

Ayvazoğlu, Beşir. *Peyami: Hayatı Sanatı Felsefesi Dramı*. Istanbul: Kapı, 2008.

———. "'Saatleri Ayarlama Enstitüsü' yahut Bir İnkıraz Felsefesi." *Töre* 169–170 (June–July 1985): 29–34.

Baer, Marc David. *The Dönme: Jewish Converts, Muslim Revolutionaries, and Secular Turks*. Stanford: Stanford UP, 2010.

Bakhtin, Mikhail. "Discourse in the Novel." *The Dialogic Imagination: Four Essays*. Ed. Michael Holquist. Trans. Caryl Emerson and Michael Holquist. Austin: U of Texas P, 1981. 259–422.

————. "Slovo v romane." *Voprosy literatury i estetiki.* Ed. S. Leibovich. Moscow: Khu-dozhestvennaia literatura, 1975. 72–233.

Bali, Rıfat. *Cumhuriyet Yıllarında Türkiye Yahudileri: Bir Türkleştirme Serüveni (1923–1945).* Istanbul: İletişim, 1999.

Balibar, Étienne. *The Philosophy of Marx.* Trans. Chris Turner. London: Verso, 2007.

————. "Racism and Nationalism." *Race, Nation, Class: Ambiguous Identities.* By Étienne Balibar and Immanuel Wallerstein. Trans. Chris Turner. New York: Verso, 1991. 37–85.

Baltacıoğlu, Ismayil Hakkı. "İslâm Yazıları." *Tedrisat-ı İbtidaiye Mecmuası* 1.9 (15 Teşrinievvel 1326/28 Oct. 1910): 111–124.

————. "İslâm Yazılarının Tarihçesi." *Tedrisat-ı İbtidaiye Mecmuası* 2.17 (15 Kanunievvel 1327/28 Dec. 1911): 175–184.

————. "İslâm Yazılarının Tarihçesi: Sülüs Nevi." *Tedrisat-ı İbtidaiye Mecmuası* 2.18 (15 Kanunisani 1327/28 Jan. 1912): 213–222.

————. "Türk Yazılarının Tetkikine Methal." *Darülfünun İlâhiyat Fakültesi Mecmuası* 2.5–6 (June 1927): 111–168.

————. *Sanat: Estetik, Yaratma, Türk Sanatı, Dil, Edebiyat, Temsil, Musiki, Resim, Mimarlık, Tezyinî Sanat, Şehircilik Üzerine Görüşmeler.* Istanbul: Semih Lûtfi, 1934.

————. *Türklerde Yazı Sanatı.* Ankara: Mars T. ve S. A. S. Matbaası, 1958.

Başvekalet İstatistik Umum Müdürlüğü. *Maarif 1928–1933: Millet Mektepleri Faaliyeti İstatistiği.* Istanbul: Devlet Matbaası, 1934.

Baymur, Fuat. *İlk Okuma ve Yazma Öğretimi.* Istanbul: İnkılâp Kitabevi, 1954.

Bayramoğlu, Zeynep. *Huzursuz Huzur ve Tekinsiz Saatler: Ahmet Hamdi Tanpınar Üzerine Tezler.* Istanbul: Yapı Kredi Yayınları, 2007.

Belge, Murat et al., eds. *Modern Türkiye'de Siyasî Düşünce.* 9 vols. Istanbul: İletişim, 2001–2009.

[Bengü], Memet Fuat. *Nâzım Hikmet: Yaşamı, Ruhsal Yapısı, Davaları, Tartışmaları, Dünya Görüşü, Şiirinin Gelişmeleri.* Istanbul: Adam, 2000.

————. "Nâzım Hikmet'in Türk Şiirindeki Yeri." *Gösteri* (Nov. 1984). Rpt. in *Nâzım Hikmet Üstüne Yazılar.* Istanbul: Adam, 2001. 107–111.

Benjamin, Walter. "Die Aufgabe des Übersetzers." *Illuminationen* 50–62.

————. *Illuminationen.* Ed. Siegfried Unseld. Frankfurt am Main: Suhrkamp Verlag, 1974.

————. *Illuminations.* Ed. with an intro by Hannah Arendt. Trans. Harry Zohn. New York: Schocken Books, 1968.

————. "On Some Motifs in Baudelaire." *Illuminations* 155–200.

————. "The Task of the Translator." *Illuminations* 69–82.

————. "Über einige Motive bei Baudelaire." *Illuminationen* 185–229.

Berktay, Halil. "Neredeyse Ahd-i Atik'ten kalma . . ." *Taraf Gazetesi* 11 Sept. 2008. Web. 5 June 2010. <http://www.taraf.com.tr/halil-berktay/makale-neredeyse-ahd-i-atikten-kalma.htm>.

Beyatlı, Yahya Kemal. *Çoçukluğum, Gençliğim, Siyâsî ve Edebî Hatıralarım.* Ed. Yahya Kemal Enstitüsü. Istanbul: Istanbul Fetih Cemiyeti, 1999.

Bilgegil, M. Kaya. *Edebiyat Bilgi ve Teorileri.* Ankara: Sevinç Matbaası, 1980.

Birinci Türk Dili Kurultayı 1932–Tezler, Müzakere Zabıtları. Türk Dili Tetkik Cemiyeti. Istanbul: Devlet Matbaası, 1933.

Blanchot, Maurice. *The Infinite Conversation.* Trans. Susan Hanson. Minneapolis: U of Minnesota P, 1993.

[Bodrumlu], Avram Galanti. *Arabî Harfleri Terakkimize Mâni Değildir*. 1927. Translit. by Fethi Kale. Istanbul: Bedir Yayınevi, 1996.

Boratav, Pertev Naili. "İlk Romanlarımız." *Folklor ve Edebiyat*. Vol. 1. Istanbul: Adam, 1982. 304–319.

Bowen, H. "Aḥmad Ḏjewdet Pasha." *Encyclopaedia of Islam, Second Edition*. Eds. P. Bearman et al. Brill, 2009. Brill Online. Pennsylvania State U. 4 June 2009. <http://www.brillonline.nl/subscriber/entry?entry=islam_SIM-0406>.

Bozdoğan, Sibel, and Reşat Kasaba, eds. *Rethinking Modernity and National Identity in Turkey*. Seattle: U of Washington P, 1997.

Braude, Benjamin, and Bernard Lewis, eds. *Christians and Jews in the Ottoman Empire*. 2 vols. New York: Holmes & Meier Publishers, Inc., 1982.

Brands, H. W. "Āk̲h̲und-zāda, Mīrzā Fatḥ ʿalī." *Encyclopaedia of Islam, Second Edition*. Eds. P. Bearman et al. Brill, 2009. Brill Online. Pennsylvania State U. 05 June 2009. <http://www.brillonline.nl/subscriber/entry?entry=islam_SIM-0475>.

Bruinessen, Martin Van. *Agha, Shaikh, and State: The Social and Political Structures of Kurdistan*. Atlantic Highlands, NJ: Zed Books, 1992.

Calichman, Richard F., ed. and trans. *Overcoming Modernity: Cultural Identity in Wartime Japan*. New York: Columbia UP, 2008.

Casanova, Pascale. *The World Republic of Letters*. Trans. M. B. DeBevoise. Cambridge: Harvard UP, 2004.

Chatterjee, Partha. *The Nation and Its Fragments: Colonial and Postcolonial Histories*. Princeton: Princeton UP, 1993.

———. "Anderson's Utopia." Cheah and Culler 161–170.

Cheah, Pheng, and Jonathan Culler, eds. *Grounds of Comparison: Around the Work of Benedict Anderson*. New York: Routledge, 2003.

Chow, Rey. *The Age of the World Target: Self-Referentiality in War, Theory, and Comparative Work*. Durham: Duke UP, 2006.

Chyet, Michael L. *Kurdish-English Dictionary=Ferhenga Kurmancî-Inglîzî*. New Haven: Yale UP, 2003.

Comte, Auguste. "Reşit Paşa'ya Mektup." *İslâmiyet ve Positivism*. Ed. Christian Cherfils. Trans. Özkan Gözel. Istanbul: Dergâh, 2008. 23–27.

Cündioğlu, Dücane. *Meşrutiyet'ten Cumhuriyet'e Din ve Siyaset*. Istanbul: Kaknüs, 2005.

Davison, Roderic H. *Reform in the Ottoman Empire, 1856–1876*. Princeton: Princeton UP, 1963.

De Man, Paul. "Aesthetic Formalization: Kleist's *Über das Marionettentheater*." *The Rhetoric of Romanticism*. New York: Columbia UP, 1984. 263–290.

———. *Allegories of Reading: Figural Language in Rousseau, Nietzsche, Rilke, and Proust*. New Haven: Yale UP, 1979.

———. *Blindness and Insight: Essays in the Rhetoric of Contemporary Criticism*. 2nd rev. ed. Minneapolis: U of Minnesota P, 1983.

———. "The Concept of Irony." *Aesthetic Ideology*. Ed. Andrzej Warminski. Minneapolis: U of Minnesota P, 1996. 163–184.

———. "Conclusions: Walter Benjamin's 'The Task of the Translator.'" Messenger Lecture, Cornell University, March 4, 1983. *The Lesson of Paul de Man*. Spec. issue of *Yale French Studies* 69 (1985): 25–46.

———. "Dialogue and Dialogism." *Resistance* 106–114.

————. "Excuses (*Confessions*)." *Allegories* 278–302.

————. "Literary History and Literary Modernity." *Blindness* 142–165.

————. "The Rhetoric of Temporality." *Blindness* 187–228.

————. "Rhetoric of Tropes (Nietzsche)." *Allegories* 103–118.

————. "The Resistance to Theory." *Resistance* 3–20.

————. *The Resistance to Theory*. Minneapolis: U of Minnesota P, 1986.

De Maria, Luciano, ed. *Teoria e invenzione futurista*. Milano: A. Mondadori, 1983.

Deleuze, Gilles. *Foucault*. Trans. Seán Hand. Minneapolis: U of Minnesota P, 1988.

————. *Foucault*. Paris: Les Éditions de Minuit, 1986.

————. *Nietzsche and Philosophy*. Trans. Hugh Tomlinson. New York: Columbia UP, 1983.

Demir, Yavuz. *Zaman Zaman İçinde/Roman Roman İçinde: Müşâhedât*. Istanbul: Dergâh, 2002.

Demiralp, Oğuz. *Kutup Noktası*. Istanbul: Yapı Kredi Yayınları, 1993.

Demircioğlu, Cemal. "From Discourse to Practice: Rethinking 'Translation' (*Terceme*) and Related Practices of Text Production in the Late Ottoman Literary Tradition." Diss. Bosphorus U, 2005.

Deny, Jean. *Grammaire de la langue turque*. Paris: Imprimerie nationale, Éditions E. Leroux, 1921.

Derrida, Jacques. *De la grammatologie*. Paris: Les Éditions de Minuit, 1967.

————. "Freud and the Scene of Writing." *Writing and Difference*. Trans. Alan Bass. Chicago: U of Chicago P, 1978. 196–231.

————. *Le monolinguisme de l'autre ou la prothèse d'origine*. Paris: Galilée, 1996.

————. *The Gift of Death*. Trans. David Wills. Chicago: U of Chicago P, 1995.

————. "Introduction to Kojin Karatani's 'Nationalism and Écriture.'" *Surfaces* V.201.1 (1995). Web. 17 July 2009. <http://www.pum.umontreal.ca/revues/surfaces/vol5/derrida.html>.

————. "İstanbul Mektubu." Trans. Elis Simson. *Derrida: Yaşamı Yeniden Düşünürken*. Ed. Zeynep Direk. Spec. issue of *Cogito* 47–48 (Summer–Fall 2006): 17–36. Istanbul: Yapı Kredi Yayınları, 2006.

————. *Monolingualism of the Other; or, the Prosthesis of Origin*. Trans. Patrick Mensah. Stanford: Stanford UP, 1998.

————. *Of Grammatology*. Trans. Gayatri Chakravorty Spivak. Baltimore: Johns Hopkins UP, 1997.

————. "Signature événement contexte." *Marges de la philosophie*. Paris: Les Éditions de Minuit, 1972. 365–393.

————. "Signature Event Context." *Margins of Philosophy*. Trans. Alan Bass. Chicago: U of Chicago P, 1982. 307–330.

————. *Specters of Marx: The State of the Debt, the Work of Mourning, and the New International*. Trans. Peggy Kamuf. New York: Routledge, 1994.

————. *Spectres de Marx: l'État de la dette, le travail du deuil et la nouvelle Internationale*. Paris: Éditions Galilée, 1993.

————. "'This Strange Institution Called Literature': An Interview with Jacques Derrida." Trans. Geoffrey Bennington and Rachel Bowlby. *Acts of Literature*. Ed. Derek Attridge. New York: Routledge, 1992. 33–75.

Develi, Hayati. *Osmanlı'nın Dili*. Istanbul: 3F Yayınevi, 2006.

Dilâçar, Agop. "Gramer: Tanımı, Adı, Kapsamı, Türleri, Yöntemi, Eğitimdeki Yeri ve Tarihçesi." *Türk Dili Araştırmaları Yıllığı Belleten* (1971): 83–145.

———. "Atatürk ve Yazım." *Türk Dili* 35.307 (Apr. 1977): 315–316.

Dino, Güzin. "Recaî-zade Ekrem'in *Araba Sevdası* Romanında Gerçekçilik." *Türkiyat Mecmuası* XI (1954): 57–74.

———. *Türk Romanının Doğuşu.* Cem Yayınevi, 1978.

Dirlik, Arif. "Modernity as History: Post-revolutionary China, Globalization and the Question of Modernity." *Social History* 27.1 (Jan. 2002): 16–39.

Ebüzziya Tevfik. "Hayreddin Bey'e Cevap." *Terakkî* 2, 3, 4 Aug. 1869. Translit. in Yorulmaz 32–40.

Eliot, Sir Charles. *Turkey in Europe.* London: Edward Arnold, 1900.

Emre, Ahmet Cevat. "Güneş-Dil Teorisi." Korkmaz 321–324.

Enginün, İnci, and Zeynep Kerman, eds. *Günlüklerin Işığında: Tanpınar'la Başbaşa.* Istanbul: Dergâh, 2007.

Ergil, Başak. *The Image of Nâzım Hikmet and His Poetry in Anglo-American Literary Systems.* Istanbul: Nâzım Hikmet Culture and Art Foundation, 2008.

Ergin, Osman Nuri. *İstanbul Mektepleri ve İlim, Terbiye ve San'at Müesseseleri Dolayısıyla Türkiye Maarif Tarihi.* 5 vols. in 3. Istanbul: Eser Neşriyat ve Dağıtım, 1977.

Ersanlı, Büşra. *İktidar ve Tarih: Türkiye'de "Resmi Tarih" Tezinin Oluşumu (1929–1937).* Istanbul: İletişim, 2006.

———. "Naming Turkish Language Politically: Ottoman Language, Sun-Language, Azerbaijan Language." *Études balkaniques* 3 (2004): 108–120.

Ertem, Rekin. *Elifbeden Alfabeye: Türkiye'de Harf ve Yazı Meselesi.* Istanbul: Dergâh, 1991.

Ertürk, Nergis. "Modernity and Its Fallen Languages: Tanpınar's *Hasret,* Benjamin's Melancholy." *PMLA* 123.1 (Jan. 2008): 41–56.

———. "Surrealism and Turkish Script Arts." *Modernism/modernity* 17.1 (Jan. 2010): 47–60.

———. "Those Outside the Scene: *Snow* in the World Republic of Letters." *New Literary History* 41.3 (Summer 2010): 633–651.

Esen, Nüket, comp. "Ahmet Mithat Bibliografyası." *Karı Koca Masalı ve Ahmet Mithat Bibliografyası.* Ed. and translit. by Nüket Esen. Istanbul: Kaf, 1999. 191–215.

———. "The Narrator and the Narratee in Ahmet Mithat." *Edebiyât: Journal of Middle Eastern Literatures* 13.2 (2002): 139–146.

Etimoloji, Morfoloji ve Fonetik Bakımından Türk Dili. Ankara: Ulus Matbaası, 1935.

Evin, Ahmet Ö. *Origins and Development of the Turkish Novel.* Minneapolis: Bibliotheca Islamica, 1983.

Eyüboğlu, Sabahattin. "Yeni Türk San'atkârı yahut Frenkten Türke Dönüş." *İnsan* (15 Apr. 1938): 31–38.

Fahd, T., W. P. Heinrichs, and A. Ben Abdesselem. "Sadj.'" *Encyclopaedia of Islam, Second Edition.* Eds. P. Bearman et al. Brill, 2008. Brill Online. Brown U. 28 Oct. 2008. <http://www.brillonline.nl/subscriber/entry?entry=islam_COM-0959>.

Fazlıoğlu, İhsan. "Osmanlı Döneminde 'Bilim' Alanındaki Türkçe Telif ve Tercüme Eserlerin Türkçe Oluş Nedenleri ve Bu Eserlerin Dil Bilincinin Oluşmasındaki Yeri ve Önemi." *Kutadugubilig Felsefe-Bilim Araştırmaları Dergisi* 3 (Mar. 2003): 151–184.

Fazlıoğlu, Şükran. "Language as a Road to the Being: Language Analysis and Practice of Arabic in the Ottoman Period." Paper presented at the Middle East Studies Association Annual Meeting, Washington D.C., 22 Nov. 2002. *Şükran Fazlıoğlu Publications.*

Ed. İhsan Fazlıoğlu. Web. 10 Nov. 2008. <http://www.ihsanfazlioglu.net/EN/Sukran_ Fazlioglu/>.

———. *"Manzûme Fî Tertîb El-Kutub Fî El-Ulûm* ve Osmanlı Medreselerindeki Ders Kitapları." *Değerler Eğitimi Dergisi* 1.1 (2003): 97–110.

Feldman, Walter. "Time, Memory and Autobiography in *The Clock-Setting Institute* of Ahmet Hamdi Tanpınar." *Edebiyât: Journal of Middle Eastern Literatures* 8.1 (1998): 37–61.

Ferguson, Charles A. "Diglossia." *Word* 15 (1959): 325–340.

Findley, Carter Vaughn. *Bureaucratic Reform in the Ottoman Empire: The Sublime Porte, 1789–1922*. Princeton: Princeton UP, 1980.

———. *Ottoman Civil Officialdom: A Social History*. Princeton: Princeton UP, 1989.

Finn, Robert P. *The Early Turkish Novel, 1872–1900*. Istanbul: Isis, 1984.

Fleisch, H. et al. "Iḍāfa." *Encyclopaedia of Islam, Second Edition*. Eds. P. Bearman et al. Brill, 2010. Brill Online. Pennsylvania State U. 21 July 2010. <http://www.brillonline. nl/subscriber/entry?entry=islam_COM-0349>.

Fortna, Benjamin. *Imperial Classroom: Islam, the State, and Education in the Late Ottoman Empire*.New York: Oxford UP, 2002.

Foucault, Michel. *Les mots et les choses: Une archéologie des sciences humaines*. Paris: Gallimard, 1966.

———. *The Order of Things: An Archaeology of the Human Sciences*. New York: Vintage Books, 1994.

Freud, Sigmund. *Gesammelte Werke: Chronologisch Geordnet*. Ed. Anna Freud. 17 vols. London: Imago Publishing, 1940–1952.

———. "A Note Upon the 'Mystic Writing-Pad.'" *Standard Edition* XIX 227–232.

———. *The Standard Edition of the Complete Psychological Works of Sigmund Freud*. 24 vols. Ed. James Strachey et al. London: The Hogart Press and the Institute of Psychoanalysis, 1953–1974.

———. "Thoughts for the Times on War and Death." *Standard Edition* XIV 273–302.

———. "The 'Uncanny.'" *Standard Edition* XVII 219–256.

———."Das Unheimliche." *Gesammelte Werke* XII 227–268.

———. "Zeitgemäßes über Krieg und Tod." *Gesammelte Werke* X 323–355.

Gabrieli, F. "Adab (a.)." *Encyclopaedia of Islam, Second Edition*. Eds. P. Bearman et al. Brill, 2010. Brill Online. Pennsylvania State U. 26 Apr. 2010. <http://www.brillonline. nl/subscriber/entry?entry=islam_SIM-0293>.

Georgeon, François. "L'Économie politique selon Ahmed Midhad." *Première rencontre internationale sur l'Empire Ottoman et la Turquie moderne*. Ed. Edhem Eldem. Istanbul: İsis, 1991. 461–479.

———. *Osmanlı-Türk Modernleşmesi (1900–1930)*. Trans. Ali Berktay. Istanbul: Yapı Kredi Yayınları, 2006.

Gerçek, Selim Nüzhet. *Türk Matbuatı*. Ed. Ali Birinci. Ankara: Gezgin Kitabevi, 2002.

Göksu, Saime, and Edward Timms. *Romantic Communist: The Life and Work of Nazım Hikmet*. New York: St. Martin's Press, 1999.

Green, Martin. Introduction. *Brave New World and Brave New World Revisited*. By Aldous Huxley. New York: Harper & Row, 1965. v–xii.

Grenoble, Lenore A. *Language Policy in the Soviet Union*. Boston: Kluwer Academic Publishers, 2003.

Grunebaum, G. E. von. "Balāgha." *Encyclopaedia of Islam, Second Edition*. Eds. P. Bearman et al. Brill, 2008. Brill Online. Brown U. 07 Nov. 2008. <http://www.brillonline.nl/subscriber/entry?entry=islam_SIM-1123>.

"Günlüklerin Işığında Tanpınar'ı Değerlendirdiler." *Kitap Zamanı* 24 7 Jan. 2008: 10–11.

Gürbilek, Nurdan. "Dandies and Originals: Authenticity, Belatedness, and the Turkish Novel." Irzık and Güzeldere 599–628.

———. "Kurumuş Pınar, Kör Ayna, Kayıp Şark." *Kör Ayna, Kayıp Şark*. Istanbul: Metis, 2004. 97–138.

———. *Yer Değiştiren Gölge: Denemeler*. Istanbul: Metis, 1995.

Gürsel, Nedim. *Dünya Şairi Nâzım Hikmet*. Istanbul: Doğan Kitap, 1992.

Hacımüftüoğlu, Nasrullah. "Ahmet Cevdet Paşa'nın *Belâgat-ı Osmaniye*'si ve Yankıları." *Ahmet Cevdet Paşa (1823–1895): Sempozyum (9–11 Haziran 1995)*. Ankara: Türkiye Diyanet Vakfı, 1997. 185–222.

Hanioğlu, M. Şükrü, *The Young Turks in Opposition*. New York: Oxford UP, 1995.

———. *Preparation for a Revolution: The Young Turks, 1902–1908*. New York: Oxford UP, 2001.

Harootunian, H. D. "Ghostly Comparisons: Anderson's Telescope." Cheah and Culler 171–190.

Hayreddin Bey. "Maarif-i Umûmiye." *Terakkî*, no. 192 31 July 1869. Translit. in Yorulmaz 29–31.

Heidegger, Martin, "The Age of the World Picture." *The Question Concerning Technology and Other Essays*. Trans. William Lovitt. New York: Harper & Row, 1977. 115–154.

———. "Die Zeit des Weltbildes." *Holzwege*. Frankfurt am Main: Vittorio Klostermann, 1950. 75–113.

Heyd, Uriel. *Language Reform in Modern Turkey*. Jerusalem: Israel Oriental Society, 1954.

Hilâv, Selâhattin. "Nâzım Hikmet Üzerine Notlar." *Türkiye Defteri* (July 1974): 29–60.

Holbrook, Victoria Rowe. *The Unreadable Shores of Love: Turkish Modernity and Mystic Romance*. Austin: U of Texas P, 1994.

Huxley, Aldous. *The Perennial Philosophy*. New York: Harper & Row, 1970.

Irzık, Sibel, and Güven Güzeldere, eds. *Relocating the Fault Lines: Turkey Beyond the East-West Divide*. Spec. issue of the *South Atlantic Quarterly* 102.2–3 (Spring/Summer 2003): 283–666.

"Islâh-ı Resm-i Hatta Dâir Bazı Tassavvûrat." *Mecmûa-yı Fünûn* cüz 2, sene 2, no. 14 (Safer 1280/July 1863): 69–74. Translit. and introd. by Suavi Aydın. "Mehmet Münif Paşa, Mirzâ Feth'ali Ahûndzâde." *Tarih ve Toplum* 14.82 (Oct. 1990): 223–224.

Ives, Ernest L. Dispatch No. 550 of the Embassy of the United States of America. Constantinople, 24 Oct. 1928. Rpt. in *Türk Harf Devrimi Üzerine İncelemeler*. Ed. Bilâl N. Şimşir. Ankara: Atatürk Araştırma Merkezi, 2006. 75–78.

İbrahim [Grantay] (in the name of Dil Encümeni). "Elifba Raporu." Istanbul, 1928.

İbrahim Şinasi. "Mukaddeme." *Tercüman-ı Ahvâl* 6 Rebiülahir 1277/ 22 Oct. 1860: 1.

İğrek, Musa. "Hangi Tanpınar?" *Kitap Zamanı* 24 7 Jan. 2008: 8–9.

İnalcık, Halil. *The Ottoman Empire: The Classical Age, 1300–1600*. Trans. Norman Itzkowitz and Colin Imber. London: Weidenfeld and Nicolson, 1973.

[İnan], Afet et al. *Türk Tarihinin Ana Hatları*. Istanbul: Devlet Matbaası, 1930.

İrem, Nâzim C. "Kemalist Modernizm ve Türk Gelenekçi-Muhafazakârlığın Kökenleri." *Toplum ve Bilim* 74 (Fall 1997): 52–101.

———. "Turkish Conservative Modernism: Birth of a Nationalist Quest for Cultural Renewal." *International Journal of Middle East Studies* 34.1 (2002): 87–112.

———. "Undercurrents of European Modernity and the Foundations of Modern Turkish Conservatism: Bergsonism in Retrospect." *Middle Eastern Studies* 40.4 (July 2004): 79–112.

İz, Fahir. "Ekrem Bey, Redjāʾīzāde Maḥmūd." *Encyclopaedia of Islam, Second Edition*. Eds. P. Bearman et al. Brill, 2010. Brill Online. Pennsylvania State U. 14 Apr. 2010. <http://www.brillonline.nl/subscriber/entry?entry=islam_SIM-2176>.

———. *Eski Türk Edebiyatında Nesir*. Istanbul: Osman Yalçın Matbaası, 1964.

İzgi, Cevat. *Osmanlı Medreselerinde İlim*. Vol. 1. Istanbul: İz Yayıncılık, 1997.

Jacobs, Carol. "The Monstrosity of Translation." *Comparative Literature: Translation: Theory and Practice*. Spec. issue of *MLN* 90.6 (Dec. 1975): 755–766.

Kabacalı, Alpay. *Başlangıçtan Günümüze Türkiye'de Basın Sansürü*. Istanbul: Gazeteciler Cemiyeti Yayınları, 1990.

Kafadar, Cemal. "Mütereddit Bir Mutasavvıf: Üsküp'lü Asiye Hatun'un Rüya Defteri, 1641–1643." *Rüya Mektupları*. By Asiye Hatun. Translit. and ed. by Cemal Kafadar. Istanbul: Oğlak, 1994. 9–47.

———. "Self and Others: The Diary of a Dervish in Seventeenth Century Istanbul and First-Person Narratives in Ottoman Literature." *Studia Islamica* 69 (1989): 121–150.

Kandiyoti, Deniz. "End of Empire: Islam, Nationalism and Women in Turkey." *Women, Islam & the State*. Ed. Deniz Kandiyoti. Philadelphia: Temple UP, 1991. 22–47.

Kaplan, Mehmet. "Saatleri Ayarlama Enstitüsü." *Edebiyatımızın İçinden*. Istanbul: Dergâh, 1978. 140–143.

———. et al., eds. *Yeni Türk Edebiyatı Antolojisi*. Vol. 3. Istanbul: Edebiyat Fakültesi Matbaası, 1979.

———. "Makinalaşmak." *Şiir Tahlilleri II: Cumhuriyet Devri Türk Şiiri*. Istanbul: Baha Matbaası, 1965. 339–356.

Karabacak, Esra. "Bergamalı Kadri'nin *Müyessiretü'l-Ulûm*'u ile Ahmed Cevdet Paşa'nın Dilbilgisi Kitaplarındaki Terimler Üzerine Bir İnceleme." *Türklük Araştırmaları Dergisi* (1997): 253–283.

Karaömerlioğlu, M. Asım. *Orada Bir Köy Var Uzakta: Erken Cumhuriyet Döneminde Köycü Söylem.* Istanbul: İletişim, 2006.

Karatani, Kojin. "Nationalism and Écriture." Trans. Indra Levy. *Surfaces* V.201 (1995): 4–25. Web. 17 July 2009. <http://www.pum.umontreal.ca/revues/surfaces/vol5/karatani.pdf>.

———. *Origins of Modern Japanese Literature*. Trans. ed. by Brett de Bary. Durham: Duke UP, 1993.

Karataş, Mehmet et al., eds. *Heşt Bihişt*. 2 vols. By İdris-i Bitlisi. Trans. Abdülbakî Sa'di. Ankara: Bitlis Eğitim ve Tanıtma Vakfı, 2008.

Karpat, Kemal H. "*Millet*s and Nationality: The Roots of the Incongruity of Nation and State in the Post-Ottoman Era." Braude and Lewis, vol. 1 141–170.

———. "Ömer Seyfeddin and the Transformation of Turkish Thought." *Revue des études sud-est Européennes* X.4 (1972): 677–691.

Kasaba, Reşat. *The Ottoman Empire and the World Economy: The Nineteenth Century*. Albany: SUNY P, 1988.

Kazancıgil, Ali, and Ergun Özbudun, eds. *Atatürk: The Founder of a Modern State*. Hamden, CT: Archon Books, 1981.

Keyder, Çağlar. *State and Class in Turkey: A Study in Capitalist Development.* New York: Verso, 1987.

Khlebnikov, Velimir. *The King of Time: Selected Writings of the Russian Futurian Velimir Khlebnikov.* Trans. Paul Schmidt. Ed. Charlotte Douglas. Cambridge: Harvard UP, 1985.

Kınış, Mustafa. *Peyami Safa'nın "Matmazel Noraliya'nın Koltuğu" ile Hermann Hesse'nin "Step Kurdu" Adlı Eserlerinde Arayış ve Kendini Gerçekleştirme Sorunu.* Istanbul: İnsan Yayınları, 2000.

Kittler, Friedrich A. *Discourse Networks 1800/1900.* Trans. Michael Metteer, with Chris Cullens. Stanford: Stanford UP, 1990.

Koç, Haşim. "Osmanlı'da Tercüme Kavramı ve Tanzimat Dönemindeki Edebî Tercümelere Dair Çalışmalar." *Türkiye Araştırmaları Literatür Dergisi* 4.8 (Fall 2006): 351–381.

Koloğlu, Orhan. *Osmanlı'dan 21. Yüzyıla Basın Tarihi.* Istanbul: Pozitif Yayınları, 2006.

Korkmaz, Zeynep, ed. *Atatürk ve Türk Dili: Belgeler.* Ankara: Türk Tarih Kurumu Basımevi, 1992.

Koz, M. Sabri. "Ahmet Mithat Efendi'nin Eserleri." *Kitap-lık* 54 (2002): 160–173.

[Köprülü], Mehmed Fuad. "Harf Meselesi." *Milli Mecmua* 1 December 1926. Translit. in *Yorulmaz* 233–236.

———. *Millî Edebiyat Cereyânının İlk Mübeşşirleri ve Divân-ı Türkî-i Basit: XVIıncı Asır Şairlerinden Edirneli Nazmi'nin Eseri.* Istanbul: Istanbul Darülfünunu, Türkiyat Enstitüsü (Istanbul Devlet Matbaası), 1928.

Krenkow, F. et al. "Ḳaṣīda." *Encyclopaedia of Islam, Second Edition.* Eds. P. Bearman et al. Brill, 2008. Brill Online. Brown U. 04 Nov. 2008. <http://www.brillonline.nl/subscriber/entry?entry=islam_COM-0461>.

Kushner, David. *The Rise of Turkish Nationalism, 1876–1908.* Totowa, NJ: Frank Cass and Co., 1977.

Kütükoğlu, Mübahat S. *Osmanlı Belgelerinin Dili: Diplomatik.* Istanbul: Kubbealtı Akademisi Kültür ve San'at Vakfı, 1994.

Kvergić, Hermann F. "Türkoloji İncelemeleri." Atatürk's Private Library, no. 184. Anıtkabir, Ankara.

Lacoue-Labarthe, Phillippe. *Heidegger and the Politics of Poetry.* Trans. Jeff Fort. Urbana: U of Illinois P, 2007.

———. "Typography." *Typography: Mimesis, Philosophy, Politics.* Ed. Christopher Fynsk. Stanford: Stanford UP, 1989. 43–138.

Landau, Jacob M., ed. *Atatürk and the Modernization of Turkey.* Boulder: Westview Press, 1984.

Laut, Jens Peter. *Das Türkische als Ursprache?: Sprachwissenschaftliche Theorien in der Zeit des erwachenden türkischen Nationalismus.* Wiesbaden: Harrassowitz, 2000.

Lawton, Anna, vol. ed. *Russian Futurism through Its Manifestoes, 1912–1928.* Texts trans. and ed. by Lawton and Herbert Eagle. Ithaca: Cornell UP, 1988.

Lähteenmäki, Mika. "Nikolai Marr and the Idea of a Unified Language." *Language and Communication* 26.3/4 (July–Oct. 2006): 285–295.

Lenin, Vladimir I. "On the National Pride of the Great Russians." *V. I. Lenin: Collected Works.* Vol. 21. Moscow: Progress Publishers, 1974. 102–106. Marxists Internet Archive. 16 July 2010. <http://www.marxists.org/archive/lenin/works/1914/dec/12a.htm>.

Lennon, Brian. *In Babel's Shadow: Multilingual Literatures, Monolingual States.* Minneapolis: U of Minnesota P, 2010.

Levend, Agâh Sırrı. *Türk Dilinde Gelişme ve Sadeleşme Evreleri*. 2nd ed. Ankara: Türk Tarih Kurumu Basımevi, 1960.

Lewis, Bernard. *The Emergence of Modern Turkey*. 3rd ed. New York: Oxford UP, 2002.

Lewis, Geoffrey. *The Turkish Language Reform: A Catastrophic Success*. New York: Oxford UP, 1999.

Malečková, Jitka. "Ludwig Büchner versus Nat Pinkerton: Turkish Translations from Western Languages, 1880–1914." *Mediterranean Historical Review* IX.1 (1994): 73–99.

Mallarmé, Stéphane. "The Book: A Spiritual Instrument." *Mallarmé* 24–28.

———."Crise de vers." *Divagations* 204–213.

———. "Crisis of Poetry." *Mallarmé* 34–42.

———. *Divagations*. 1897. *Oeuvres complètes* II. Ed. Bertrand Marchal. Paris: Gallimard, 2003. 81–277.

———. "Le livre, instrument spirituel." *Divagations* 224–228.

———. *Mallarmé: Selected Prose Poems, Essays, and Letters*. Trans. and ed. Bradford Cook. Baltimore: Johns Hopkins UP, 1956.

Mango, Andrew. *Atatürk: The Biography of the Founder of Modern Turkey*. Woodstock, NY: Overlook Press, 2000.

———. "Münīf Pasha, Meḥemmed Ṭāhir." *Encyclopaedia of Islam, Second Edition*. Eds. P. Bearman et al. Brill, 2010. Brill Online. Pennsylvania State U. 14 Mar. 2010. <http://www.brillonline.nl/subscriber/entry?entry=islam_SIM-5514>.

Mardin, Şerif. *Continuity and Change in the Ideas of the Young Turks*. Istanbul: School of Business Administration and Economics, Robert College, 1969.

———. *The Genesis of Young Ottoman Thought: A Study in the Modernization of Turkish Political Ideas*. Princeton: Princeton UP, 1962.

———. "The Modernization of Social Communication." *Propaganda and Communication in World History*. Eds. Harold D. Lasswell et al. Vol. 1. Honolulu: U of Hawaii P, 1979. 381–443.

———. "Playing Games with Names." *Fragments of Culture: The Everyday of Modern Turkey*. Eds. Deniz Kandiyoti and Ayşe Saktanber. New Brunswick: Rutgers UP, 2002. 115–127.

———. "Projects as Methodology: Some Thoughts on Modern Turkish Social Science." Bozdoğan and Kasaba 64–80.

———. *Religion and Social Change in Modern Turkey: The Case of Bediuzzaman Said Nursi*. Albany: SUNY P, 1989.

———. "Some Consideration on the Building of an Ottoman Public Identity in the Nineteenth Century." *Religion, Society, and Modernity in Turkey*. Syracuse: Syracuse UP, 2006. 124–134.

———. "Some Notes on an Early Phase in the Modernization of Communications in Turkey." *Comparative Studies in Society and History* 3 (1961): 250–271.

———. "Super Westernization in Urban Life in the Ottoman Empire in the Last Quarter of the Nineteenth Century." *Turkey: Geographical and Social Perspectives*. Eds. Peter Benedict, Erol Tümertekin, and Fatma Mansur. Leiden: E. J. Brill, 1974. 403–446.

Marinetti, F. T. "Destruction of Syntax-Imagination without Strings-Words-in-Freedom." *Futurist Manifestos*. Ed. and with introd. Umbro Apollonio. Trans. Robert Brain et al. New York: The Viking Press, 1973. 95–106.

———. "Distruzione della sintassi Immaginazione senza fili Parole in libertà." De Maria 57–70.

―――. "Manifesto tecnico della letteratura futurista." De Maria 40–48.

―――. "Technical Manifesto of Futurist Literature." *Let's Murder the Moonshine: Selected Writings*. Ed. R. W. Flint. Trans. Flint and Arthur A. Coppotelli. Los Angeles: Sun & Moon Classics, 1991. 92–97.

Marx, Karl. *Capital: A Critique of Political Economy*. Vol. 1. Trans. Ben Fowkes. New York: Penguin Books, 1990.

McLuhan, Marshall. *Understanding Media: The Extensions of Man*. Cambridge: MIT Press, 1994.

Meeker, Michael E. *A Nation of Empire: The Ottoman Legacy of Turkish Modernity*. Berkeley: U of California P, 2002.

―――. "Once There Was, Once There Wasn't: National Monuments and Interpersonal Exchange." Bozdoğan and Kasaba 157–191.

―――. "Oral Culture, Media Culture, and the Islamic Resurgence in Turkey." *Exploring the Written: Anthropology and the Multiplicity of Writing*. Ed. Eduardo P. Archetti. Oslo, Norway: Scandinavian UP, 1994. 31–64.

Mehmed Münif Pasha. "Cemiyet-i İlmiye-yi Osmâniye'nin 1278 Senesi Zilkadesinin Onüçü Tarihinde Münif Efendi'nin Husûs-ı Mezkûre Dâir Telâffuz Eylediği Makaledir." *Mecmûa-yı Fünûn* cüz 2, sene 2, no. 14 (Safer 1280/July 1863): 74–77. Translit. and introd. by Suavi Aydın. "Mehmet Münif Paşa, Mirzâ Feth'ali Ahûndzâde." *Tarih ve Toplum* 14.82 (Oct. 1990): 224–225.

Messick, Brinkley. *The Calligraphic State: Textual Domination and History in a Muslim Society*. Berkeley: U of California P, 1993.

―――. "Genealogies of Reading and the Scholarly Cultures of Islam." *Cultures of Scholarship*. Ed. S. C. Humphreys. Ann Arbor: U of Michigan P, 1997. 387–412.

Milâslı İsmail Hakkı. *Yeni Yazı ve Elifbası*. Istanbul: A. Asaduryan Matbaası, 1327/1911.

"Millet Mektepleri Talimatnamesi." Law no. 7284. 11 Nov. 1928. *Resmi Gazete* 1048 24 Nov. 1928. Rpt. in Korkmaz 84–92.

Mitchell, Timothy. *Colonising Egypt*. Berkeley: U of California P, 1991.

Moran, Berna. *Türk Romanına Eleştirel Bir Bakış*. Vol. 1. Istanbul: İletişim, 2005.

Moretti, Franco. "Conjectures on World Literature." *New Left Review* 1 (Jan.–Feb. 2000): 54–68.

Morris, Rosalind C. *In the Place of Origins: Modernity and Its Mediums in Northern Thailand*. Durham: Duke UP, 2000.

―――. "Returning the Body without Haunting: Mourning 'Nai Phi' and the End of Revolution in Thailand." *Loss: The Politics of Mourning*. Eds. David L. Eng and David Kazanjian. Berkeley: U of California P, 2003. 29–58.

Mufti, Aamir R. *Enlightenment in the Colony: The Jewish Question and the Crisis of Postcolonial Culture*. Princeton: Princeton UP, 2007.

―――. "Orientalism and the Institution of World Literatures." *Critical Inquiry* 36.3 (Spring 2010): 458–493.

Namık Kemal. *İntibah*. 1293/1876. Ed. Yakup Çelik. Ankara: Akçağ, 2005.

―――. "Kırâat ve Islâh-ı Hurûf Mes'elesi." *Hürriyet*, no. 14 23 Aug. 1869. Translit. in Yetiş, *Ölümünün* 30–37.

―――. "Mukaddime-i Celâl." 1302/1884–1885. Translit. in Yetiş, *Ölümünün* 341–379.

―――. "Ta'lim-i Edebiyat Üzerine." Translit. in Yetiş, *Ölümünün* 278–339.

―――. "Usûl-i Tahsîlin Islâhına Dâir." *Tasvir-i Efkâr*, no. 403 26 Safer 1283/10 July 1866. Translit. in Yetiş 1–5.

Nancy, Jean-Luc. *The Inoperative Community*. Ed. Peter Connor. Trans. Connor et al. Minneapolis: U of Minnesota P, 1991.

Navaro-Yashin, Yael. *Faces of the State: Secularism and Public Life in Turkey*. Princeton: Princeton UP, 2002.

Necipoğlu, Gülru. "The Suburban Landscape of Sixteenth-Century Istanbul as a Mirror of Classical Ottoman Garden Culture." *Gardens in the Time of the Great Muslim Empires: Theory and Design*. Ed. Attilio Petruccioli. Leiden: E.J. Brill, 1997. 32–71.

Nietzsche, Friedrich. "On Truth and Lying in an Extra-Moral Sense." *Friedrich Nietzsche on Rhetoric and Language*. Ed. and trans. with a critical introd. by Sander L. Gilman, Carole Blair, and David J. Parent. New York: Oxford UP, 1989. 246–257.

Nutku, Özdemir. *Meddahlık ve Meddah Hikâyeleri*. Istanbul: İş Bankası Kültür Yayınları, 1976.

———. "On *Aşık*s (Tale Singers) and *Meddah*s (Story Tellers)." *The Traditional Turkish Theater*. Ed. Mevlüt Özhan. Ankara: Ministry of Culture Publications, 1999. 53–68.

Oğuzertem, Süha. "Unset *Saat*s, Upset *Sıhhat*s: A Fatherless Approach to *The Clock-Setting Institute*." *Turkish Studies Association Bulletin* 19.2 (Fall 1995): 3–18.

Okay, M. Orhan. *Batı Medeniyeti Karşısında Ahmed Midhat Efendi*. Ankara: Baylan, 1975.

———. *Beşir Fuad: İlk Türk Pozitivist ve Naturalisti*. Istanbul: Hareket Yayınları, 1969.

Oktay, Ahmet. *Toplumcu Gerçekçiliğin Kaynakları: Sosyalist Realizm Üstüne Eleştirel Bir Çalışma*. Istanbul: İthaki Yayınları, 2008.

Olgun, Tahir. *Edebiyat Lügatı*. Istanbul: Enderun Kitabevi, 1973.

Oran, Baskın. *Türkiye'de Azınlıklar: Kavramlar, Teori, Lozan, İç Mevzuat, İçtihat, Uygulama*. Istanbul: İletişim, 2004.

Osmanlıcadan Türkçeye Söz Karşılıkları: Tarama Dergisi. 2 vols. Türk Dili Tetkik Cemiyeti. Istanbul: Devlet Matbaası, 1934.

Osmanlıcadan Türkçeye Cep Kılavuzu. Türk Dili Araştırma Kurumu. Istanbul: Devlet Basımevi, 1935.

Ömer Seyfeddin. "Ali Canip'e Mektuplar." Yöntem 11. Rpt. in *Bütün Eserleri 5* 329–335.

———. *Ashab-ı Kehfimiz: İçtimaî Roman*. Istanbul: Kanaat Kütüphanesi, 1918. Translit. in *Bütün Eserleri 3* 111–157.

———. "Balkan Harbi Hatıraları." Translit. in *Bütün Eserleri 5* 269–310.

———. *Bütün Eserleri 2: Hikâyeler 2*. Ed. Hülya Argunşah. Istanbul: Dergâh, 2007.

———. *Bütün Eserleri 3: Hikâyeler 3*. Ed. Hülya Argunşah. Istanbul: Dergâh, 2007.

———. *Bütün Eserleri 4: Hikâyeler 4*. Ed. Hülya Argunşah. Istanbul: Dergâh, 2007.

———. *Bütün Eserleri 5: Şiirler, Mensur Şiirler, Fıkralar, Hatıralar, Mektuplar*. Ed. Hülya Argunşah. Istanbul: Dergâh, 2000.

———. *Bütün Eserleri 6: Makaleler 1*. Ed. Hülya Argunşah. Istanbul: Dergâh, 2001.

———. *Bütün Eserleri 7: Makaleler 2—Tercümeler*. Ed. Hülya Argunşah. Istanbul: Dergâh, 2001.

———. *Efruz Bey: Fantazi Roman*. Istanbul: Vakit Matbaası, 1919.

———. "Fon Sadriştayn'ın Karısı." *Yeni Mecmua* 1.26 (3 Jan. 1918): 513–517. Translit. in *Bütün Eserleri 2* 248–261.

———. "Fon Sadriştayn'ın Oğlu." *Yeni Mecmua* 2.30 (31 Jan. 1918): 76–80. Translit. in *Bütün Eserleri 2* 300–314.

———. "'Hatırat' Defterinden." *Yeditepe* 7.127 (15 Mar. 1957): 6. Rpt. in *Bütün Eserleri 5* 253–256.

————. *Harem.* Türk Kadını Mecmuası Yayınları. Istanbul: Orhaniye Matbaası, 1918. Translit. in *Bütün Eserleri 3* 15–49.

————. "Hürriyete Layık Bir Kahraman." Translit. in *Bütün Eserleri 4* 47–92.

————. *Mektep Çocuklarında Türklük Mefkûresi.* Çocuk Dünyası Mecmuası Neşriyatı. Istanbul: Şems Matbaası, 1914. Translit. in *Bütün Eserleri 6* 351–363.

————. "Nakarat." *Yeni Mecmua* 3.63 (3 Oct. 1918): 216–220. Translit. in *Bütün Eserleri 3* 50–68.

————. "Osmanlıca Değil Türkçe." *Türk Sözü* 5 (21 May 1914): 33–35. Translit. in *Bütün Eserleri 6* 227–230.

————. "Tuhaf Bir Zulüm." *Yeni Mecmua* 3.66 (26 Oct. 1918): 278–280. Translit. in *Bütün Eserleri 3* 69–77.

————. "Türkçeye Karşı Enderunca." *Türk Sözü* 4 (14 May 1914): 25–27. Translit. in *Bütün Eserleri 6* 216–220.

————. *Vatan! Yalnız Vatan . . .* Yeni Hayat Kitapları 2. Selanik: Rumeli Matbaası, 1911. Translit. in *Bütün Eserleri 6* 141–159.

————. "Yeni Lisan." *Genç Kalemler* 2.1 (29 Mar. 1327/11 Apr. 1911): 1–7. Translit. in *Bütün Eserleri 6* 102–113.

————, trans. "İlyada." Translit. in *Bütün Eserleri 7* 331–368.

————, trans. "Kalevala." Translit. in *Bütün Eserleri 7* 369–436.

"Ömer Seyfettin İçin." *Küçük Mecmua* 1.1 (5 June 1922): 11–13. Translit. in *Küçük Mecmua I.* Ed. Şahin Filiz. Antalya: Yeniden Anadolu ve Rumeli Müdafaa-i Hukuk Yayınları, 2009. 19–21.

Özkırımlı, Atilla. "Nazire." *Türk Edebiyati Ansiklopedisi.* Vol. 3. Ed. Atilla Özkırımlı. Istanbul: Cem Yayınevi, 1982. 899.

Özön, Mustafa Nihat. *Türkçede Roman Hakkında Bir Deneme.* Vol. 1. Istanbul: Remzi Kitabevi, 1936.

Öztürk, Muhsin. "Tanpınar Telif Davası AİHM'de." *Zaman Online* 15 Dec. 2006. Web. 15 May 2008.

Paker, Saliha. "Translation as *Terceme* and *Nazire:* Culture-bound Concepts and Their Implications for a Conceptual Framework for Research on Ottoman Translation History." *Crosscultural Transgressions: Research Models in Translation Studies II; Historical and Ideological Issues.* Ed. Theo Hermans. Northampton, MA: St. Jerome Pub., 2002. 120–143.

————. "Turkish Tradition." *Routledge Encyclopedia of Translation Studies.* Ed. Mona Baker. London: Routledge, 1998. 571–582.

Pamuk, Orhan. "Ahmet Hamdi Tanpınar ve Türk Modernizmi." *Defter* 23 (Spring 1995): 31–45.

Parla, Jale. *Babalar ve Oğullar: Tanzimat Romanının Epistemolojik Temelleri.* Istanbul: İletişim, 1990.

————. "Car Narratives: A Subgenre in Turkish Novel Writing." Irzık and Güzeldere 535–550.

————. "The Object of Comparison." *Comparative Literature Studies* 41.1 (2004): 116–125.

Parla, Taha. *The Social and Political Thought of Ziya Gökalp, 1876–1924.* Leiden: E. J. Brill, 1985.

Parlatır, İsmail. *Recaî-zade Mahmut Ekrem: Hayatı-Eserleri-Sanatı.* Ankara: Atatürk Kültür Merkezi Yayınları, 1995.

Perloff, Marjorie. *The Futurist Moment: Avant-garde, Avant guerre, and the Language of Rupture*. Chicago: U of Chicago P, 1986.

Perry, John R. "Language Reform in Turkey and Iran." *International Journal of Middle East Studies* 17.3 (Aug. 1985): 295–311.

Poggioli, Renato. *The Theory of the Avant-garde*. Trans. Gerald Fitzgerald. Cambridge: Belknap Press of Harvard UP, 1968.

Quataert, Donald. *The Ottoman Empire, 1700–1922*. 2nd ed. Cambridge: Cambridge UP, 2005.

Rafael, Vicente L. *The Promise of the Foreign: Nationalism and the Technics of Translation in the Spanish Philippines*. Durham: Duke UP, 2005.

Ran, Nâzım Hikmet. *835 Satır: Şiirler 1*. Istanbul: Adam, 1992.

———. *Benerci Kendini Niçin Öldürdü?: Şiirler 2*. Istanbul: Adam, 1992.

———. *Beyond the Walls: Selected Poems*. Trans. Ruth Christie, Richard McKane, Talât Sait Halman. London: Anvil Press Poetry, 2002.

———. *Bursa Cezaevinden Vâ-Nû'lara Mektuplar*. Istanbul: Cem Yayınevi, 1970.

———. "The Epic of Sheik Bedreddin." *Poems of Nazım Hikmet* 40–71.

———. *Human Landscapes from My Country: An Epic Novel in Verse*. Trans. Randy Blasing and Mutlu Konuk. New York: Persea Books, 2002.

———. *İlk Şiirler: Şiirler 8*. Istanbul: Adam, 1995.

———. *Kemal Tahir'e Mahpusaneden Mektuplar*. Ankara: Bilgi Yayınevi, 1968.

———. "Makinalaşmak." *835 Satır* 22–23.

———. *Memleketimden İnsan Manzaraları: Şiirler 5*. Istanbul: Adam, 1990.

———. "Öz Türkçe Düşünceler." *Sanat, Edebiyat, Kültür, Dil: Yazılar 1*. Istanbul: Adam, 1992.

———. *Poems of Nazım Hikmet*. Trans. Randy Blasing and Mutlu Konuk. New York: Persea Books, 2002.

———. "Regarding Art." *Poems of Nazım Hikmet* 4–5.

———. "San'at Telâkkisi." *835 Satır* 36–37.

———. *Selected Poems*. Trans. Taner Baybars. London: Jonathan Cape, 1967.

———. "Simavne Kadısı Oğlu Şeyh Bedreddin Destanı." *Benerci* 221–265.

———. "Simavne Kadısı Oğlu Şeyh Bedreddin Destanı'na Zeyl Millî Gurur." *Benerci* 267–273.

———. "Taranta-Babu'ya Mektuplar." *Benerci* 179–216.

Recâizâde Mahmud Ekrem. *Araba Sevdası*. Istanbul: Alem Matbaası, 1314/1896.

———. *Araba Sevdası*. Translit. in *Bütün Eserleri* III. Eds. İsmail Parlatır, Nurullah Çetin, and Hakan Sazyek. Istanbul: Milli Eğitim Basımevi, 1997. 205–445.

———. *Tâlim-i Edebiyat*. 1296/1879. Istanbul: Mihran Matbaası, 1299/1882.

Redhouse Türkçe/Osmanlıca-İngilizce Sözlük (Redhouse Turkish/Ottoman-English Dictionary). Eds. U. Bahadır Alkım et al. Istanbul: SEV Matbaacılık ve Yayıncılık, 1999.

Rimbaud, Arthur. *Complete Works, Selected Letters* (A Bilingual Edition). Trans. with an introd. and notes by Wallace Fowlie. Updated and revised ed. with a foreword by Seth Whidden. Chicago: U of Chicago P, 2005.

Ross, Kristin. *The Emergence of Social Space: Rimbaud and the Paris Commune*. Minneapolis: U of Minnesota P, 1988.

Rutherford, Danilyn. "Why Papua Wants Freedom: The Third Person in Contemporary Nationalism." *Public Culture* 20.2 (Spring 2008): 345–373.

Sadoğlu, Hüseyin. *Türkiye'de Ulusçuluk ve Dil Politikaları*. Istanbul: Bilgi İletişim Grubu, 2003.

Safa, Peyami. "Allahım, Bu Ne Anarşidir!" *Tasvir-i Efkâr* 5 Feb. 1941. Rpt. in *Osmanlıca* 66–67.

———. "Bölge Dilleri ve Ortak Dil." *Türk Yurdu* 1959. Rpt. in *Osmanlıca* 243–246.

———. "Cingöz Recai'den Nâzım Hikmet'e." *Hafta* 77 23 Sept. 1935. Rpt. in Ayvazoğlu 217–221.

———. "Dost ve Düşman Kelimeler." *Tasvir-i Efkâr* 13 Dec. 1941. Rpt. in *Osmanlıca* 96–97.

———. "Düetto." *Cumhuriyet* 8 Apr. 1937: 3.

———. "İlk Basamak." *Cumhuriyet* 30 Mar. 1940. Rpt. in *Osmanlıca* 55–57.

———. "Kanunsuz Olmaz!" *Cumhuriyet* 22 Dec. 1936: 3.

———. *Matmazel Noraliya'nın Koltuğu*. Istanbul: Nebioğlu Yayınevi, 1949.

———. *Millet ve İnsan*. Istanbul: Halk Basımevi, 1943.

———. *Osmanlıca, Türkçe, Uydurmaca*. Istanbul: Ötüken, 1990.

———. "Türk Gramerinin Esasları." *Tasvir-i Efkâr* 16, 20, 26, 31 July and 6 Aug. 1941. Rpt. in *Osmanlıca* 79–96.

———. *Türk İnkılabına Bakışlar*. Ankara: Kültür Bakanlığı, 1981.

———. "Türk Olmak Şartı." *Büyük Doğu* 1.8 (21 Dec. 1945): 3.

Said, Edward W. *The World, the Text, and the Critic*. Cambridge: Harvard UP, 1983.

Samih Rıfat. *Türkçede Tasrif-i Huruf Kanunları ve Tekellümün Menşei: Ankara Maarif Vekaleti Telif ve Tercüme Encümeninde 3 Nisan 1338 Tarihinde Heyet Reisi Samih Rıfat Bey Tarafından Okunan Rapor*. Ankara: Matbuat ve İstihbarat Matbaası, 1338/1922.

Sandfeld, Kristian. *Linguistique balkanique*. Paris: E. Champion, 1930.

Saraçoğlu, Mehmet Safa. "Reality with a Moral Twist: Ahmed Midhat's *Müşahedat* as an Image of an Ideal Ottoman Society." *Critique: Critical Middle Eastern Studies* 15.1 (Spring 2006): 29–47.

Schleiermacher, Friedrich. "On the Different Methods of Translating." Trans. Susan Bernofsky. *The Translation Studies Reader*. 2nd ed. Ed. Lawrence Venuti. New York: Routledge, 2004. 43–63.

———."Über die verschiedenen Methoden des Übersetzens." *Kritische Gesamtausgabe: Akademievorträge*. Vol. 11. *Schriften und Entwürfe*. Eds. Martin Rössler and Lars Emersleben. Berlin: Walter de Gruyter, 2002. 67–93.

Şemseddin Sami. "Lisân-ı Türkî-i (Osmanî)." *Hafta* 12 (10 Zilhicce 1298/3 Nov. 1881): 177–181. Translit. in *Şemsettin Sami*. Ed. Agâh Sırrı Levend. Ankara: Ankara Üniversitesi Basımevi, 1969. 152–157.

Seyhan, Azade. *Tales of Crossed Destinies: The Modern Turkish Novel in a Comparative Context*. New York: Modern Language Association of America, 2008.

Shafak, Elif. "Accelerating the Flow of Time: Soft Power and the Role of Intellectuals in Turkey." *World Literature Today* 80.1 (Jan./Feb. 2006): 24–26.

Shaw, Stanford J. *From Empire to Republic: The Turkish War of National Liberation, 1918–1923: A Documentary Study*. 6 vols. Ankara: Türk Tarih Kurumu Basımevi, 2000.

Shaw, Wendy M. K. "Whose Hittites, and Why? Language, Archaeology and the Quest for the Original Turks." *Archaeology under Dictatorship*. Eds. Michael L. Galaty and Charles Watkinson. New York: Kluwer Academic/Plenum Publishers, 2004. 131–153.

Siegel, James T. *Fetish, Recognition, Revolution*. Princeton: Princeton UP, 1997.

——— *Naming the Witch*. Stanford: Stanford UP, 2006.

Somel, Selçuk Akşin. *The Modernization of Public Education in the Ottoman Empire (1839–1908): Islamization, Autocracy and Discipline*. Leiden: Brill, 2001.

Spitzer, Leo. "En apprenant le turc." *Bulletin de la Société de Linguistique de Paris* 35 (1934): 82–101.

———. "Türkçeyi Öğrenirken." Trans. Sabahattin Rahmi [Eyüboğlu]. *Varlık* 19 (15 Apr. 1934): 296–297; 35 (15 Dec. 1934): 163–164; and 37 (15 Jan. 1935): 194–196.

Spivak, Gayatri Chakravorty. *A Critique of Postcolonial Reason: Toward a History of the Vanishing Present.* Cambridge: Harvard UP, 1999.

———. "Ghostwriting." *Diacritics* 25.2 (Summer 1995): 64–84.

———. *Imperatives to Re-Imagine the Planet.* Vienna: Passagen, 1999.

———. "Harlem." *Social Text* 22.4 (Winter 2004): 113–139.

Stepanyan, Hasmik A. *Ermeni Harfli Türkçe Kitaplar ve Süreli Yayınlar Bibliyografyası (1727–1968).* Istanbul: Turkuaz, 2005.

Steuerwald, Karl. *Untersuchungen zur türkischen Sprache der Gegenwart 1: Die türkische Sprachpolitik seit 1928.* Berlin-Schöneberg: Langenscheidt, 1963.

Strauss, Johann. "Diglossie dans le domaine ottoman: Évolution et péripéties d'une situation linguistique." *Revue du mondes musulman et de la Méditerranée* 75.1 (1995): 221–255.

———. "Konuşma." *Osmanlı İmparatorluğu'nda Yaşamak: Toplumsallık Biçimleri ve Cemaatlerarası İlişkiler (18.–20. yüzyıllar).* Eds. François Georgeon and Paul Dumont. Trans. Maide Selen. Istanbul: İletişim, 2008. 307–386.

———. "Who Read What in the Ottoman Empire (19th–20th centuries)?" *Middle Eastern Literatures* 6.1 (2003): 39–76.

Şener, Nedim. *Dink Cinayeti ve İstihbarat Yalanları.* Istanbul: Güncel Yayıncılık, 2009.

Şimşir, Bilâl N. *Türk Yazı Devrimi.* Ankara: Türk Tarih Kurumu Basımevi, 1992.

Tanpınar, Ahmet Hamdi. "Antalyalı Genç Kıza Mektup." *Yaşadığım Gibi.* Ed. Birol Emil. Istanbul: Dergâh, 2005. 348–353.

———. *Beş Şehir.* Ankara: Ülkü, 1946.

———. *Beş Şehir.* 2nd ed. Ankara: Türk Tarih Kurumu Basımevi, 1960.

———. *Huzur.* Istanbul: Remzi Kitabevi, 1949.

———. *A Mind at Peace.* Trans. Erdağ Göknar. Brooklyn, NY: Archipelago Books, 2008.

———. "Ne İçindeyim Zamanın." Rpt. in *Bütün Şiirleri.* Ed. İnci Enginün. Istanbul: Dergâh, 2007. 19.

———. *Ondokuzuncu Asır Türk Edebiyatı Tarihi.* Revised and expanded 2nd ed. Istanbul: Çağlayan Kitabevi, 1956.

———. *Saatleri Ayarlama Enstitüsü.* Istanbul: Remzi Kitabevi, 1961.

———. *The Time Regulation Institute.* Trans. Ender Gürol. Madison: Turko-Tatar Press, 2001.

———. "Türk Edebiyatı'nda Cereyanlar." *Edebiyat Üzerine Makaleler.* Ed. Zeynep Kerman. Istanbul: Milli Eğitim Basımevi, 1969. 102–131.

———. *Yahya Kemal.* Ed. Mehmet Kaplan. Istanbul: Dergâh, 2007.

Tansel, Fevziye Abdullah. "Arap Harflerinin Islahı ve Değiştirilmesi Hakkında İlk Teşebbüsler ve Neticeleri (1862–1884)." *Belleten* 17.66 (Apr. 1953): 223–249.

Taşköprülüzâde Ahmed. *Mevzuat'ül Ulûm.* Vol. 1. Trans. Kemaleddin Mehmed Efendi. Translit. and simplified by Mümin Çevik. Istanbul: Üç Dal Neşriyat, 1966.

Tekin, Mehmet. *Romancı Yönüyle Peyami Safa.* Istanbul: Ötüken Neşriyat, 1999.

Tinckom-Fernandez, W. G. "Changing Alphabet Obsesses Kemal." *New York Times* 2 Sept. 1928: 26.

"Türk Harflerinin Kabul ve Tatbiki Hakkındaki Kanun." Law no. 1353. 1 Nov. 1928. *Resmi Gazete* 1030 3 Nov. 1928. Rpt. in Korkmaz 71–72.

"Türk Dili Birinci Kurultayınca Kabul Edilen Çalışma Programı." *Türk Dili* 1 (Apr. 1933): 6.

"Türk Dili Tetkik Cemiyeti Nizamnamesi." *Türk Dili* 1 (Apr. 1933): 4–5.

Türkiyede Halk Ağzından Söz Derleme Dergisi. Vol. 1: A-D. By Türk Dil Kurumu. Istanbul: Maarif Matbaası, 1939.

Trix, Frances. "The Stamboul Alphabet of Shemseddin Sami Bey: Precursor to Turkish Script Reform." *International Journal of Middle East Studies* 31.2 (May 1999): 255–272.

Troupeau, G. "Naḥw." *Encyclopaedia of Islam, Second Edition.* Eds. P. Bearman et al. Brill, 2008. Brill Online. Brown U. 16 Nov. 2008. <http://www.brillonline.nl/subscriber/entry?entry=islam_COM-0838>.

Uçarlar, Nesrin. *Between Majority Power and Minority Resistance: Kurdish Linguistic Rights in Turkey.* Diss. Lund U, Sweden, 2009.

Uzunçarşılı, İsmail Hakkı. *Osmanlı Devletinin İlmiye Teşkilatı.* Ankara: Türk Tarih Kurumu Basımevi, 1965.

Üçüncü Türk Dil Kurultayı 1936—Tezler Müzakere Zabıtlar. Türk Dil Kurumu. Istanbul: Devlet Basımevi, 1937.

Ülkütaşır, M. Şakir. *Atatürk ve Harf Devrimi.* Ankara: Türk Dil Kurumu, 2000.

Üyepazarcı, Erol. *"Korkmayınız Mr. Sherlock Holmes": Türkiye'de Yayınlanmış Çeviri ve Telif Polisiye Romanlar Üzerine Bir İnceleme (1881–1928).* Istanbul: Göçebe Yayınları, 1997.

Venuti, Lawrence. "Invisibility." *The Translator's Invisibility: A History of Translation.* London: Routledge, 1995. 1–42.

Versteegh, C. H. M. "Ṣarf." *Encyclopaedia of Islam, Second Edition.* Eds. P. Bearman et al. Brill Online. Brown U. 16 Nov. 2008. <http://www.brillonline.nl/subscriber/entry?entry=islam_SIM-6636>.

Weil, G., and Meredith-Owens, G. M. "'Arūḍ." *Encyclopaedia of Islam, Second Edition.* Eds. P. Bearman et al. Brill, 2008. Brill Online. Brown U. 28 Oct. 2008. <http://www.brillonline.nl/subscriber/entry?entry=islam_COM-0066>.

[Yalçın], Hüseyin Cahid. "Arnavut Hurufatı." *Tanin* 7 Kânunusani 1325/20 Jan.1909.

[Yaltkaya], Mehmed Şerefeddin. *Simavne Kadısı Oğlu Şeyh Bedreddin.* Istanbul: Evkaf-ı İslamiye Matbaası, 1340/1924.

Yavuz, M. Hakan. "Print-Based Islamic Discourse: The Nur Movement." *Islamic Political Identity in Turkey.* New York: Oxford UP, 2003. 151–178.

Yeğen, Mesut. "Turkish Nationalism and the Kurdish Question." *Ethnic and Racial Studies* 30.1 (2007): 119–151.

Yetiş, Kâzım. *Belâgattan Retoriğe.* Istanbul: Kitabevi, 2006.

———. *Talîm-i Edebiyatın Retorik ve Edebiyat Nazariyâtı Sahasında Getirdiği Yenilikler.* Ankara: Atatürk Kültür Merkezi Yayınları, 1996.

———, ed. *Ölümünün 100. Yıldönümü Münasebetiyle Nâmık Kemal'in Türk Dili ve Edebiyatı Üzerine Görüşleri ve Yazıları.* Istanbul: Edebiyat Fakültesi Basımevi, 1989.

———, ed. *Atatürk ve Türk Dili 3: Atatürk Devri Yazarlarının Türk Dili Hakkındaki Görüşleri (Dergilerden Seçmeler).* 3 vols. Ankara: Türk Dil Kurumu, 2005.

Yıldız, Ahmet. *"Ne Mutlu Türküm Diyebilene": Türk Ulusal Kimliğinin Etno-Seküler Sınırları (1919–1938).* Istanbul: İletişim, 2004.

Yorulmaz, Hüseyin, ed. *Tanzimat'tan Cumhuriyet'e Alfabe Tartışması.* Istanbul: Kitabevi, 1995.

Yöntem, Ali Canib. *Ömer Seyfeddin: Hayatı, Karakteri, Edebiyatı, İdeali ve Eserlerinden Nümuneler.* Istanbul: Remzi Kitabevi, 1947.

Ziya Gökalp. *Türkçülüğün Esasları.* Istanbul: Varlık Yayınları, 1963.

———. "Türkleşmek, İslamlaşmak, Muasırlaşmak 1." *Türk Yurdu* 3.11 (Mar. 1329/1913): 331–337.

———. *The Principles of Turkism.* Trans. Robert Devereux. Leiden: E. J. Brill, 1968.

Zürcher, Erik J. *Turkey: A Modern History.* 3rd ed. London: I.B. Tauris, 2004.

INDEX

Made in United States
North Haven, CT
05 May 2022

18925439R00145